THE WAR ON WORDS

THE WAR ON WORDS

Slavery, Race, and Free Speech
in American Literature

MICHAEL T. GILMORE

THE UNIVERSITY OF CHICAGO PRESS
CHICAGO AND LONDON

The University of Chicago Press, Chicago 60637
The University of Chicago Press, Ltd., London
© 2010 by The University of Chicago
All rights reserved. Published 2010.
Paperback edition 2014
Printed in the United States of America

23 22 21 20 19 18 17 16 15 14   2 3 4 5 6

ISBN-13: 978-0-226-29413-1 (cloth)
ISBN-13: 978-0-226-10169-9 (paperback)
ISBN-13: 978-0-226-29415-5 (ebook)
DOI: 10.7208/chicago/9780226294155.001.0001

Library of Congress Cataloging-in-Publication Data

Gilmore, Michael T.
 The war on words : slavery, race, and free speech in American literature /
Michael T. Gilmore.
    p. cm.
 Includes bibliographical references and index.
 ISBN-13: 978-0-226-29413-1 (cloth : alk. paper)
    ISBN-10: 0-226-29413-1 (cloth : alk. paper)   1. American literature—19th century—
History and criticism.   2. American literature—20th century—History and criti-
cism.   3. Slavery in literature.   4. Race in literature.   5. Style, Literary—Social
aspects—United States. I. Title.
 PS217.S55G55 2010
    810.9'3552—dc22

                                                          2009048709

CONTENTS

ACKNOWLEDGMENTS

Many friends and colleagues contributed to this book, and it is much the better for their insights and learning. I should begin by acknowledging the wise stewardship of Alan Thomas at Chicago and the two anonymous readers who made important suggestions for revision. It was my good fortune to know three other people who took time from their own work to read the manuscript in its entirety and give me both needed encouragement and vital ideas for improvement. I wish to express my gratitude to Larry Buell, Robert Ferguson, and Cindy Weinstein; they were, collectively, the most supportive and intelligent critics one could hope for.

Others read individual portions and/or gave generously of their expertise and ideas. Among present and former colleagues at Brandeis, I owe thanks to John Burt, Eugene Goodheart, Caren Irr, Jackie Jones, Ramie Targoff, and Steve Whitfield. I am also thankful for the help of Phil Fisher, Ed Folsom, Eric Foner, Brooke Hopkins, Alex Keyssar, John Stauffer, Sam Otter, and Ross Posnock. Editors of journals and collections who spurred me to sharpen my thinking and prose include Millicent Bell, Gordon Hutner, Jackson Lears, and, once again, Cindy Weinstein.

One of the most pleasurable things about working on a scholarly book is the opportunity to deliver lectures at various venues and get the benefit of the questions, disagreements, and reflections of listeners. I feel particularly blessed in this respect, having presented pieces of *The War on Words* in five countries before consistently challenging and thoughtful audiences. At the University of California, Berkeley, I was the guest of Martin Jay and Catherine Gallagher; they were, as always, model hosts as well as probing interlocutors. I spoke at the John F. Kennedy-

Institute for North American Studies at the Free University of Berlin and had stimulating conversations with Heinz Ickstadt and Winfried Fluck. At Oxford University, my hosts were Ron Bush and Paul Giles; a remarkably spirited discussion followed my presentation of an overview of the entire project. I delivered three lectures on the book in Japan: at the annual meeting of the English Literary Society of Japan in Hiroshima; at Keio University in Tokyo; and at Doshisha University in Kyoto. The hospitality and intellectual rigor of Ichiro Hayashi, Noriko Ishizuka, Toshiyuki Owada, Keiko Shirakawa, Hisao Tanaka, and Takayuki Tatsumi made my trip an unforgettable experience. Finally, I tried out parts of the manuscript at Hebrew University in Jerusalem and at Tel Aviv University; thanks are due to Ilana Pardes, Shira Wolosky, Michael Zakim, and especially Milette Shamir, whose dissertation I directed at Brandeis over a decade ago.

Past and current undergraduates and graduate students at Brandeis patiently endured my argument, and I have learned from their resistance and concurrence. Among those who stand out are Sari Edelstein, Holly Jackson, Scott Moore, and Rekha Rosha.

I must mention a few additional friends whose tolerance and support were more personal: Mark Goldberg and Phyllis Emsig, Dave and Deirdre Rosenberg, David and Janna Smith, Richard and Donna Vinter, and Lewis Wurgaft and Carol Colsell. My daughters, Emma and Rosa, are scattered far from home, but they sustained me with their love. As for my wife, Deborah Valenze, I can barely put into words the depth of my gratitude. She is my best reader, best critic, best advocate, and best friend.

A longer version of "'Speak, man!': *Billy Budd* in the Crucible of Reconstruction" appeared in *American Literary History* 21, no. 3 (Fall 2009): 492–517. Grateful acknowledgment is made to Oxford University Press, the publisher of *ALH*.

Portions of the "Slavery" section of Part I first appeared as "A Plot against America: Free Speech and the American Renaissance" in *Raritan* 26 (Fall 2006): 90-113. Reprinted with permission.

A slightly different version of "Hawthorne and the Resilience of Dissent" was published as "Hawthorne and Politics: Words and Deeds in the 1850s" in *Hawthorne and the Real: Bicentennial Essays*, ed. Millicent Bell (Columbus: Ohio State University Press, 2005), 22–39. Reprinted with permission.

The treatment of *Uncle Tom's Cabin* in "Stowe: From the Sacramental to the Old Testamental" originally appeared as part of a larger essay,

"*Uncle Tom's Cabin* and the American Renaissance: The Sacramental Aesthetic of Harriet Beecher Stowe," in *The Cambridge Companion to Stowe*, ed. Cindy Weinstein (Cambridge: Cambridge University Press, 2004), 58–76. © Cambridge University Press, 2004. Reprinted with the permission of Cambridge University Press.

INTRODUCTION

This book makes a large claim about the continuity of nineteenth-century American literature, one that adds an element of complication to our usual understanding of the subject. Nobody can doubt that the Civil War marks a watershed between radically distinct cultural formations. On the antebellum side, the age of slavery, romanticism thrives; on the postwar side, Reconstruction—denounced by critics as romanticism in politics—fails to take root, and realism holds sway. Emerson, Fuller, Douglass, and Melville give way to James, Twain, Jewett, and Chesnutt. It would seem foolhardy to argue for a commonality among writers so obviously remote in historical context, gender, race, temperament, and popular reception. Beyond the (banal) fact of authorial nationality, what could possibly connect *The Scarlet Letter* (1850) to the *Adventures of Huckleberry Finn* (1885), or allow us to generalize about the rhetorical flights of Henry David Thoreau and Verena Tarrant and the aphonia of Babo and Dr. Trescott (from Crane's *The Monster* [1898])?

While I take seriously the differences between the two epochs, and propose a way to describe them as a transition from comedy to tragedy, I also want to insist on a shared predicament: the perseverance of the censor's presence. The pronounced rupture between the two formations makes it all the more remarkable that linguistic constriction can be seen as a defining feature of both. The policing takes multiple forms over the course of the century. Sometimes it is literal, restraining what can be said by external force, such as a physical assault (Charles Sumner), a threat of prison (Lincoln), or a lynching (blacks in the 1890s). Sometimes the expurgation is figurative and internalized, a self-regulating apprehension about the risks of impermissible speech; this auto-checking afflicted Melville in the antebellum decades and a host of authors after Reconstruction. Plainly, fear of offending one's audience (and losing one's livelihood) can enter into this second equation. But what ultimately lies behind the censorial continuity is the culture's experience with slavery and then race. These two facts—and they are arguably the central facts for the nineteenth-century United States—exerted coercive pressure on freedom of expression in spite of the enshrinement, in the Constitution's First Amendment, of a foundational right to speak. The deterrence began in earnest by targeting abolitionism in the 1830s, was briefly overthrown during and after the Civil War, and, redirecting its animus toward racial equality, acquired fresh life that lasted into the next century.

Prior to Lincoln's election, the planter class and its allies—vilified by abolitionists as the Slave Power—controlled the federal government and were the dominant force in the nation's polity. They used legislation and bullying to stifle agitation against the South's labor regime, portraying debate on the subject as a threat to the Union's survival. An ideological *cordon sanitaire* was erected around the Mason-Dixon line, but the campaign did not relent at the region's borders: it extended throughout the country, reaching as far into the free states as New York City and Concord, Massachusetts, and it did not end until Secession. Armed conflict temporarily abolished Dixie's rule along with slavery, but if the North won the war, the historically closed and illiberal South won the peace. After a decade-long effort at democratic revolution, the post-Appomattox republic developed a virulent bigotry toward the ex-bondsmen. It repudiated the rights promised in the war amendments and embraced a new self-definition predicated on the hierarchical thinking of laissez-faire economics and global imperialism. The reunited country gave its blessing to resurgent southern attitudes barring public defense of racial equality, and the hostility to dissent proved to be, if anything, more thoroughgoing than it was during the slavery era. In short, demands for excision survived the reality of change, and no more than in the past did they confine themselves to the narrow arena of political life. They left indelible marks on the literary imagination and molded some of the principal themes and strategies of American romanticism *and* American realism.

The insights do not just flow in one direction, from history to literature. If the climate(s) of intolerance can tell us something about the American classics, the texts in their turn can reveal a good deal about the extent and intensity of repression. Indeed, they may be our best guide to a cultural phenomenon that did not always assume the concrete form of governmental actions or popular mobbing but, operating as a shadowy inhibition, insinuated itself into consciousness and, above all, into discourse. The particulars of oppression, to be sure, are not a secret; in the case of the Old South, they have long been known. A spate of studies published in the 1940s first documented the story, and there is no doubt that the rise of national monoliths abroad sharpened sensitivity to their simulacra in slaveholding Georgia and South Carolina. (The parallel to totalitarianism, at times explicit, is hyperbolic. No powerful state hounded independent thought in the antebellum South, although, as Tocqueville famously claimed, majoritarian intimidation could be at least as effective.)[1]

Russel B. Nye, in *Fettered Freedom: Civil Liberties and the Slavery Controversy* (published in the same year, 1949, as George Orwell's *1984*), showed that the campaign to harass disagreement spread northward. Later scholars have filled in the details of riots against abolitionists, attacks on the post and press, the "gag rule" against antislavery petitions in the House of Representatives, the antidemocratic provisions of the Fugitive Slave Law, the role of Supreme Court decisions such as *Dred Scott v. Sandford*, which would have disbanded the Republican Party, and numerous other restrictive measures. We know that many Northerners pushed back against the assaults; the eventual success of the Republicans testified to their resolve (though Lincoln would win the White House with less than 40 percent of the popular vote). And the antislavery coalition had no doubt about what was at stake. The slogan of the Free Soil Party was "Free Soil, *Free Speech*, Free Labor, Free Men" (emphasis added), and when the Republicans, with Lincoln as their standard-bearer in 1860, refurbished the motto, they put the relevant phrase at the head of the list: "Free Speech, Free Home, Free Territory."[2]

The situation is less satisfying when we turn to research on the postbellum years. Historical scholarship has made it clear that the reunionist concordat stripped away black gains as the price of sectional harmony, and recent work on the South's defiance of Reconstruction has unearthed long-forgotten material on the violence and terror used to restore conservative white hegemony. Much attention has been paid to lynching, the especially lurid form of terror that flourished in the 1890s. (Readers of Albion W. Tourgée's carpetbagger novels, or of Thomas Dixon's racist Reconstruction trilogy for that matter, will not be surprised at even the most shocking details.) W. J. Cash argued as far back as 1941 that the New South outdid the Confederacy in its intellectual regimentation. Former slaves were the initial victims of this despotism, but the denial of liberties applied to whites as well. Calling this imposed conformity "the savage ideal," Cash contended that it was established "almost as truly as it is established today in

Fascist Italy, in Nazi Germany, in Soviet Russia—and so paralyzed Southern culture at the root."[3]

White supremacy gradually conquered the North, where it had always been tacit anyway: C. Vann Woodward called the Mississippi Plan of disenfranchisement and segregation "The American Way."[4] Though direct violence had a lesser part in colonizing opinion outside Dixie, it never entirely disappeared. Lynchings, for example, occurred in California, Indiana, and New York, and Mark Twain expected to see one in Union Square, with fifty thousand in attendance. But the degree to which white Northerners were discouraged from breaching the limits of acceptable discussion on race has received a paucity of notice. Although Eric Foner has commented on the narrowing of discursive latitude that accompanied "the re-racialization of American freedom," most work on the conformist and/or coercive atmosphere that emerged in the last quarter of the nineteenth century has centered on beliefs and idioms having little or nothing to do with the former slaves. The Comstock Act of 1873, termed by critics the "National Gag-Law," banned radical material on sex and religion from the mails. Government and business joined hands to demonize unions, and judicial travesties such as the Haymarket hangings demonstrated all too plainly that certain criticisms of the political and economic order would not be allowed. David M. Rabban's volume *Free Speech in Its Forgotten Years* (1997) contains important information about the Free Speech League, which was founded in 1902 after McKinley's assassination led to wholesale arrests of anarchists. Coeval with Dixon's best-selling defense of lynching, *The Leopard's Spots* (1902), the organization would go on to defend Margaret Sanger, Emma Goldman, and the International Workers of the World. The league took no interest in racial subjugation and its curtailment of free speech, and Rabban's index contains no entry for either race or Reconstruction.[5]

Literature, which is made up of words, can be an unusually sensitive barometer of attempts to regulate them. It can cast light, as I believe it does for the postbellum experience, on subtle, and not so subtle, contractions of discursive possibility that might otherwise be missed. Certainly nineteenth-century literary texts themselves provide fruitful entry into the culture's struggles with proscription. They abound in acts of silencing and self-silencing, and that which is not there is frequently as illuminating as that which is. Some "extratextual" examples of erasures would include Melville's bowdlerizing of sections from *Typee* (1846) and James's failure to publish another novel set in America after *The Bostonians* (1886).

There is good—not to say melodramatic—precedent in venerable political writing for attentiveness to such gaps. Consider the inaugural texts of American nationhood, the Declaration of Independence and the Constitution. Both documents present themselves as models of openness, bravely submitting their claims to the judgment of "a candid world" (the Declaration) or the scrutiny of the citizens of the United States (the Constitution). But both lapse into silence or evasion when they come up against the realities of bondage and race. Thomas Jefferson's original draft for the Declaration contained a long paragraph assailing the Crown for introducing African slavery into the colonies and then vetoing every legislative attempt to halt the traffic; objections from fellow Southerners caused him to remove the passage. The delegates to the Constitutional Convention could not avoid the forbidden topic in their blueprint for government but shrank from naming it. In the three-fifths clause on representation, they referred to slaves as "those bound in Service for a Term of Years," and they euphemized runaways as persons "held to service or Labor in one State" who flee into another. Repression and self-repression over black people marked the new republic's entrance into public speech.[6]

The foundational reflex evokes a moment of mimicry in nineteenth-century imaginative literature: in "Benito Cereno" (1855), the silent and morose Spaniard whose ship was overrun in a slave revolt accounts for his reticence with an ominous signifier, "The Negro." It would not be difficult to cull examples of such dumbness from the fiction, nonfiction, and poetry of both eras. I will review a few selections here to indicate how pervasive the pattern is, and also to prepare the reader for the pages that follow, which offer many detailed readings of canonical texts. The slave narrative and related works are inevitable candidates for a starting point, because blacks in antebellum culture had no recognized right to speak at all. A motif in these volumes is an attack on the mouth or throat, an outbreak of violence against the organs of speech. David Walker's diatribe *Appeal to the Coloured Citizens of the World* (1829) complains bitterly that Americans "have their feet on our throats." A Boston-based free man of color, Walker predicts that he will be murdered for presuming to expose white hypocrisy—which may in fact have happened, given the mysterious circumstances of his death. The heroine of Harriet A. Jacobs's *Incidents in the Life of a Slave Girl* (1861) distills the verbal condition of all black people, enslaved or not, into her plight as a hideaway in her grandmother's garret. She is unable to speak for fear of revealing her location and soon contracts, from immobility, stiffness in the face and tongue: "I lost the power of speech."[7]

The forcible muzzling is not limited to black-authored works. On the

contrary, it shows up with some regularity in compositions by whites—
hardly surprising in view of the Slave Power's crusade to stamp out dissidence in the North—and is aimed at white characters, too. It can be found
in texts without minority figures. The act makes a remarkably brutal entrance in stories by the transplanted Southerner Edgar Allan Poe, where
violent bridling under the shadow of slavery tends to operate in tandem
with undisguised misogyny. In Poe's "Murders in the Rue Morgue," a tale
alluding to sectional tensions, an escaped orangutan strangles one woman
and cuts the throat of a second so viciously that her head falls off.[8] Babo,
the recaptured slave in "Benito Cereno," refuses to testify before the tribunal that sentences him to death by beheading, and he has a precursor
of sorts in Captain Ahab, a contender for our greatest fictional orator and
another object of censorship, this time by Melville. The whaleman dies
by strangulation when his harpoon line catches him around the throat at
the end of *Moby-Dick* (1851). Whitman's preface to *Leaves of Grass* (1855)
protests against the cross-racial virus of muteness: "the strong throats are
choked with their own blood."[9] The same conceit, with a notably different
valence, shows up in Hawthorne's *The House of the Seven Gables* (1851),
a novel that hardly glances at the North-South divide but strongly favors
verbal policing. Colonel and Judge Pyncheon are punished for their rapac-
ity by the Maule curse: they choke on their own blood.

Silencing, violent or otherwise, resumes its epidemic proportions with
Reconstruction's demise and migrates, as usual, from blacks to whites. A
fictionalized memoir published before the fighting, Harriet E. Wilson's
Our Nig (1859), proves prophetic of the lot of the former slaves after the
peace. The family that takes the free mulatta protagonist as a servant into
their "Two-Story White House, North" (a prototype for the nation) resents
her candor as insolence and retaliates by "propping her mouth open with a
block of wood."[10] Wilson's treatment would pale beside that meted out to
the freed people, typically but not always male, who gained a reputation
for being uppity in the defeated South. Lynching was the preferred penalty.
That grisly ritual not only killed but destroyed the throat, and it represented an extreme manifestation of the linguistic disempowerment that
accompanied the ex-bondsmen's return to near slavery. The aged Douglass
had no doubt of lynching's symbolic significance. Its victims were charged
with the "unspeakable" crime of rape, and white "delicacy" forbade the
black man "a chance to be heard in his own defense." Conspicuously dis-
played corpses with broken necks, like the severed head of Babo, acted as
terrifying deterrents to future temptations to verbal impudence. Douglass
had no doubt, either, that the rationale for the mob killing was intended

to cow whites as much as blacks. Its purpose was "to divest the Negro of his friends by giving him a revolting and hateful reputation." Who would dare speak out on behalf of a "moral monster" who ravaged spotless white women?[11]

One person who did object was Tourgée, though a pertinent if commonly overlooked detail is that the carpetbagger in *A Fool's Errand* (1879), Comfort Servosse, descends into stillness after North Carolina is "redeemed." That once-intrepid reformer ends up mumbling incoherently on his deathbed. Not all realist fiction, of course, touches on Reconstruction and the freedmen, even obliquely, and Tourgée was always something of an anomaly in his forthrightness. But he turns out to be more central than one might think, and some of the high-water marks of American realism replicate the dynamic of minority persecution spawning white quiescence. The model operates in the *Adventures of Huckleberry Finn* (1885): during the protracted episode at the Phelps farm, where Jim is humiliated, the voice of Tom Sawyer, the juvenile redeemer, overwhelms that of the hero. In *The Monster*, Whilomville's scapegoating of the colored hostler, Henry Johnson, results in the ostracism and stutterlike repetitions of his protector, Dr. Trescott. We get still another version in *The Bostonians*, which has no black characters: an ex-Confederate and defender of slavery, Basil Ransom, silences the object of his affection, the northern activist Verena Tarrant. The "not there" in this case is Verena's long-awaited address at the Music Hall. The last three novelists, Twain, Crane, and James, all deserted the intellectually straitened United States for extended residences abroad.

It should be evident, then, that my concern in this study is not with slavery and race per se, but with their effects on free speech and with how the atrophying of that right plays out in society and culture. In some respects, the project seconds Toni Morrison's argument, in *Playing in the Dark* (1992), about the "Africanist presence" in the American canon—a presence, according to Morrison, that functions as a kind of surrogate or screen onto which whites project their own fantasies and anxieties.[12] My more historicist approach, focused on the nineteenth century, emphasizes the ubiquity of a species of oppression that crossed racial boundaries (though striking far more brutally at blacks). Some white authors resisted the prohibitions and allied themselves with nonwhites, others consented or equivocated, but all wrestled with the admonition to guard one's speech. The Africanist presence, on this view, is not so much a displacement as a carrier of the real—not imaginary—dangers of indiscreet or defiant discourse. Resistance clustered in the period before the war; its "strong" advocates included Emerson, Thoreau, Fuller, Longfellow, Whittier, Lowell, Stowe, and, for a time, Whitman. As Douglass stated in 1855, "The poets are with us."[13] That sort of overt opposition was seldom heard from later realists. Except for minority writers and a few white radicals—Douglass again, Chesnutt, and Tourgée—post-Reconstruction culture gravitated toward silence and obfuscation on race. Its banner, to crib from the barber's sign in Melville's *The Confidence-Man* (1857), was inscribed with "No trust." The diminishing number of mainstream voices raised in protest is more evidence, drawn from literature, of the greatly reduced horizons of reunionist comity.

I now wish to reassert the importance of historical change by taking up my previous suggestion that the nexus of slavery, race, and free speech yielded two quite opposed types of stories. The stories correspond to two different ideas of "free speech." As I have intimated, the concept of discursive liberty did not remain constant throughout the century. In the romantic or antebellum period, it signified prophecy, active intervention, and political agency. Conscious of handling explosive ingredients, those who decried slavery's wrongs often framed their words as the deliberate supplanting of an obsolete or enervated textuality. They knew that their utterances, in confronting prohibitions enforced by law, custom, and popular sentiment, threatened the maintenance of societal peace. Some, like Stowe, may have shrunk from that result, but most understood that their voicing was a form of acting. Curiously, a nonliterary figure who was otherwise astute about the verbal's power may have underestimated its effects on his adversaries. Lincoln fearlessly inveighed against the slave system's transgressions, but one feels that he could not quite believe in the probable impact of his eloquence. He miscalculated the potency of his language in driving the South to make good on its promise to leave the Union if he were elected.

After the bloodshed, as Reconstruction came undone, free speech acquired a rather different meaning. It lost its effectiveness and devolved into something like discredited utterance. For the realist author, the risk was not so much that one's words imperiled the republic's tranquility, but rather that the affirmation of civil equality for the freedmen would spend itself without consequence. Dissenting from the hegemonic conclusion about minority capability or from the South's dominance of the terms of national reconciliation would be more likely to affect the speaker than it would the object of his or her criticism. Verbal forthrightness still had a certain kind of power, but it was increasingly the power to marginalize, to damage the career or reputation of the writer. Against the impregnable wall of white supremacy, it could do little to advance justice or destabilize the status quo. Free speech as expressive agency, the signature of romantic idealism, gave way to free speech as inexpedient advocacy—or, even worse, to free speech as mere sound.

Our two stories track this linguistic declension and are intertwined with it. The stories follow the Aristotelian model. The first, which has a happy ending, is a comedy; the second, at which even "God wept," according to W. E. B. Du Bois,[14] qualifies as a tragedy. Admittedly, one might hesitate to apply the label "comic" to the antislavery movement's thirty-year struggle against the plantocracy. The war to preserve the Union, and ultimately to free the slaves, cost the lives of 620,000 Americans and turned out to be longer and more sanguinary than anyone imagined possible. But the proscribed vocabulary of abolition became efficacious, and in a remarkably short time it evolved into a syntax of minority rights. To that extent, the first narrative has a gratifying outcome. "Incendiary" utterance, as the slavocracy had termed it, marched to triumph in the amendments abolishing involuntary servitude and conferring citizenship and the suffrage on the freedmen. What is more, the North put muscle behind that language, now part of the nation's permanent obligation. Breaking with the Bill of Rights pattern of forbidding governmental action, the amendments stipulated that Congress "shall have the power to enforce this article by appropriate legislation."[15] The ruling Republicans were as good as their word. When the South tried to annul black freedoms through violence and fraud, the party of Lincoln passed the legal infrastructure of Reconstruction: federal laws divided the region into military districts (1867), dismantled the Ku Klux Klan (1871), and prohibited discrimination in public accommodations (1875).

As we know, the upbeat resolution was short lived. Reconstruction's visionary program unraveled, and a collateral casualty was the idiom of racial justice. The war—like many wars—had sown a suspicion of rhetoric even before the South surrendered.[16] Bloodletting on such a vast scale discredited words in two ways: it made them seem insignificant beside the numberless dead, and it pronounced them culpable for having precipitated the carnage in the first place. At Gettysburg, where thousands of Union soldiers had perished, Lincoln famously demoted language to a secondary, commemorative position, the unworthy appendage of events: "The world will little note, nor long remember what we say here, but it can never forget what they did here." That initial disaffection assumed a darker hue as the nation gradually eviscerated its pledges to the freedmen. Commitment to fairness for the ex-slaves did not just disappear; it lingered on after its unofficial expiration date of 1876–77, when the last federal troops were withdrawn from the defeated section. Some protections were still in place as late as the 1890s, when the South, with the blessing of the whole country, used the "color-blind" Mississippi Plan (literacy tests, poll taxes, and the like) to strip away the freedmen's remaining rights.

These policies, by rescinding the Fourteenth and Fifteenth Amendments, left a whole generation's noble sentiments in tatters. They rendered empty the language of equality and effectively banished it from the public sphere. Denied the vote, African Americans lost their "voice" in the polity; spatially confined and quarantined, they could express their opinions only to each other. Most members of the dominant caste embraced the new dispensation. The peace of the nation seemed to require allegiance to it, and the depth of American prejudice meant that few people did not internalize its supremacist suppositions. Challenges to the agreed-upon parameters about race could be articulated, but with diminishing prospects of being listened to. A reign of censorship established itself, "not," as Ralph Ellison has said of this ideological landscape, "by an apparatus set up in Washington, but within the center of the American mind."[17] So the second story has the contour of a tragedy, and its unfolding redefined the meaning of free speech with respect to race. The betrayal of the African American was the tragedy of linguistic impotence. In duration and scope, that unhappy narrative may be *the* tragedy of our history. Its denouement lasted well into the next century, when the Civil Rights and Voting Acts of the mid-1960s, seeking to reverse the history of injustice, sparked the battle over the Second Reconstruction that has continued, arguably, to this day.

After a first part laying out the argument for the antebellum and postbellum eras, I turn to the fiction, nonfiction, and poetry of major writers who confronted or, especially after the war, evaded the problem of free speech with respect to slavery and race. I analyze an array of texts, and my goal is to reveal dynamics of coercion and self-monitoring, operative within those texts and within the larger culture, that have been underestimated or ignored. If this approach constitutes a "privileging" of the literary, I accept the charge to the extent that literature, as a medium of language, has a heightened interest in, and insight into, measures intended to censor what people think and say. Another feature of my approach, its close attentiveness to historical events, leads to some inevitable restatement of facts, as different authors try to come to terms with the implications of, say, the Compromise of 1850 or the Supreme Court's acceptance of "separate but equal." I ask the reader's indulgence for these repetitions, which I believe are necessary to mapping my subjects' engagement with the pressures shaping their times.[18]

The section on prewar literature commences in the 1830s with Emerson and includes Thoreau, Fuller, Hawthorne, and Stowe. Three figures who produced significant work in both epochs, Douglass, Whitman, and Melville, occupy the middle section. A glance at Melville's short story "Bartleby, the Scrivener," which I read as prescient of later attitudes, prefaces the consideration of post-Reconstruction literature. In that final section I examine Tourgée, James, Twain, Crane, Chesnutt, and Dixon. As my outline indicates, chronology governs the book's organization, but the structure has a cognitive logic as well. Emerson, with whom I start, set the agenda for most antebellum writers by reinvigorating the prophetic voice, a breakthrough that he associated with the recovery of sight. Emerson's idea of the poet-actor, his powers no longer vitiated by blindness or retrospection, dominates the American Renaissance. The postwar sequence, from Tourgée to Dixon, tracks the actual progress (or regress) of American culture, from advocacy for racial enlightenment to the enthronement of Jim Crow. Twain attacked Sir Walter Scott as the rebarbative voice of the slaveholding South, but Dixon would emerge as an American Scott who shaped the country's sensibility as a whole. That "continuity" could also be expressed as the fate of *Uncle Tom's Cabin*. Stowe, the writer-hero gendered female, shattered the taboo on antislavery protest with her blockbuster in 1852. But in 1903, a year after *The Leopard's Spots*, the New York City public school system removed *Uncle Tom's Cabin* from its approved reading lists for children. Stowe's fictionalized attack on the South's domestic institution was deemed unsuitable for young people at the outset of the twentieth century.[19] *The War on Words* tells the story of how censorship, American style, came full circle.

Race in this study refers to African Americans. My focus is on the confrontations over hereditary bondage and the place of the ex-slaves in the polity because free speech was at the center of those battles. I am well aware that other races suffered from the Anglo-Saxon juggernaut, but attempts to manage public discourse did not have the same urgency in the suppression of Hispanics and Native Americans.[20] The North-South binary remained hegemonic until late in the century, and the South had an overriding stake in containing criticism about its way of life. The West and its peoples could be an accessory to that goal, a point I touch on briefly in discussing Helen Hunt Jackson's *Ramona* in conjunction with Tourgée's defense of the freedmen.

A few additional comments will conclude this introduction. First, a word about my title: I borrow it from the contemporary American poet Rafael Campo. Campo begins his "Patriotic Poem": "The war on words had been declared. A voice / was now considered dangerous / and could be confiscated by police." The piece, which is based on earlier verses composed by Pablo Neruda to protest the overthrow of the Spanish Republic, was reacting to the climate of intimidation adopted in the United States after the invasion of Iraq,[21] and I freely confess that the perilous state of civil liberties under the Bush administration contributed to my analysis of nineteenth-century literature. But I would defend myself against the charge of anachronism by pointing out that developments in the present often illuminate aspects of the past that have been overlooked or whose importance has been slighted. They challenge us to fruitful rethinking. The fresh understanding of Reconstruction that emerged in the 1970s through the 1990s, and was made possible by the Civil Rights movement, is a relevant case in point.

Second, some readers may feel that this study is guilty of a glaring omission. Where, they may ask, is the literature produced during Reconstruction itself, works such as John de Forest's *Miss Ravenal's Conversion from Secession to Loyalty* (1867) or Anna Dickinson's *What Answer?* (1868)? I believe that bracketing such material can be justified on the same grounds that I have little to say about the incipient romantics, Cooper, Irving, and Sedgwick, who came before Emerson. The cultural and political configurations I am interested in exploring—romanticism and antislavery, and realism and the repudiation of racial equality—were not firmly in place before 1836 in the first case, and did not become rooted until after 1876–77 in the second. For the most part, the omitted writers operated outside these chronological boundaries. The problematic of silencing and resistance certainly occurs in their work, but it does not assume the importance it was to hold in the prewar decades and the last quarter of the century.[22]

Finally, a necessary qualification or disclaimer seems in order. A book such as this one, which aspires to present a forceful argument, inescapably emphasizes some claims while discounting or minimizing others. Its insights come at the price of a certain blindness. So I should acknowledge at the outset that apprehension about speaking out on slavery or race is not the only motive for textual ambiguity or hypercomplexity. Other subjects held dangers too. Religious iconoclasm could be particularly hazardous: Melville's story "The Two Temples" was judged offensive to churchgoers and rejected by *Putnam's*. It did not see print until the twentieth century. Novelists from Cooper to James watched their words because of the presumed disapproval of the female reader (the "Iron Madonna," in H. H. Boyesen's phrase), and control of late nineteenth-century publishing by a coterie of "genteel" literary men imposed restrictive standards of prudery and decorum.[23]

Further, writers could have more personal, self-generated reasons for guarding their language. Savvy artists could be trying, through their editorial decisions, to put their best face before the general public. They could value complication as an aesthetic choice. Or they could refrain from taking a public stand on a controversial issue because they simply were indifferent to it. Thoreau, who went to jail for his beliefs, is an invaluable witness from the 1840s. As he observed in—of all places—his manifesto of engagement, "Resistance to Civil Government," "It is not a man's duty, as a matter of course, to devote himself to the eradication of any, even the most enormous wrong; he may still properly have other concerns to engage him."[24] I do not mean to suggest that Melville *should* have been an abolitionist like Stowe, or that James somehow owed it to posterity to be as unambiguous on reunion as Chesnutt. But I do believe that many of the writers I discuss chose not to express themselves openly on these issues because they took stock of the likely consequences of candor. On slavery and race, career-based strategies and the self-censorship that came from attunement to societal proscriptions were all but indistinguishable. Authorial obliqueness may have been overdetermined, but external factors played a role; and that role, far from negligible, left traces, or scars, from the romantic era into the reaches of modernity.

PART I

Slavery, Race, and Free Speech

Slavery

Our point of entry is an incident that has no visible connection to the cultural ferment of the antebellum period, a flowering famously designated the "American Renaissance" in 1941 by the literary critic F. O. Matthiessen. Considered as a group, Matthiessen's subjects entered the literary lists in 1836, with Emerson's *Nature,* and they achieved their apogee in the 1850s, a decade launched by *The Scarlet Letter* and *Moby Dick* and more or less capped at the middle with *Walden* and *Leaves of Grass.* The literary marvel had pretty much spent itself by the end of the decade, and the date with which we begin is 1860, almost a boundary line between our two eras. The principal actors are not writers. They are the politicians Abraham Lincoln and Stephen A. Douglas, and the stage is not a lyceum or a pond or even a customhouse, though it does encompass the same Manhattan of which Melville mused and Whitman sang. The scene opens on the campaign trail, at New York's Cooper Institute, and then shifts to the floor of the United States Senate and to a proposal offered by Douglas to quash unfettered speech. This obscure piece of legislation, menacing fiction and poetry as surely as it aimed a dagger at democratic discourse, reveals how the antebellum struggles over slavery helped to shape the romantic imagination. Years of attacks on free inquiry created an atmosphere of intimidation that affected every literary work produced in the United States between the 1830s and the Civil War.

Lincoln had journeyed to the East to expound his position on slavery before the New York intelligentsia; his goal was to establish himself as a leader of the Republican Party and a dark-horse candidate for the presidential nomination. His audience, numbering fifteen hundred, included such opinion makers as Horace Greeley, Henry Ward Beecher, and William Cullen Bryant. Lincoln went into great historical detail to show that the Founders had regarded slavery as an evil and, while reluctantly accepting its existence in the southern states, had opposed its extension into the territories. He did not directly revive his charge, from the "House Divided" speech, of a high-level conspiracy to spread the "peculiar institution" throughout the republic. But neither did he mince words about the Slave Power's aggression, and he called upon his listeners to resist pressure "to unsay what Washington said, and undo what Washington did."[1]

The rhetorical flourish was rooted in Lincoln's belief that nothing less than recantation would propitiate the South. It will not be enough, he asserted, to yield to them on the territories. It will not even suffice to desist from belaboring the slavery issue and simply leave them alone. For the South to be satisfied, Lincoln argued, we must

> cease to call slavery *wrong*, and join them in calling it *right*. And this must be done thoroughly—done in *acts* as well as in *words*. Silence will not be tolerated—we must place ourselves avowedly with them. Senator Douglas's new sedition law must be enacted and enforced, suppressing all declarations that slavery is wrong, whether made in politics, in presses, in pulpits, or in private. We must arrest and return their fugitive slaves with greedy pleasure. We must pull down our Free State constitutions. The whole atmosphere must be disinfected from all taint of opposition to slavery, before they will cease to believe that all their troubles proceed from us.[2]

On ten further occasions, as he traveled throughout New England delivering versions of his speech, Lincoln repeated this attack on Douglas. Notice his language: the senator from Illinois would ban all *declarations* that slavery is wrong. The subliminal allusion to the founding document of American liberty, almost certainly intended, resonated with the widespread northern fear that the "lords of the lash" would not rest until they had repealed the Declaration of Independence.

Lincoln's suspicions of a Slave Power conspiracy against civil liberties have generally not fared well with historians. Scholars have dismissed, even ridiculed, the idea of a concerted plot to overthrow the rights guaranteed in the First Amendment to the Constitution. But that is too literal a way of thinking about the matter. No one denies that Southerners had political differences among themselves, or seriously charges that a coterie of slave owners, headed by, say, John C. Calhoun, sat in a smoke-filled room and hatched a scheme to dominate the North. But what *did* exist in pre–Civil War America was a widespread resolve to muzzle opposition to slavery by arresting the free flow of information. Southerners initiated that repressive drive, but they would not have achieved the success they did without allies from the free states like Stephen Douglas.[3]

There has been surprisingly little discussion of Douglas's extraordinary sedition law. In 1860 the Illinois senator was the most formidable politician in the United States. Later that year, as the candidate of the northern Democrats, he received the second highest number of popular votes for the presidency and lost the election, not because he defied southern extremism, but rather because he did not go far enough to satisfy it. (Southern Democrats, irked by Douglas's refusal to back a blanket slave code for the territories, ran their own candidate, John C. Breckinridge.) Yet only a handful of sources mention the Senate resolution, and perhaps the fullest treatment still remains that of Henry Wilson, a Republican senator from Massachusetts whose *History of the Rise and Fall of the Slave Power in America*, a massive three-volume work consisting of more than two thousand pages, was published in 1874. Wilson was present in the Senate at the time of the proposed law, and he had not forgotten its trampling on democratic freedoms.[4]

The impetus for Douglas's bill was the recent raid on Harpers Ferry. John Brown's plot, though it failed to ignite a slave insurrection, had crystallized southern grievances at antislavery agitation in general and at the Republican Party in particular. For all their anti-intellectualism, slaveholders had never deluded themselves about the fecklessness of words. They may have mocked northern "isms," but they recognized their potency, and they knew that unless they silenced unfriendly speech, that airy nothing would depose their way of life. Although Douglas did not always see eye to eye with the South, his Senate measure, titled the "Invasion of States" resolution, fully endorsed the region's outrage against linguistic malfeasance. As he laid out his indictment, the "Little Giant" drew an equation between the murderous violence of Brown and his followers and the verbal pillorying of chattel bondage. Condemnation of the South's property and institutions incited criminal behavior and was as guilty as action itself. Douglas did not flinch from identifying those responsible for this lethal and seditious discourse:

> I have no hesitation in stating my firm and deliberate conviction that the Harper's Ferry crime was the natural, logical, inevitable result of the doctrines and the teachings of the Republican party, as explained

and enforced in their platform, their partisan presses, their pamphlets and books, and especially in the speeches of their leaders in and out of Congress.

This accusation was greeted by "Applause in the galleries."[5] The Illinois senator proceeded to name Lincoln and William Seward of New York as the principal rhetorical conspirators he had in mind, Lincoln for his statement in the "House Divided" speech that the Union could not endure half slave and half free, and Seward for his "Irrepressible Conflict" speech asserting that the two sectional labor systems could not peacefully coexist.

Nor did Douglas stop there. Having singled out two leading political adversaries as dangers to the country, he went on to enunciate a fit penalty for all verbal wrongdoers whose object was "to alarm the people of the other section, and drive them to madness." As Lincoln was to warn at Cooper Institute, it would not be sufficient under Douglas's plan simply to disavow acts of lawlessness like Brown's. Antislavery agitators must "also repudiate and denounce the doctrines and teachings which produced the act." They must cease speaking words and thinking thoughts that would "molest" the domestic institutions of the southern states. Should they persist in their intemperate recriminations, Douglas would treat them as felons guilty of undermining the public safety: "I will open the prison doors to allow conspirators against the peace of the Republic and the domestic tranquility of our States to select their cells wherein to drag out a miserable life as a punishment for their crimes against the peace of society." Everyone in the United States Senate knew that Lincoln and especially Seward stood high on the list of possible Republican candidates for president. The senator from Illinois, likely candidate of the Democrats, was proposing that his rivals be jailed for holding and voicing opinions contrary to his own.[6]

Douglas scoffed at the charge, leveled by some of his fellow lawmakers, that the South's aggressiveness toward northern freedoms was fueling the Republican onslaught. A man proud of his evenhandedness, as critical of the proslavery Missourians who had swarmed into Kansas in 1855 as of the New England backers of Brown, Douglas acknowledged that Southerners had committed trespasses too. But he had no doubts about assigning the lion's share of the blame for worsening conditions to the antislavery movement, or, as he put it, to the "revolutionary and treasonable" opinions circulated by "the Abolition or Republican party." It was this partisan outpouring, this avalanche of books, tracts, newspapers, and public oratory, which had provoked "the South to assail and abuse and traduce the North." Acts of retaliation by slaveholders being "essential to the Republican cause," the party's spokesmen routinely ratcheted up their rhetoric until they secured the violent reaction they desired and could justify themselves "upon the plea of self-defense."[7] Republican language, then, bore a double responsibility. It instigated not only the Harpers Ferry raid, but also the assaults on northern rights of which Republicans were constantly complaining. The North, if it were serious about protecting basic liberties, simply had to agree to cease criticizing slavery.

As Lincoln would later say about a related argument, "That is cool." In fact the logic was typical of slaveholders: since all the country's ills stemmed from agitation or utterance, the only way to restore harmony between the sections was to extinguish the verbal irritant. Put the Republican leadership behind bars, Douglas waxed to a peroration, and you halt the torrent of insults aimed at the South and "strike terror into the hearts" of other troublemakers. "Then we shall get to the root of the evil."[8] Douglas's deployment of this antidemocratic reasoning prompted an immediate response on the Senate floor. Two Republican legislators rose to answer in ways intended to underline the difference between antislavery rhetoric and a more primitive use of language to bully and intimidate—words as an instrument or adjunct of physical force.

The two senators, William P. Fessenden of Maine and Wilson of Massachusetts, anticipated Lincoln's similar if more vivid retort at Cooper Institute. Fessenden spoke first and challenged Douglas to take a stand against the real agents of linguistic transgression—not those who voiced their dislike of slavery without offering violence, but those who repeatedly vowed to dissolve the Union unless the majority did their bidding. This refrain, thundered by southern fire-eaters since the 1830s, had become an "electioneering trick" trundled out every four years to browbeat critics into renouncing their rights. The tactic, said Fessenden, was nothing less than an attempt to enslave the North. If citizens couldn't cast their ballots without threats of retaliation, without fearing that, if they voted their consciences, their political opponents would dismantle the country, they were no longer free men but groaned under "heavier bonds . . . than ever were placed on an African." Wilson, two days later, added his own protest against warnings of disunion. These "disloyal and revolutionary threats" were not political dialogue in any meaningful sense of the term. Their sole purpose was "to intimidate the people."[9]

Lincoln, addressing the New York gathering a month later, took the Republican critique of slaveholder speech to its end point. He followed up the debates in the Senate by suggesting that the southern threat to secede moved out of the category of discourse and into that of lawless and violent behavior. It was not linguistic persuasion; rather, it amounted to armed coercion. And blaming antislavery oratory for the crime merely compounded the culpability of the perpetrator. "In that supposed event" of a Republican being elected in November, Lincoln declared to the South, in a passage I have already cited, "you say, you will destroy the Union; and then, you say, the great crime of having destroyed it will be upon us! That is cool. A highwayman holds a pistol to my ear, and mutters through his teeth, 'Stand and deliver, or I shall kill you, and then you will be a murderer!'" There is no difference in "principle," Lincoln continued, between "the threat of death to me, to extort my money, and the threat of destruction to the Union, to extort my vote." The threat was not worthy of a democratic polity, and neither the South's bluster of intimidation, nor the comparable tyrannizing represented by Douglas's proposed sedition law, would succeed in stifling discussion. The man whose surprise elevation to the White House would ignite a civil war concluded by exhorting his listeners: we Republicans must not be frightened from our duty by "menaces of destruction to the Government nor of dungeons to ourselves."[10]

The "Invasion of States" resolution was tabled a week after its introduction and never came to a vote. Many reasons contributed to the decision to let it die. Southern legislators rightly regarded Douglas's bill as a belated sop to win their support for his presidential bid, and in 1860 they were in no mood to forgive him for past failures to embrace their positions. No doubt, too, after days of Republican rebuttal, slaveholders saw the potential danger to themselves in the measure, which, in banning seditious speech, could easily have been turned against their own cries of disunion. But the proposed law's burial in the Senate does not palliate its undemocratic content and should not deflect us from appreciating its political—and, yes, literary—significance.

Had it passed, the resolution would have culminated the slave interest's long battle to impose intellectual conformity on the Republic, a campaign that, refusing to accept the verdict of the ballot box, reached its climax with the bombardment of Ft. Sumter in 1861. Although the assault on free speech specifically targeted abolitionist protest, it had, and it was meant to have, a chilling effect on all discourse. The chain of events stretching from physical attacks on editors and printers in the 1830s to Douglas's bill outlawing Republican rhetoric constituted a history of coercion against the literary as well as the political imagination, a sustained attempt to throttle the openness necessary, not simply for people to debate politics, but for them to think and write as free individuals. Suppression weighed on everyone who earned a living from language, and its influence can be discerned as readily in works that scarcely glance at the subject of slavery as in those that take the peculiar institution as their polemical and thematic centerpiece.

No one living in the mid-nineteenth century would have presumed an absolute right to free speech. The scope of permissible utterance has always been contested in this country, from John Adams's Sedition Act in 1798 to Woodrow Wilson's in 1918, and the positive modern understanding of the concept did not achieve canonical status until the twentieth century.[11] But rarely has the antidemocratic resolve been so fraught with peril for literary culture. The furor over intellectual freedom is the historical reality that connects Matthiessen's handful of major (white, male) artists with their women and minority contemporaries. Emerson, Thoreau, Hawthorne, Melville, and Whitman, the makers of the American Renaissance, may have stood on the political sidelines for many, or, in some cases, all of the antebellum years, but they could not insulate themselves from the crusade to censor speech. When a few errant sentences could destabilize the status quo, land those who inscribed them in jail, or even get their authors killed, nobody could pretend that literature was an inconsequential pastime (though Hawthorne desperately tried to). An expanding slave regime, intolerant of dissent within its own borders and eager to strangle it in the North, cast a shadow upon *Typee* and *The Blithedale Romance* no less than upon the *Narrative of the Life of Frederick Douglass, an American Slave* and *Uncle Tom's Cabin*. Along with more popular and controversial contemporaries such as Stowe, Douglass, and Fuller, the American Renaissance writers understood that the ordeal of the Union had transformed the nature of utterance. Whether they were reformers or conservatives, whether they sought to mobilize the verbal for social change or to check its power, the men and women who penned the classic texts of the mid-nineteenth century held a common belief in the efficacy of words. Language had acquired the force of deeds, and they knew that it could bring about results in the real world, for good or ill.

Just how closely antebellum literary culture tracked the crisis over slavery can be seen in the historical convergences. The pressures on civil liberty reached some of their highest levels at the very moments when the landmarks of the era were being produced. In 1834, just as Emerson began his career as a writer, slaveholders in the South seized and burned abolitionist documents sent through the mails. In 1836 the Concord philosopher announced his Transcendentalist credo in *Nature*, and slaveholders in Congress chose the same moment to violate the First Amendment.

They pushed through the gag that automatically tabled antislavery petitions without a hearing. A decade later, in 1845, slavery supporters joined with advocates of Manifest Destiny to annex Texas as a slave state, and President Polk, covetous of still more territory, began fomenting war with Mexico. Fuller simultaneously brought out *Woman in the Nineteenth Century*, and Douglass published his *Narrative* detailing the inhumanity of southern bondage.

The Compromise of 1850, which contained unprecedented incursions on northern liberties, was coterminous with Hawthorne's first novel, *The Scarlet Letter*. The Compromise's key provision, the Fugitive Slave Law, required all citizens, regardless of their beliefs, to assist federal agents in apprehending runaways, and it denied suspected fugitives the writ of habeas corpus and the right to trial by jury. Protests erupted throughout the free states, whereupon doughfaced Democrats and Cotton Whigs joined Southerners in demanding that all further agitation of the slavery question instantly cease. To continue speaking out, fumed Daniel Webster, was "treason and nothing else."[12] Great literature arose out of this conjuncture of majoritarian repression and impassioned dissent. Hawthorne followed his masterpiece with *The House of the Seven Gables* in 1851 and *The Blithedale Romance* in 1852. Melville's greatest work, *Moby-Dick*, was also published in 1851, and Stowe stated explicitly in the preface to *Uncle Tom's Cabin* (1852) that the Fugitive Slave Law had roused her to utterance.

Two years later, in 1854, Thoreau saw *Walden* through the press and delivered an impassioned lecture on slavery in Massachusetts, and Stephen Douglas persuaded Congress to pass his Kansas-Nebraska Bill. Douglas's legislation, crafted in close consultation with Southerners, included a clause revoking the Missouri Compromise, which, by proscribing slavery north of the line 36°30', had kept an uneasy peace between the sections for a quarter of a century. Free Soilers, and plenty of Whigs and Democrats too, saw the change as the most brazen attempt yet by slaveholders to spread their economic system, and with it their annulment of constitutional rights, into lands formerly reserved for freedom. By 1855 the act had triggered a rehearsal for civil war in Kansas, where the proslavery legislature passed a "Border Ruffian Code" (as Republicans labeled it). The law called for two years at hard labor for individuals who should "print, publish, write, circulate, or cause to be introduced into this Territory" any opinion hostile to the "right of persons to hold slaves." Douglas may have opposed the code as a violation of popular sovereignty, but his Senate resolution five years later would have nationalized its interdict on agitation.[13]

In faraway Manhattan, Whitman picked July 4, 1855, as the date to self-publish his torrent of untrammeled poetic speech, *Leaves of Grass*. The year after that, 1856, brought Stowe's *Dred* and the near-fatal beating of Charles Sumner on the floor of the United States Senate. Sumner had incurred the wrath of a South Carolina Congressman named Preston Brooks by giving a speech on Bleeding Kansas. Brooks believed that the speech had insulted his uncle, Senator Andrew P. Butler, and he determined to respond with violence rather than words. He stole into the Senate chambers with a gutta-percha cane while Sumner sat writing at his desk and rained blows on his unarmed victim until the Massachusetts senator collapsed to the floor, blood crimsoning his papers. The southern press hailed the attack as an act of courage, and Brooks' constituents presented him with a replacement cane as a token of their approbation.[14]

Could there be a better parable of the clash between civilizations? Emerson did not think so: he reacted to Sumner's caning with horror. "We must get rid of slavery," he said, "or we must get rid of freedom." Whitman, in *The Eighteenth Presidency!* (1856), excoriated southern masters who have "pistol'd, bludgeoned, yelled and threatened America, . . . into one long train of cowardly concessions, and still not enough, but rather at the commencement." A popular lithograph (see figure) perfectly captured the sectional polarity. Brooks leans over the supine Sumner with his cane

SOUTHERN CHIVALRY — ARGUMENT versus **CLUB'S**.

Figure 1. John L. Magee, "Southern Chivalry—Argument versus Club's [*sic*]" (1856)

raised to deliver another blow. Sumner holds up a quill pen as his only resistance. The contrast between club and pen is reiterated in the illegible script of blood on Sumner's forehead and the readable script of ink on the scroll on which he had been writing ("Kansas"). In the background stand members of the Senate, some with looks of dismay but two smiling broadly and none daring to intervene. In John L. Magee's print, violence and bloodshed are the "discourse" of the South, and they have taken over the republic's citadel of deliberation. Or, in the unintentional commentary of Alexander H. Stephens, later vice president of the Confederacy, "I have no objection to the liberty of speech, when the liberty of the cudgel is left free to combat it."[15]

The *Dred Scott* decision, handed down in 1857, coincided with the last work of fiction Melville completed, *The Confidence-Man*, which is also his most pessimistic. This ruling, from a court with a southern majority, held that Congress had no constitutional authority to prohibit the extension of slavery into the territories and effectively pronounced the Republican Party null and void. Lincoln believed that the decision was readying public sentiment for the legalization of slavery nationwide. At this point events hurtled toward armed conflict: Southerners lobbied for purchasing Cuba and reopening the African slave trade, while the Republicans cohered as a regional coalition intent on preserving free soil, free opinion, and free men. The Democrats splintered at Charleston in 1860, and northern delegates could no longer delude themselves that their cohorts from the slave states would settle for anything less than complete submission. A journalist, Murat Halstead, caught the flavor of slaveholder intransigence through the comments of exasperated Northerners. According to an Ohioan, the fire-eaters were saying "in effect they [the northern Democrats] must put their hands in their mouths and their mouths in the dust." The fissure assured Lincoln's victory, and the 1860 election results reconfirmed the South's nature as a closed society. Lincoln's name was not permitted on the ballot in the Deep South, and fresh waves of violence and intimidation so depressed Republican turnout that even in the border states, he received barely 3 percent of the total votes.[16]

Three years after Melville fell silent as a novelist, the equation of words with deeds had passed into commonplace. Thoreau acknowledged as much in a paper prepared for John Brown's memorial service at North Elba, New York, in 1860. Reflecting on the hanged insurrectionist's final speeches, Thoreau compared the talent of composition to a firearm aimed at the heart of slavery. We have come back, as it were, to the "Invasion of States" resolution: the Concordian happily embraced Douglas's charge that after Harpers Ferry, linguistic interference with the southern way of life amounted to an act of revolution. Douglas and those like him had helped to create that situation with their war on words, and the romantics—including those who, like Hawthorne and Melville, feared the consequences for national unity—accepted it as axiomatic. All were attracted to the consummate modes of effective speech, prophecy and the curse, and Hawthorne no less than Frederick Douglass trafficked in maledictions against injustice.[17]

The two clusters of prewar authors should be discussed in tandem, then, because the escalating tension over slavery, convulsing the polity as repeated forays against intellectual freedom, impressed them all with the reality of performative utterance. And the shared perspective points to another unexpected affinity, this time linking them as a group with the revolutionary past. Figures as different as Emerson, Fuller, and Lincoln complained of a declension from their forebears and saw their task as becoming once again, as Whitman put it, "the voice and exposition of liberty."[18] The American Renaissance did not simply, as in Matthiessen's understanding, emulate the artistic splendor of the European Renaissance. The designation has a double aptness: it conveys the high quality of antebellum literature, while at the same time it suggests that the works composed in those years sought to resuscitate the revolutionary template of verbal activism.[19]

Eighteenth-century polemicists drew on two storehouses of influential discourse, the religious and the ideological. The language of Protestant theology, or rather the Bible as filtered through that theology, held pride of place. The conviction that speech—the Word of God, as revealed in the scriptures, and the ministerial word, as preached from the pulpit—could produce dramatic change both in the individual and in society united colonial divines from John Cotton to Jonathan Edwards. Edwardsian piety in turn flowed into and nurtured the questioning of established authority that became the hallmark of the American Enlightenment. On the political side, the paramount sources were Old Whig or Commonwealth thought, with its suspicion of arbitrary power, and the writings of John Locke, who emphasized the consent of the governed. These ideas evolved into an ethos of republicanism, and their circulation provided the motor of revolution. And the acme of that welter of speeches, books, and broadsides, a precursor of the agitation deplored by Douglas in 1860, was Jefferson's Declaration of Independence, composed with assistance from John Adams and Benjamin Franklin. Jefferson's words, imitating the Deity of Genesis ("And God said, let there be light, and there was light"), summoned a new nation into existence.

Even this capsule summary reminds us that the American literary past differed significantly from that of long-established European nations, with their histories of patronage and professional authorship. America's principal indigenous writers were not really literary figures at all. They were preachers like Edwards and politicians and statesmen like Jefferson and Franklin. Their most celebrated productions were not fictions and poems but world-transforming speech acts: the Declaration and the Constitution, sermons such as "Sinners in the Hands of an Angry God," and Franklin's didactic *Autobiography*, which helped teach generations of readers how to be good members of civil society.

The works just cited are examples of rhetorical writing; and the movement from the American eighteenth to the nineteenth century is usually seen as a transition from rhetoric to romanticism. No one can deny that a distinction exists between texts calculated to persuade, to move to action, and those that deal in symbolic action and show characters grappling with imaginary situations: the difference, say, between a tract and a novel. But the difference is not absolute. Kenneth Burke, the modern thinker with whom the terms are most commonly associated, points out that while the rhetorical and the symbolical may occupy opposite ends of the spectrum in a theoretical sense, in practice they often overlap. A represented event may be a substitute for a real action, but it may also be a clue to the text's rhetorical strategies and an incitement to, or prophecy of, their actualization. Burke mentions the case of John Milton, whose verse seems unrelated to his political writings until one looks more closely at the content and context of the poetry. An instance would be the scene from *Samson Agonistes* (1671) where Samson conquers in his blindness. Burke reads this as a promise that despite the defeat of the English Commonwealth, the blind Milton (and his party) "will *conquer*" too.[20] To return to the American context, Stowe was a creator of fictitious characters and episodes who changed the course of history with a story. She patterned her novel on the Bible, a cornerstone of antebellum culture that does away altogether with the separation of rhetoric from aesthetics.

Lincoln, as the second advent of the founding fathers, should be enrolled in the census of the American Renaissance. This is to say nothing more, really, than that the tumult over slavery generated its own version of the literary-civic symbiosis of the revolutionary period, a coupling that had elevated Jefferson into one of the major writers, if not *the* major writer, of the American Age of Reason. In uncanny respects, the six-teenth president—not the eighteenth, as Whitman has it in his visionary chapbook—was the fulfillment of the romantic prophecies. These oracles, as we shall see in the discussions of individual writers, often centered on a charismatic truth teller who would combine "Saying" and "Doing," in Emerson's well-known formulation from "The Poet." Or, to use Thoreau's variant of the wished-for leader, he would be a hero-bard, a sighted Homer who could fight as well as sing, and who would not simply imagine a reno-vated future but bring it into being through his speech and actions. Or, again, he would materialize as a more benign Captain Ahab, arousing his countrymen with Shakespearean, scripturally inflected oratory and steer-ing them into a millennium purged of evil. Whitman's treatise went so far as to envision the "Redeemer President" as a Lincoln look-alike, a bearded westerner whose hands were rough from toil but who was also "shrewd" and "fully informed."[21]

Lincoln delivered on the promises: his "songs" proved to be mightier weapons than anything in John Brown's armory, and, despite his fealty to the founders, he imparted his own prophetic dimension to the polity. From the beginning of his career, the Illinois Republican had dedicated himself to maintaining, as accurately as he could, the nation's ideological patri-mony. He would inherit the mantle of the founders because he would al-ways seek to honor their "propositions." The Springfield Lyceum Address of 1838 was no different in this respect from the Gettysburg Address of 1863: both paid lavish tribute, in the cadences of the former speech, to "the legacy bequeathed us, by a *once* hardy, brave, and patriotic but *now* la-mented and departed race of ancestors."[22] One point of Lincoln's growing a beard, which he did after his election but before the inauguration, was to make himself look older and thus to underline his connection to those ancient heroes.[23] The continuity was thoroughly researched. Lincoln did extensive reading to support his claim that the founders meant to confine slavery to the original southern states. The Cooper Institute speech was a scholarly tour de force, and its wide circulation was instrumental in gain-ing him the Republican nomination. He ran, and won the presidency, as the candidate of succession.

Yet he transfigured what he inherited, and his words were the instru-ment of change. Lincoln *wrote* and *spoke* himself into executive authority, convincing the people that his mind and art uniquely qualified him to guide them through the crisis of the Union.[24] For him, as for the found-ers, leadership was as much a matter of utterance as of decision making: recall his flourish at Cooper Institute, where he warned that the enemies of freedom wanted Americans to "unsay what Washington said, and undo what Washington did." As Lincoln explained at Gettysburg, his compatriots had inherited both "a new nation" and a statement, "the proposition that all men are created equal," and they were waging war not just to save the territorial republic, but also, and most urgently, to ensure the perpetuation of the principle. More than that, they were fighting to expand the meaning of the proposition, to give it "a new birth of freedom" that would include not just whites, but black people too. Lincoln left his lasting mark on history less through an act of legislation than through his own piece of writing. The politician who had alerted his listeners to a sedition law "suppressing all declarations that slavery is wrong" came to issue a declaration that vies, in its importance for the nation, with Jefferson's original document: the 1863 Emancipation Proclamation freeing the slaves (technically only those behind Confederate lines).

A clarification is in order before we turn to the decades after Appomattox. Repression of literary dissent in the antebellum years had inherent limits that would weaken or dissolve in the nationalizing fervor of Union triumphalism. (The very term "Union" would recede as a desideratum, to be replaced by the more all-encompassing "nation"—a shift already detectable in Lincoln's wartime speeches.)[25] Lincoln's shorthand, the "house divided," caught the flavor of the decentralized, sectional society of the mid-nineteenth century. The country consisted of "island communities" linked but not integrated by uneven flows of trade and information.[26] Unifying mechanisms were few: no national currency or taxes, no United States bank, no mass-circulation newspapers that bridged the sections, and a military that numbered barely seventeen thousand when Lincoln took office. Political parties and religious denominations aspired to inclusiveness but could not escape the antagonism over slavery. The uproar over the territories sharpened divisions between North and South to the point where the Whigs dissolved, the Democrats fractured, and the Baptists and Methodists split into sectional wings. Four years of bloodshed were needed to fulfill Lincoln's prediction that the United States would "become *all* one thing, or *all* the other."[27]

Dispersion ensured a certain amount of security from outside dangers. Sectionalism, until it reached white heat in the mid- to late 1850s, could be a form of insulation. Paradoxically, the technological improvements that made possible the American Renaissance threatened these protections. Mechanized presses, cloth and then paper binding, turnpikes, canals, and finally the railroad meant that books and pamphlets could be released in pressruns of thousands and disseminated over vast distances.

John Tyler of Virginia, a slaveholder who was later president and still later a member of the Confederate Congress, warned that a cabal of abolitionists was exploiting cheap paper and the postal system "to despoil us of our property."[28] In the absence of sturdy national institutions, however, these modernizing inroads could not dispel the country's persistent localism. The Charleston mobs and postmasters who intercepted Garrison's *Liberator* also kept Emerson's essays out of the hands of South Carolinians. Although Stowe's first choice as a publisher for *Uncle Tom's Cabin*, Lee and Shepard, rejected the book for fear of offending their southern trade, another Boston firm, John P. Jewett, promptly accepted it, and readers in the free states turned it into an unprecedented best seller.[29]

A network of northeastern publishers and, less grandly, presses guaranteed an outlet for the radical voices the South wanted to still. The Anti-Slavery Office of Boston issued Douglass's *Narrative*; "Civil Disobedience" made its first appearance in the same city, in Elizabeth Peabody's *Aesthetic Papers*; and Whitman arranged to have *Leaves of Grass* printed at his own expense in Brooklyn, New York. Boston's many publishers included Houghton and Mifflin; Ticknor and Fields; Little, Brown; and Phillips, Samson (the publishers of *Dred*), while the more pro-southern metropolis of New York had Putnam's, Scribner's, E. P. Dutton, and the largest house of all, Harper and Brothers. It is no accident that Melville, a New Yorker and the romantic who most resembled the realists in self-monitoring, brought out *Moby-Dick* under the Harper's imprint. Among antebellum booksellers, Harper's came closest to commanding, and thus having to satisfy, a national audience.

Race

From prospects to retrospect: Emerson's formula from *Nature*, inverted, provides as good a synopsis as any of the transition from prewar advocacy to postbellum pullback and indeterminacy. The prophetic impulse was supplanted by the propensity to gaze backward, and language renounced its ambitions, or, as Twain might have said, its unwarranted pretensions, to intervene in history. The reformist texts produced during the realist period sought, by diagnosing the causes of social ills, to inspire readers to remedy them. The "retrospective" strain could even be turned on its head in order to recruit it for a reformist agenda: Edward Bellamy's utopian novel *Looking Backward* (1888) reflects on the failings of the present from the more broad-minded vantage of the year 2000. But on the subject of race, language as a force for progress had played itself out in the struggles over slavery and civil equality, and the mainstream writers considered in this study subordinated purposefulness to "Evasion," in Tom Sawyer's apt term for the charade through which he puts Jim and Huck at the end of the *Adventures of Huckleberry Finn*.[30] And by the dawn of the new century, culture would switch allegiances and ally itself with the South and reaction.

The recoil from the verbal's agency began well before the killing stopped. The war, as I have noted, seemed to convict words of recklessness, for few wars have been so clearly the result of discursive confrontation. Lincoln, whose speeches hastened disunion, articulated the inevitable reaction at the ceremonies dedicating the Gettysburg cemetery. He described the oratory of the occasion, his own brief statement included, as a "poor power," unable "to add or detract" from the sacrifices of the dead. Though Lincoln was mistaken about his address, his stark separation of speech from deeds, of "what we say here" from "what they did here," would evolve into a consensus among his countrymen, Northerners as well as Southerners, who would remember the toll of the war far more vividly than the ideological commitments that produced it. At least Lincoln, assassinated less than a week after Lee's surrender, did not lose sight of the fact, as he said in his Second Inaugural Address, that the slave interest "was, somehow, the cause of the war." Others, appalled by the desolation and increasingly indifferent to the plight of the freedmen, began to place the blame on verbal incitement alone. Whitman, representative in this as in his earlier indignation, looked back in 1879 with equal disgust at the "hot passions of the South" and "the incendiarism of the abolitionists." The evenhanded logic proved so convincing that it came to dominate historiography on the subject for almost a century. Before the 1960s, most historians agreed that the overheated rhetoric of proslavery fire-eaters and northern extremists precipitated the slaughter. Ignored or deprecated were the Slave Power's expansionism and its endangering of civil liberties throughout the republic.[31]

Lincoln's remarks imply a devaluation of language for an apparently opposite reason, what might be called the sequential indictment, and Emerson's "sepulchers of the fathers" have special relevance here. The amnesia of the Gilded Age regarding the war's causes had a corollary in the cult of memory that enabled Yankees and Rebels to reconcile by cherishing every detail of heroism and suffering on both sides of the conflict. For the rest of the century (and beyond), aging veterans—at first in separate gatherings, and then jointly—would assemble to share memories and pay homage to fallen comrades. These occasions evolved into national ceremonies replete with marches, speeches, and the decorating of graves. (The holidays show up in resolutely irenic literary works, such as Jewett's *Country of the Pointed Firs*.) Retrospective commemoration of Union and Confederate valor took it for granted that events were prior to the description of them. Utterance, being necessarily supplemental and parasitic, did not originate heroism. It could do no more than express reverence for the feats of bravery that had happened earlier.

And so, as the mood of filiopietism spread, the two figures whom the prophetic paradigm had joined, the warrior and the poet, were again sundered, the one to do, the other to say. The writer-hero of "Song of Myself" now regularly performed his memories of the nation's "Captain" and "dear father" in his eulogy, "Death of Abraham Lincoln" (1879).[32] Stephen Crane published his classic novel about the Civil War, *The Red Badge of Courage*, in 1895, a full three decades after hostilities ended. Crane's tale, a major document of American realism, incarnates the ex post facto spirit. Its author had not been born yet when the fighting occurred, and the extreme belatedness of his fictionalized "Episode of the American Civil War" confirms that words are distant appendages of the deeds they narrate.

Besides the war, the failure of Reconstruction dealt a crushing blow to the authority of language. In a sense, the three amendments ratified between 1865 and 1870 marked the apogee of the word-deed dynamic of the American Renaissance—the apogee, and the repudiation. These measures, intended by their Republican sponsors as a positive, governmental intervention into the civic arena, were an act of writing, or of rewriting, that could have transformed American culture. But beyond abolishing involuntary "Service" (as the original Constitution characterized slavery), the amendments did little for their ostensible beneficiaries, the freedmen. Most Southerners, though resigned to the loss of their chattel, would not give an inch in their opposition to equality and the ballot. Murder, fraud, and KKK terrorism reasserted white supremacy and returned African Americans to their customary place at the bottom of the social order, with no political rights at all. Although in the 1880s and 1890s black males lynched for rape might be castrated, under Reconstruction the dead sometimes had their tongues cut out as an emphatic demonstration of their silencing as a people. The likelihood of permanent northern opposition to such outrages can be gauged from the election results of 1868. Grant beat the flamboyantly racist Democratic ticket headed by Horatio Seymour with a scant 53 percent of the vote, and the South took the measure of its erstwhile adversaries. Northerners would go to war to get rid of slavery and save the Union, but they would not fight very long for a people with skin pigment unlike their own.[33]

Reconstruction foundered for many reasons, and racial prejudice, if an indisputable factor, may not have been the most important. As the ex-Confederacy's recalcitrance mounted, the healing of the nation seemed to hinge on appeasing the defeated region's long-held beliefs. (Southerners, as Tourgée was not the only one to observe, had a more martial spirit than their northern conquerors.) Without peace, there could be no prosperity, and in a rapidly industrializing society hit by severe depressions in 1873–78 and again in 1893–97, people understandably craved security. The economic upheavals led to worker unrest, and northern elites, alarmed by unionizing and strikes, discovered newfound sympathy for the Bourbon ruling class in the South. Republicans backed off from proposals for land redistribution and winked at harsh forms of labor control, such as sharecropping, that severely restricted black freedoms. Moreover, the ideological armature of the emergent industrial system clashed with Reconstruction's fundamental premises. Laissez-faire economics barred state action on behalf of the less fortunate, and scientific racism, an outgrowth of social Darwinist thought, lent an aura of inevitability to the subordination of minorities. Finally, the United States needed sectional accord to assume its rightful place on the world stage as an imperial power, a goal realized when Georgians and New Yorkers fought side by side at San Juan Hill in the Spanish-American War of 1898.

Unlike during the pre–Civil War period, after Appomattox legislation played a secondary role in abridging the sense of linguistic possibility. It was the *undoing* of statute and amendment, the conspicuous proof of their emptiness, that encouraged skepticism about words and what they could achieve. Perhaps the most significant federal laws passed to implement Reconstruction, those enacted between 1870 and 1872 to suppress the KKK and protect voting rights, lost all credibility after the withdrawal of occupying forces abandoned the Negro to his own devices. The Justice Department gave little aid to election officials in the South, and in 1891 the last attempt to enforce the Fifteenth Amendment went down to defeat in the Senate. The would-be legislation's name in historical memory, the "Lodge Force Bill," indicates how southern Redeemers were gaining control of language. Two years later, the Democrats under President Cleveland repealed enforcement altogether.[34]

Party planks and speeches further eroded confidence in language's trustworthiness. Today we put little stock in such avowals, but in an era when oratory still mattered, it came as a shock to many that political pledges counted for nothing. These were *Republican* utterances, it must be emphasized—pronouncements by members of the party that prided itself on speaking truth to power. "It is what we say, which dissatisfies them," Lincoln had declared at Cooper Institute, signaling his refusal to retreat. "They will continue to accuse us of doing, until we cease saying."[35] The falling off after reunion was palpable. One Republican platform after another vowed—in the words of the 1880 plank—"a faithful performance of every promise which the nation has made to the citizen. . . . To this end the honest voter must be protected against terrorism, violence or fraud." Similar platitudes ornamented the inaugurals of every president from Hayes to McKinley. The 1892 platform, released a year before Republicans capitulated to disenfranchisement, was, if anything, more fervent than its predecessors in its paeans to the integrity of the ballot.[36]

Republicans and Northerners, not Democrats from Dixie, also formed the majority on a Supreme Court whose decisions consistently hobbled the ex-slaves' constitutional safeguards. A series of rulings, beginning in 1873 with the *Slaughter-House Cases* and peaking in 1905 with *Lochner v. New York*, effectively transferred the rights guaranteed to actual persons in the Fourteenth and Fifteenth Amendments to the artificial person of the corporation. The decisions were a confession that the United States government did not mean what it said. The Fourteenth Amendment had scripted esteem for speech into its section on oaths, barring from public office any individual who had sworn to uphold the Constitution and then engaged in insurrection. That clause, like the amendment itself, was more honored in the breach than in the observance; Congress was prolific of exceptions.

Two other notable rulings that caught the attention of nineteenth-century authors deserve mention. The *Civil Rights Cases* of 1883 held unconstitutional the Civil Rights Act, which made it illegal to deny access to public facilities on the basis of race. Congress had passed the act in 1875 as a tribute to the memory of Charles Sumner. Stunned by the Court's finding, Frederick Douglass compared it to the "surrender of the national capital to Jefferson Davis in time of the war." The most "pernicious" decision—the word is Justice Harlan's, who dissented—may have been *Plessy v. Ferguson*, which gave the national seal of approval to racial segregation. Lead counsel for the plaintiff, Homer Plessy, was the novelist and jurist Albion W. Tourgée, on another of his "fool's errands." Forty years earlier an outcry had greeted the *Dred Scott* decision; the reunited republic hardly noticed *Plessy*, which merely reinforced the post-Reconstruction climate of consensus and constriction. Protest seemed futile against social realities that had the imprimatur of the universe: as Justice Brown, writing for the majority, explained, it was not "in the nature of things . . . to abolish distinctions based upon color."[37]

Trends at home were solidified by developments outside the United States, and the difference from the age of slavery is instructive. In the eighteenth and nineteenth centuries, the impetus for abolition often came from abroad. Milestones included the *Somerset* decision of 1772, outlawing slavery in England; the Haitian Revolution, establishing the world's first independent black republic (1791–1804); and "The Emancipation of the Negroes in the British West Indies" on August 1, 1834, a date, and a harbinger, that Emerson hailed as "singular in the history of civilization" in his address on its tenth anniversary. English antislavery pioneers such as William Wilberforce and Thomas Clarkson were revered on both sides of the Atlantic. The names most likely to be spoken of in admiring tones after the Civil War were Queen Victoria, designated Empress of India in 1876, coeval with Reconstruction's last breath, and Herbert Spencer, the English philosopher who translated "natural selection" into the doctrine that only the strongest races and individuals ought to survive. Crucial dates announced the Western powers' resolve to extend their dominance over the inferior nonwhites who inhabited the rest of the planet. Representatives of the European nations, convening in 1884–85 at Berlin, and without consulting the Africans whose fates they decided, agreed to apportion the "dark continent" among themselves.[38] The World's Columbian Exposition, held at Chicago's "White City" a decade later, showcased national and international attitudes toward racial hierarchy. Before a global audience, the fair's organizers permitted American blacks a single, segregated exhibit and created ethnographical displays or "imperial spectacles" depicting the primitiveness of indigenous peoples.[39]

A passage from the "dean" of American letters, a man who labored tirelessly to promote the realist aesthetic, William Dean Howells, inadvertently captures the dwindling of "reputable" support for black rights. The passage, from a letter Howells wrote to the editor of the New York *Tribune* but probably didn't send, has nothing to do with Reconstruction. Howells had been campaigning for some time against the prosecution of the Haymarket anarchists. In his letter, occasioned by their executions in November 1887, he imagines what might have happened if the kind of conspiracy charges that held four workers accountable for the deaths of the Chicago policemen killed in a riot had been applied to the militants of the antislavery cause:

We had a political execution in Chicago yesterday. The sooner we realize this, the better for us. By such a perversion of law as brought the
Anarchists to their doom, William Lloyd Garrison who published a paper denouncing the constitution as a compact with hell and a covenant
with death, and every week stirred up blacks and their friends throughout the country to abhor the social system of the South, could have
been sent to the gallows if a slave had killed his masters. Emerson,
Parker, and Howe, Giddings and Wade, Sumner and Greeley, and all
who encouraged the war against slavery in Kansas, and the New England philanthropists who supplied the Free State men with Sharp's rifles could have been held "morally responsible," and made to pay with
their persons, when John Brown took seven Missourians out of their
beds and shot them. Wendell Phillips and Thoreau, and the other literary men whose sympathy inflamed Brown to homicidal insurrection at
Harper's Ferry, could have been put to death with the same justice that
consigned the Anarchists to the gallows in Chicago.[40]

One can easily quibble with Howells's analysis: extralegal acts of violence
did seek to hold high-profile abolitionists such as Garrison and Sumner
"morally responsible" for their denunciations of slavery, and the "Invasion
of States" resolution inspired by Brown's raid would have made Republican rhetoric a felony punishable by prison.

But as a commentary on his own time, Howells's letter reveals a good
deal in both what it does and doesn't say. First of all, it testifies to the
level of contemporaneous repression. The Haymarket affair was part of a
general crackdown on undesirable speech in a society where white anarchists were hanged for their political beliefs and black men and women
lynched for their race, essentially to keep their race out of politics. Few
figures of Howells's eminence dared to put their reputations on the line
for the sake of the convicted workers, and he himself did not publish his
letter. Fewer still raised their voices against the lynchings, whose numbers spiked sharply in the late 1880s. Mark Twain suppressed his piece
on lynching, and the antilynching crusader Ida B. Wells reported that she
had to travel to Great Britain to tell her story, *Southern Horrors*. "Only in
one city—Boston—had I been given even a meager hearing," she wrote in
her autobiography, "and the press was dumb." Wells had to appeal to "the
Afro-American women of New York and Brooklyn" for the funds to have
her pamphlet published in 1892.[41]

What stands out most vividly for our purposes is a contrast extraneous to Howells's intention—the contrast between white involvement on the subjects of slavery and race. The novelist's roster of antebellum notables who championed emancipation, sometimes at the risk of their safety, exemplifies the change from past to present. His letter features two of the pillars of American Transcendentalism, Emerson and Thoreau, and it includes, among others, two renowned stalwarts of reform, Garrison and Phillips; a prominent United States senator, Sumner; one of the best-known preachers of the day, Theodore Parker; the founder of the New England Asylum for the Blind and the husband of Julia Ward Howe, Samuel Gridley Howe; and a former editor of the New York *Tribune*, Horace Greeley, who published Margaret Fuller in his newspaper and would run for the presidency in 1872 as the nominee of the Democrats and Liberal Republicans.

One would be hard pressed to produce an array of late nineteenth-century defenders of racial justice equivalent to Howells's distinguished list of antislavery activists. It is another of those absences that stretch back to the Declaration of Independence. Howells did not refer to Douglass or Sojourner Truth; he didn't have to name African Americans, because white opponents of hereditary bondage were so plentiful. White fighters for equality after Reconstruction amounted to barely a handful, and none could claim the cultural visibility of Emerson or Greeley. As the historian Rayford W. Logan pointed out long ago, one looks in vain for an implacable firebrand like Garrison, whose defiant motto from the first issue of the *Liberator*, "I WILL BE HEARD," aroused no echo in the postbellum media. On the basis of his detailed study, Logan asserts that a magazine rivaling Garrison's for fearless devotion to the black cause did not exist in the postwar United States until W. E. B. Du Bois founded the *Crisis* in 1911; the *African Methodist Episcopal Review*, with a predominantly black circulation and a quite different mission, came the nearest. The (white) intellectual landscape was silent or opaque.[42]

In literature, the rule of discretion did not require the threat of legal prosecution. Internal curbs accomplished the objective, even when, or perhaps especially when, the writer's heart was in the right place. White authors approached the fraught subject of race gingerly and in ways that make evident their self-reflexive awareness of the prohibitions on candor. Howells, who ended his career writing fictionalized defenses of socialism and was a founding member of the NAACP, had the courage to portray an interracial courtship in his novel *An Imperative Duty* (1892). Dr. Olney and fair-skinned Rhoda Aldgate decide to wed despite societal disapproval. At this point, either Howells's bravery falters or he "realistically" accedes to American mores; perhaps the two possibilities are the same. The novelist cannot imagine his married lovers on native grounds, in the land where it was not "in the nature of things" to cross racial boundaries. We learn on the final page that the couple has settled abroad, in Rome, and that Rhoda, happily, can pass for Italian. Literary works from the realist period, unlike those from before the war, seldom calibrate with violations of civil liberties; background events tend to be less causative.[43] But Howells was sensitive to the general tenor of opinion, and it may be relevant that *An Imperative Duty* appeared two years after the Mississippi Plan tightened the lines between the races.

Or consider a writer who routinely wrestled with black-white relations, George Washington Cable. His two ambitious Reconstruction novels, *The Grandissimes* (1880) and *John March, Southerner* (1894), are studies in polysemy. In *The Grandissimes*, Cable's masterpiece, character, plot, and dialogue all conspire to confound what Thoreau called "easy reading." The first chapter, set at a masked ball, establishes the atmosphere of mystification. Cable, a New Orleans–born racial progressive who ended up deserting the South for New England, displaces his story to 1803, the time of the Louisiana Purchase. Two half brothers, one white, the other a "free man of color" (as were all blacks after slavery's abolition), have the same name, Honoré Grandissime, and readers, as well as the other characters, have trouble knowing which one is being referred to; a chapter titled "Was It Honoré Grandissime?" only compounds the difficulty. Language is the principal agent of obstruction. The Creoles of New Orleans speak broken and often indecipherable English, but that is the least of it: like the author, no one in the novel says what he or she means. The American immigrant, Joseph Frowenfeld, complains of a world of "hints, allusions, faint unspoken admissions, ill-concealed antipathies, unfinished speeches, mistaken identities, and whisperings of hidden strife." Instead of clearing things up, the concluding chapter reaffirms the text's investment in encoded communication: in it, Aurore Nancanou responds to Honoré Grandissime's marriage proposal by bursting into tears and crying, "No!" She means "yes."[44]

At least *The Grandissimes* got by reunion's cultural gatekeeper, the editor George Watson Gilder, and was serialized in *Scribner's Magazine;* Gilder rejected *John March, Southerner,* which had the misfortune of being set in the present. Yet the later novel, produced in the security of Northampton, Massachusetts, surpasses its precursor in equivocation, to the point where the elisions spoil the book. Cornelius Leggett, the villainous mulatto who often has right on his side, is not so much a complex character as an incoherent one. The courtship between John March and Barbara Garnet (both white) completely submerges the Reconstruction theme, and in the end the mysteries of the plot baffle everyone, including Cable's wife, who makes a cameo appearance in order to complain to her husband that he "leaves too much to be inferred." Cable tries to wrap things up with some unsatisfactory explanations, and one cannot help but agree with Mrs. Cable that the racial chasm of the 1890s had turned the country's second-best southern-born novelist into "a very poor story-teller."[45]

The best southern-born novelist, of course, was Cable's fellow performer on the "twins of genius" lecture tour, Mark Twain, another refugee from the former Confederacy who settled for a time in Hartford, Connecticut. *Adventures of Huckleberry Finn* (1885) and *The Tragedy of Pudd'nhead Wilson* (1894) contain some of the most famous black characters in American literature—Jim, Roxy, and Tom Driscoll—and the two books are widely studied for their insight into the problem of race after Reconstruction. Except that neither story dares to address the topic in the present. Instead, the reader is returned to the 1830s or 1840s, and slavery, an issue settled definitively on the battlefield at least two decades earlier, emerges as the focus of interest. Twain's novels replicate the postwar passion for looking backward: he also composed three historical romances set in the Middle Ages. His stratagems (and Cable's in *The Grandissimes*) inevitably remind one of Hawthorne's use of Puritanism in *The Scarlet Letter*, but with a crucial difference. Hawthorne aimed to disable the linguistic agency unleashed by antislavery by holding it at a safe temporal distance. The antebellum conservative imagined an eloquent Massachusetts preacher (shades of Theodore Parker!), showed him to be morally compromised, and relegated him to the remote origin of colonial settlement. The two realists reverted to the past to create room for their imaginations at a protective remove from the atmosphere of intellectual closure in which they lived. Hawthorne wanted to abort speech; they wanted to express themselves, however warily.

Even the activist Tourgée acknowledged that racial equality was a toxic subject in turn-of-the-century America. One could advocate for the promise of Reconstruction, but only by consigning oneself to marginality and churning out dead (i.e., unread) communications like those Bartleby sorted through in his Washington office, something that Twain in particular was unwilling to do. Tourgée, who deplored the Confederate bias of contemporary literature, eventually found himself persona non grata with the reading public and with the Republican "wise men" whom he had served loyally since 1865. He gave up calling on the government to fulfill its obligations to the freedmen, repaired to Europe—where Twain composed *Pudd'nhead Wilson* and Crane *The Monster* (1898)—and titled his last collection of short stories *The Man Who Outlived Himself* (1898).[46]

Crane's novella of a black stable hand who loses his face while saving a white child alerts us to another element in the postbellum détente that hampered dissent: the modernized reach of the *doxa*. Again, a comparison to a Hawthorne text proves illuminating. *The House of the Seven Gables*, set at mid-century, possesses a vein of discourse that operates outside official channels like newspapers and volumes of history and law. Hawthorne variously identifies this stratum as gossip, rumor, "fireside tradition," and "the woman's, the private and domestic," view of things. What gives unlicensed speech its peculiar potency in the romance is its subversiveness: whereas public opinion pronounces the characters of Colonel Pyncheon and his descendant, the Judge, to be unimpeachable, the linguistic undercurrent, invariably "murmured . . . under the narrator's breath," tears away the cover of respectability and exposes the two men as grasping and corrupt.[47] It seethes with contempt for the status quo. Plainly uncomfortable with this perspective, Hawthorne makes his "lawless" reformer, Holgrave, renounce it and conform to society's ordinary practices. Yet the idea of antiestablishment "murmuring" retains its prestige in the book as a counterdiscourse to the banality of convention.

The Monster, a portrait of the 1890s, also foregrounds private talk as a mighty force in the community. But whereas rumor offsets orthodoxy in *The Seven Gables*, in this tale it infiltrates the homes and minds of all the characters with the deadening clichés of culture. "Everybody says so" governs both the public and private spheres and allows no space for independent thought. The communications revolution—transcontinental railroads, wire services, mass circulation dailies, even the bicycle on which the local reporter rides in search of the latest news—ensures that a small town such as Crane's imaginary Whilomville (based on his upstate New York hometown, Port Jervis) cannot escape the pervasiveness of national and global attitudes. Martha Goodwin, a dynamo of gossip, has "adamantine opinions" about the Turkish atrocities in Armenia, the state of women in China, a quarrel in the Baptist Sunday school, and a scandalous "flirtation between Mrs. Minster of Niagara Avenue and young Griscom." And "everybody" has absorbed the racial stereotypes that brand Henry Johnson first as a "coon" and then as a monster and ostracize Dr. Trescott for sheltering the faceless black man. In Crane's fictional America, the "outside" of countervailing discourse doesn't exist anymore; as Carrie's fellow gossips insist, "you can't go against the whole town."[48]

The modernizing developments glanced at in Crane's tale—telegraph, electric lights, post office, and streetcars—had become as much second nature to fin-de-siècle Americans as the decree against racial commingling delivered by the Supreme Court. A quick review of those advances, all tending to the end of a standardized or centralized culture, should probably begin with the radically increased powers of the federal government. The war was pivotal here. In the absence of southern Democratic representatives, who had long blocked nationalizing measures, Congress passed high protective tariffs, rebuilt the banking system, issued a uniform paper currency, imposed the first income tax in American history, and authorized land grants and loans to establish colleges and finance the construction of rail lines spanning the continent (and with them, telegraph lines enabling instantaneous communication between California and Maine). The Union army, fed by regular drafts, brought young men from all over the country into contact with each other. (Over 100,000 Southerners fought on the side of the Union.) By the close of the contest, and with the total defeat of the more agricultural, dynastic Confederacy, a dispersed society had been welded into an integrated industrial power. Once a plural subject, as in "the United States are," the reunified republic emerged from the war, according to James M. McPherson, as a singular noun: "the United States is."[49]

During the next three decades, a flood of innovations enhanced the circulation of words among Americans, and old enclaves evaporated before the scope and speed of the changes. The spurt in railroad and telegraph mileage brought demands for greater precision in scheduling. In 1883 (the same year as the *Civil Rights Cases*), Standard Railway time, an extragovernmental enactment, replaced local times with graduated zones, a major symbolic step in cultural consolidation. The invention of the web rotary press and the linotype machine expedited the production of newspapers and magazines, and the introduction of rural free delivery in 1896 meant that publications, including mail-order catalogs offering books for sale, could penetrate remote corners of the country. By 1901 the United States boasted more than 76,000 post offices, the highest total in its history and more than any other country in the world. Magazines with national audiences flourished under the direction of editors attuned to popular tastes and prejudices. With Gilder at its helm, *Scribner's*, later renamed *Century Magazine*, printed James and Twain and ran an enormously influential series of wartime recollections. Electronic media, representing still newer and more immediate forms of communication, included the telephone, patented in 1876; the phonograph, invented a year later; and the kineto-scope, already on display in 1893 at the World's Columbian Exposition.[50]

Some of the most important changes for literature occurred in publishing. New York, with its long history of close ties to Dixie (the song was composed there, and every Democratic candidate for president from Seymour to Cleveland resided in the Empire State), emerged as the unchallenged hub of book and magazine publication, with Chicago taking second place. Boston, the erstwhile bulwark of New England literature and the city where American bookselling began, faded as the cultural capital, a process whose implications James pondered in *The Bostonians*. The number of leading Boston houses shrank to just two, Houghton, Mifflin and Little, Brown, and the latter firm did not handle fiction until 1896, long after New York had established its preeminence. Harper's, Melville's press before the war and still the country's largest publisher, claimed a surfeit of literary riches by the 1890s. The firm picked up Twain after the failure of his subscription business, Howells after he relocated from Boston to New York, and James after the bankruptcy of his Boston firm, Osgood and Company.[51] The shift in the culture's center of gravity to Manhattan, with its southern sympathies and hypersensitivity to the national market, was inextricable from the withering of dissent on race.

It might seem almost to have been preordained, then, that the postwar narrative should close with a resurgence of verbal power on the side of white supremacy. Whereas realist fiction took refuge in multivalency, a more romantic strain arose at the turn of the century to muster the reflex of "looking backward" for outright reaction. Words made a comeback, as it were, in a series of hugely popular novels by Southerners committed to racial hierarchy. These fictions, collectively known as the Lost Cause or plantation school, seized the ground formerly occupied by New England reformers. They replayed the Civil War as a literary rivalry between the sections, with the southern imagining of slavery and race victorious this time and heretics converted, silenced, or killed.[52] Thomas Nelson Page and Thomas Dixon Jr. carried the rewriting of history into the Reconstruction era itself. With two decades worth of hindsight, they pronounced the experiment a grotesque miscarriage of justice and its proponents the offspring of the devil. Page rode the revisionary ethos to best-sellerdom (and to regular appearances in the pages of the *Century*). His novel *Red Rock* (1898) features the usual flurry of intersectional marriages, and on the last page the Union veteran, Captain Thurston, is accepted into the home of his beloved Elizabeth on condition that he dance to the strains of "Dixie." He can sing "The Star-Spangled Banner," but only in the privacy of his own room. Love has reunited Lincoln's house divided, and the conquering Southerners call the tune.

The more sensational romances of Dixon would not permit even Page's concession. Dixon makes the wresting of literary efficacy from its historic possessors a self-conscious theme in his work, and he co-opts the two staples of abolitionist rhetoric, the Protestant Bible and Jefferson's Declaration, for the cause of white "redemption." In *The Leopard's Spots* (1902), the first volume of his Reconstruction trilogy, the Invisible Empire of the KKK is a prefiguration of the millennial reign on earth. When Charles Gaston delivers the speech "that fixed the history of a state [North Carolina] for a thousand years," he identifies the Saxon race with "Israel of old," raised up by God to vanquish the "semi-barbaric black man."[53] Dixon calls the chapter in which the Klan overthrows the horror of Negro rule "Another Declaration of Independence." And lest we miss the point, in *The Clansman* (1905), the second volume of the trilogy, the carpetbagger Austin Stoneman has a clubfoot—that is, a figurative cloven hoof.[54] D. W. Griffith, who would turn Dixon's saga into cinematic power, gives the otherworldly elect a visual form. Griffith's film *The Birth of a Nation* (1915) concludes with a heavenly sequence in which adoring whites congregate under the watchful eyes of Jesus: paradise for Anglo-Saxons only. The reconfiguration of American publishing hovers in the background of this image. *Red Rock* was an imprint of the New York house of Scribner's; Doubleday, Page, another of the city's enterprising firms, published *The Leopard's Spots* and *The Clansman*.

PART II

Antebellum

Emerson: Prospects

Although Emerson's turn toward reform has been copiously documented in recent years, repairing the overemphasis on his Transcendentalist aversion to the social, the full extent of his relationship, witting and unwitting, with the controversy over slavery has not been recognized. The consensus is that Emerson did not awaken to the magnitude of the nation's original sin until August 1844, when he committed himself to abolition with his "Address on . . . the . . . Emancipation of the Negroes in the British West Indies."[1] The claim is accurate, but it neglects the extent to which his grappling with language issues, a concern from the outset of his career, merged with the larger political drama of the antebellum years. A major part of Emerson's project in the 1830s, to restore the freshness and potency of words, set him against the regnant ideological suppositions of his time. Those suppositions were taken as axiomatic save by a few mavericks, and while Emerson said little about slavery in the 1830s, his aesthetic and philosophical allegiances had myriad affiliations with the voices of dissent. Eventually he came to see the commonalities and to feel that the prophetic hopes of his pre-activist writings were being fulfilled in the political realm. And he understood all along that respectable society's antagonism to free discussion of the South's labor regime posed a danger not merely to one-issue men like William Lloyd Garrison, physically attacked for his beliefs in 1835, or Elijah Lovejoy, murdered for his in 1837. The taboos on agitation would sap the vibrancy of intellectual and literary life as a whole.[2]

Emerson's development instructively intersects with that of Lincoln, a coupling that proves relevant, as we shall find in the next chapter, for Thoreau as well. The Emerson-Lincoln comparison begins in radical disagreement but ends in the coming together of the literary and the civic; it reveals how the Concord thinker's quarrel with the past evolved into the explicit policy of the republic. Lincoln became the leader who transformed and revitalized the legacy of the fathers, and that result could be seen as a testament to the power of "the deedful word" that a generation of writers and activists wielded against the stasis of remembrance. (The quoted phrase, a succinct description for prophetic utterance, comes from Johann Gottfried Herder, a German critic well-known to the American Transcendentalists).[3] Lincoln was at once the hero of an epic crafted by others and the poet whose own eloquence produced a second birth of American liberty. The paradoxes are plentiful, starting, no doubt, with the fact that Lincoln—anything but a Transcendentalist—revered the past and rewrote the Founders' monument under the sign of loyalty. A more tragic paradox, one that completes and reverses the Emersonian program, has to do with what a later generation of Americans made of the martyred president. They turned him into the first among the fathers whose apotheosis dictated an end to prophecy.

The "long foreground" to Emerson's first book, *Nature*, included not simply the intellectual currents, often continental in genesis, that stimulated questioning of traditional religion.[4] Also crucial was the complex of attitudes and events that lay behind *Nature*'s opening salvo against the fathers and their hagiography—"fathers" connoting, among a battery of authority figures, the forebears whose achievements in creating and sustaining the United States seemed to tower over an age in decline. The 1830s combined intense filiopietism with the initial rustlings of the antislavery movement and brought the two phenomena into open conflict. In 1831 Garrison established the organ of abolitionism, the *Liberator*, and seven months later James Monroe, the second-to-last revolutionary titan, died. (A month after that, Nat Turner launched his famous rebellion in Southampton County, Virginia.) Garrison singled out the framers' textual blueprint, the Constitution, as the principal impediment to reform, constantly inveighing against the concessions to the South that stitched injustice into the very fabric of the country: the provision requiring the return of fugitive slaves, the three-fifths clause conferring an advantage in representation, and the transfer of the national capital from Philadelphia to Washington D.C., adjacent to the slaveholding states of Virginia and Maryland.[5]

Garrison's patricidal bluntness exiled him to the cultural margins; far more common was deference to the founders' solutions and a growing sense, as sectional friction increased, that so much as broaching the subject of slavery would imperil the whole republican structure. Reverence for what was said in the past supplied a convenient pretext for holding one's tongue in the present. Daniel Webster, in his "Second Reply to Hayne" (1830), was unambiguous about the logic. Referring to the compromise on representation, he denounced agitation against slavery and its appurtenances as a crime against origins: "It is the original bargain, the contract; let it stand. . . . I go for the Constitution as it is, and for the Union as it is." In 1836, the year of Emerson's manifesto, the last surviving founder, James Madison, died, and a grieving republic redoubled its devotion to the past. When abolitionists demurred, flooding Congress with petitions to outlaw the slave trade in the District of Columbia, a coalition of planters and doughfaces led by John C. Calhoun demanded that the pleas not even be allowed inside the door. Such petitions insulted the southern way of life and were an affront to the Constitution, which gave the federal legislature no power to tamper with the institution in any shape or form. Northern delegates overwhelmingly agreed, and the House adopted a ban that remained in force for eight years.[6]

Submission before the eighteenth-century "bargain" grew so extreme that it threatened to ossify the federal charter itself. The amendment clause was a lever of structural reform that had been allowed to atrophy. At the time Emerson was working on *Nature*, more than thirty years had elapsed since the country dared to tinker with the Constitution, no amendment having been added since 1804, when the Twelfth, revising the process for electing the president and vice president, was ratified. A grand total of two amendments had been passed since the ten that made up the Bill of Rights, and both were more procedural than substantive. (The Eleventh, adopted in 1798, prohibited suits against a state by citizens of another state.) The Thirteenth Amendment abolishing slavery, the first postrevolutionary-generation adjustment in the governmental text and the most decisive change in the document since its inception, had to wait until 1865. Sixty-one years thus separated the Thirteenth Amendment from the Twelfth, and that gap remains the longest Constitutional hiatus in the history of the United States. Petrifaction of the Constitution, like the congressional refusal to hear antislavery petitions, enthroned the "Party of the Past" (Emerson's phrase) in antebellum society. Memory crowded out hope and insisted on being the only narrative permitted in the public forum.[7]

The filiopietistic fixation of the times weighed heavily on the younger Emerson, as did the curbs on articulation which that belief system put in place. His first public comment about slavery, given in Concord in 1837, makes evident that he viewed the restrictions as an assault on all discourse and a polluting influence on language. The bedrock of New England cultural life, the lyceum, finds itself so "bandaged and muffled that it threatens to be silent." Emerson's tone is defiant: "If the motto on all palace-gates is 'Hush,' the honorable ensign to our town-halls should be 'Proclaim.'" No abolitionist at this stage, he claims to have more pressing obligations at home than in the Carolinas, but he does not relent from his insistence on protecting free opinion. We must not be dissuaded, he tells his neighbors, in terms redolent of *Nature*, from "calling things by their right names."[8]

Two years earlier, as he was pondering the inaugural statement of his Transcendentalism, Emerson prepared a lecture on John Milton in which the kinship between civil and artistic imperatives is again a subtheme. Though he distinguishes between Milton the disputant and Milton the writer of *Paradise Lost*, he never forgets that "the opinions, the feelings, even the incidents, of the poet's life" inform his greatest work. Ranking Milton higher than Shakespeare because of his "power to *inspire*," Emerson pays homage to the English Puritan as an unparalleled example of a writer and activist who tolerated no constraints on the human voice—whether that voice sang of expulsion from Eden or decried the tyranny of the Stuarts. Milton was of course blind, but for Emerson he could "see" in his blindness because of his attunement to mankind's potential. In book 3 of *Paradise Lost*, he argued for the illumination of inward or spiritual sight, and his visual defect did not prevent him from serving the Commonwealth. He is at once an image of what Emerson would like to be and a preview of the American's development. Emerson was living on the cusp of his own era of internecine conflict, and he, too, would emerge as "an apostle of freedom" and a defender of "freedom of speech" and "freedom of the press." Above all, Milton represents the possibility of a dynamic speech, and Emerson would translate the Miltonic prototype into the oracular visionary of *Nature* who returns men to sight and words to efficacy.[9]

Nature grew out of Emerson's disaffection from Unitarianism and its emphasis is on men's spiritual condition; yet it links up unmistakably with the age's discursive and political embargo and maps an exit from that impasse. "Our age is retrospective," Emerson declares in the first line. "It builds the sepulchers of the fathers." A backward-looking culture favors a particular brand of literature: "It writes biographies, histories, and criticism." Such works are by definition secondary, focusing on what *did* happen, not on what *will* or *should* happen; they remember and commemorate and do not incite to action except by imitation. Resignation to belatedness amounts to being blind, according to Emerson, for it means that people see through the eyes of others rather than relying on their own perceptions. (Emerson had personal experience of such loss of vision when he was a student at Harvard's Divinity School. He suffered a bout of psychosomatic blindness while immersing himself in the theology of the "foregoing generations.") The author of *Nature* implores his readers to cease groping "among the dead bones of the past" and instead join him in calling for "a poetry and philosophy of insight and not of tradition." "There are new lands," concludes the introductory paragraph, "new men, new thoughts. Let us demand our own works and laws and worship" (3).[10]

Emerson moves on from this polemical opening to dissect the state of rhetoric in 1836. A pervasive "corruption of language," he contends, is the corollary to a cult of retrospection. Ancestor worship seeps into and takes a toll on words, depleting them of their power to originate, converting them into empty and weightless signifiers: "Old words are perverted to stand for things which are not," much as "a paper currency is employed, when there is no bullion in the vaults." Because they have lost their rootedness in the world, words can no longer "stimulate the understanding or the affections." They are instruments of stagnation ("new imagery ceases to be created"), not weapons of truth and change (17).

To redeem language from immobility, then, is to break its subservience to the past. *Nature* aims to reorient us to the present and the future by building on a pair of models that recall the Milton essay: the unfallen Adam who names natural objects according to their essence, and the prophetic poet whose words shape the course of events. Emerson remarks in the essay that "Adam and Milton are often difficult to be separated." The two figures, the epic hero and the poet who imagined him, are basically different sides of the same coin of effectual articulation.[11] Adam as the first man has neither past nor parents: his idiom arises from unmediated experience of the physical world. Like him, the eloquent speaker must "fasten words again to visible things" (17). He must reattach the signifier to the referent and so endow his discourse with the heft and substance dissipated by concentrating on the past. Emerson explains that because material objects are emblematic of spirit and subordinate to its laws, the word as thing is simultaneously the word as deed, inheritor to the mind's mastery over nature. A reenergized tongue can command as well as nominate, and it can have immediate consequences in history for the poet or orator who employs it:

Amidst agitation and terror in national councils—in the hour of revolution—those solemn images shall reappear in their morning luster, as fit symbols and words of the thoughts which the passing events shall awaken. At the call of a noble sentiment, again the woods wave, the pines murmur, the river rolls and shines, and the cattle low upon the mountains, as he saw and heard them in his infancy. And with these forms, the spells of persuasion, the keys of power are put into his hands. (18)

Nature traces a path from retrospect to "Prospects," from works of memory to acts of prophecy. The prophetic, language at its most interventionist, is the antidote to biographies, histories, and criticism. Emerson's Orphic poet, who steps forth in the final section, rivals the biblical first man as an exemplar of proactive utterance. This oracular speaker traffics in a mode of discourse that does not solely foretell events but acts as a midwife to bring them into being. His songs of lordship are "both history and prophecy": history, because they have been achieved in the past, in miracles and revolutions, and prophecy because they "reappear to every bard" and will be realized in the future (39).

Emerson closes his little book with an ecstatic paragraph in which his own voice, merging with that of his oracle, assumes a vatic idiom. "So shall we come to look at the world with new eyes," he proclaims, and promises the fulfillment of "what my poet said," the restoration of Adamic possibility through the "kingdom of man over nature." The text's conquest of retrospective disability culminates with the Orphic poet's invocation of the gospel miracle in which Jesus enables the blind man to see. The poet's rhapsody, taking over *Nature*, lays claim to the same transformative power, and the prophetic dimension is underscored by the profusion of "shalls": "shall be no more seen," "so shall the advancing spirit," "shall enter without more wonder." The last three words, spoken by the oracle, are "restored to sight" (42).

Emerson's attempt to free language from filiopietistic impotence continues in the lecture he gave a year later at Harvard's Phi Beta Kappa Society, "The American Scholar" (1837). Again, the new piece barely glances at politics, but it comes down hard on abasement before the past. The sense of decline is more muted than in *Nature* but still unmistakable, as when Emerson complains, "Men are become of no account" (58), or when he attributes the timidity of "the literary class" to their unease at finding "themselves not in the state of mind of their fathers" (60).[12] The most sustained analysis of retrospection's crippling effects appears in the reflections on reading. Emerson lists books as a vital resource for the scholar, second only to nature, but he esteems the writings of older periods exclusively for their ability to inspire and warns that they must not be allowed to tyrannize over the present. Unthinking idolatry degrades the understandable "love of the hero" into "worship of his statue," and it makes us satellites of the "past utterance of genius," rather than originating thinkers and speakers in our own right (49–50). Read the past, Emerson says, but read it creatively, taking from books "only the authentic utterances of the oracles" and leaving the rest as dross (51).

Like *Nature*, "The American Scholar" proceeds from impatience with secondhandedness to a demand for generative speech. "We hear, that we may speak," says Emerson (50), and he advocates self-trust as the secret to discursive renewal. The orator who has the courage to communicate his truest thoughts, eschewing repetition of what others have written or said, gains access to a power that can sway multitudes. He imparts the "oracles" of the human heart, and his auditors "drink his words because he fulfills for them their own nature" (56–57). The note of prophecy returns, as does a fascination with the "hour of revolution" (*Nature*, 18) as a time of world-changing eloquence and events. Emerson begins by asking, "Who can doubt that poetry will revive and lead in a new age [?]," and he concludes by asserting that the celebration of human capability "belongs, by all motives, by all prophecy, by all preparation, to the American Scholar" (45 and 62). His own epoch, he insists, can repossess the élan of the American Revolution if his contemporaries learn to trust themselves:

> If there is any period one would desire to be born in, is it not the age of Revolution; when the old and the new stand side by side and admit of being compared; when the energies of all men are searched by fear and by hope; when the historic glories of the old can be compensated by the rich possibilities of the new era? This time, like all times, is a very good one, if we but know what to do with it. (60)

Emerson's appeal to revolutionary experience demands comparison to the political thinker who was at this stage his virtual opposite, Lincoln. In the 1830s Lincoln was an Illinois state representative with a thoroughgoing commitment to textual antecedents; at the same time, he rigorously differentiated the revolutionary period from antebellum America, which he viewed as a society that had the duty to cherish its inheritance, not the license to engage in creation. The best-known of Lincoln's early speeches, "The Perpetuation of Our Political Institutions" (1838), decries the recent wave of mob violence against blacks and abolitionists as a threat to the liberties of all that can be averted only by abject "gratitude to our fathers"

(28).[13] The patriots of 1776 founded a republican form of government at the risk of their lives, and many of them, surviving into the nineteenth century, have been living reminders of those heroic deeds. But the "field of glory is harvested," according to Lincoln, and now that the fathers are dying off, our charge, as their descendants, is the more modest and secondary one of maintaining what they established (34). Just as they rallied "to the support of the Declaration of Independence, so to the support of the Constitution and Laws, let every American pledge his life, his property, and his sacred honor." Lincoln might almost be offering a rebuttal, in a civic register, to Emerson's spiritual discontent with the past; his enthusiastic acceptance of belatedness veers toward a conflation of the political with the religious. Respect for law must "become the *political religion* of the nation," and all Americans who would protect the founders' legacy should "sacrifice unceasingly upon its altars" (32–33).

Lincoln, a moderate, had no use for slavery's apologists, and his defense of the federal compact could be read as an affirmation of the right of free expression. A year earlier, Lovejoy had been killed in Illinois for publishing an abolitionist newspaper, a crime that lay behind Lincoln's condemnation of those who destroy printing presses and "shoot editors" (31). Yet his call for ancestral piety, and his relegation of the Declaration to a sealed-off past, coalesced with the filiopietism that could, in other hands, be used for antidemocratic purposes. Lincoln himself adduces "the blood of the Revolution" to advocate for a discursive universe in which repetition banishes novelty. He wants reverence for the Constitution to be the lingua franca of American culture: "let it be taught in schools, in seminaries, and in colleges; let it be written in Primers, spelling books, and in Almanacs;—let it be preached from the pulpit, proclaimed in legislative halls, and enforced in courts of justice" (32). Lincoln's voice is hortatory, but there is little room for "shall" in his iterative chorus, and he permits no political analog to Emerson's Orphic poet. The address's circumscribing of the Declaration effectively eliminates the prophetic element in the founders' documentary armature from contemporary relevance.

Emerson and Lincoln would gravitate toward compatibility as the sectional rupture widened, the former by coming to see the political as the home of prophecy, the latter by embracing the Declaration as a harbinger of democratic renovation. The turning point for Emerson came in 1844, a year that brought two relevant publications, though on the surface they have little in common. The address on West Indian emancipation announces his conversion to antislavery; "The Poet," an essay written between 1841 and 1843, affirms the interchangeability of speech and action—or, in the case of the epic poet, the dominion of speech over action. The essays share an emphasis on literary power, a force that, during the next two decades, Emerson would locate in the public domain. He would conclude that the narrative climaxing in the freeing of the slaves was the epic poetry of the American people and the rebirth of the revolutionary paradigm in the present. In the address he is already moving in this direction, and although in 1844 British antislavery is the formidable tongue, he feels confident that his countrymen will shed their myopia, and that the voice of liberty will resound in America.

Involuntary servitude met its nemesis in the British movement's resolution to expose and discuss it: what muteness had shielded for so long, language eradicated. The drama of colonial abolition started with something as apparently trivial as "a country-boy or girl" in the Islands observing the cruelties inflicted on Negroes and having "the indiscretion to tell of them." This breach in the wall of silence led to further revelations, and the campaign gathered momentum from an endless supply of "shocking anecdotes" and reports of "things not to be spoken" (10).[14] In England proper, "the Quakers got the story" (11) and saw to it that "every horrid fact became known" (13). Emerson makes much of the conversion of the philanthropist Thomas Clarkson, an early opponent of the slave trade. While at Cambridge, Clarkson composed a prizewinning essay against slavery, and his own words were so persuasive that they changed his life. He "wrote too well for his own good" and "began to ask himself, if these things could be true" (12). Deciding that they were, the privileged scion of wealth became an advocate of the oppressed and could not rest until the evil commerce was outlawed.

The British example stands as a reproach to the United States and a "chapter of history" (26) to be emulated. But slavery's virulence as a knotter of tongues—the institution "does not love the newspaper, the mailbag, a college, a book, or a preacher" (21)—presents grave obstacles to American progress, more resistant, Emerson implies, than those confronted by the English. In contrast to Parliament's willingness to investigate, here outrages such as the southern seizure and imprisonment of free black sailors, many of them natives of Massachusetts, are "hushed up," and the politicians who should raise a protest are "dumb" (24). The disorder of compulsively looking backward, familiar from the earlier, philosophical essays, emerges as the besetting sin of the political class, whose loyalty to "the old order of things" makes them tremble at the possibility of change. Refusing to speak out against slavery's crimes themselves, they "would fain silence every honest voice, and lock up every house where liberty and innovation can be pleaded for" (29). Indeed, as Emerson wrote, congressional leaders were just coming to the end of their nearly decade-long suppression of the petition campaign, and the address includes a tribute to the "one eloquent old man," John Quincy Adams, who "has defended the freedom of speech, and the rights of the free, against the usurpation of the slave-holder" and done more than anyone else to overturn the interdict (25–26).

Adams's defiance of bullying in government constitutes a positive omen, and Emerson threads throughout his essay symptoms of a shift in attitudes. The change is in him too, of course, and he introduces the address by apologizing for his own "weakness" or belatedness in not joining "this work of humanity" sooner. But the subject of freedom for the enslaved overrides hesitation; it has the virtue "of making dull men eloquent" (7). Emerson picks up the theme of compelling language in his comments on the antislavery societies, and the remarks anticipate by a decade his explicit conception of those gatherings as a kind of collective seer. Quoting the adage that "eloquence is dog-cheap at the anti-slavery chapel," he praises the meetings for "the free and daring discussions" that catch, as it were, "God's truth . . . like a bolt from a cloud" (27–28). In the final pages, he recurs to the long uneasiness with reformers that kept him on the sidelines. Believers may despair at such failures of vision, but Emerson assures them from his own experience that the "coldness and blindness will pass away." At the very end of the lecture, his diction turns oracular, reprising the prophetic buoyancy of *Nature* and "The American Scholar." The "blazing eye" of the intellect, gazing on "this blot" of bondage, will cause it to disappear. Justice cannot be retarded "because it is the voice of the universe," and "in the history of the First of August," the governing Power or Spirit "has made a sign to the ages, of his will" (32–33).

The irresistibility of a divinely inspired vocabulary is the connective between the address and "The Poet," and the second piece adumbrates the prospect of an epic singer of the civic sphere. The focus is very different: it now falls on the aesthetic, allotting linguistic force not to the antislavery movement, but to the poet who transcribes snatches of the cosmic voice's orisons. At first Emerson seems more intent on distinguishing his subject, whom he calls the Sayer, from the Knower and the Doer. The Knower treasures truth; the Doer, good; and the Sayer or Poet is "the man of Beauty" (320–21).[15] But as the argument develops, these distinctions are eroded: the poet's sayings are shown to be cognate with doings and, in the case of epic, to rule over them. An "emperor in his own right," the epic bard, like Homer, does not trail behind the passage of events searching for the topic of his song. The scenarios that he devises in his imagination catalyze the warrior's exploits; they start the action into life:

> The poet does not wait for the hero or the sage, but, as they act and think primarily, so he writes primarily what will and must be spoken, reckoning the others, though primaries also, yet, in respect to him, secondaries or servants, as sitters or models in the studio of the painter, or as assistants who bring building-materials to an architect. (321–22)

Emerson rejects the prejudice that exalts those who do and disparages those who say, "a cant of materialism" that implicitly prioritizes looking backward in the act of artistic creation (321). In the terms of *Nature*, it turns the poet into a historian or biographer, a passive recorder of what others did and not a precipitator or oracle of what must be done.

The poet, in short, is a Doer through the medium of language, whose visions attain consummation in the real. Emerson proceeds to deconstruct the division with which he began, insisting that on a closer view words and deeds reveal their true nature as congeneric, not opposite. They "are quite indifferent modes of the divine energy. Words are also actions, and actions are a kind of words" (322). Emerson's equivalence invites a similar reading of the relationship between "The Poet" and the address, or between Emerson the Sayer and Emerson the Doer, Emerson the lover of beauty and Emerson the fighter for good. The two positions, enunciated in the same year, are forms of each other, and a discourse of freedom operates in both. Poets are described—twice—as "liberating gods," and Emerson imputes to them a "power of emancipation": "They are free, and they make free" (334–35). In 1844 Emerson professes disappointment that a figure of genius has not appeared in America: "I look in vain for the poet whom I describe" (338). Emerson was the first to call for such a Sayer/Doer, but he was far from the last. From one perspective, his expectations were realized in the host of antebellum authors, Fuller, Thoreau, and Whitman among them, whom he helped to stir into speech. From another, they were met in Lincoln, the leader whose words proved to be inseparable from deeds in the nation's brewing crisis.

Emerson's subsequent antislavery writings grow more forthright about the meshing of the civic with the aesthetic and furnish a running commentary on the milestones in the sectional breakdown. The essays scout all the landmarks of Slave Power aggression—the Fugitive Slave Law, the Kansas-Nebraska Act, the clubbing of Charles Sumner, and so on—and in every case Emerson vows that the repressive measures will be met with redoubled protest. Attempts to muzzle openness, the pieces stress, invariably provoke the linguistic backlash that, by gaining adherents for antislavery, will destroy the South's hateful institution. At times the Concordian can sound like Lincoln at Cooper Institute in 1860, as when he dismisses planter charges that "the friends of freedom" are the cause of all the troubles because they presume to speak their minds: "If you starve or beat the orphan, in my presence, and I accuse your cruelty, can I help it?" ("Address to the Citizens of Concord," [1851], 61). The free-speech motif reaches a finale in 1861, during remarks Emerson delivered in Boston on the recent Republican victory at the polls. Deploring the intractability of southern "ophthalmia" or "blindness" (126), he vowed an end to concessions such as those made at the Constitution's formation. An angry mob shouted him down, and he had to cut short his address.

People who can't see the light of emancipation, according to Emerson, are hostage to the past, and he reiterates the problematic of *Nature* in which regression produces the decay of language. In 1851, adopting the fierceness of Thoreau,[16] he lambastes Daniel Webster for his March 7 speech endorsing the Fugitive Slave Law and labels the senator "a man of the past, not a man of faith or hope." That acolyte of memory, Emerson speculates, would have opted out of the American Revolution's "rich possibilities" ("The American Scholar," 60) and sided with the Tories. "What he finds already written," that only will he defend (66). Three years later, Emerson would still be assailing those who with "heads reverted" to the past, "to the dying Demosthenes, or Luther, or Wallace," ignore the urgent questions of the age ("The Fugitive Slave Law," [1854], 88). And an inevitable casualty of the refusal to face the current "dragons" (88) is the integrity of words, an effect noted by Emerson as far back as 1836. Let us not falsify utterance, he says, and call the stealing of men and women "by any fine names, such as 'union' or 'patriotism'" ("To the Citizens of Concord," 71). In an appeal for Kansas relief from 1856, he devotes a full paragraph to how "language has lost its meaning in the universal cant." Manifest Destiny, Union, representative government: all have become misnomers, and what the slavers praise as "otto of rose and lavender," Emerson doesn't hesitate to call "bilge water" (113–14).

Perhaps the clearest token of the integration of earlier conceits with the political is Emerson's now insistent foregrounding of the prophetic or epic component in agitation. The ending of "The Fugitive Slave Law" proclaims this note emphatically. After berating those who avert their eyes from the present, Emerson declares that in the United States of 1854—the year *Walden* was published—the cause of liberty demands the support of "all brave and conscientious men. It is the epic poetry, the new religion, the chivalry of all gentlemen." If liberty is the *Iliad* or *Odyssey*, where is the Homer? In whom or what is the prophet, the epic poet, instantiated? Emerson goes on in the concluding passage of the essay to hail the American Antislavery Society as the living sibyl, "the Cassandra that has foretold all that has befallen, fact for fact, years ago—foretold it all, and no man laid it to heart." If, for so long, too many could neither hear the warnings nor read the signs, the Fugitive Slave Law unglued "the eyes of men, and now the Nebraska Bill leaves us staring" (88–89). Twenty years after *Nature*, Emerson's all-seeing oracle has metamorphosed into the abolitionist movement and the irrevocable transit of events.

Emerson and Lincoln found common ground in their appreciation of the Declaration as a civic lodestar.[17] The Illinois Republican never backtracked from his adoration of the founding fathers, but, alarmed by the belligerence of the slavocracy, he made room in his filiopietism for other writings besides the Constitution.[18] At Cooper Institute, he invoked the Northwest Ordinance to justify the idea that the revolutionary generation meant to pen up slavery in the South, there to let it die. (Emerson said much the same thing in 1851: "confine slavery to slave states, and help them effectually to make an end of it" ["To the Citizens of Concord," 68–69].) Above all, Lincoln upheld the Declaration against those who dismissed the document as a theoretical absurdity. In 1852, when he was concentrating largely on his law practice, he took issue with the growing number of slavery apologists who "[were] beginning to assail and to ridicule the whiteman's charter of freedom—the declaration that 'all men are created free and equal.'" Lincoln's point was that Jefferson's manifesto was not limited to whites but, as is plain from its language, applied to all men. Six years later, in debates with Stephen A. Douglas, he would concede that while the two races were not equal in every respect, they shared an inalienable right to "life, liberty, and the pursuit of happiness."[19] The Declaration's core maxim was an eruption of prophecy into the humdrum world of politics, not a description of things as they are but an ideal toward which the republic should strive.

The text was also the culture's supreme example of result-producing discourse, a model for the Emancipation Proclamation that Lincoln would issue in the midst of the war. As president, Lincoln kept before his countrymen, directly and tacitly, the Declaration's importance for the struggle against slavery and secession (the latter, he always insisted, being a case of anarchistic disregard for an electoral decision, not an exercise in self-government). He called Congress into special session on July 4, 1861, to ratify his measures to save the Union; and at Gettysburg in 1863 he mentioned not the Constitution, but Jefferson's "proposition that all men are created equal." This left no doubt that Lincoln had become a man of 1776, not 1787: his speech's first line refers to the nation brought forth by the founders "fourscore and seven years ago." To ensure the effectiveness of his proclamation freeing the slaves, he incorporated into it a section authorizing the enlistment of any blacks who escaped to the Union armies. These soldiers proved essential to the victory over slavery. The proclamation has a good claim to being Emerson's "epic poetry" of liberty, and Lincoln was determined to guarantee that its promise would outlast the bloodletting. He had a constitutional amendment abolishing involuntary servitude included in the 1864 Republican platform, and he worked hard for its passage after his reelection. Under the guise of fidelity to "our fathers," Lincoln rewrote their governmental legacy: within five years of his death, his fellow Republicans enacted the Fourteenth and Fifteenth Amendments as necessary enlargements of the Thirteenth's assurance of freedom. Thus did the Constitution itself acquire a vatic strain with the additions of citizenship rights and a color-blind franchise, egalitarian pledges that were not actualized for more than a century.

Emerson, meanwhile, took his own path to Jefferson's words, the rediscovered relevance of which he would identify with a second American Revolution. In 1854, smarting from the repeal of the Missouri Compromise, he exhorted the anti-Websters, the forward-looking shock troops of liberty: "You must be citadels and warriors, yourselves Declarations of Independence, the charter, the battle, and the victory" ("The Fugitive Slave Law," 83). About the chaos in Kansas, Emerson was unambiguous: it foreshadowed "the new revolution of the nineteenth century" ("Kansas Relief Meeting," 115). The war embodying that revolution overthrew the slave interest's control of the federal government, making it again possible to call things by their rightful names, and the currency of the Declaration testified to the renewed vigor of speech. Its visionary proposition was coming to pass, and Emerson enthusiastically welcomed the Emancipation Proclamation as the proof of that. In Lincoln, he saw "the poet, the orator, bred in woods," who "in the hour of revolution" had the "keys of power" put into his hands (*Nature*, 18). The president's measure was "the Second Declaration of Independence, the proclaiming of liberty . . . for all men" ("Fortune of the Republic" [1863], 140). It was "a poetic act," "a sally of the human mind into the untried future" that restored the United States to moral primacy among the nations ("The President's Proclamation" [1862],

129). With many of England's foremost men of letters sympathetic to the Confederacy, Emerson believed that the New World's erstwhile laggard on slavery had overtaken its model. Assuming Great Britain's leadership role in the struggle for freedom, the republic bore the world's hopes and represented "the future of mankind," the seer-vanguard all others would have to follow ("Fortune of the Republic," 139.)

Lincoln was simultaneously the epic poet and the epic hero of the narrative of liberty. Author of emancipation, he was also, as Emerson said in his eulogy for the slain president, "a heroic figure in the centre of a heroic epoch." Like Achilles or Odysseus, like Aeneas or Milton, he embodied the spirit of his land and countrymen, being "the true history of the American people in his time." Always true to his word, he vowed to abolish slavery and "lived long enough to keep the greatest promise that ever man made to his fellow men" (920).[20] In all this, of course, he resembled the leaders of 1776 who initiated the Revolution with their discourse and carried it to success with their deeds. Emerson's eulogy, which he gave on April 19, 1865, the anniversary of the Battle of Lexington and Concord, accentuated the succession. Lincoln, he said, had earned the sobriquet "father of his country," and he had no equal in the annals of American patriotism except for Washington (920–21). This was not, or not principally, a reversion to the retrospective mood of *Nature*'s first sentences. Lincoln's achievement did not slavishly imitate the fathers but updated them, and he redeemed their textual edifice, the Constitution, by infusing it with the Declaration's egalitarianism.[21]

Other Americans, though, were more than happy to fetishize the worship of the fathers in the aftermath of Reconstruction. They turned the cult of the Civil War dead into an obsessive display of remembrance that had the effect, as it was intended to, of burying racial progress under an avalanche of "biographies, histories, and criticism." And no one stood higher in the pantheon of fallen heroes than Lincoln, for whom Congress began planning a memorial in 1867.[22] Southern opponents of the Republican agenda were particularly unscrupulous in recruiting the Kentucky-born president to the cause of reunion and retrospection. This backward turn, which resulted in the annulling of the Fourteenth and Fifteenth Amendments, not only disregards Lincoln's growth on the subject of race, but also casts him as a friend of lawbreakers and an enemy of the Constitution, the defense of which, at this time if not in 1838, would have perpetuated racial justice in our political institutions.

Thoreau: Words as Deeds

Thoreau is usually regarded as the most militant of the literary Transcendentalists. Nothing published by Emerson or Fuller (in her American phase, anyway) quite equals the fiery partisanship of "Civil Disobedience," "Slavery in Massachusetts," and the late group of essays dealing with John Brown. Some of the stridency of these addresses comes from Thoreau's sense that pressures on free speech have divorced words from deeds and left his fellow New Englanders paying no more than lip service to their ideals, a state of affairs that he regularly castigates as a want of manliness and a declension from the founding fathers. Overcoming the rupture is, for him, a project in two parts: people must be persuaded to act on their best professions, and language must be reinvigorated in the face of fears that it can accomplish nothing. The scholar-poet should be cognate with the hero, unafraid to implement his values, and he should be a creator of words to galvanize his countrymen for civic action.

Thoreau's belief in the power of oratory to move multitudes preceded and came after the publication of *Walden*, but the greatest of his writings does not share that confidence. The account of his life at the Pond self-consciously narrows its appeal from the imperfect but educable audience of 1849 to the handful still capable of understanding him in the early 1850s. Why did Thoreau's development as a writer follow this course? What lay behind his disaffection from the American public? Was it the marketplace, where his first book, *A Week on the Concord and Merrimack Rivers*, had fared so poorly?[1] Or was it just a logical outcome of his independent, environmentally centered worldview?[2] Without minimizing such factors, I wish to propose another reason: the inevitable overlapping of the political with the aesthetic at a time when words, the lifeblood of literature, were under extreme duress from institutional and consensual forces. Demands for an acceptance of the status quo and a halt to dissent on slavery culminated in the years between the passage of the Fugitive Slave Law and the legislation opening Kansas to chattel bondage, which rekindled northern opposition to the direction of American society. Parallels with Abraham Lincoln's career suggest that Thoreau's avoidance or withdrawal from civic issues in *Walden*, mostly written in these years, was implicated in the republic's political impasse. He recoiled from his country, and the possibility of awakening it, because the country seemed to have subsided into quiescence over slavery. Thoreau did not give up during this period, any more than Lincoln did, and the dormant social dimension of his thought surged back to prominence just at the moment he completed his masterpiece. But the ebbs and flows of the slavery controversy, and their implications for literary activism, had a greater impact on his artistic development than has previously been imagined.

Encounters with censorship shadowed Thoreau's career as a writer. An attempt by "respectable" Concordians to block the prominent abolitionist Wendell Phillips from speaking at the local lyceum coincided with his venture at the Pond (52).[3] Conservatives objected to the airing of controversial opinions in the town-sponsored venue, and Thoreau joined forces with Emerson to fight this would-be prohibition. In March 1845—the month, as he says in *Walden*, when he first "went down to the woods" (40),[4] and also the month of the annexation of Texas by a Congress dominated by Southerners—he composed a letter to the *Liberator* commending "the people," his townsmen and -women, for defying the censors and turning out in substantial numbers to listen to Phillips; the auditors, he notes, made a point of "being very silent so they *might* hear" (59–60). The lesson he draws is one of demotic receptivity: "the readiness of the people at large, of whatever sect or party, to entertain, with good will and hospitality, the most revolutionary and heretical opinions, when frankly, and in some sort, cheerfully expressed" (62).

Thoreau not only invested faith in a popular hearing; he also nurtured a vision of the poet as sparking communal reformation. In *A Week*, convinced that good books "make us dangerous to existing institutions," he summons an archive of examples of the transformative character of language (96).[5] He cites Sir Walter Raleigh as a "captive knight" who, when thrust into prison, transcended confinement with his pen. Making "his words his deeds," Raleigh transferred "to his expression the emphasis and sincerity of his action" (105). Thoreau would strive to duplicate Raleigh's achievement in "Civil Disobedience," where he describes the night he spent in jail for refusing to pay his poll tax. *A Week* also retells the New England legend of Hannah Dustan, who was seized by Indians and, rising while her captors slept, slew every one of them with a tomahawk and took their scalps. This prompts the reflection that Dustan's escape "happened since Milton wrote his Paradise Lost," and the further observation that the "talent of composition is very dangerous"—comparable to "striking out the heart of life at a blow, as the Indian takes off a scalp" (324 and 329).

Political liberals such as Thoreau esteemed the Puritan Milton as the voice of the defeated English Commonwealth; he sang of spiritual liberty and Eden forsaken in a time of monarchical restoration. By invoking the author of *Paradise Lost*, the Concord dissident was tapping into a tradition of adversarial bards. Nineteenth-century readers ranked Milton alongside Homer and Ossian; the three represented the poetry of resistance, in contrast to the Virgilian epic of imperialism.[6] The blind poet of the *Iliad* and the *Odyssey* was perceived as a kind of pre-Virgilian naïf; his episodic, digressive narratives possessed none of the forward thrust and patriotic agenda of the *Aeneid*. Thoreau's meandering account of his weeklong river journey with his brother John echoes the Homeric archetype. Perhaps even more vital as an exemplar is Ossian, the apocryphal voice of Scottish nationalism described in the final "Friday" section of *A Week*. "It was his province," says Thoreau, "to record the deeds of heroes," but the customary primacy of the warrior over the sightless poet, unable to act because of his optic impairment, has no place in this account. Though often depicted as blind and infirm, Thoreau's Ossian is himself a young champion, a "hero-bard" or "sighted singer"[7] who rebukes in his own person the modern division of labor in which the Doer is separated from the Sayer (345–48). Excelling in both domains, the son of Fingal can perform courageous exploits on the battlefield as effortlessly as he breaks into verse. The current-day poet, however, falls far short of this ideal. Thoreau laments the diminution of the writer: "He no longer has the bardic rage, and only conceives the deed, which he formerly stood ready to perform" (367). Now a denizen of the study, this reduced scrivener haunts the romantic age.

Ossian's integrated office establishes the benchmark for Thoreau's advocacy of "resistance to civil government," the original title of "Civil Disobedience." In the essay, the gulf between believing or saying something and acting in support of it is a symptom of national decay. The second paragraph denominates the American government as a tradition whose integrity has been eroded by time, and Thoreau routinely sets the pusillanimity of the present against the revolutionary past. His contemporaries, the "children of Washington and Franklin," acknowledge as universal the right to revolution against unjust authority, but they limit the relevance of that principle to 1775, the date when Concord militiamen fired the first shots against the Crown. However opposed *"in opinion"* to the war and slavery, they take no real steps to end such policies and "postpone the question of freedom to the question of free trade." At best they vote and petition, but voting, according to Thoreau, is only "feebly" expressing a wish for the right to prevail (69). It is a substitute for action, not action itself, and does not close the gap between convictions and deeds.

Thoreau's gesture to the founding generation is not a backward-looking call for filiopietism. He distinguishes between the resistance to colonial rule and the state builders of 1787; what he wants his neighbors to emulate is their ancestors' knack for "action from principle" (72). Like Emerson, he seeks a "poetry and philosophy" that will resuscitate the revolutionary spirit in antebellum America and, in doing so, restore Northerners to the manhood they once possessed but have ceded to the South.[8] "Oh for a man who is a *man*," Thoreau cries, and he describes his neighbors, the farmers and merchants of Massachusetts, as being so cowed by the fear of offending southern customers that they invariably "co-operate with, and do the bidding of those far away" (70 and 68). Thoreau does not underestimate the difficulty of getting people to believe in their own agency. It is a challenge that he himself faces, with all of society apparently arrayed against him, and he poses the inevitable question: Why bother to oppose "this overwhelming brute force," the millions of men and women who, ignoring their consciences, implicitly consent to slavery and the Mexican-American War? One might as well resist "the winds and the waves," so little chance is there of making a difference against such odds. Thoreau responds to this naturalizing of the political with an assertion of human freedom:

> just in proportion as I regard this as not wholly a brute force, but partly a human force, and consider that I have relations to those millions as to so many millions of men, and not of mere brute or inanimate things, I see that appeal is possible, first and instantaneously, from them to the Maker of them, and, secondly, from them to themselves. (85)

Unlike Orpheus, Thoreau continues, he does not have the ability to change nature, but he will be an Orpheus to his countrymen and energize them through the power of his argument and example.

The idea that righteousness can trump coercion—can itself be an irresistible force—constitutes a central tenet of "Civil Disobedience." A decade later, in the Cooper Institute speech, Lincoln would confront northern immobility by taking a similar position: he would exhort his New York audience to "HAVE FAITH THAT RIGHT MAKES MIGHT."[9] Thoreau develops a contrast in his essay between the power of truth, which operates upon men's minds, and the institutional might of the state, which always confronts just their bodies. He argues that the majority rules in a democracy not because it has justice on its side, but rather because it is "physically the strongest" (64). But "superior physical strength," while it can lock up dissenters behind stone walls, cannot approach "superior wit or honesty" as an instrument of persuasion. "They only can force me who obey a higher law than I," contends Thoreau; "they force me to become like themselves" (81).

To inspire his contemporaries, Thoreau demonstrates his own willingness to act on his principles. Ossian-like (or founding father–like), he performs the deed that he imagines. He declines to pay the tax that, directly or indirectly, sponsors slavery and imperialism, and he goes to jail for his commitment. But being incarcerated does not end his project of renovation. Besides being "the only house in a slave-state where a free man can abide with honor," prison, as Raleigh discovered in the Tower of London, is an ideal launching pad for dissent. Thoreau embeds in his essay three or four pages on his night in the Concord jail in order to dramatize "how much more eloquently and effectively he can combat injustice who has experienced a little in his own person" (76). This is the crucial second stage in his argument: he doubles his act of civil disobedience by turning it into "Civil Disobedience." By taking the state's exercise of force against his body and using it as a piece of literature to encourage others to resist, he proves that truth can vanquish blind compulsion. The Doer and the Sayer are interchangeable in his account: he converts his deed into words in order to make his word the deed that will defeat the state.

The jail incident introduces another theme important to Thoreau's conception of the bard as instigator rather than parasitic copier. Immurement paradoxically confers a defamiliarizing distance on the community where he has spent almost his whole life; suddenly Concord seems far removed from him in both space and time. Being confined proves as eye-opening as "traveling into a far country" or being transported back into the Middle Ages. The Concord River alters into "a Rhine stream," while "visions of knights and castles" swim before his eyes. "I had never seen its institutions before," Thoreau says of his native village, and the fresh vantage disabuses him of the illusion that his fellow Concordians can be trusted. "In their sacrifices to humanity," he realizes, "they ran no risks, not even to their property" (82–83). They are as alien to his values as the members of another race.

Thoreau's emphasis on distancing as enlightenment looks ahead to *Walden*, where he settles "a mile from any neighbor" (3), and to the nature of writing as he describes it in that text, as the antithesis of speech's proximity. In "Civil Disobedience," he returns to the estrangement motif in his concluding section on the shortcomings of American politicians. His principal target is Daniel Webster, still revered in New England but increasingly viewed by abolitionists as a trimmer on slavery. A defender of the Constitution who uncritically follows "the men of '87," Webster's credo is "not Truth, but consistency, or a consistent expediency." The senator, with his long years as an elected official, stands too deeply within the institution of government to perceive its failings "distinctly and nakedly"; as a result, he cannot "speak with authority about it." He has no prospect of instigating genuine change in society because he has "no resting-place without it" (86–87). To Thoreau, Webster exemplifies the depletion of language in a slaveholding republic, and the essay offers an alternative to him, and to all the rest of the country's leaders, in its vision of an outsider who governs through words and not the statute book. Only a person who does not hold office, who sees the state's inadequacies lucidly because he observes them from afar or from a prison cell, can have the moral and political leverage to precipitate a reformation in his countrymen. Such a writer-legislator would be a hero for the ages:

> There are orators, politicians, and eloquent men, by the thousand; but the speaker has not yet opened his mouth to speak, who is capable of settling the much-vexed questions of the day. We love eloquence for its own sake, and not for any truth which it may utter, or any heroism it may inspire. (88)

Thoreau would suffer a loss of certitude in his ability to transform the status quo with his voice and pen and would eventually relocate this ambition in John Brown. After *A Week*'s conspicuous failure to reach a popular readership, he put aside his manuscript of *Walden*, which he had begun at the pond, and did not resume work on it until the end of 1851 or early 1852.[10] The demoralizing political climate of 1850–54, when sectional differences were subordinated to Slave Power conciliation, contributed to his disillusionment. The major parties, the Whigs and the Democrats, acclaimed the omnibus Compromise of 1850 as a definitive resolution of the causes of strife; their 1852 platforms agreed to embargo further discussion of slavery's place in the polity. As the Whigs put it: "We deprecate all further agitation of the question thus settled, as dangerous to our peace; and will discountenance all efforts to continue or renew such agitation whenever, wherever, or however the attempt may be made." The Democratic platform, employing nearly identical language, warned of "alarming and dangerous consequences" if extremists breached the pact of silence. A "final settlement" had secured the Union's survival; nothing more on the subject needed to be said.[11]

It was no surprise that the usual suspects—Democratic doughfaces and Cotton Whigs—backed the legislation and pronounced it permanent; the extent of support was what made the ban demoralizing. A relieved public overwhelmingly consented rather than rising in protest. With Pierce as their standard-bearer, the Democrats swept to victory, and the strenuously objecting Free Soil Party, which had done well in 1848, was soundly repudiated by the voters. Charles Sumner, who after Webster's resignation in 1851 replaced him in the Senate, had to fight for a hearing against the "rule of silence" that blanketed the upper chamber. Nor did the atmosphere of intolerance soon lift. Looking back on this period from the 1870s, the abolitionist historian Henry Wilson complained of "Northern paralysis" lasting right up to the repeal of the Missouri Compromise.[12] Thoreau completed *Walden* and rediscovered activism as Anthony Burns was remanded to Virginia and the Kansas-Nebraska Bill wended its way through Congress, the crucial events in the breakup of the sectional armistice.

As Thoreau was shaping his Pond experience into a book, disappointment with the civic sphere weighed on the minds of antislavery advocates. A man who had more conventional political aspirations, Abraham Lincoln, followed a career path with surprising affinities to the Concord radical's. Indeed, Lincoln has as good a claim as John "Osawatomie" Brown to having realized Thoreau's prophecy of the principled outsider. An opponent of the war with Mexico, he made a name for himself in his single term as a Whig congressman by demanding to know "the spot" where Mexican forces had supposedly crossed into American territory and initiated hostilities. He said that he had voted forty times for the Wilmot Proviso, the amendment of a Pennsylvania Democrat to exclude slavery from lands acquired in the war. Lincoln's hatred of the South's labor system was if anything more visceral than Thoreau's. As a young man, he had observed slavery firsthand, and he never budged from his conviction that it was wrong and a blot on the republic's honor.

But the building of pressure for sectional peace, and the widespread retreat from antislavery advocacy that accompanied the Compromise of

1850, brought a hiatus in Lincoln's political vocation. He did not run for reelection to Congress after his term ended, and "from 1849 to 1854," as he explained in several autobiographical sketches composed for the 1860 campaign, he lost interest in the national arena and "practiced law more assiduously than ever before." The legal profession "had almost superseded the thought of politics in his mind" when the Kansas-Nebraska Act "aroused him as he had never been before," and he returned to the stump for candidates opposed to slavery's encroachments.[13] Lincoln's progression coincides exactly with the pattern of Thoreau's writing, from "Civil Disobedience" through *Walden* to the renascent partisanship of "Slavery in Massachusetts." Moreover, the future president's evolution endowed him with a certain distance on the makeshifts and horse-trading of electoral careerism. His years outside the government enabled him, like Thoreau's "legislat[or] for all time" (87), to utter the truth because he was not beholden to those in power. When he made his bid for the White House, Lincoln did so from the independent position of a citizen and nothing more, not having occupied public office for over a decade; and, as his Cooper Union address illustrates, he felt free to articulate a message integral to "Civil Disobedience": the primacy of right over might.

Thoreau, for his part, put political agitation away to craft an epic of deracinated questing. He tells us that he took up residence at Walden "by accident" on July 4, 1845 (84), and the disclaimer of patriotic motivation proves significant. It sets the tone for a globalized, at-home-everywhere-and-nowhere perspective that deliberately contracts its audience from the "*not* few" who heard Wendell Phillips lecture to the select few who cherish literature (*Reform Papers*, 59). The loss of faith is not so much in linguistic agency as in the judgment of the people. Or rather, Thoreau has ceased to believe in the United States. It would take John Brown's intervention to restore him to a measure of hope. In *Walden*, he spurns the Virgilian model of corporate teleology for a defense of individual heroism in an epic of wandering. "Thank Heaven, here is not all the world," he exclaims in the "Conclusion," and he defines "the only true America" as any place or country where one can do without the luxuries that "sustain slavery and war" (320 and 205). But Thoreau's reaction to the discursive stasis of the early 1850s is twofold, and the second part, more in the spirit of that patriotic epic *Leaves of Grass*, is a renewed determination to "say" in the face of censorship. The Thoreau who salutes writing as a medium that weeds out the unworthy also engages in direct dialogue with the reader, from the first sentence of *Walden*, "When I wrote the following pages . . . ," to the last paragraph, which begins, "I do not say that John or Jonathan . . ."

(3 and 333). If Whitman supplies the tumult of the city in his poetry, *Walden* reproduces the polyphony of nature combined with the sound of a human voice, an undercurrent (or perhaps overcurrent) of continuity with the essays.[14]

Water is crucial to Thoreau's enterprise and, more than his beanfield, forms the endlessly changing site of opposition to the instrumentalism of modern life.[15] *Walden* introduces its speaker as a "sojourner," formerly at the Pond, now in "civilized life," but always in motion, a traveler who sends tidings "from a distant land" (3). Better to be a "sailor" or a "fugitive slave," he says, than to entomb oneself in a permanent dwelling (71). Thoreau does much of his wandering by boat, and he repeatedly tropes his condition in nautical or fluvial terms: "Time is but a stream I go a-fishing in" (98); "I had withdrawn so far within the ocean of solitude" (144); "the life in us is like the water in a river" (332). But although he calls the Pond his most treasured companion and devotes pages to its irregular shoreline and "wonderful purity" (197), his pleasure in the local always reaches outward, away from Concord and toward the global. Walden's ice is shipped to other continents, and its water mingles "with the sacred water of the Ganges" and arrives at "ports of which Alexander only heard the names" (298).

Thoreau's migratory cosmopolitanism allies his narrative with the great classic of seafaring, Homer's *Odyssey*. In "Where I Lived, and What I Lived For," he speaks of Homer's works as songs of "wrath and wanderings" (89); the two halves of the description perfectly fit "Slavery in Massachusetts," where the anger is directed openly against the United States, and *Walden*, whose emphasis on homelessness abstracts this most American of books from its native realm. What the Concord native relishes most is the adventure of setting sail and losing his way. After a visit to the village, he heads for "his snug harbor in the woods," but the most valuable part of the experience is "going astray," for not until "we have lost the world," Thoreau moralizes, "do we begin to find ourselves" (169–71). The Odysseus he admires is the mariner who sails on by, "looking the other way, tied to the mast" (97). The voyaging motif culminates in the "Conclusion," where he urges his readers to travel inwardly, "opening new channels, not of trade, but of thought," and tells us that the siren he would escape is the "restless, nervous, bustling Nineteenth Century" (321 and 329). And what better way to make good his exit from antebellum America than through the world's heroic writings?[16]

Thoreau's chapter on reading spells out his reverence for the classical texts and contrasts those demanding pages with the current fad of "easy reading." Scope and potency demarcate the heroic books. Like Odysseus, they "circulate around the world" and carry their "serene and celestial atmosphere into all lands" (99 and 102). Imaginative equivalents to a night in Concord's jail, they possess the "remoteness" necessary to effect change in the few who can appreciate them (101). Their authors are always outsiders, as far away as the stars, and they form "a natural and irresistible aristocracy in every society, and, more than kings or emperors, exert an influence on mankind" (103). Thoreau makes much of the fact that the distance of these works is a function of their writtenness. Whereas easy reading suggests a textuality as easily digested as conversation or speech, the hallmark of ancient literature is that it has exchanged the unconscious "mother tongue" of orality for the "father tongue" of script, "a reserved and select expression, too significant to be heard by the ear, which we must be born again in order to speak" (101). The classics conjure heroic readers out of the effort to understand their wisdom.

In the "Conclusion," Thoreau circles back to the theme of abstruseness and escalates it into inaccessibility. Previously, in "Economy," he warned of obscurities in his account, owing to the "secrets of my trade" (17), and said that some matters of importance would have to be withheld. Now, as he reflects on his experiment as a whole, he emphasizes how few concessions he has made to potential readers: "It is a ridiculous demand which England and America make, that you shall speak so that they can understand you. Neither men nor toad-stools grow so." Most who open the book will inevitably fall away, daunted by its complexity, but there will always be "enough to understand you without them" (324). It is clear that Thoreau no longer contemplates "moving society," as he did in 1849 (*Reform Papers*, 86); the "enough" whom he hopes his words will inspire is a minuscule group of individuals. There is manifest aggression in such passages, and the object of Thoreau's wrath is his fellow-citizens whose proclaimed beliefs had been so tarnished by their compromises with the Slave Power. Even before he published his new book, he was berating the moral obtuseness of his compatriots, the ruled as well as the rulers, and describing his natal land as "the empire of hell" ("Slavery in Massachusetts," 107). The failure of America in the early 1850s is the subtext of *Walden*'s privatism and discriminations.

Let us look briefly at the most bitter of all Thoreau's writings, "Slavery in Massachusetts," before taking up the more conciliatory side of *Walden*.[17] The temporal propinquity of the essay and the book, issued weeks apart, implies a concert of concerns; and no other lecture Thoreau composed seethes with comparable fury at "the cowardice and want of principle of Northern men" (108). Occasioned most immediately by the forced return of the runaway Burns from Boston, the outburst inveighs against the inhabitants of Massachusetts as white slaves who ring bells and fire cannons to celebrate the liberty of their forefathers but whose own "liberty went off with the smoke" (95). "We have used up all our inherited freedom," Thoreau asserts (108), and he predicts that a government such as the American one, which professes liberty and equality while it enacts injustice at the behest of slaveholders, will end by becoming "the laughing-stock of the world" (96). The events of 1854 have put the devil in charge of the Commonwealth and turned him and all his neighbors into dwellers in hell.

Thoreau enigmatically complains in *Walden* of having lost "a hound, a bay horse, and a turtle-dove" (17). In "Slavery in Massachusetts," anger overshadows loss: when he steals away to the ponds, the "remembrance" of the government's misdeeds spoils his delight in nature, and his "thoughts are murder to the State" (108). But feelings of privation also suffuse the essay, and here they have an explicitly national reference. For a long time, according to Thoreau, he has been living with a sense of "vast and indefinite loss" that should be familiar to every American still capable of patriotic sentiments. At first he does not know what is missing. Then he realizes "that what I had lost was a country" (106).

A passage in the "Visitors" chapter of *Walden* dramatizes Thoreau's privileging of writing over speech. He describes sitting in his house and conversing with an unnamed guest. Since "big thoughts in big words" require plenty of space, the two push their chairs to opposite corners, and even then they feel cramped. For the most meaningful interchanges, Thoreau states, "we must not only be silent, but commonly so far apart that we cannot possibly hear each other's voice" (140–41). The paragraph converts spoken discourse into the separation and soundlessness of written communication and can be taken as a metaphor for Thoreau's objective of limiting his auditors.[18] But it is not his last thought on colloquy in his cabin. A later section, "Former Inhabitants; and Winter Visitors," identifies a poet as the guest, and this time Thoreau and his companion make "that small house ring with boisterous mirth and resound with the murmur of much sober talk" (268). Animated, intimate conversation happily dispels the solitude of the snow-covered woods.

Thoreau's zest for spirited exchange with interlocutors is the antithesis of his wish to emulate the obscurity of the pond's ice. It is the thread connecting *Walden* to the adjacent polemics, evidence not of an intention to banish the common herd of readers but of a refusal to submit to the aphasia of post-Compromise America. Although Thoreau pays relatively little attention to slavery in the text—he does refer, contemptuously, to "the passage of Webster's Fugitive-Slave Bill" (232)—he is insistent about making as much noise as possible, if only, like chanticleer at dawn, "to wake my neighbors up" (84). Often noted for its silences, *Walden* at the same time is one of the loudest works in the American canon, with countless moments of direct address and imaginary confabulation, and numerous chapters— "Sounds," "Brute Neighbors," "Winter Animals," "The Pond in Winter," and "Spring"—that incorporate the babel of nature. As Thoreau himself points out on the first page, he will retain the "I" in his narrative and not let us forget "that it is, after all, always the first person that is speaking" (3). Whitman's fondness for "saying" in "Song of Myself"—not a bad subtitle for *Walden*—has a rival in Thoreau's similar habit of foregrounding his voice. He does a great deal of saying in his own right: "I would fain say" (4), "I may say it without boasting" (18), "I have to say" (65), "I am obliged to say to you, Reader" (164), and "I do not hesitate to say" (73). Variations are legion, among them "I would gladly tell" (17), "I will speak a good word for the truth" (50), and "I can assure my readers" (285).

Perhaps the most arresting feature of these moments, given Thoreau's reputation for prickliness, is their dialogic quality. Time and again he relates conversations with people he knows or meets during his experiment, such as the Canadian woodchopper or the poet of "Brute Neighbors." He endeavors to draw his readers into talk by asking questions ("Are you one of the ninety-seven who fail? or of the three who succeed?" [38]); giving advice ("explore your own higher latitudes" [321]); and assuming a mutuality of interest ("The reader will perceive" [61]). Constructions like "Let us" appear frequently, and Thoreau encourages us to speak without inhibition: "Say what you have to say, not what you ought" (327). Moreover, he does not restrict dialogue to human beings but represents it as constitutive of the universe. An "irresistible voice" calls him away from societal conventions and into dialogue with matter (10). "I awoke to an answered question, to Nature and daylight" (282), he tells us at one point; "all things and events speak without metaphor," he writes at another (211). The soil and the sand are particularly prolific of utterance. When the Deep Cut thaws in the spring, the sand foliage shapes itself into letters and speaks in "living poetry" (309).

Besides these human and almost-human speakers, the text overflows with the sounds and pronouncements of nature. Thoreau hears foxes barking, a loon laughing, and owls hooting, a note he calls "the very *lingua vernacular* of Walden Wood" (272). He comments at length on the crowing of an actual chanticleer, which drowns out "the feebler notes of the other birds" and "would put nations on the alert" (127). The arrival of spring brings a fresh round of sounds, from the "chuckling and chirruping and vocal pirouetting and gurgling" of the red squirrels (310) to the cracking and booming of Walden's ice as it breaks up in the warming weather.

The list could go on, but the import should be evident. Thoreau's stake in difficult writing never extinguishes the "free speech" strain in *Walden* that echoes and prefigures his engagement with the political. "Sounds" and "Visitors" jostle "Solitude" among his chapter titles, and "the language heard" (101), the speaking voice, is everywhere in his manual of mysteries. This seeming contradiction between proximity and unapproachability can be partially resolved by thinking of *Walden* as a text of immediacy within distance. Thoreau the "I" strives to be there for the handful who will labor to fathom his meaning. In this, he emulates the ancient authors who manage to meet their readers on the page as living, breathing presences. As Thoreau insists in his account of the classics, the written word "is the work of art nearest to life itself. It may be translated into every language, and not only read but actually breathed from all human lips;—not be represented on canvas or in marble, but be carved out of the breath of life itself" (103). Although its creators may be separated from us by tracts of space and time, they have the power to "inspire" because they come alive for "the alert and heroic reader" (106). They are forever near in their remoteness. (Variations of this presence/agency dynamic will appear in Whitman, Fuller, and the Stowe of *Uncle Tom's Cabin*.)

Thoreau's dialogic commitment would eventuate in a renewed interest in the possible redemption of his neighbors, as can be seen in the orations on Brown. Thoreau met Whitman in Brooklyn in 1856 and reported saying to the poet, "in answer to him as representing America, that I did not think much of America."[19] Yet within three years Brown's attempt to foment a slave insurrection helped to ignite a volte-face in the Concord individualist's attitude toward his country and toward the civic efficacy of language and example.[20] In *Walden*, Thoreau speaks of planting the seeds of truth, sincerity, and heroism in his auditors. But the seeds, he continues, "if indeed they *were* the seeds of those virtues, were wormeaten or had lost their vitality, and so did not come up" (164). "A Plea for Captain John Brown" retrieves the metaphor and gives it a markedly different inflection. Thoreau says that "when you plant, or bury, a hero in his field, a crop of heroes is sure to spring up" (119). That seed infallibly germinates, and Brown, shortly to be hanged, fills the role of the speaker-warrior whose announced values are synonymous with his actions.

Thoreau first delivered his lecture on Brown at the Concord Town Hall at the end of October 1859; it was published the next year (along with the fragment "Martyrdom of John Brown") in an anthology edited by James Redpath entitled *Echoes of Harper's Ferry*. "Slavery in Massachusetts" began with an expression of annoyance at his neighbors, who seem eager to discuss the situation in Nebraska but "are not prepared to stand by one of their own bridges" (91). In "A Plea," the hero of Harpers Ferry emerges as the rebirth of the revolutionary spirit, "like the best who stood at Concord Bridge" (113), and his self-sacrifice for principle makes him a greater *man*—a word Thoreau accentuates in describing Brown—than either Franklin or Washington, the exemplary forebears of "Civil Disobedience." Brown, "the most American of us all" (125), is the long-awaited catalyst for national change who has "quickened the feeble pulse of the North" (135). In a subsequent piece, "The Last Days of John Brown" (1860), written for his memorial service in North Elba, New York, Thoreau claims that Brown's life and death will end by touching off a second revolution. He quotes from the martyr's testimony before the Virginia court, and he predicts that historians will record the scene and poets sing of it. Emerson deplored a retrospective age that memorialized the dead fathers in biographies and histories; Thoreau's Brown is a father *redivivus*, a hero of our own age, whose achievements will be celebrated by future generations.

As his comment about the "crop of heroes" indicates, Thoreau cedes to Brown the dual mission, once claimed for himself, of the Scottish poet Ossian: to inspire with language as well as to act. At Harpers Ferry, despite the raid's ostensible failure, Brown put into practice the war against slavery that he had conceptualized. His written and recorded statements are already functioning as decisive blows against the South's system of injustice. Thoreau, who endorses violence against slaveholders in "A Plea," sees in Brown a consummation of the word-as-deed activism that defined the whole antebellum period, from the gag rule of the 1830s to Lincoln's imminent election. In Brown's "undying words" in the improvised courtroom, the power of the verbal reaches a lethal climax: "In his case there is no idle eloquence, no made, nor maiden speech, no compliments to the oppressor. Truth is his inspirer, and earnestness the polisher of his sentences. He could afford to lose his Sharps' rifles, while he retained his faculty of speech, a Sharps' rifle of infinitely surer and longer range" (127). "Last Days" reiterates the idea of linguistic armament. Thoreau alludes to the recent death of Washington Irving, and, noting how Brown's truth telling dwarfs the writings of that lapidary stylist, he declares: "The *art* of composition is as simple as the discharge of a bullet from a rifle, and its master-pieces imply an infinitely greater force behind them" (151).

So was Thoreau really the most militant of the Transcendentalists? In some respects, yes, but not while Stowe was writing *Uncle Tom's Cabin*, nor when Emerson, disgusted by Webster's call for silence after the Fugitive Slave Law, said that antislavery voices merely raised the decibel level. The irony is that Thoreau's return to agitation finally resonated with the elusive northern public that venerated Emerson and devoured the "easy reading" of Stowe's fiction. The author who had hoped for a large audience in "Civil Disobedience" and the first draft of *Walden* found it with "A Plea for Captain John Brown." He was heard, and his words contributed their mite to slavery's downfall. Redpath's *Echoes of Harper's Ferry*, hurried into publication, sold 33,000 copies by February 1860, just three months after the lecture in Concord, and little more than a year before Ft. Sumter's surrender, making it the first and only best seller Thoreau ever wrote.

Fuller: History, Biography, and Criticism

In "The Literati of New York City" (1846), Poe has left a portrait of Margaret Fuller that is too often glossed as negative. "Her acts are bookish," Poe says, "and her books are less thoughts than acts." The description may seem mocking, but Poe expresses respect for his subject—a figure of "high genius," he calls her—and if we read his words sympathetically, they contain some important insights about the author of *Woman in the Nineteenth Century* (1845). Poe's appraisal intimates both Fuller's propinquity and her departure from her Transcendentalist compeers, Emerson and Thoreau.[1]

Most obviously, Poe singles out the conflation of discourse and deed in Fuller. He thus calls attention to her ties with the Emerson who avowed the equivalence of words and actions in "The Poet" and with the Thoreau whose essay on civil resistance constituted an act of subversion against the state. But, equally noteworthy, Poe's emphasis on Fuller's bookishness crystallizes her separation from the two Concordians. It reminds us of her commitment to scholarship or literary criticism as a mode of communication that, far from being an encumbrance on the present, as Emerson declares at the outset of *Nature*, is in actuality inspirational and causative.[2] Like Thoreau, Fuller possesses a polemical strain, and her feminist classic, which helped catalyze the women's rights movement that gathered at Seneca Falls in 1848, had a greater influence on antebellum culture than the unread "Civil Disobedience." But whereas Thoreau's style is direct and aphoristic, Fuller's is anything but: dense and often knotted in its constructions, allusive, crammed with quotations, many in foreign tongues, and concluding with not one but eight arcane appendices. How could such an irremediably "bookish" piece of writing be construed as an action?

How could the recitation and explication of history, biography, and literature be an impetus for change?

For Fuller, the sectional controversy always took second place to the issue of women's rights, and in *Woman* she does not complain directly of
Slave Power censorship. Yet like the other antebellum authors considered
here, she was consumed by the question of language's efficacy, and she
sought a renovated tongue on behalf of her sex. From personal history and
recent events, Fuller knew that antislavery and feminism often moved in
concert; opposition to the one commonly coalesced with resistance to the
other. The threat to (white) women from the slavocracy is a subdued or
background motif for most of her book, but it moves to the forefront in
the portions written in 1844. As she readied her text for publication, en-
larging it from the initial essay of 1843, "The Great Lawsuit. Man *versus*
Men. Woman *versus* Women," the Lone Star State's application to enter
the Union as a slave state convinced Fuller that the cause of women could
not withstand the expansion of bondage. The heightened passion and outspokenness of these pages convey her realization that the two forms of
liberation, always associated, were now inseparable, and that all reformist
discourse would be shackled if the antidemocratic forces in the country
had their way.

Within *Woman*, an early dialogue between Fuller and an "irritated
trader" first raises the question of silencing. The exchange also underlines
how hostility to antislavery tends to merge into patriarchal oppression. To
the trader, the two great reform movements of the mid-1840s are "Jacobin"
assaults on nation and home: "It is not enough that you have done all you
could to break up the national union, and thus destroy the prosperity of
our country, but now you must be trying to break up family union, to take
my wife away from the cradle and the kitchen hearth to vote at polls, and
preach from a pulpit." The trader does stop at maintaining that belief; like
the upholders of slavery, he would preclude any talk on the subject. When
Fuller asks if he has consulted his wife, the trader explains that there is no
need to because he is the head of the household, and her place is to serve
and obey him: "I would never consent to have our peace disturbed by any
such discussions" (15).[3]

Fuller was well aware of the overlapping condition of women and slaves.
According to her book, they are alike in their subordination, their wiles
of the weak, and their lack of control over their own bodies and minds;
they are alike, too, in their right to be free. The pairing seemed to define
the historical moment: Douglass published his *Narrative of the Life of an*

American Slave in the same year as *Woman*, and the meeting at Seneca Falls coincided with the formation of the Free Soil Party in the nearby city of Buffalo. As Fuller observes, abolitionists have been actively involved in the feminist movement, partly because of women's prominence in opposing slavery, and "partly from a natural following out of principles" (15). Support for both species of emancipation had a long tradition in her family. Fuller's father, Timothy, appears lightly disguised in *Woman* as a firm believer "in the equality of the sexes" who, recognizing that "one man by right cannot hold another in bondage," applied the same truth to gender relations and raised his daughter "not as a plaything, but as a living mind" (20–21).[4]

The senior Fuller's experience may well have been Margaret's introduction to the campaign to suppress antislavery ideas. Timothy had been a Federalist congressman and vocal restrictionist (that is, a proponent of forbidding slavery's spread into the territories) at the time of the Missouri Compromise, perhaps the last moment when slavery was discussed openly in the halls of government until the clashes over Texas. He advocated the position later adopted by Lincoln: that the peculiar institution be confined to the South, there eventually to expire. But restrictionism was sufficiently incendiary in 1820–21 to draw down the wrath of no less a figure than Thomas Jefferson, then in full flight from his eighteenth-century revolutionary credo. Jefferson believed that the founders' edifice was being destroyed by the fanaticism of the sons, and he raged against "this act of suicide on themselves, and of treason against the hopes of the world." Southerners, joined by northern moderates, emerged from the crisis certain that the Union could be preserved only by saying nothing at all about slavery.[5]

A similar concurrence of emancipatory concerns with struggles over speech distinguished John Quincy Adams, the best-known victim of the legislative compact to disallow further antislavery protest. In *Woman*, Fuller quotes at length from a lecture Adams gave at Hannah Foster's boarding school championing female education. The duty of men, the enlightened former president told his youthful audience, was to love and honor women, but *"not to flatter them"* (84). Elsewhere in the book, Fuller praises Adams as "the Phocion of his time" (17). Phocion was a Greek statesman who won renown by standing alone in opposition to the entire Athenian political class, an act of bravery comparable to Adams's lonely fight against the congressional refusal to hear antislavery petitions. For that defense of constitutional liberties, Adams's colleagues sought to censure and expel him. The attempted muzzling made enough of an impression on Fuller for her to return to it in "New Year's Day," an essay published right before *Woman* and right after the Tennessee slaveholder James K. Polk won the White House.[6]

Fuller understood that such developments threatened the political warrant for American exceptionalism. They would nullify the text in the country's documentary archive that confers special hopes on the United States. Slavery and the subjugation of women make a mockery of the Declaration's foundational "verbal statement" that "All men are born free and equal." Jefferson's pronouncement is the "golden certainty" at the core of American nationhood that, however disregarded in practice, promises "an independence of the encroachments of other men" as the equivalent to the republic's "external freedom" (13–14). Notice Fuller's deliberate revision or rewriting of the famous words: not "all men are created equal," but "all men are born free and equal"—a substitution of birth by woman for creation by God, and a reminder that Jefferson's formula implies freedom as well as equality, an end to both racial slavery and gender hierarchy. The Declaration, on this reading—or rereading—is the oracular element in the polity, the riposte to the often blocking provisions of the Constitution and the analog in the civic arena to the omens or tokens that Fuller will cull from her storehouse of mythological, historical, literary, and global sources. Fuller's gloss puts before us in embryo all the principal themes of her book: the centrality of women, the role of prophecy in the reanimation of language, the reordering of genres, and the importance of quotation and interpretation to her program of liberation.[7]

The defense of woman entails the rehabilitation of scholarship because they are notoriously the gender and the genre of the supplement. In popular thinking, they do not initiate or stand alone but are the diminished reflection of some other. Fuller's trader is representative: he takes it for granted that "woman was made *for man*" (20). Most men assign the "second sex" to a lower order of capability and view them as deficient in "the gift of reason, man's highest prerogative." They presume to do their thinking and speaking for them (18). This derisory attitude gains crucial support from the formative religious myth of Western culture. In the account of mankind's beginning found in the Old Testament, the human race forfeited its paradisiacal estate "through the fault of a woman," and Eve, that first and guilty female, exists so far beneath her mate in the order of being that she is said to have been created "from but a small part of himself" (25 and 32). Adam is the original, Eve and her descendants the adjuncts or flawed copies.

So the first step in Fuller's transvaluation of feminine and critical speech is to dislodge the supposition of woman's belatedness. Or rather, it is to rupture the very notion of a stable origin followed by a declension into afterthought. Fuller proceeds to do this by putting her chosen methodology into practice, interpreting and rebutting the Genesis narrative with an array of historical and textual evidence illustrating woman's self-sufficiency. Most notably, she counters the convention of the Fall with the even more prestigious idiom of the gospels. The New Testament supplies the conclusive rejoinder to the Hebraic judgment on the first woman; it immortalizes a story of female precedence in "Mary as the bride of the Holy Spirit" (26). As the mother of Jesus, Mary inverts the chronological order of the Old Testament creation fable. She comes before, and is the necessary precondition for, the appearance of the male god, and this reversal of roles makes the assignment of priority impossible. Fuller cites a similar circularity in classical mythology, where the female deities have as good a claim to origination as the males: "Jove sprang from Rhea, Pallas from Jove" (70). As she also observes, in a phrase recalling her feminist rewording of the Declaration, the fact that every "man is of woman born" (17) ought to induce a salutary modesty about masculine fantasies of primacy.

Fuller's deft maneuver reprieves those linked stepchildren, woman and the scholarly enterprise, from the imputation of inadequacy. She demonstrates that commentary on a predecessor text, or series of texts, along with citation from them, can still "speak with authority" (89) in the present. Fuller wants to establish herself as the compiler and exegete who can guide us through the discursive past and present, identifying the effectual signs that herald "the future Eden" while exposing the "prejudices and passions . . . continually obstructing the holy work" (7 and 5). She frequently juxtaposes passages and puts them into dialogue with each other, as when she comments on the moral shortcomings of George Sand by reprinting a pair of sonnets on Sand by the English poet Elizabeth Barrett. Her Appendix D consists of a long "unawakened" extract by Spinoza (115) that Fuller answers with poems by William Ellery Channing and Philip James Bailey and a prose description by Eugène Sue. Fuller even assumes the task of explicating her own book. She admits that her many illustrations and repetitions may have confused some readers and proposes to clarify her meaning by retracing, "once more, the scope of my design in points, as was done in old-fashioned sermons" (99). The culminating example of this method occurs during a complex reading of Madame Necker. "I know not how the subject could be better illustrated," Fuller writes, than by separating the wheat from the chaff in Madame Necker's book; place them in two heaps and then summon the reader to choose; giving him first a near-sighted [i.e., magnifying] glass to examine the two; it might be a Christian, an astronomical, or an artistic glass, any kind of good glass to obviate acquired defects in the eye. I would lay any wager on the result. (95)

The author of *Woman* is the "good glass," able to obviate the blind spots that mar our perception. She is the "transparent eyeball" that can show us the working of spirit or the law, not, as Emerson did, in the bare common, but in culture and society.

Yet what gives those yellowing extracts, stretching from Plato and Xenophon to Goethe and Catharine Maria Sedgwick, their power to persuade in 1845? Fuller musters Eve, Mary, Jesus, and the Hebrew prophets, but unlike Stowe (to whom I shall return), she does not look to the Christian scriptures as the sole or chief purveyor of providential design. Nor, like Emerson, does she find it in nature. She affirms an irresistible teleology or destiny in the world, leading to the longed-for future of gender equality, and she reiterates her conviction that "[man's] happiness is secure in the end" (9). (This "truth," a favorite term of Fuller's, resembles the divine communication that Emerson would invoke in his abolitionist phase, "the God's truth . . . like a bolt from a cloud" that he saw as empowering the antislavery movement in his "Address on the Emancipation.") The "signs" (7) and "tokens" (37) that assure Fuller of the coming jubilee appear in a multiplicity of sites: the high place of women as muses and sibyls in Greek mythology; the life of Emily Plater, "the heroine of the last revolution in Poland" (24); and the numerous "triumphs of female authorship" in the nineteenth century (55). Above all, the promises appear "as prophecy or as poesy" (69) in the inspired utterances of the women and few men whose finely tuned sensibilities can receive the spiritual messages. And because those words are the emanation of a higher power, they are, if properly understood, as efficacious now as when they were spoken years or centuries ago. However "past in time," their freshness cannot fade; they "have been translated into eternity by thought" (7).

Fuller elaborates these ideas in her discussion of male and female nature, and, as she converts woman's perceived shortcoming into strength, the potency of secondhand or copied language moves to center stage. At first her reflections on sexual identity seem unexceptional. She argues that female nature comprises two elements, one of which, Minerva, or wisdom, can be seen as the masculine component in women. It has been allowed to

atrophy, leading to a greater exfoliation of the other element, denominated
the Muse. This feminine capability, which is present to a lesser degree in
men, especially poets, is synonymous with insight or clairvoyance. Fuller
claims to want to nurture her female readers' Minerva side in order to
right the internal balance, but it quickly becomes apparent that her real
fascination is with the other, stereotypically female side. She defines the
Muse as "the unimpeded clearness of the intuitive powers" and says that
certain women possess it in unusual abundance. Two examples she mentions often are the Trojan princess Cassandra, who can "foresee the results
of actions passing around her," and the Seeress of Prevorst (discussed at
length in *Summer on the Lakes* [1844]), who can penetrate more deeply
than others into the spiritual realities hidden behind daily routine (69).
Such women, joined by the occasional male poet, are endowed with a kind
of electrical "genius" (68), "fluid" (61), or "element" (95) that gives them an
instinctive attunement to the energy of the world spirit. It puts them in
touch with the ineluctable unfolding of truth in history.

What they can see, they announce; they give voice to the reasons for
hope that the new era is approaching, and they warn their hearers of the
disastrous consequences of obstruction. But the trademark of their speech
is that it derives from somewhere else; its efficacy consists precisely in its
being an echo or repetition of another source. None can match Cassandra,
the daughter of Priam and Hecuba, in "superior susceptibility to magnetic
or electric influence" (68), and she, along with the sibyls at Delphi, "told
[that is, announced] the oracle of the highest god" (31). Cassandra is an archetype of prophetic truth telling because Apollo spoke through her. Her
forebodings, though ignored by mistrustful auditors, invariably came to
pass, and her Trojan countrymen paid the price for their refusal to listen:
their homeland was destroyed.

The sibyls establish the pattern for divinely inspired utterance. In
the Hebrew Bible, the motif persists: the Lord speaks through his chosen
prophets and puts his commands into their mouths. For Fuller, too, the
"disclosures" (64) are an announcement from the world spirit; the "copy"
is cognate with its origin. Scholarship, feminine receptivity, and inspired
eloquence all come together in *Woman*'s compulsive reproducing of the
words of previous speakers. What other text by an antebellum author relies
so heavily on quotation and paraphrase to make its argument? (Many, as it
happens, from *Moby-Dick* to Lincoln's Cooper Institute address.) Take the
long quoted selection from Xenophon on the love of Panthea and Abrada-
tus. Fuller prepares us for this moment by promising, some fifteen pages in
advance, "This picture I shall copy by and by" (35); and when she arrives at

the appropriate place in her text, she chooses two memorable passages, declaring, "I shall copy both." And quote them both she does, thickening her book with four or five pages taken verbatim from the Greek historian. The passages will be familiar to many readers, Fuller concedes, but this does not lessen the value of reprinting and explicating them, "for never were the heroism of a true woman . . . painted in colors more delicate or more lively" (51).[8] It would be superfluous to review all these "borrowings," as she unashamedly refers in *Summer on the Lakes* to material drawn from elsewhere;[9] but one other example seems noteworthy. In her Appendix G, Fuller quotes an earlier passage of herself quoting Euripides' *The Trojan Women*; the subject, fittingly enough, is Cassandra, "singing wildly her inspired song" (133 and 63).

Indeed, the idea of the productive facsimile or copy is a constant in Fuller's thinking. According to Caroline Healey Dall, she discussed Mercury, the god of thieves and rhetoric, in her conversations on mythology and affirmed that "eloquence was a kind of thieving."[10] In "A Short Essay on Critics" (1840) from the *Dial*, she observed that the quotation and analysis of a piece of writing can "give more pleasure then the original production . . . , as melodies will sometimes ring sweetlier in the echo."[11] She excelled at translation—repeating someone else's words in a second tongue—and saw the practice as dynamic, not a mere transcription but the forming of something unique.[12] And she was not unusual among the romantics in fortifying her argument with the vibrant language of others. Coleridge, a writer she admired, exhibits a comparable "ventriloquism of the divine" in his fondness for scriptural quotation and redaction.[13] Even Emerson, as committed as Fuller to the oracular, defers to the inspired word: he turns over practically the entire last paragraph of *Nature* to his Orphic poet and encloses the appropriated sentences in quotation marks.

Yet Emerson, at least the Emerson of *Nature*, opposes the prophetic voice to an obsolete textuality; for Fuller, on the contrary, "the historian is a prophet turned backward" (the phrasing is Friedrich Schlegel's),[14] and past omens lose none of their might. Moreover, her view of the enduring agency of "biographies, histories, and criticism" had wide appeal among antislavery advocates of both races and genders. The borrowed, stolen, and quoted words had proven their worth before—why not again? In his emancipation address, Emerson himself quotes liberally from Clarkson, Wilberforce, and other English pioneers in the antislavery movement. Douglass takes heart from Sheridan's speeches and a dialogue between master and slave that he discovers in the *Columbian Orator*; reading them "over and over again with unabated interest" solidifies his hatred of racial bondage, which might otherwise have "died away for want of utterance."[15] And when Douglass revises his memoir into *My Bondage and My Freedom* (1855), he quotes freely from his earlier account to preserve the freshness of his first impressions.

But perhaps the best comparison is to a novelist with whom Fuller seems to share little: Harriet Beecher Stowe. In *Uncle Tom's Cabin* and *Dred*, Stowe strives to create "the magic of real presence" on the page—a miracle, she believes, for which the Bible is the model. She fills the later novel with paraphrastic jeremiads from the Hebrew prophets and the Book of Revelation. The more secular Fuller anticipates Stowe by deploying quotations pulsating with electrical and magnetic currents. She sets those passages, infused with supernatural presence, as close to the reader as she can, with nothing between them and us, and lets the charges flow unobstructed from the original sources. Like Stowe, moreover, she discriminates between skeptics who will scoff and readers with the capacity to understand. She writes that "to appreciate such disclosures one must be a child, and here the phrase 'women and children' may, perhaps, be interpreted aright, that only little children shall enter into the kingdom of heaven" (64). For those with feminine susceptibility to the "page of prophecy" (77), Fuller's difficult and learned volume achieves an influence akin to Stowe's sentimental dramas. It is a triumphant example of retrospect as prospect.

Fuller does more then assemble and interpret the signs discerned by others. Like the sibyls in the grip of the god, she foretells the shape of the future in her own voice. Her genius, too, is intuitive: of her self-portrait, Miranda, she explains that the young woman had "a strong electric nature" which "attracted" those like her and "repelled" the unsympathetic (21). "'Sight comes first,'" Fuller insists in a passage on Linnaeus (69), and near the conclusion of *Woman* she offers a vision of an inspired band of young men and women, residing throughout the globe, whom she names the exalted ones, Los Exaltados and Las Exaltadas: "I have in my eye a youth and a maiden whom I look to as the nucleus of such a class"; they will serve as "the harbingers and leaders of a new era" (91). Although insight is the first step, annunciation is the necessary corollary: the words must be spoken for the future to be actualized. Saying makes it happen, according to Fuller:

> Could we indeed say what we want, could we give a description of the child that is lost, he would be found. As soon as the soul can affirm clearly that a certain demonstration is wanted, it is at hand. When the

Jewish prophet [Isaiah] described the Lamb, as the expression of what was required by the coming era, the time drew nigh. (10)

Occurrences in the present were about to test Fuller's buoyancy about the future. The election as president of the proslavery Democrat Polk, a supporter of Texas annexation, shook her faith in the United States and in the inexorable progress of truth in history. Slavery, the scourge of free speech, had resumed its march, and its lengthening shadow darkens the final section of *Woman*. The impending acquisition, Fuller exclaims in dismay, will "rivet the chains" of slavery on the republic and destroy the whole "tissue of prophecies" leading to the spot where all men were to "be born free and equal." It will strengthen the hands of conservatives everywhere, and voices raised in protest against gender inequity as well as the South's patriarchal institution will come under redoubled attack. Fuller no longer distinguishes between women's rights and the bondmen's rights. "This cause is your own," she tells her female readers; the resurgence of Manifest Destiny, unless checked, means that both forms of liberation "will have no more a nation, no more a home on earth" (97–98).

American women represent the last, best hope of preserving the millennial dream. Fuller's tone assumes a fresh urgency and determination as she beseeches her audience to ceaselessly lobby their husbands, fathers, and sons to see the light. Here her faith in reinvigorated speech unites her antislavery and feminist commitments. Above all, she asserts, women must use their tongues to thwart the designs of the Slave Power. They must "reprove," "check," "convince," "tell," and raise "their voice in public" in order to save their nation and "lift off the curse incurred by Eve." You will be accused of immodesty, she warns her readers, and critics will try to shame you into muteness. But "you would not speak in vain" (98).

A few pages later, *Woman* reverts to the prophetic mode. Fuller reprints—copies from herself—the vatic paragraph with which she closed "The Great Lawsuit":

And will she not soon appear? The woman who shall vindicate their birthright for all women; who shall teach them what to claim; and how to use what they obtain? Shall not her name be for her era, Victoria, and for her country and life, Virginia? Yet predictions are rash; she herself must teach us to give her the fitting name. (104)

This self-quotation marks the text's oracular acme. Fuller places her unmediated words before us, their electromagnetic conductivity unobstructed, and her passage leaves us with the inevitable question: Does not her utterance of this visionary portrait, her giving voice to "what was required of the coming era," signal that the reality "is at hand"? Is not the prophecy, so clearly a manifestation of the world spirit, destined to come true? For the architects of the Declaration of Sentiments at Seneca Falls, a convention attended by Frederick Douglass, the answer was yes, and the teacher's name was Margaret Fuller.

Fuller did not relinquish the idea of impactful speech after her feminist scripture. Yet even before the next season of her life, as a correspondent in Italy during the Roman revolution, *Woman*'s confidence began to metamorphose into Old Testament-style anathemas or sibylline prophecies of doom. In political pieces from around the time of Texas's annexation, America as "the ark of human hopes" competes with images of an "Avenging Angel," sometimes sable-hued in a hint of race war, and always furious at a people who have betrayed "the purposes of Heaven" for their land. An article entitled "First of August, 1845," published a year after Emerson's, denounces the Texas annexation as the "most shameful deed . . . that ever disgraced a nation" and warns that God cannot "much longer pardon" the country's crimes.[16] Fuller's reporting from abroad continues the theme of national judgment. Caught up in the battle for the Roman republic, she declares that the divine promises have deserted her homeland for Europe. The Mexican-American War and "this horrible cancer of Slavery" have so soiled the West's first modern republic that it no longer qualifies as "the advance-guard of Humanity." It trails far behind Rome in commitment to freedom and brotherhood, and the "Future" is "more alive here at present than in America."[17]

Fuller left Italy after the Roman republic's downfall, embarking for the United States in the summer of 1850, within months of the passage of the Fugitive Slave Law and the reopening of the sectional schism. Her Roman experience had helped convert her from antislavery to outright abolitionism. Like Emerson before his radicalization, she had considered the movement "tedious" and "rabid"; she now judged it "something worth living and dying for to free a great nation from such a terrible blot."[18] Many of her friends feared she would not have fit in if, instead of drowning off the coast of Fire Island, she had returned safely to her country. That seems unlikely. One can imagine Fuller throwing herself into the antislavery cause and "speaking with authority" in the tempestuous 1850s. Cassandra-like, she would doubtless have added her prophetic warnings to those of Thoreau (in his John Brown essays), Douglass, and Stowe's *Dred*.

A writer who dreaded this kind of epilogue for Fuller was Nathaniel Hawthorne, and she was to have an afterlife in his fiction as a radical female speaker in need of disciplining. We have seen Fuller's investment in productive facsimiles; Hawthorne's use of her might be said to constitute "obstructive facsimiles," copies or quotations meant to retard the emancipation of women and slaves rather than hastening that future. Zenobia, the feminist turned jilted lover of *The Blithedale Romance*, who, like Fuller, dies by drowning, is an obvious debt. Hester Prynne echoes *Woman* in her final avatar as a consoler of women and imaginer of a female redeemer. Hester of course is chastened into penitence, and her misgivings about her own role paraphrase Fuller on the controversial George Sand. Because she is "stained with sin," Hawthorne's heroine admits, she will not "be the destined prophetess" and will not see the better world materialize.[19] But perhaps the final word belongs to the author of *Woman in the Nineteenth Century*. Her facsimiles, reworked by Hawthorne, would not give up their potency quite so easily. They can still be heard in the dissident murmurings that the novelist could not altogether purge from his writing.

Hawthorne and the Resilience of Dissent

The consensus on Hawthorne and politics goes something like this: unlike Emerson and Thoreau, unlike Douglass and Stowe, activists all, Hawthorne was an *inactivist* who fetishized deferral. His campaign biography of Franklin Pierce is said to provide a retroactive template for his fiction. Hawthorne the artist contemplated subversion—most notably in the person of Hester Prynne—only in order to break its spirit, and he regarded idealistic political action, whether against slavery or any other injustice, as a wrongful arrogation of God's power to dispose of human affairs when and how he saw fit. *The Scarlet Letter, The House of the Seven Gables, The Blithedale Romance*—Hawthorne's three "American" novels gave fictional form to the age's ethical and legislative impasse, the Compromise of 1850.[1]

In this chapter, I do not so much want to overturn this consensus as to deepen and complicate it by foregrounding Hawthorne's connection to the dissenting ferment that he, like his friend Pierce, saw as a menace to sectional peace. The novelist was out of the country during much of the 1850s, first as Pierce's consul in Liverpool and then as a resident in Italy;[2] but during his creative heyday, from 1850 to 1852, he was acutely conscious of the mounting pressures on free speech. Indeed, his book on Pierce placed him at the center of those pressures. He hoped the prohibitions would prevail and stifle the seditious ferment of anti-slavery oratory. His "little biography" (23:273),[3] as he disparagingly calls it, concludes with a frank endorsement of the end of partisan debate—almost, one might say, the end of politics. Hawthorne reports that the two national parties, Whigs and Democrats, have ceased to differ over principles. They have put aside their disagreements to unite "in one common purpose—that of preserving our sacred Union, as the immovable basis from which the destinies, not of

America alone, but of mankind at large, may be carried upward and consummated." The result, greeted by the text with relief, is "unwonted quiet and harmony," a blanket of stillness happily descending on all regions of the country (23:369–70).

Hawthorne's position, to put it mildly, is highly anomalous: he is himself a storyteller, a man of words, and yet the performative power of speech menaces the societal stasis he cherishes. One way to circumvent the anomaly, perhaps, would be to purify nomination of deceptive artifice. A reclusive type with no competence in politics, Hawthorne contends that his sole qualification for writing of Pierce is that he knows the general personally and will "tell the truth" about him (23:274). His campaign biography bristles with antipathy toward verbal cleverness, a revulsion from the mastery of language possessed by so many characters in Hawthorne's fiction. Pierce emerges from his portrait as a kind of anti-Dimmesdale. Unlike *The Scarlet Letter*'s adulterous pastor, whose intoxicating oratory catapults him ahead of his seniors as the foremost preacher of Puritan Boston, Pierce scrupulously avoids pushing himself forward in debate. He will not open his mouth to say anything if some "other and older man could perform the same duty as well as himself" (23:289). Nor, when he does bring himself to address the people, does the Democratic candidate resort to manipulation and half-truths—again, the special province of Arthur Dimmesdale. Pierce "never yet was guilty of an effort to cajole his fellow citizens, to operate upon their credulity, or to trick them even into what was right" (23:349–50). Hawthorne goes so far as to compare his old college friend to the representatives of the Continental Congress, paragons of moral probity whose earnestness supposedly trumped their linguistic polish. Today, he adds, eloquence has degenerated into something other than a medium of truth; it has become "a knack, a thing valued in itself" (23:298).

But it would be a mistake to construe Hawthorne's quarrel in *The Life of Franklin Pierce* as being directed exclusively against verbal glitter or the use of language to beguile and mislead. Language itself is the object of his strictures, and he praises Pierce not simply for eschewing rhetorical excess, but for having "no fluency of words" whatever (23:289). As we have seen, the general is reputed to be a speaker of rare integrity. Yet the extraordinary fact about the biography is how infrequently it quotes from its subject's public pronouncements—perhaps a score of paragraphs in all, and most of those not from addresses but from two relatively minor sources, a letter declining President Polk's offer of the attorney generalship and a brief communication accepting the Democratic nomination. Hawthorne offers no direct testimony of his own, in that age of oratory, to Pierce's linguistic prowess. He confesses that he has none to offer:

> It has never been the writer's good fortune to listen to one of Frank-
> lin Pierce's public speeches, whether at the bar or elsewhere; nor, by
> diligent inquiry, has he been able to gain a very definite idea of the
> mode in which he produces his effects. To me, therefore, his forensic
> displays are in the same category with those of Patrick Henry, or any
> other orator whose tongue, beyond the memory of man, has mouldered
> into dust. (23:305–6)

Several individuals are summoned as eyewitnesses to Pierce's exploits at the bar and in the forum. One, a Professor Edwin D. Sanborn of Dartmouth College, relates that during the revision of the New Hampshire state constitution, Pierce conducted himself with "eloquence" and "magnanimity" (23:359). The reader has to take the declaration on trust, however, because nothing is quoted as corroborating evidence. As for his famous rallying behind the Compromise of 1850, Pierce's support was consistent with his long-held convictions. From the time of his first election to Congress, Hawthorne tells us, again without illustration, his friend always "raised his voice against agitation" (23:351).

Hawthorne's reticence projects an image of Pierce as "a man of deeds, not words" (23:290), a legislator so disgusted by contemporaneous "agitation" that he would rather wrap himself in silence than condescend to utterance. It is as though language has been so debased by antislavery militancy that it has no proper place in politics at all. A political biography rightly honors this separation by relegating glibness to the margins or, better yet, expunging it from the text almost completely. Indeed, Hawthorne's preface suspends judgment on the accuracy of his rendition of Pierce's sentiments. So few of the candidate's actual words and ideas appear in the book that Hawthorne's speculations "may, or may not, be in accordance" with his subject's opinions. The reader can best glean Pierce's views not from the author's sketch of them, but from his "straight-forward and consistent deeds," which are superior to any public statement as a register of what he thinks (23:273–74). Thus does Hawthorne invert the word-deed dynamic of the antebellum years; he presents the Democratic nominee for president as a verbal lightweight whose acts do his talking for him, and who expressly refrains from deranging the culture's equilibrium with flights of oratory.

It is true, though, that Hawthorne inserts a long selection from the private journal Pierce kept while he was serving with the Ninth Regiment in Mexico, "hasty jottings-down in camp" that allegedly reveal more about him than "any narrative which we could substitute" (23:319). (Chapter 4 of the biography is titled "The Mexican War.—His Journal of the March from Vera Cruz.") But here, once again, the journal entries—more copious than any extracted speech—subordinate rhetoric to action. They consist of a tedious chronicle of events: we proceeded with eighty wagons, we encountered enemy fire, so-and-so's horse was shot from under him, we bivouacked near the river, we broke camp at dawn, etc., etc. The doer of Pierce's war journal records no memorable ideas or insights, and he puts on display no talent for language. In this, as in so much else, the Democrat was the opposite of the eloquent Republican standard-bearer who followed him eight years later into the White House. Pierce, Hawthorne implies, should be elevated to the presidency because he grasps the aversion of patriotism to empty phrase making.

Let us, following critical fashion, take the campaign book as our template. The imperative that Hawthorne's text urges most forcefully is the quarantining of discursive agility from the practical realm of politics. Ostensibly, the two domains, the verbal or aesthetic and the worldly or civic, share little and fare best in isolation from each other. Hawthorne, as a well-known novelist and "the Author of this Memoir," disavows any connection to politics and makes much of his unfitness to represent a "public man" to the electorate, that being a "species of writing too remote from his occupations—and, he may add, from his tastes"—for him to carry out satisfactorily (23:273). He acknowledges, moreover, that there have been large gaps in his intercourse with Pierce. Their "modes of life" have simply been too different, their "culture and labor" too unlike: "There was hardly a single object or aspiration in common between us" (23:302). Yet this seemingly natural division between the man of words and the man of action masks a fearful recognition that on some deeper level they are not only entangled with each other—after all, Hawthorne, for all his protests of unsuitability, compiled *The Life of Franklin Pierce*—but that the literary possesses an anarchic energy dangerous to civic peace. The pose of linguistic and artistic innocence or impotence is just that, a pose, founded on the mid-century reality that abolitionist agitation, and southern efforts to crush it, were hurrying the nation toward internecine warfare.

To turn to Hawthorne's longer fiction at this point—to approach it, as he invites us, through the entryway of "The Custom House"—is to reencounter the segregation of the aesthetic from the functional, and from the arena of politics in particular. The man who would become Pierce's biographer began his career as a novelist by positing an absolute breach between literature and public life. In the introduction to *The Scarlet Letter*, he comes before the reader as a representative of "Uncle Sam's government" (1:5), a political appointee to the Salem customhouse. (Polk, the annexationist Southerner who fomented the Mexican-American War, named him to the post.) But as a romancer turned Surveyor of the Revenue, Hawthorne is a fish out of water, gasping for survival in an element thoroughly inhospitable to the creative imagination. His fellowship once included intellects of the caliber of Emerson, Thoreau, Alcott, Ellery Channing, and Longfellow; it now consists of aging public functionaries, former military officers, and an unnamed "man of business," few of whom have read or even heard of his literary accomplishments. The effect on his productivity is disastrous. Even after he discovers the packet belonging to Surveyor Pue, with its dozen or so yellowed pages on Hester Prynne and its moth-eaten scarlet letter, Hawthorne cannot reanimate his powers of invention. His imagination is "a tarnished mirror" (1:34). Employment by the United States government has extinguished his ability to write.

It must be among the oddest introductions on record to a major work of art, a narrative of the author's failure to compose the very text we are holding in our hands. The paradox of American literary culture in the age of slavery's expansion is that it almost expires in a writer's block. Hawthorne details the paralysis that gripped his mind while he was pocketing Uncle Sam's wages, and he recounts the miraculous dissolving of that obstruction as soon as he escaped from his position with the state. Verbal fluency and politics, we are instructed, do not mix. "So little adapted is the atmosphere of a Custom-House," Hawthorne says, "to the delicate harvest of fancy and sensibility, that, had I remained there through ten Presidencies yet to come, I doubt whether the tale of 'The Scarlet Letter' would ever have been brought before the public eye" (1:34). Only expulsion from office—a figurative beheading, as he conceives it—liberates him from his protracted silence. Restored to his customary occupation of man of letters, Hawthorne regains his voice and dashes off the novel in a blaze of creativity.

The ensuing tale reconstitutes the introduction's polarities with a significant variation. The wrinkle, which recurs in *The House of the Seven Gables* and *The Blithedale Romance*, is the presence of a tertium quid, a wielder of words whose morally problematic or dissident speech hovers on the margins of the rupture between language and politics, and whose eventual acquiescence leaves a residue of discontent. For the moment, I want to defer discussion of these figures, who disconcertingly evoke their creator, Hawthorne, in order to concentrate on the pattern familiar from the Pierce book. The speaker in *The Scarlet Letter* is the narrator or author of the introduction, finally rid of his customhouse duties and able to set his words down on paper. We are constantly aware of his addressing us. He offers reflections on the contrast between Puritan New England and the nineteenth century, muses about the motivations of his characters, and calls attention to his verbal mannerisms. These last include an addiction to asking questions ("could it be true?" [1:59]; "what imagination would have been irreverent enough to surmise that the same scorching stigma was on them both?" [1:247]) and a habit of announcing when he is about to tell us something ("we have as yet hardly spoken of the infant . . ." [1:89]; "we have a matter of business to communicate to the reader" [1:261]).

At the opposite extreme from this voluble and highly articulate figure are the ruling elders of Boston, leaders who orate or preach before the multitude but fail to do so with distinction. Like Pierce, they have "no fluency of words." Hawthorne reiterates that while the community's eminent men possess dignity and respectability, they lack the gift of imagination: "They would have vainly sought—had they ever dreamed of seeking—to express the highest truths through the humblest medium of familiar words and images" [1:143]. When their senior member, the Reverend John Wilson, delivers his sermon on Hester's sin, we are not permitted to eavesdrop on his actual disquisition but are provided only a summary.

Also on the side of taciturnity is Hester Prynne. The heroine is a subverter of societal norms, an apostate from the Puritan state, but, unlike the abolitionist protesters of the antebellum era, she lives under a sentence of virtual silence. Practically her first words in the text are "I will not speak!" [1:68], and although we have access to her thoughts, she seldom gets to enunciate them aloud. Chapters such as "The Interior of a Heart" and "Another View of Hester" investigate consciousness, not assertion or action. Except for one or two scenes—the meeting with Dimmesdale in the forest, for instance—Hester says about as little as any protagonist in American fiction. And when she does attain utterance, the setting is invariably a confidential location distant from the public sphere, such as a prison cell or the primeval woods. She relies on Dimmesdale, her former pastor, to argue her case for retaining Pearl to the Puritan magistrates. Her credo, as she cautions her daughter, is, "We must not always talk in the market-place of what happens to us in the forest" [1:240].

The split between politics and the aesthetic continues in *The House of the Seven Gables* (1851). The two positions are embodied in Clifford

Pyncheon and Judge Jaffrey Pyncheon, the first a lover of the beautiful, the second a prominent jurist and prospective candidate for governor of Massachusetts. (The consanguinity between these adversaries hints at unacknowledged affinities.) Clifford has returned to Salem after serving a thirty-year prison sentence for a murder he did not commit. He is a shattered spirit who nevertheless possesses a hyperactive imagination and "an exquisite taste" (2:108). When he and Hepzibah flee their ancestral home, he delivers a tirade against convention to a "gimlet-eyed old gentleman" on the train, who dismisses his "wild talk" of social upheaval as "all a humbug!" (2:259, 262–63). As in his previous romance, Hawthorne would banish such indecent speech from the public concourse. Unflattering "stories," "fables," "traditions," and "gossip" about the community's eminent citizens circulate in chimney corners and byways, but this "hidden stream of private talk" never makes its way into print (2:122–24, 310). Like Clifford's questioning of the status quo, it is apparently without consequence, a muffled whispering that leaves those in power unaffected.

Clifford's nemesis, the judge, is a figure of solidity whose smiling exterior conceals a "hot fellness of purpose, which annihilated everything but itself" (2:129). Two objectives drive Jaffrey: he wants to be the chief magistrate of the Commonwealth, and he wants to coax or bully his cousin into revealing the secret of the Pyncheons' missing wealth. When he tries to force an entrance into the house to confront Clifford, the latter cries out for mercy in an "enfeebled voice," his "murmur of entreaty" no more capable of dissuading the hard-hearted judge than the wail of a "frightened infant" (2:129). Jeffrey's political ambitions were to be realized on the evening he dies from the family's inherited liability. He planned to dine with the "little knot" of influential schemers who regularly "steal from the people" the right of selecting their rulers (2:274). Hawthorne sums up the disproportionate strength of his two characters—and, by implication, of the literary sensibility and the world of politics—by observing that Clifford could never have survived a face-to-face encounter with the judge: "It would be like flinging a porcelain vase, with already a crack in it, against a granite column" (2:242).

The Blithedale Romance (1852), Hawthorne's third and last novel set in America, takes as its inspiration the socialist experiment at Brook Farm. Literature and politics are once again sharply differentiated from each other. Hawthorne's preface finds "the author" (as he repeatedly calls himself) disavowing any intention, "favorable or otherwise, in respect to Socialism." The setting is nothing more than a "theatre . . . where the creatures of his brain may play their phantasmagorical antics" (3:1). Haw-

thorne erects a barrier between his own voice—the voice of the apolitical artist—and those of the activists at Blithedale. The minor poet Miles
Coverdale relates the adventures of the community and thus, for the first
time in the fiction we have been examining, displaces Hawthorne himself
as the narrator. Similarly, the various proposals for political change can
be traced back not to the name on the title page, but to the zealots who
assemble at the would-be utopia. Besides Coverdale, two other major characters dream of reform and traffic in language. They are the feminist and
writer Zenobia, who declaims against woman's oppression with the eloquence of "a stump-oratress," and the former blacksmith Hollingsworth
(3:44). Zenobia frames female victimization as an act of physical silencing:
"Thus far, no woman in the world has ever once spoken out her whole
heart and her whole mind. The mistrust and disapproval of the vast bulk
of society throttles us, as with two gigantic hands at our throats" (3:120).
Hollingsworth has come to Blithedale to recruit disciples for his project
of prison reform. He is constantly exhorting his fellow philanthropists
at the boulder-pulpit where John Eliot preached to the Indians. "No other
speech of man," comments Coverdale of his friend's performances, "has
ever moved me like some of those discourses" (3:119).

All three characters end up dead or defeated, and it is hard not to read
their unfortunate outcomes as Hawthorne's vengeance on his utopians
for daring to advocate societal renovation. For all her feminist rhetoric,
Zenobia proves to be another dependent woman; she kills herself when
Hollingsworth rejects her. The prison reformer is overwhelmed by guilt
and abandons his ambitious plans in order to focus on a single criminal,
himself. And Coverdale, soured by his experience at Blithedale, renounces
his political ideals altogether. He would be ready to join the struggle for
Hungarian rights, he confides to the reader, only if Kossuth pitched the
battlefield "within an easy ride of my abode" and arranged the conflict for
"a mild, sunny morning, after breakfast. . . . Further than that, I should
be loth to pledge myself" (3:247). If Coverdale does eventually write the
romance we have just finished reading, the preface's tone of authorial fas-
tidiousness should not surprise us. The erstwhile radical has, in his disaffection from activism, become one with his creator.

The problem with these readings of Hawthorne's fiction should be evident.
In every case, a charismatic speaker or linguistic rebellion has been omitted. This is the complicating factor persistently slighted by the current
consensus: Hawthorne's politics of pacification always contain an un-
pacified dimension. Even though the potent wordsmith is discredited or

subdued and the dissident rhetoric muted, "the power of words" (the title of one of Poe's stories) haunts Hawthorne's narratives as a resilient and unruly force. Furthermore, the watertight compartmentalization between the imagination and politics keeps springing leaks. The aesthetic exercises authority over practical areas that seem to be immune from its effects.

Perhaps the most obvious example of this intersecting is the introduction to *The Scarlet Letter*. Hawthorne may be speechless in the customhouse, but he discovers there, preserved by his "official ancestor," Surveyor Pue (1:33), the ancient documents that fertilize his fancy after his expulsion. The brick building flying "the banner of the republic" (1:5) *originates* the story that follows; structurally, the political sphere serves as the anteroom to the opening of the verbal floodgates, much as, in mid-nineteenth-century culture at large, the polity's attempted suppression of "agitation" gives rise to the American Renaissance. An embargo on discourse, either external or internally generated (and for Hawthorne, the distinction is blurred), is in both cases the necessary precondition for artistic prodigality.

As for the oppositions of the romance, they are eroded by the very existence of the Reverend Dimmesdale. His singular standing as at once a brilliant orator and a leader of the settlement folds into one individual the seemingly antithetical principles of linguistic ingenuity and worldly influence. The young divine has the gift "of addressing the whole human brotherhood in the heart's native language," the "Tongue of Flame" denied his elders (1:142); and his skill in the pulpit deconstructs the divide between speaker and ruler. Hawthorne has emphasized all along that the Puritan magistrates lack literary or intellectual distinction. None of those officials could preach effectively. Dimmesdale, on the other hand, is a man of eloquence who could also be a man of action:

> His was the profession, at that era, in which intellectual ability displayed itself far more than in political life; for—leaving a higher motive out of the question—it offered inducements powerful enough, in the almost worshipping respect of the community, to win the most aspiring ambition into its service. Even political power—as in the case of Increase Mather—was within the grasp of a successful priest. (1:238)

Of course, Dimmesdale is a morally compromised character whose boundary transgressions might be taken to vindicate the lesson: words and deeds overlap at their peril. His parishioners receive the minister's oratory with rapture, but his speeches are exercises in equivocation. Cunning delivery turns his vague confessions in church into falsehoods; his "revelation of the scarlet letter" in the final scaffold scene is similarly evasive and ambiguous, and the Puritans disagree about its meaning. Are we to conclude, then, that when verbal fluency crosses into public space, it automatically mutates into verbal treachery? Is the Pierce biography, Hawthorne's own venture into political speech, another example of linguistic turpitude, or is it the exception that proves the rule? Certainly Dimmesdale's inspired tongue refutes the idea that the literary sensibility is dysfunctional when it colludes with power. And what of the minister's election sermon? That discourse, which owes its "deep, sad undertone of pathos" to Dimmesdale's guilt, culminates in a prophecy that has to count as truthful because it is realized in history. Though we are not permitted to hear the sermon—an indication of Hawthorne's continuing uneasiness with language as power—we learn that the preacher's mission was "to foretell a high and glorious destiny for the newly gathered people of the Lord" (1:249). Hawthorne, speaking of the United States two centuries after Dimmesdale's death, declares in the Pierce book that on the welfare of the Union rest the destinies of all mankind.

Prophecy is performative utterance at its most dramatic. The "old prophets of Israel" (1:249) whom Hawthorne cites did not deal in feckless sentences; their judgments, backed by the omnipotence of the Deity, summoned events into being. Dimmesdale's announcement of the future is the first of a number of such predictions in Hawthorne's work, some positive, others much more ominous, all marked by a deedlike impact on the actual. The minister's flair for prophetic speech passes on to Hester. The two characters have ventriloquized each other before: Dimmesdale at Governor Bellingham's mansion, where he pleaded with the colony's leaders to let Hester keep Pearl; and Hester in the forest scene, where the emotionally and physically drained pastor implored her, "Think for me. . . . Thou art strong. Resolve for me!" (1:196). (Hester's counsel to her lover, "Preach! Write! Act!" [1:198], suggests her stake in articulation as intervention.)

In the novel's conclusion, the heroine picks up the mantle of seer that Dimmesdale has left behind—or half picks it up. The final pages are a study in ambiguity. Hawthorne explicitly states that Hester will *not* be the prophetess of a new truth about gender roles. But he also says that the wearer of the scarlet letter firmly assures her listeners of a "coming revelation" in which "the whole relation of man and woman" will be placed "on a surer ground of mutual happiness" (1:263). He has her publicize that belief in precisely the kind of marginalized but quasi-open forum favored by emergent political movements, such as the antebellum struggle for emancipation. Hester, until this moment, has done all her speaking in clandestine or solitary spaces; now she addresses a gathering or, perhaps, a succession of women in her cottage near the settlement, at meetings that could not possibly escape the notice of the governing elders. As with Dimmesdale's election sermon, Hawthorne does not provide us access to Hester's conversations. He gives us only a digest. Is his restraint another attempt to muzzle the voice of dissent—whose intuition of the future has arguably come true, in our day if not in his? Or does Hawthorne's secondhand account paradoxically betray an awareness of his own lack of distance from the age's polemical tumult, his inevitable implication as a writer in the transformative power of speech?

What is undeniable is that the motif of prophecy moves to center stage in Hawthorne's fiction, and that it acquires ever-greater ascendancy over the real. In *The House of the Seven Gables*, the young boarder in the Pyncheon house, Holgrave, is a writer, lecturer, daguerreotypist, and reformer whose "lawless" (2:85) words bend others to his will. More generally, the members of the Maule family, from whom the pseudonymous Holgrave is descended, have always known how to use language as a weapon. The tradition dates back to Matthew Maule, the progenitor of the line. Maule, wrongly convicted of witchcraft, pronounced a "prophecy" against his persecutor, Colonel Pyncheon. "God will give him blood to drink!" (2:8), the condemned man cried on the scaffold, and his prediction was fulfilled in the manner of the colonel's sudden death, with his beard and ruff drenched in blood. The Maule family medium, in short, is the curse, the dark twin of oracular utterance.

The inheritance has taken a slightly less lethal turn in Holgrave. The "artist" or "author," as Hawthorne calls him, rails in Emersonian fashion against the past's hold on the present. After haranguing Phoebe Pyncheon about "Dead Men's houses" such as that of the seven gables (2:183), he proceeds to read aloud to her one of his magazine contributions, entitled "Alice Pyncheon." The story revisits the "chimney-corner legend" (2:197) of the curse and has the grandson of the original wizard, also named Matthew Maule, assert hypnotic sovereignty over the haughty Alice. This venture into subterranean discourse, into the sort of scandalous "superstition" the novel as a whole relegates to the domestic sphere, casts a spell over Phoebe similar to the one that subjugated Alice. While Holgrave toys with the thought of "empire over the human spirit," Hawthorne adverts to his real target in this scene, the specter of political speech. In an otherwise mysterious aside, he mentions the moon melting into the dusk, "like an ambitious demagogue, who hides his aspiring purpose by assuming the prevalent hue of popular sentiment" (2:212–13). The "artist" catches himself in time to waken the half-conscious girl and refuse the mastery conferred by his narrative.

Hawthorne, another artist averse to verbal power, brings Holgrave to heel in the remainder of the novel, just as he returned the wearer of the scarlet letter to Puritan Boston and a life of penitence. Holgrave's renunciation can no more cleanse the text of disruptive discourse than Hester's could, however. The descendant of the Maules recants his radicalism and proposes marriage to the utterly conventional Phoebe, promising her that he "will conform [himself] to laws, and the peaceful practice of society" (2:307). Yet this apostasy, which presumably means that Holgrave will also abandon authorship, could not have happened without the reassertion of linguistic dominion. The two young people bond with each other, and declare their love, over the corpse of Judge Pyncheon; and that grasping hypocrite, like his forebear the colonel, was felled by Maule's curse. (According to Holgrave, the judge's "mode of death has been an idiosyncrasy with his family, for generations past" [2:304].) Not even departure from the family mansion can quell the "legendary." After the lovers drive off into the sunset, the Pyncheon elm is heard to whisper "unintelligible prophecies" (2:319). As in *The Scarlet Letter*, the oracular voice hovers unconciliated over the novel's final pages, and conservatism triumphs without getting the better of verbal agency.

The Blithedale Romance transfers the imperialism of the curse to Zenobia, and Hawthorne, as I have suggested, retaliates against his "dark lady" by sentencing her to a histrionic death. Not only that, but the entire novel exposes clairvoyance as a humbug. The subplot of the Veiled Lady, the "Sibylline" (3:6) medium concealed behind a strip of white cloth, brings out the close link between mesmeric soothsaying and the "cold and dead materialism" of Professor Westervelt (3:200). Zenobia is tainted by her collusion with this mountebank, and Priscilla's supposed second sight draws a blank outside the contrived setting of the public stage: she is quite stumped by Coverdale's inquiry, "What is about to happen" at Blithedale? (3:143). Hawthorne would have us believe that prophetic intimations, conveyed through speech, are fraudulent when they are not positively evil.

But it is a nice question as to who gets the last word in the narrative, the author or the female character he tries so hard to confound. Hawthorne's final statement is Miles Coverdale's weariness with political activism, as well as his equivocal confession of his love for Priscilla—equivocal (and Dimmesdale-like) because Coverdale has seemed completely obsessed with Zenobia. The storytelling and fiery speeches of the antiheroine, who, though not an accomplished writer, possesses a voice both "living" (3:120) and "inimitable" (3:107), prove much more efficacious. Chapter 13, significantly called "Zenobia's Legend," takes up the *House of the Seven Gables'* theme of disreputable but potent speech. Zenobia relates a "wild, spectral" tale (3:107) about "Theodore" and the Veiled Lady that in one possible interpretation predicts Coverdale's pining for Priscilla and so "certainly accorded with the event" (3:6). (The quoted phrase is the poet's own formulation, from the first time he watched Priscilla perform.)

Zenobia's presentiments, scattered throughout the text, escalate in the final pages and assume an unerring authority. She foretells her death—a bit cryptically, perhaps, but such is the nature of oracles—when she announces to Coverdale that he will next see her face "behind the black-veil" (3:228). The river in which she drowns during the night is a "broad, black, inscrutable depth" (3:232); and Zenobia, one might say, has donned the prophetic veil that formerly covered her sister's countenance, in the process altering its color from silver to the darkness of the curse. (Interestingly, Zenobia's gift for forecasting seems to be contagious; following the confrontation at Eliot's Pulpit, no less a character than Coverdale has a dream-premonition in which he correctly divines her suicide.) The clairvoyant-oratress herself waxes bolder and more imperious. After Hollingsworth jilts her for Priscilla (and Priscilla's money), she exclaims to Coverdale, "Tell him he has murdered me! Tell him that I'll haunt him!" According to our narrator, Zenobia "spoke these words with the wildest energy" (3:226), and it is not long before they achieve their purpose. We next encounter Hollingsworth several years later near the retired cottage where he dwells with Priscilla. Suffering has reduced him to childlike dependency on his wife, and when he tells Coverdale that he has been busy with but "a single murderer," the poet instantly recalls Zenobia's imprecation: "I knew what murderer he meant, and whose vindictive shadow dogged the side where Priscilla was not" (3:243). In the Hawthorne universe, otherwise so dismissive of human action, "mere" words outlive their speaker and prostrate the object of their spite.[4]

A much-quoted passage from *The House of the Seven Gables*—quoted, rightly, as evidence of Hawthorne's conservative recoil from human schemes of improvement—urges resignation to the principle that "God is the sole worker of realities" (2:180). But all three of Hawthorne's American novels qualify that Pierce-like hostility to reform. The not-so-hidden message of the novels, culminating in Zenobia's curse, is that language rivals God as an engine of transformation. The Deity, Hawthorne would no doubt prefer us to forget, is the model for this conception of speech. The first chapter of the Book of Genesis is the touchstone: "And God said, Let there be light: and there was light. . . . And God said. . . . And God said . . . and it was so."

Toward the end of *The Blithedale Romance*, Hawthorne has Zenobia liken herself to "an hereditary bond-slave" (3:217). The comparison reverberates. Is it nothing more than coincidence, a topical reference with no subtext? Or does the analogy amount to an equivocal confession on Hawthorne's part that the prophetic voice he most feared, heralding the Civil War within a decade, was that raised on behalf of the enslaved?

Stowe: From the Sacramental
to the Old Testamental

If Hawthorne, in his prefaces, tries to disable agitation by wrenching the literary away from the political, Stowe's prefaces lie at the antipodes: they assume the fraternity of the two domains. As she puts it in the preface to *Uncle Tom's Cabin*, the "influence of literature, of poetry and art" has begun to awaken "sympathy and feeling" for the dispossessed African (1).[1] A literature worthy of "our times" can do no less, according to Stowe, and she dedicates her own "representations" to "the great cause of human liberty" (2). The nub is how to make that objective efficacious in a work of fiction. The drama of what a piece of writing can do, and the mystery of how it does it, gripped this novice author as she produced her account of "life among the lowly" in a burst of outrage against the Fugitive Slave Law. Clearly viewing her culture's most vibrant textual inheritance as devotional, Stowe turns to what is for her, more than any political document, the warranty of freedom: the word of God as revealed in the scriptures. There, in the archetypical narrative of redemption, she finds her own empowerment. The biblical template of the Israelites escaping from "the house of bondage" in Egypt (2) has an inspiriting afterlife in her two novels on American slavery as she moves from the Christian sacrament to Hebraic prophecy as the catalyst for societal change.

I want to begin with a crucial scene from *Uncle Tom's Cabin*, one in which Stowe's novel self-reflexively ponders its capacity for intervention in history. The moment occurs in chapter 9, "In Which It Appears That a Senator Is But a Man." Eliza has told her harrowing story of flight over the Ohio River, and now Senator Bird must decide whether to help the fugitive or uphold his oath as a state official and return her to captivity. The senator, a master at political "eloquence," has previously persuaded his colleagues, as well as himself, that patriotism requires obedience to the law. But "then," says Stowe,

> his idea of a fugitive was only an idea of the letters that spell the word,—or, at the most, the image of a little newspaper picture of a man with a stick and bundle, with "Ran away from the subscriber" under it. The magic of the real presence of distress,—the imploring human eye, the frail trembling human hand, the despairing appeal of helpless agony,—these he had never tried.

Confronted with the reality of a frantic mother and her terrified child, Senator Bird does "penance" for his political sinning and defies the law to lead Eliza and Harry to safety (90).[2]

The "magic of . . . real presence" is the ideal toward which all representation in Stowe's narrative strives. The living person is the antonym both of "dead letters," the black marks on the page that convey only the idea of a fugitive, and of empty images, newspaper drawings that flatten the runaway into a series of black lines and white spaces. Real presence alone can awaken readers and listeners out of their sleep of law and custom and rouse them to act in the name of conscience.

To say this much is merely to pose the problem, however, not to solve it. Stowe is, after all, providing a verbal approximation of Eliza's escape from bondage. The technology of print cannot literally place the physical mother and child before us. It cannot supply the unmediated fact of Eliza's being there, the "trembling" hand and "imploring" eye that overcome Senator Bird's scruples. As Stowe often states, she regards the ocular as an especially affecting rhetorical strategy. In a preview of the cinema's mass appeal, her style aspires to the vividness of "moving picture[s]" (144). But, again, this is to frame the dilemma, not to indicate an exit from it. What causes the image rendered in language to come alive, to transcend the inertia of the newspaper cartoon and attain the *"living dramatic reality"* (442) that can change hearts and minds? How can a textual proxy duplicate the alchemy of presence? How can it galvanize readers to purge the land of slavery?

Political oratory, Stowe makes clear, has no prospect of sparking the needed renovation. It has been too debased by politicians. For Stowe, politics has devolved into the craft of self-promotion. (The senator's harangue in the state legislature did him no honor, as Mrs. Bird points out.) The story Eliza relates to the Birds is but one of at least three renditions of her experience included in *Uncle Tom's Cabin*, and we are invited to evaluate the other two for their rhetorical effectiveness—to ask whether those secondhand versions can even begin to approach the transformative pressure of Eliza's own words, delivered in person, on the senator. A second account comes from Black Sam, the Shelbys' factotum, who is dispatched to help Haley recover his property. The role Sam plays is purely instrumental, calculated to advance his own standing with his mistress and narrated so as to advertise his oratorical skills. Stowe calls him "an electioneering politician," and he rehearses the day's adventures to the assembled slaves "with all kinds of ornament and varnishing which might be necessary to heighten its effect." When Andy objects to the self-congratulatory speech, reminding Sam that he originally intended to apprehend Eliza, the old slave sniffs that "dat ar was conscience." And it was conscience, too, when he realized that Mrs. Shelby didn't want the runaway caught and changed course in order to obstruct the chase. Sam's "principled" credo is a burlesque of every antebellum lawmaker, Stowe implies. He defends his consistency by explaining, "I'm persistent in wantin' to get up which ary side my larder is; don't you see, all on yer?" (75–77). It is Thoreau's Daniel Webster, from "Resistance to Civil Government" (1849), in blackface: his "truth is not Truth, but consistency, or a consistent expediency."[3]

Not all political rhetoric in the novel is subjected to this kind of parody. Stowe herself invokes the republican/revolutionary tradition on behalf of George Harris, although she also suggests that secular nationalism has been so sullied by hypocrisy and legal obfuscation that it can no longer, on its own, inspire heroism among white people. She suspects that "Liberty!—electric word!" has become, to "the men and women of America," nothing more "than a name—a rhetorical flourish" (381). Canada, not the United States, is in 1852 the "shores of refuge" (429) for those seeking emancipation, and George, who delivers a stirring "declaration of independence" to his pursuers (197), eventually elects to abandon the New World altogether and return to Africa. Moreover, those who shield the Harris family are invariably devout Christians, such as the Quaker network around the Hallidays. For such individuals, abolition is rooted in religious faith, and to deprive someone of liberty is above all to commit a crime against God. A Christianized vocabulary, not a political one, has moved them to risk their welfare for the bondsman.

Which brings us to the third representation of Eliza's escape, the one inscribed by Stowe herself. This is the first version in order of appearance, and it is addressed to us, the readers of *Uncle Tom's Cabin*. It may come as a surprise to realize that the actual flight across the Ohio, along with Eva's death perhaps the novel's best-known scene, consists of a single paragraph.

(The previous paragraph tracks the pursuit to the water's edge, with the trader Haley after his quarry "like a hound after a deer," and records Eliza's wild leap "over the turbid current by the shore, on to the raft of ice beyond.") The description is graphic, its kinetic energy conveyed by dashes, by the "ing" endings of the verbs—"stumbling—leaping—slipping—springing upwards again!"—and by the sudden change of tense to the present in the clause "Her shoes are gone . . ." (61). Stowe relates the entire incident in three moderately sized sentences, and it takes less time to scan than Eliza must have needed to make her dash across the ice. Brief as it is, the moment is indelible, and though we, the novel's readers, are not standing on the Kentucky shore watching the fugitive bound for freedom, we almost feel as though we are. Something approaching "real presence" has been achieved; and it was achieved even more powerfully for Stowe's contemporaries, who so relished the episode that they insisted on seeing it regularly reproduced on stage for the next half century.[4]

The breathless quality of the writing is part of it, but only part. What lifts the scene out of the category of lifeless words are the biblical and eucharistic resonances. Eliza's escape is an unmistakable echo of the flight from Egypt. Her miraculous crossing of the frozen river, with the slave catchers at her heels, commemorates the parting of the Red Sea for the fleeing Israelites. The scene's original telling in chapter 7, "The Mother's Struggle," is already a retelling, Stowe's imitation of, and variation on, God's deliverance of his chosen people. The vivifying spark inheres in the scriptural source, the authentic Word whose lessons for the antebellum present too many Christians, according to *Uncle Tom's Cabin*, have refused to heed.

For Jews, the release from bondage is remembered in the Passover feast;[5] for Christians, salvation from sin is celebrated in the Lord's Supper, the consuming of bread and wine in memory of Christ's death. For well over a thousand years, Catholics described that sacrament as the "real presence." They believed that at the moment of communion, the elements were quite literally transubstantiated into the body and blood of the Savior. Protestantism is a history of disagreement with this doctrine. As Emerson observed, in the sermon in which he resigned from the pulpit, "The famous question of the Real Presence was the main controversy between the Church of England and the Church of Rome."[6] The disputes are too technical to canvass here, but the key point is that for post-Calvinists such as Stowe, the Supper was a sort of hybrid: neither merely symbolic nor the actual physical substance of the crucified God. Jesus was indeed there when worshippers received the sacraments; he suffused the rite not as a figure of flesh and blood, but as a living spirit.

Stowe had her first intimation of the story of *Uncle Tom's Cabin* in a pew in the First Parish Church in Brunswick, Maine, while she watched the celebration of the Eucharist. The "real but spiritual presence" (the formula that descends from Calvin) of the suffering Christ in the bread and wine kindled in her mind the image of a bleeding slave, and when she reached home after the service, she jotted down her vision.[7] The rite was her model for the abolitionist narrative she went on to write over the next year, the impetus for her own effort to create a text of "real presence" that would, as an *imitatio Dei*, bring to life the letters on the page. Stowe knew that she could not produce the physical Eliza for her readers. The Lord's Supper, and the Bible, assured her that she didn't have to. She could simulate—no, she could tap into and capture—the spiritual reality that infused the ordinance and the Word and that, after eighteen hundred years, still had the power "to stir up the soul from its depths, and rouse, as with trumpet call, [enough] courage, energy, and enthusiasm" to remake the world (118–19).

Without presence, neither salvation, nor healing, nor transformative action can occur. Stowe reiterates this premise throughout *Uncle Tom's Cabin*. George Harris, like his wife, Eliza, is the subject of a newspaper advertisement promising a reward for the capture of a runaway. The empty words are obliterated by the "real presence" of the fugitive himself, who, disguised as a Spanish gentleman, reveals his true identity to the manufacturer, Wilson. George's passionate self-defense—"delivered with tears, and flashing eyes, and despairing gestures" (114)—persuades his otherwise proslavery but good-natured former employer to switch allegiances. Deeply moved by the black man's plight, Wilson breaks down and cries and offers George a wad of bills to aid him in his flight.

Then there is the education of Miss Ophelia. As St. Clare points out, Northerners recoil from physical proximity to blacks even as they reproach the South for the wrongs of slavery. You would send them all to Africa, "out of your sight and smell" (178), he tells his cousin. Topsy's unruly antics around Ophelia stem from the same perception: she rightly senses that the Vermonter can't bear to touch her. Eva softens the hearts of both her aunt and the black child and in doing so lives up to her nickname of "The Little Evangelist" (the title of chapter 25, where the incident takes place). Laying her "little thin, white hand on Topsy's shoulder," she as-

sures the slave girl that she loves her—loves her as Jesus does, precisely because she is black and friendless. The effect on Topsy is instantaneous—"a
ray of real belief" penetrates her soul, and she vows to reform—and Ophelia learns a lesson that enables her to overcome her prejudice. "If we want
to give sight to the blind," St. Clare summarizes for Stowe, "we must be
willing to do as Christ did,—call them to us, and *put our hands on them*"
(italics in the original; 280–81). Fastidious distance leaves the heart untouched; nothing less than being fully there, as the Savior was for the suffering and infirm, can make a difference.

The indispensable book of spiritual presence, and the template for
But presence, as we have seen, doesn't have to be corporeal. It is possible to be present without being visible in the flesh, just as the risen Christ
is immanent spiritually but not materially in the Eucharist—or, perhaps
better yet, just as he is present in the Word and in the life around us, dis-
cernible not by the five senses but by the insight that comes from faith.
Stowe is contemptuous of the notion that things lack reality unless they
can be physically seen and heard. To her, such literalism betrays an utter
poverty of imagination, like that shown by the servants who misinterpret
the parental reactions to Eva's death. These people are "the slave of their
eye and ear" (298); they foolishly assume that Marie suffers more than
St. Clare because his eyes remain dry while she makes a great show of sobbing and complaining.

The indispensable book of spiritual presence, and the template for
Stowe's story, is the Bible. For those who attend to that ancient volume, the
letters on the page pulsate with life; they undergo a categorical sea change
similar to that which overtakes the signifier "runaway" when one comes
into contact with the real human being, the woman Eliza or her husband,
George. Eva, her health failing, faces death without misgiving because of
her immersion in the sacred text: "In that book which she and her simple
old friend had read so much together, she had seen and taken to her young
heart the image of one who loved the little child; and, as she gazed and
mused, He had ceased to be an image and a picture of the distant past, and
come to be a living, all-surrounding reality" (273). When, on her deathbed,
St. Clare asks his daughter how she can love someone she has never set
eyes on, Eva has her answer ready. "That makes no difference," she replies;
"I believe him, and in a few days I shall *see* him" (289).

Eva is Stowe's exemplary reader, the standard to be emulated by the
antebellum audience. She opens herself to the salvational narrative and
not only is transfigured as a consequence, but perceives divinity where
others are incapable of sight. Indeed, Eva internalizes every affecting story
she reads or is told about, including those she encounters at second hand,

like Tom's history of Prue and St. Clare's recollection of Scipio, the slave who nursed him back to health from cholera and then died of the disease himself. Eva rejects her father's suggestion that she ought not to hear such things because they impress her much too deeply. We must allow these "sad stories" to "sink into our hearts," she says more than once, because only by listening to them without reserve can we truly empathize with the "pain and suffering" of their victims (216–18, 233, and 275).

The dynamic of reception is double-sided, then: the text must appropriate the spiritual truth of the scriptures, and the reader must be prepared to accept that truth with his or her entire being. Taken together, these two desiderata impart spiritual life to the rite of narrative incorporation. The parallel to the Protestant Lord's Supper holds firm: in Reformed sects, as opposed to the Catholic church, the miracle of the sacrament is never independent of the parishioner. For the bread and wine to be effective, communicants must take the Savior into their souls. The ordinance can do nothing with a congregant whose heart is closed against it, any more than the story of Prue, or Uncle Tom, or Jesus Christ can move a Haley or a Simon Legree to repentance. How one responds to the story is what separates the sheep from the goats.[8]

That Eva expires from, as it were, too much sensitivity to others' suffering does not mean that the novel's internal narratives issue in stasis or inaction. On the contrary, the stories are a crucifixion for the child heroine, and Eva's fate is one of two cases of sacrificial death that have a profound and lasting effect on survivors and are presented by Stowe as fictional imitations of Christ. Topsy and Ophelia, whose awakenings were cited above, are never the same after watching the heroine die. The older woman, having "learnt something of the love of Christ" from Eva, tells Topsy that she loves her, and no longer shrinks from her charge's touch. "From that hour," according to Stowe, "she acquired an influence over the mind of the destitute child that she never lost" (297). Even the cynical St. Clare starts to change. He studies his daughter's Bible with growing seriousness and announces a resolve to free his slaves before his life is cut short in a brawl. But no one experiences Eva's example more intensely than Uncle Tom, for whom her goodness proves contagious. Inheriting the mantle of *imitatio*, the eponymous hero evolves into that cliché of literary criticism, a black Christ figure. What interests us here is how Stowe conceives this metamorphosis as molding response to the text. Tom becomes the fulcrum or relay through whom invisible presence flows on its passage from the scriptures to her readership.

Tom's accession to preternatural sight and hearing begins in earnest immediately following Eva's death. St. Clare reads aloud to his servant from the gospel of St. John, and the two men have this exchange:

> "Tom," said his master, "this is all *real* to you!"
> "I can jest fairly *see* it, Mas'r," said Tom.
> "I wish I had your eyes, Tom."
> "I wish, to the dear Lord, Mas'r had!" (301).

On Legree's plantation, Tom's certainty in the reality of the unseen will be tested, in what amounts to a rewriting of Frederick Douglass's "dark night of the soul," the episode from the *Narrative* where the overseer Covey almost breaks the great abolitionist. But the moral desert of Red River also witnesses the definitive intervention of the divine on behalf of the oppressed. The Savior, in this novel, does not confine his outreach to Holy Writ; he makes himself resplendently manifest to Uncle Tom as a real but nonmaterial being.

Stowe's most explicit rejoinder to the problem of bodily nonappearance, the quandary raised by Eliza's personal plea to the Birds, comes in chapter 38, "The Victory." The moment has been thoroughly prepared for. A recurrent theme in this last quarter of the novel has been, precisely, absence or apparent emptiness. When Tom reads his Bible to Legree's slaves, they refuse to credit the words because they cannot imagine that God is there in Red River. They are versions of the skeptical reader-auditor for whom the verbal, being powerless to reproduce presence, cannot bring about conviction. "The Lord never visits these parts," says Cassy; and when Tom, his spirit almost crushed, cries out to Jesus, she tells him not to bother: "There's no use calling on the Lord,—he never hears, . . . there isn't any God, I believe" (353 and 358). Even Stowe, appalled by the misery on Legree's farm, wonders, "Is God HERE?" (348). But this section also abounds in hints of an approaching revelation. At one point, Tom's hopes are strengthened by an "invisible voice" (336); at another, he has a dream of Eva reading to him from the scriptures. The intimations culminate at the lowest moment of Tom's ordeal, when God's silence seems complete and Legree taunts him with the failure of his religion.

The dejected hero suddenly has a vision of the crucified Jesus; and as he gazes "in awe and wonder," the thorns change into "rays of glory," and a voice assures him of salvation. Is the apparition real? Stowe, anticipating readerly disbelief, musters "psychologists" to justify the incident. According to these unnamed experts, the "affections" can grow so strong "that they press into their service the outward senses, and make them give tangible shape to the inward imagining." And who, Stowe adds, can doubt that "an all-pervading Spirit" can do this with human capabilities? (388–89). (One psychologist whom Stowe foreshadows is William James, particularly his merger of pragmatism and religious faith. In *The Varieties of Religious Experience* [1902] and "The Will to Believe" [1896], James argued that truth comes into existence because of one's willingness to believe it. *"Faith in a fact can help create the fact,"* he wrote, supplying the italics for incredulous modern readers.)[9]

The scene is a watershed for Uncle Tom and the climactic instant in his creator's sacramental aesthetic. With "an ever-present Saviour" in his heart (390), the protagonist turns his mind entirely to heaven and becomes a source of redemption for the other slaves. To Cassy, "this lowly missionary" breathes Holy Writ (392); his sufferings convert even Sambo and Quimbo, Legree's most degraded henchmen, who relieve his agony with a cup of water, as Jesus was succored on the cross. Here "real but spiritual presence" emigrates from the Bible, through spectral visitations, to the "man that was a thing" (the novel's original subtitle) whom Stowe pictured being whipped while communion was celebrated in her family church. And from Tom, spiritual being radiates outward to members of the reading public. If the novel has taught these readers to *"feel right,"* "in harmony with the sympathies of Christ" (443–44), they will give "tangible shape" to their imagining of Stowe's hero. They will experience him as being as unforgettably present as Eliza was to Senator Bird and the Almighty was in Tom's vision, as real as Jesus proved to be when Tom was murdered, and Sambo and Quimbo felt divinity "a standin' by you so, all this night!" (412). Transformed by their encounter with invisible presence, the novel's readers, again like Senator Bird, will no longer allow themselves to be lulled by dead letters but instead, energized by faith, help to cast out the sin of slavery from America.

Not everyone will hear and "follow me," as Tom, copying the Savior, pleads with the slaves at Red River (416). Stowe, whose imagination had room for a Simon Legree, could not have been more mindful of this fact. Her Christ is a God of love; but he is a good deal more than that: He is a God of wrath and vengeance, too. Her novel, which teems with apocalyptic references to the Last Judgment, incorporates an alternative mode of storytelling that makes greater use of fear than of belief. Cassy, playing on Legree's superstitions with singular "words and language" (398), persuades the villain that spirits inhabit the upper regions of his house. She and Emmeline then hide out in the garret while awaiting their moment to flee. In chapter 42, "An Authentic Ghost Story," she masterminds a spectral visitation of her own, the complement and opposite of Tom's exultant revelation. A ghostly white figure assaults Legree's "spiritual eyes" (420) as he lies half awake in bed, and the vision so fills him with terror that he absolutely refuses to search the garret, thus allowing the two women to make good their escape. The threat of damnation lurks in the background of this staged act of spooking.[10]

It is an efficacious fiction, as potent as the eucharistic narratives of Eva and Uncle Tom—and in history, arguably more so. While *Uncle Tom's Cabin* undoubtedly helped turn northern opinion against slavery's sinfulness, and so, as Lincoln supposedly said, made war between the sections inevitable, the impact of Stowe's sacramental novel was long-term and cumulative. The fighting lay almost a decade in the future, and much would have to happen for that climax to be reached. The idiom of prophecy, inflected by the jeremiad and the curse, would prove more relevant to the divisive atmosphere of the 1850s. Stowe would make that cataclysmic strain of literary agency the centerpiece of her successor fiction on slavery, which she produced in 1856, near the acme of southern hegemony over the national government.

Dred did not repeat the influence of *Uncle Tom's Cabin*; the book sold decently but not spectacularly, and it had no lasting effect on the popular imagination. But it has been recuperated in recent years as an unabashed turn toward activism, with a black revolutionary hero who lays to rest Uncle Tom's counsel of submission.[11] Paralleling Whitman, whose verse fragment "Says" also dates from 1856, Stowe vowed "to make a voice to say" the anguish and anger that burned within many Northerners in the wake of Bleeding Kansas and Bleeding Sumner.[12] The voice indisputably exists in the novel, but its principal locus is the black insurgent, and his message of vengeance is never actualized.

Dred registers Stowe's disillusioned sense that the sectional crisis has so worsened by the time of her writing that no meaningful change can arrest the slide toward catastrophe. Christ's gospel of love and the spirit that enabled *Uncle Tom's Cabin* to maintain hopefulness in the face of the Fugitive Slave Law had not borne fruit, and that vocabulary emerges in the new work as a largely privatized discourse with no consequences for the nation. Nominally, it gets the better of the prophetic idiom wielded by the titular protagonist. But this outcome signals not so much the resilience of the Christian perspective as Stowe's pessimism about the country's present and future; it is a triumph with all the earmarks of defeat. And the voice of doom, lingering on in the figure of Harry Gordon, whom Dred nominates as his successor, broods over the text's ending with its intimation of an American Armageddon. The force of "Hebraistic" speech proves too powerful for Stowe to pacify (211),[13] even as it would prove too explosive to contain in the culture as a whole.

The hard facts of the Slave Power's ascendancy impend over *Dred*, which is set in the early 1830s but imbued with the apocalyptic mood of 1856. Stowe's North and South Carolina can be taken, with minor qualification, as a synecdoche for a United States that has been corrupted and degraded by "all the aggressions of slavery" (593). Brutalized men such as Tom Gordon lord it over this increasingly closed society, using violence and majoritarian intimidation to silence opposition. Gordon incites a mob to "lynch" (i.e., whip) an antislavery clergyman, and he replays the Sumner-Brooks affair by assaulting both his mulatto half brother, Harry, and the white lawyer, Edward Clayton, with a gutta-percha cane. The insertion of the historical present into the fictional past dramatizes the urgency of the threat, and Clayton's friend, Frank Russel, underlines the danger when he describes the slaveholding class as the rulers of the republic, their dominion rendered impregnable by their advantage in congressional representation:

> Those among us who have got the power in their hands are determined to keep it, and they are wide awake. They don't mean to let the *first* step be taken, because they don't mean to lay down their power. The three fifths vote they get by it is a thing they won't part with. They'll die first. . . . These men are our masters; they are yours; they are mine; they are masters of everybody in these United States. They can crack their whips over the head of any statesman or clergyman, from Maine to New Orleans, that disputes their will. They govern the country. Army, navy, treasury, church, state, everything is theirs. (465)

When Clayton objects that Northerners will not long submit to such tyranny, Frank assures him that protest is futile: "The mouth of the North is stuffed with cotton, and will be kept full as long as it suits us" (537).

What is to be done when economic self-interest, religion, law, and government all conspire to crush efforts at reform? In *Uncle Tom's Cabin*, Stowe believed that sympathy, energized by faith, could produce social change. While warning in her own voice that God would punish an America unwilling to repent the sin of slavery, she had concluded on an affirmative note: "A day of grace is yet held out to us."[14] Four years later, it was evident that she had failed.[15] *Uncle Tom's Cabin*, for all its success, had done little to stem the forces of reaction. The novel enjoyed unparalleled sales in the United States, the largest English-speaking book market in the world, but Americans were notably less enthusiastic than the English, and Southerners were almost uniformly hostile.[16] In Great Britain, where slavery had been abolished a quarter of a century earlier, sales reached at least a million and a half (there were many pirated copies), but not one of those readers could vote in American elections.[17] Emancipation at home looked more remote than ever. The number of blacks held in bondage in the United States had multiplied, not lessened, and the planter oligarchy, with northern backing, had repealed the Missouri Compromise. Slavery was spreading into the territories, establishing itself, as Stowe complains in the preface, "over broad regions, where till now, you [the American people] have solemnly forbidden it to enter" (3–4). Pierce occupied the White House, and Sumner was convalescing from the injuries that would prevent him from resuming his Senate seat until 1859. In Kansas, Border Ruffians from the slave states harassed and murdered settlers from the North, their "fiend-like proceedings . . . connived at and protected, if not directly sanctioned and in part instigated, by our national government" (593). The *Dred Scott* decision, six months away but widely publicized while Stowe wrote, was in the pipeline from a Supreme Court with a southern bias.

Dred entertains two main paths of action against the hardening carapace of slavery's control: the gradualist nonviolence of the Christian characters on the one side, and the revolutionary, totalized agenda of Dred and his swamp-based community of maroons on the other.[18] The first narrative, with which Stowe's book begins (and continues for two hundred pages before the Dred story materializes), centers on the abortive courtship of Nina Gordon and Edward Clayton. Sister of the monstrous Tom, Nina evolves from an empty-headed coquette who hates books to a passionate protector of her slaves who converts herself to Christianity by reading the Bible aloud to Tiff ("Everything is changed, and it is the beauty of Christ that has changed it" [346]). She falls in love with the reformer Clayton but dies from cholera before the two can marry; her defenseless slaves fall into the possession of her brother.

Clayton embodies the possibility of a South redeemed piecemeal by change from within, but Nina's death is a harbinger of his frustration. The lawyer pursues several strategies of amelioration. He initiates a suit on behalf of Milly against the master's unchecked power over his slaves, a fictional reenactment of an actual legal case, *State v. Mann* (1829). Clayton also endeavors to teach his slaves to read and write, and eventually, disgusted with the inhumane economy, he resolves to free them and employ them as wage laborers. Not one of his objectives can be realized in the United States. The legal decision, handed down by his own father, goes against him. His neighbors refuse to allow slaves to be educated, and a mob menaces his home, Magnolia Grove, when word gets out of his emancipation scheme. Forced to flee for his life, Clayton makes his way to the Dismal Swamp, then to the North, and at last to Canada. His relocation to the Elgin colony seals the bankruptcy of reform in America.

Dred, in contrast, intends to end slavery through violence. Son of Denmark Vesey and inheritor of his father's biblical vision of divine retribution, he considers himself an Israelite among the Egyptians who has been called upon to deliver his people from bondage. According to Stowe, he possesses the gift of "second sight," a faculty standing in relation "to the future what memory is to the past," and he is endowed "with prophetic and supernatural impulses" (274). For much of the narrative, he paraphrastically pronounces Hebraic judgments on his (white American) oppressors, asserting that "The Lord is against this nation!" and that supernatural wrath will visit it with devastation (263). But Dred, unlike his father (or Nat Turner, whose *Confessions* Stowe includes as an appendix), never mounts an insurrection against the slaveholders: he spends three hundred pages of text in the modern reprint awaiting a sign that doesn't appear. He explains his immobility by saying that the "token cometh not" (451), and in the chapter with the ironically Old Testament–like title "Jegar Sahadutha," he allows himself to be vanquished by an otherworldly notion of restitution. Sounding a bit like Hester Prynne, of all people, the black rebel devolves into a prophet of deferral. A "man of unclean lips" (502), as he calls himself (presumably referring to his voice), Dred concedes that he is unworthy and will not live to see the land redeemed, and shortly afterward he is shot dead in the swamp by Tom Gordon's posse.

The extratextual catalyst for Dred's silencing is Stowe's fear about the "overpowering mesmeric force" of the prophetic language she has unleashed (450). (Her original title for the novel was "Dread.") The novelist goes to considerable lengths to counter and vanquish her black rebel's bloodthirsty imaginings. The character who opposes his vision of an earthly cataclysm most effectively is the slave Milly, who has a dematerialized understanding of the scriptures. Milly's owners sold away her fourteen children, the last of whom was murdered by an overseer. Consumed with grief and hatred, she pronounced a curse against her mistress, Aunt Nesbit; but now, with the hindsight of faith, as she explains to Nina, she recognizes the wrongness of her outburst: "I was in Egypt den. I was wandering in the wilderness of Sinai. I had heard de sound of the trumpet, and de voice of the de words; but, chile, I hadn't seen de Lord" (181). After she finds faith, Milly repents her anger and embraces her mistress as a "sister in Jesus" (183).

To Milly, the correspondences with Israel and Egypt are states of mind, and she overcomes Dred with the "better way" of "de new covenant" (461). According to her, the swamp dweller is in a wilderness of his own making, as she was before her conversion; he may imagine himself a leader of Israel, but he "han't come to de heavenly Jerusalem." Milly, who knows as well as anyone the horrors of slavery, goes so far as to discount the bondsman's temporal suffering: "Jerusalem above is *free*—is *free*, honey; so, don't you mind, now, what happens in *dis* yer time" (201). But while Milly disavows requital in this world, she does not renounce the idea of wrath altogether. Rather, she postpones it to the judgment day. "Leave the vengeance to him," she pleads with the community of fugitives. "Vengeance is mine—I will repay, saith de Lord" (462). It is this appeal to heavenly justice that fatally weakens Dred's resolve, and Stowe's Christology fervently endorses the position: divine retribution is the corollary to divine love. Christ as the principle of intercession has "in reserve this awful energy of wrath," the novelist writes (497). The wicked will be punished in eternity, and Dred's imprecations on the American Egypt will be consummated in the next world, not in this one.

But with the vanquishing of prophecy, the narrative runs out of options for large-scale societal transformation. The "Christian" injunction, Stowe's earlier panacea, can make no headway against the behemoth of slavery, and her surviving characters take refuge in personal good works and fantasies of eschatological redress. Milly and Tiff escape to the North to put into practice modest projects of caring for others. Both head interracial "families," in Milly's case a New York City orphanage for "blacks, whites, and foreigners" (546).[19] The concluding chapter in which we learn these details is titled "Clear Shining after Rain," but its satisfactions are tempered by the radically circumscribed quality of the two ex-slaves' enterprises. Clayton's more ambitious settlement has been spatially displaced across the Canadian border. As for the villainous Tom Gordon, he experiences no punishment in *Dred* and casts his shadow over the future. He is sovereign below the Mason-Dixon Line, leader of a class, "supported by special constitutional privileges" (394), that will not peacefully yield an iota of its wealth or authority. The last page of Stowe's last appendix, which decries the inexorable march of the slave interest, implicitly seconds Frank Russel's warning: Tom Gordon reigns in the North as well.

Stowe herself would turn away from the "impending crisis." After *Dred*, she would renounce her protagonist's oracular gift or "second sight" and devote her energies to memorializing the past in historical fictions. Her next novel, *The Minister's Wooing* (1859), does touch on slavery, but at a safe temporal and physical remove: it examines the institution in the eighteenth-century northern city of Newport, Rhode Island. This shift away from the fraught present—a pattern Stowe would continue after the war with stories such as *Oldtown Folks* (1869)—evokes an author she greatly admired, Nathaniel Hawthorne. It is no accident that the influence of that proponent of quiet can be felt on every page of her novel of memory and clerical courtship, issued within a year of secession.

Yet we do *Dred* a disservice if, in noting Stowe's retreat, we underestimate her mobilizing of discursive energies that would, in fact, help to bring about slavery's death. Her text resonates with other voices in the decade that, despairing of reform, ratcheted up the level of confrontation. For all her anxieties about race war, the novelist does not entirely uproot the possibility of militancy from her narrative. She keeps the rhetorical flame alive by inserting a bridging figure, Harry Gordon, who perpetuates and intensifies the prophetic paradigm even as he, too, appears to abandon it. Harry acts as an emissary between the two worlds of the plantation and the swamp. As his disaffection from slavery grows, he spends more time in the wilderness and begins to merge with the heroic isolato whom he regards as his mentor. Dred should be seen as Harry's long-repressed doppelgänger, someone who articulates the dreams of vengeance against America that the mulatto feels but cannot speak because of his love for Nina. Dred does not even enter the tale until Harry curses Tom Gordon, some two hundred pages into the action. Overhearing the angry words, the prophet leaps out of the woods to taunt Harry with his service to the Egyptians. Soon the embittered house slave is sounding more like Dred than Dred himself. After Nina succumbs to cholera (in the chapter "The Tie Breaks"), he pronounces a scripture-inflected curse against the oppressors of his people: "There will come a day when all this shall be visited upon you! The measure you have filled to us shall be filled to you *double*—mark my words!" (388). The target of Harry's rage is the entire nation, not just the slavocracy. As he later observes to Dred, "The North is as bad as the South! They kill us, and the North consents and justifies!" (500).

What Harry adds to the messianism of the swamp is the rhetoric of the Declaration of Independence. Stowe, who was skeptical of the republican tradition's viability in *Uncle Tom's Cabin*, may have been influenced by the rising controversy over Jefferson's principles. By the mid-1850s, proslavery apologists were routinely dismissing the fallacious doctrine that "all men are created equal," while Republicans like Lincoln rallied to the document's defense. Harry has made a thorough study of the Declaration, and he twice quotes from it at length and verbatim, once in a letter to Clayton and once to explain its meaning to an audience of maroons. Ironically, the aspect of the nation's foundational statement that especially appeals to the fugitives is *the right of the people to alter or to abolish* unjust government (435–36)—the principle that the leaders of the Confederacy would invoke after Lincoln's election to justify their withdrawal from the Union.

Harry eventually surpasses his teacher in his appetite for "immediate and precipitate action" (499). His integration of republican and biblical vocabularies, which places him squarely in the American revolutionary lineage, whets his impatience with Dred's endless delays, and by the last few chapters the pampered near-white slave has become more of a firebrand than the swamp dweller. Dred has laid the groundwork for this outcome, singling out Harry as a person whose many talents "might make him at some day a leader in the conspiracy against the whites" (212). As his dejection over the endlessly deferred sign builds, the prophet passes on to his more educated disciple the role of a Moses to the bondsmen. "Brethren," he explains to the maroons, placing the hand of succession on Harry, "the Lord caused Moses to become the son of Pharaoh's daughter, that he might become learned in the wisdom of the Egyptians, to lead forth his people from the house of bondage. . . . In like manner hath the Lord dealt with our brother" (454). Inheritor of Dred's office, and no longer inhibited by Nina, Harry will presumably ignite an insurrection pitting black against white, Israelite against Egyptian.

Except that he doesn't. He accepts the imprudence of an uprising against the better-armed whites and elects to flee rather than fight. As though still indivisible from Dred, Harry all but disappears from the narrative once the prophet falls silent. He never speaks another word after Dred addresses his dying speech to him, and his trajectory gets folded into that of the high-minded and violence-averse Clayton. Stowe writes (with evident relief) that Southerners ought to applaud the escape of such slaves via the Underground Railroad because it removes an "incendiary magazine" from under their homes (520). She contrives in the rest of the story to buy Harry off from further eruptions of wrath. He reaches New York City with his wife, Lisette, and through the patronage of benefactors attains "a situation of comfort" (542). But the North is not far enough away. Two pages later we discover that Harry has moved on to Clayton's settlement in Canada and "is rapidly acquiring property and consideration in the community" (544). Men as well-off as this are seldom at the head of armed uprisings.

End of story? Not quite. Harry is still alive, and his prophecies and curses, rather like those of Zenobia in *The Blithedale Romance*, continue to disturb the text with their lawless energy. A shocked Clayton, hearing his curse against white Americans, admonishes Harry, "You don't know what you are saying," but the incensed slave retorts, "Yes, I do, and my words will be true!" (388). Stowe's novel itself can be considered an act of prophecy. Woven into its structure are the Hebraic parallels that Milly spiritualizes but Dred takes as concrete. Chapters are titled "The Flight into Egypt," The Voice in the Wilderness," and "The Desert." The Old Testament shapes the plot of *Dred* just as its drives Harry's oracular outbursts; whereas *Uncle Tom's Cabin* was a New Testament novel, this one takes its inspiration from the Hebrews.

Moreover, Stowe enunciates a true prophecy of her own when she compares her light-skinned Moses to that Old Testament figure, John Brown. In a crucial passage, Harry broods on the fate of his friend Hark, slain by Tom's vigilantes:

> How stinging is it at such a moment to view the whole respectability of civilized society upholding and glorifying the murderer; calling his sin by soft names, and using for his defence every artifice of legal injustice! Some in our own nation have had bitter occasion to know this, for we have begun to drink the cup of trembling which for so many ages has been drank alone by the slave. Let the associates of Brown ask themselves if they cannot understand the midnight anguish of Harry! (499)

Harry's curses would be fulfilled in the veteran of guerrilla warfare in Kansas. "Osawatomie Brown" was already hatching his plans to foment precisely the sort of slave revolt that Stowe turns away from in *Dred*. The Harpers Ferry conspiracy would not spark a race war, but it would precipitate four years of bloodshed in which the measure, if not quite filled to double, would still be horrific.

That consummation could barely be imagined in 1856, but it is the nature of prophecy to telescope the future, and the nature of prophets to monitor the passage of time. For most of Stowe's story, the position of watchman is held by Dred; when he is killed, Harry inherits that role, too.[20] Dred constantly readies himself for the day when the oppressors will suffer divine wrath. Few characters, even in an age of prophetic oratory, are so profuse of the future tense: "Then shall the silver cord be loosed, and the golden bowl be broken" (270); "there shall be a cry in the land of Egypt . . ." (342); "we will slay them utterly, and consume them from off the face of the earth" (460). The black prophet chafes at the endless delays, but though he wavers before Milly's last-day theology, he refuses to relinquish the idea of retribution in sentences rife with a sense of the temporal: "Woman, thy prayers have prevailed for this time! The hour is not yet come!" (462).

Harry, hustled off to Elgin after Dred's death, has been preparing from the outset to assume the mission of watchman. The idea is casually, almost imperceptibly, introduced in the first chapter, "The Mistress at Canema." A profligate Nina has just returned home, and she includes among the bills she presents to her mulatto half brother gifts for him and his wife. "I'll tell you one thing I've got, Harry," she cries excitedly, "and that is a gold watch for you" (14). Harry later proudly displays his timepiece to Lisette, and he wears it throughout the narrative, as one character after another cautions him that the week, the day, the hour for revolution is not now. In this respect Clayton is no different from Dred: he persuades Harry of the "undesirableness . . . under present circumstances" of resorting to force, and he believes it imperative "at this time" to "prevent the development of bloody insurrection" (519–20). Though Harry capitulates, he surely still has that gold watch with him in Canada as a memento of his beloved sister and mistress, whose paternalistic Christian methods of opposing slavery came to nothing. As he says at one point to Dred, "There's no time to be lost" (389), and one imagines him consulting the watch regularly for signs that the long-awaited confrontation is at hand. Like John Brown, and like so many other antislavery watchmen after the violence in Kansas, Harry Gordon is biding his time until the Lord of Hosts indicates that the moment to strike has finally arrived.

The southern crusade to stamp out unwelcome criticism ended by making antislavery speech so powerful that disunion seemed the only option, and the result of that misstep was the bloody downfall of African bondage. Stowe's grim novel corresponds to a host of other warnings from the mid- to late 1850s, all cast in the exigent dialects of the American tradition, that foresaw the day of reckoning. Their number includes the jeremiads of Douglass, the Brown orations of Emerson and Thoreau, and Melville's *The Confidence-Man*, published a year after *Dred*. Even Fuller, who died in 1850, should be counted; as if in homage to the author of *Woman in the Nineteenth Century*, Stowe draws a Fuller-like comparison of Dred with the Trojan oracle Cassandra crying out against the moral failings of her countrymen (497). Emerson, in his speech on the soon-to-be martyr of Harpers Ferry, ascribes to Brown the same dual inheritance Stowe assigns to Harry Gordon. Brown believes in "two articles," Emerson claims, the Golden Rule and the Declaration of Independence, and he would often say, "Better that a whole generation of men, women and children should pass away by a violent death, than that one word of either should be violated in this country."[21] Melville's last prewar fiction adds its own dark omen to these pronouncements. Like *Dred*, *The Confidence-Man* contemplates an apocalyptic comeuppance for a society drifting ever more deeply into slave territory. Neither novel allows itself to picture the fateful hour. But neither doubts that "Something further may follow of this Masquerade."

PART III

Antebellum/Postbellum

Speech and Silence in Douglass

Frederick Douglass's three autobiographies stretch from the heyday of antislavery activism to the abyss of lynching and segregation. In chronological order, the texts are *Narrative of the Life of Frederick Douglass, an American Slave*, published in 1845; *My Bondage and My Freedom*, which appeared in August 1855; and *Life and Times of Frederick Douglass*, first issued in 1881 and then revised and expanded for a volume with the same title published in 1893. In each autobiography, Douglass portrays slavery as a regime of silence and repression in which the only voice permitted is that of the master. In each, he traces his emergence into speech and writing, a process inseparable from his escape to freedom; he pairs the two forms of utterance as cognate acts of resistance to social and mental extinction. The full title of Douglass's first memoir, including the phrase *Written by Himself*, captures this congruence: he will narrate or tell the story of his experiences in a book that he inscribed himself. Or, as he reiterates in *My Bondage and My Freedom*, he will wield both his voice and his pen "in the great work of renovating the public mind, and building up a public sentiment which should at least, send slavery and oppression to the grave" (389).[1] Douglass is the Sayer/Doer of Emersonian prophecy in blackface.

So much for the comedy. Yet Douglass's three texts have a tragic story to tell as well, as they move from his own rupture of the master's monotone in the *Narrative*, through the Slave Power's effort to impose the plantation ban on the country as a whole in *My Bondage and My Freedom*, to the triumph—temporary, Douglass firmly believes, but undeniable—of that undemocratic objective in *Life and Times*, where race supplants slavery as the cause of repression. It would be hyperbolic but not unwarranted to describe the last memoir as inverting the titular sequence of the second:

it could have been called *My Freedom and My Bondage*. This retrograde trajectory, highlighting the persistence of black subjugation and of white demands for silence, gives the former slave and now freedman a special relationship to reticence as an almost constitutive element of his identity. Douglass overcomes the vocal disability, but he never loses sight of the hidden power of saying nothing. The theme of aphonia, secondary but crucial in the *Narrative*, becomes utterly central to the third and final part of *Life and Times*, that composed mostly after the 1883 Supreme Court decision invalidating the Civil Rights Act of 1875. In the *Narrative*, silence functions strategically, a necessary aid to survival. In *Life and Times*, stillness has a different purpose: in a time of apparent hopelessness, it is the prefix, the enabling condition, for prophecy's return.

Even before Douglass enters his own book, prefatory remarks by the abolitionists William Lloyd Garrison and Wendell Phillips remind us that proscribed expression has a history in America reaching back to the Age of Revolution. Garrison, still marveling at Douglass's first oration delivered at a Nantucket antislavery convention in 1841, observes that "PATRICK HENRY, of revolutionary fame, never made a speech more eloquent in the cause of liberty" (4).[2] Phillips adds that just as the founding fathers "signed the Declaration of Independence with the halter about their necks," so Douglass, as a runaway slave, publishes his "declaration of freedom" in the knowledge that he can be seized and returned to bondage at any moment (12). Emerson called for a reanimation of the revolutionary paradigm in literature, and the *Narrative* takes up the challenge by arguing that the successor discourse to proselytizing against the Crown is antislavery agitation. Ever mindful of the continuity, Douglass imitates the founders and appends his signature to his text, concluding with the words, "I subscribe myself, FREDERICK DOUGLASS" (102). Nor is the fugitive the only one who braves the halter by denouncing the peculiar institution, even from the presumed safety of Massachusetts. A decade before he introduced the *Narrative*, an irate mob had dragged Garrison through the streets of Boston at the end of a rope.[3]

The actual slave who dares to speak his mind runs the gravest risk because he violates the taboo on utterance that buttresses the whole system of racial bondage. Douglass's opening paragraph lays out the prohibitions, which start from the moment of the slave's existence. Slaves, Douglass writes, have no certain knowledge of their ages or birth dates because an "authentic"—that is, written—"record" containing this information does not exist. The bondsman cannot make up the deficit by inquiring orally of the master for facts about himself; all such questions by a slave are deemed "improper and impertinent, and evidence of a restless spirit" (15). Douglass devotes much of the rest of the *Narrative* to filling in the details of linguistic proscription. "No answering back" is the law on every plantation (29), and the two Barneys who look after Colonel Lloyd's horses must stand and listen in silence while their master criticizes their performance. An unnamed black who faults the colonel for how he treats his slaves pays for the indiscretion by being sold to a Georgia trader: "This is the penalty of telling the truth, of telling the simple truth, in answer to a series of plain questions" (27). And if a master dies, blacks have "no more voice" in deciding their fates "than the brutes among whom we were ranked" (46). Literacy of course is the principal exclusion, and when Douglass's mistress, Sophia Auld, teaches him the alphabet, her husband intervenes with the warning that learning will render Douglass unfit for his duties. The slave needs only to obey and "to do as he is told to do" (37); he is the object of speech and never its agent.

Balancing the silence of the chattel is the monotone of the ruling class, and that sole proprietorship, the linguistic corollary to arbitrary power, manifests itself in multiple perversions of discourse. The sound of one voice talking, as Jefferson noted sixty years earlier in *Notes on the State of Virginia* (1787), is a license for unchecked indulgence. The master "storms," the slave quakes, and the listening child contracts the habit of indiscipline.[4] In the *Narrative*, white people make their wishes known by shouting, complaining, commanding, accusing, and cursing. Covey likes to sneak up on his field slaves and "scream out" orders to quicken their pace (57). Captain Anthony accompanies his flogging of Douglass's Aunt Hester with a volley of oaths. ("Now, you d—d b—h, I'll learn you how to disobey my orders" [19].) The aptly named overseer, Mr. Severe, is "a profane swearer" who spends his days raving and blaspheming and who dies "as he lived, uttering, with his dying groans, bitter curses and horrid oaths" (22). Other overseers, like Mr. Gore, are sparing of words; they do all their "talking" with the whip or the rifle.

In order to salvage his humanity, Douglass knows that he has to break the slaveholder monopoly on speech. When he has his transformative battle with Covey, his determination to achieve this objective is made explicit: "At this moment—from whence came the spirit I don't know—I resolved to fight; and, suiting my action to the resolution, I seized Covey hard by the throat" (64). Note the defiant gesture: Douglass grasps his tormentor's throat. Covey twice manages to call for help, but the once-mighty words of the overseer are now ineffectual.[5] Douglass drives off another white man with a well-placed kick, and another slave, Bill, flatly refuses to intervene on Covey's behalf. Douglass, on the other hand, "talks back" with impunity. He warns Covey that "he had used me like a brute for six months, and I was determined to be used no longer." The successful fight rekindles his wish for literacy. It lifts him "from the tomb of slavery, to the heaven of freedom," and he resumes reading with fresh commitment (64–65). By choking and vanquishing his oppressor, Douglass reverses the racial coordinates of a major trope of the American nineteenth century: the physical silencing of a colored person by a white one (see Melville's *Typee* [1846], Chesnutt's *Marrow of Tradition* [1901], and the lynch mobs of the 1890s). Douglass tears the halter from his own neck and places it around that of the planter class. Symbolically, he would repeat the act by publishing the *Narrative* and helping to set hereditary servitude on the course to ultimate extinction.

For Douglass does gain his voice: he learns to read and write, and he becomes a celebrated speaker for the cause of antislavery. Literacy, he claims, is "the pathway from slavery to freedom" (38), and reading *The Columbian Orator* awakens him to the full injustice of his condition. The arguments for emancipation that he encounters there "gave tongue to interesting thoughts of my own soul, which had frequently flashed through my mind, and died away for want of utterance" (42). Fortified by reading, Douglass forges a pass in his first, failed attempt at flight; later he escapes to the North and eventually makes his way to Massachusetts. The *Narrative* also traces his growing confidence in his speaking abilities as the somewhat passive observer of the first half metamorphoses into an active user of language.[6] Instead of being told what to do, he now does the telling: the construction "I told him" (43, 64, 78, 87, and 88) becomes commonplace. (Whitman, a Free Soiler, would foreground this emphasis on the speaking subject in *Leaves of Grass*.) The training helps Douglass overcome his nervousness when he addresses a white audience at Nantucket for the first time, and, swept up in the "freedom" of utterance (96), he makes the memorable impression that Garrison records in the preface.

But discursivity has its limits for Douglass; as long as slavery continues in the United States, speech cannot be wholly free. In the *Narrative*, speech remains encumbered and infiltrated by its nemesis, silence, even after Douglass flees Maryland for the free states. It might be argued that the difference between the South and the North, bondage and freedom, is that between compulsory and voluntary wordlessness; but in fact many slaves willingly maintain silence to fool their masters, and northern abolitionists faced beatings or worse for their opinions. Douglass learns the maxim "A still tongue makes a wise head" (27) while still on the Lloyd plantation. The adage stands him in good stead when his escape plan is betrayed: the captured slaves all agree to *"own nothing!"* (78), and their refusal to confess eventually secures their release from jail. Douglass adopts the same tactic after his flight to the North. Afraid "to speak to anyone for fear of speaking to the wrong one," he keeps his circumstances to himself and revises his old motto into "Trust no man!" (90). Nor does the security of writing a book in the antislavery stronghold of New England lull Douglass into complete disclosure. He omits the details of his successful escape and pointedly rejects the "very public manner" in which some abolitionists describe their involvement with the Underground Railroad. Such "open declarations," he insists, enlighten the master without doing anything to benefit future fugitives (85). Events and individuals from the more distant past have to be screened, too, and Douglass withholds the names of the two street urchins who helped him learn to read in Baltimore because teaching literacy to a slave remains "an unpardonable offence" (41). The one form of utterance Southerners allow their slaves has "silence"—the silence of not being comprehended—built into it. Although bondsmen are encouraged to sing while they work, the meaning of "those rude and apparently incoherent songs," as Douglass emphasizes, totally eludes their white auditors. "Slaves sing most when they are most unhappy," but owners and overseers, deaf to the undercurrent, believe that the sounds they hear are proof of contentment (24).

Of course, as Phillips pointed out, Massachusetts is *not* a safe haven for a runaway; Douglass cannot speak or write freely anywhere in the United States. Under the fugitive slave clause of the Constitution, an emissary from his owner could seize him by the throat and drag him back to the South. Three months after he revealed his identity in the *Narrative*, Douglass, still technically an American slave, boarded a Cunard steamer and sailed for Europe. He lectured in England, Ireland, and Scotland and did not return home for two years, by which time English sympathizers had managed to buy his freedom from Hugh Auld. As we shall see in *Life and Times*, post-Reconstruction would bring a repetition of this pattern, and Douglass would again flee his natal land as an ideological monolith that decreed muteness for blacks.

The title of Douglass's second memoir, *My Bondage and My Freedom*, erects a false binary. Bondage and its satellite attitudes pursue him into freedom and even harry him on his transatlantic voyage, where southern passengers aboard the *Cambria* "swore [he] should not speak" and had to be restrained from mobbing him by the English captain and crew (371). Abolitionists, ironically mimicking the master class on black literacy, didn't want him to start a newspaper funded by English supporters when he returned to the United States. Barely one-fifth of the revised volume deals with Douglass's "Life as a Freeman," and the longest chapter in that section describes not his experiences in the North, but his "Twenty-one Months in Great Britain." Moreover, the fragile condition of "American freedom" is a reality for more than just the ex-slave. Silence, its terrain enlarged racially and geographically, haunts *My Bondage and My Freedom*, which traces the threat of suppression as it spreads northward and aims at whites as well as blacks.[7]

The wonder is that Douglass exudes confidence in the antislavery cause's ability to surmount the blockages. By the end of the book, he himself enjoys a measure of immunity. His manumission has relieved him of the danger of rendition, and, as a prominent author and editor, he no longer finds it necessary to foreground his conquest of illiteracy. The *Narrative's* subtitle, *Written by Himself*, has been excised (it will be restored in *Life and Times*). Douglass also gives his oratorical performances a new prominence. An appendix includes extracts from half a dozen speeches delivered in the United States and abroad; with the advantage of hindsight, Douglass recognizes that he began his "public speaking" career as an educator of his fellow slaves (306). These excerpted lectures contain his bill of particulars against the South's emboldened attack on discursive liberties.

My Bondage and My Freedom was published five years after the omnibus compromise that was meant to lay sectional strife to rest and little more than a year after the Kansas-Nebraska Act became law. Douglass's public addresses make much of the idea that slavery's campaign against open discussion has pressed far beyond Dixie's borders. Douglass first raised the subject of censorship for whites at the end of the *Narrative*. There he relates the incident of his beating at a Baltimore shipyard and says that no white man dared step forward to testify against the assailants. Doing so would have incurred the charge of abolitionism, "and [the] name [of abolitionist] subjected its bearer to frightful liabilities" (83). By 1855 the intimidating of potential witnesses on the Baltimore docks seems a relatively mild transgression. With the slave interest's aggressiveness on the rise—the Fugitive Slave Law, according to Douglass, has effectively obliterated the Mason-Dixon Line, and "New York has become as Virginia" (438)—the plantation itself looms as a prototype for the nation.

The fourth chapter of *My Bondage and My Freedom*, "A General Survey of the Slave Plantation," contains a pertinent description of the Lloyd place as a closed society, a kind of totalitarian regime in embryo. This "secluded and out-of-the-way" setting constitutes a factual analog to the deck of Melville's *San Dominick*, from the coeval "Benito Cereno." It forms a world unto itself:

> To be a restraint upon cruelty and vice, public opinion must emanate from a humane and virtuous community. To no such humane and virtuous community, is Col. Lloyd's plantation exposed. That plantation is a little nation of its own, having its own language, its own rules, regulations and customs. The laws and institutions of the state, apparently touch it nowhere. The troubles arising here, are not settled by the civil power of the state. The overseer is generally accuser, judge, jury, advocate and executioner. The criminal is always dumb. The overseer attends to all sides of a case. . . .
>
> In its isolation, and self-reliant independence, Col. Lloyd's plantation resembles what the baronial domains were, during the middle ages in Europe. Grim, cold, and unapproachable by all genial communities without, *there it stands*; full three hundred years behind the age, in all that relates to humanity and morals. (160)

The ambition of the "the slavery party," as Douglass calls it, is to turn the United States into this tranquilized realm, and to ensure that the only "language" spoken and heard there is the philosophy of the owners of men.

American bondage knows that it cannot survive without muzzling its adversaries. In the mid-1850s, the lords of the lash have shown unprecedented insolence in dictating to the people of the other section: "They virtually asked them to unite in a war upon free speech, and upon conscience, and to drive the Almighty presence from the councils of the nation" (441). As always, the Slave Power's cardinal object is "to padlock the lips of the whites, in order to secure the fetters on the limbs of the blacks." They want every dissenting tongue in the nation to be stilled—"every anti-slavery organization dissolved—every anti-slavery press demolished—every anti-slavery periodical, paper, book, pamphlet, or what not, . . . searched out, gathered together, deliberately burned to ashes, and their ashes given to the four winds of heaven" (444). They will not rest until they have fastened the despotism of the overseer on the once free citizens of the North.

But bondage's concerted assault on freedom will not succeed, according to Douglass. The slavery party cannot eradicate dissent because too many voices, starting with the Deity's, are arrayed against it: "God has interposed an insuperable obstacle to any such result. 'There can be *no peace,* saith my God, to the wicked'" (444). The freedom loving refuse to be cowed. Douglass lists the many men and women of letters, from Stowe to Bryant, who have written on behalf of the Negro. They have so stamped antebellum culture with their service to the oppressed that despite the South's bluster, future generations will remember this time "as the age of anti-slavery literature." Even the "Ethiopian songs" routinely misinterpreted by the masters can awaken compassion for the slave; they, too, are formidable recruits to the banner (449). Douglass's litany concludes with the ringing assertion, in the last line of the volume, "that this anti-slavery cause will triumph" (451).

Douglass's optimism does not blind him to the complicity of the republic, North and South alike, in slavery's sins, and that consciousness gives a prophetic or jeremiadlike edge to much of his rhetoric. His sense of national responsibility can issue in passages full of wrath. These outbursts have antecedents in the *Narrative.* The appendix to the earlier memoir levels a scriptural warning from Jeremiah against the American Israel: "'Shall I not visit for these things? saith the Lord. Shall not my soul be avenged on such a nation as this?'" (100). The extracts gathered in *My Bondage and My Freedom* extend the charges, as prophecy after prophecy spills from Douglass's pen. He warns his countrymen "to BEWARE!" of divine retribution, and he reprints Thomas Jefferson's famous words, "'I tremble for my country when I reflect that God *is just,* and that his justice cannot sleep forever.'" The "spirit of patriotism" ought to encourage us to expose national wrongs, Douglass maintains, not cover them up or try to hide them from the world's sight (429–30).

Yet nationality is not an absolute for Douglass. His book appeared as Stowe was composing her novel *Dred,* and his volcanic oracles informed her conception of her eponymous hero. Like Stowe's mythical swamp dweller, the author of *My Bondage and My Freedom* can entertain a darker vision of the United States. From one perspective, the republic is a backslidden Israel, marred by its tolerance of slavery; from another, Dred's view, it is an Egypt or Babylon in which black people as latter-day Hebrews are a captive nation. Though never an outright separatist like Martin Delany, Douglass tends to oscillate between these two positions.[8] "The God of Israel is with us," he says about his decision to become an abolitionist lecturer (366); but what if America should refuse to see the light and persist in the ways of the Egyptians? Would fealty to God's edicts require abandonment of the country?[9]

By accident or not, Douglass's words echo John Winthrop's "Model of Christian Charity" ("The God of Israel is among us"), spoken at the foundational flight of the Puritans from a fallen England. Douglass's very title, *My Bondage and My Freedom*, reprises the Exodus pattern. His fiercest indictment, "What to the Slave Is the Fourth of July?," conveys a strong undercurrent of disaffection as it excoriates the United States for falseness to its anniversary.[10] The people who see themselves as a second Zion court the "irrecoverable ruin" that befell ancient Israel when its crimes aroused the Almighty's anger (431). Again, Douglass quotes scripture (Psalm 17) against a white America that betrays its principles for the consolations of Babylon: "'If I forget thee, O Jerusalem, let my right hand forget her cunning. If I do not remember thee, let my tongue cleave to the roof of my mouth'" (432). The Civil War would revive Douglass's hopes for his country, but the psalmist's sentences would have relevance again in the wake of Reconstruction, when there could be no doubt that the United States had forgotten.

Douglass himself would not forget, even at the nadir. To argue that the great abolitionist remained loyal to racial justice, as I will do here, is to run counter to a common view of *Life and Times* as the least progressive of the autobiographies. The unrevised 1881 edition lends support to this reading of Douglass as morally depleted. The bill of particulars includes his service as a ward heeler for the Republican Party of the Gilded Age; his Booker T. Washington–like advice to blacks to stay put in the South, where their labor was wanted, and not to desert to the North; and his celebration of the self-made man in a period when white racism, not character flaws, kept his people from advancing.[11] But if these attitudes suggest insensitivity to black realities, it is important to notice that in almost every case, and especially in the 1893 revision, Douglass moderates his position. He turns critical of the Republicans and the new doughfaces who lead them, and he softens his apparent embrace of laissez-faire ideology by insisting that no one can rely on just himself and that the friends who aided his rise deserve "at least an equal measure of credit, with myself" (900). The third part of the book, devoted to "Later Life," finds him removing himself from the whole country, not just the South, and records a reawakening of the prophetic imagination. Having seen the prophecies of his earlier work fulfilled in the Civil War, the abolition of slavery, and the achievements of Reconstruction, Douglass knows what language can do and what it still has to accomplish. The paradox is that speech has to defer to reticence before Jerusalem can be regained.

The prewar chapters of *Life and Times* are a primer on the South's "war upon free speech," and the North's pusillanimity before slaveholder intransigence serves as an ominous portent of the 1877 retreat. In the late 1850s, antislavery activism intensified in response to Slave Power belli- cosity, as Southerners and their allies took ever more extravagant steps to crush agitation. Douglass speaks of "the display of pistols, bludgeons, and plantation manners in the Congress of the nation," and he describes "the murderous assault" upon Senator Charles Sumner for the offense "of words spoken in debate!" (734 and 736). The South's policy of "rule-or- ruin intimidation" (767) came to a head with the threats of disunion that greeted Lincoln's nomination and then election. Northerners across the political spectrum fell over themselves in their eagerness to propitiate de- mands for slavery's protection; as Douglass puts it, they "bent before this southern storm, and were ready to purchase peace at any price," includ- ing throwing away the election results. The months before Lincoln's in- auguration brought renewed attacks on civil liberties of a kind not seen in the North since the 1830s, when Garrison had that famous "halter about his neck" (770–71). Through it all, the president-elect remained steadfast on freedom's side; at long last a leader had appeared who spoke "pregnant words" that "went straight to the heart of the nation" (736).[12] But it took the bombardment of Ft. Sumter to dispel illusions of reconciliation, and even then racism impeded the Union's victory because the government refused to enlist and arm black soldiers.

Twenty years later, in the reunited nation that erased from memory the causes of the war, northern waffling has deteriorated into a full-scale rout. Tangible signs of Douglass's disaffection appear at the end of the second part, in the 1880 speech entitled "West India Emancipation" that concludes the section's appendix. He complains of the widespread percep- tion that the abolitionists caused the war. This is true, Douglass concedes, in the sense that, had there been no agitation, southern aggression would have prevailed and slavery would have been nationalized. Now the South *has* gotten the upper hand: with Reconstruction in tatters and black rights stripped away, the "old master class is to-day triumphant." The ex-slaves have been effectively reduced to chains again; their lot is "but little above that in which they were found before the rebellion" (932). Or, as Douglass phrases it in the third part, emancipation has superseded bondage, but "it has not supplanted the spirit or power of slavery" (976). The thread that connects this abandonment to the North's earlier inconstancy is not far to seek. It was in plentiful evidence among otherwise enlightened abolition- ists in the 1850s, and it has become the defining characteristic of the post- bellum United States: the condition Douglass calls "colorphobia" (891).

Indeed, if the enslavement of blacks stamped the prewar republic with its backward, "baronial" identity, the fetishizing of race and the use of color to oppress the country's own citizens are what sets the continental colossus apart from the rest of the civilized world as a regressive outlier. White Americans cannot adjust "to the idea that a man of a different color from themselves should have all the human rights" that they enjoy (939). They take pride in having outgrown "the castes and aristocracies of the old world" but enforce discriminations at home that are "far less rational and much more ridiculous" (962). Douglass's extended travels in Europe and Egypt constantly reaffirm his awareness of this perverse exceptionalism: "nowhere, outside of the United States, is any man denied civil rights on account of his race" (980). Whatever he may have said about blacks bailing out from the South, the same motivation fuels Douglass's own wanderlust by the late 1880s: he relishes the chance to "walk the world unquestioned, a man among men," and to leave "conflict with race and color prejudice and proscription" behind (1017). The erstwhile American slave, always skeptical of his homeland's democratic pretensions, has developed into a spiritual exile, someone more at ease abroad than in his birthplace.

Douglass had felt this way before, when twice compelled to flee the United States to avoid extradition to the South: once as a runaway, and once after John Brown's raid on Harpers Ferry, in which he was suspected of involvement. During that grim era, censorship did not fully relent until the onset of armed hostilities. Now northern bigotry and cowardice have leagued with southern recidivism to reentrench the climate of repression. The iron law of black disempowerment, proscribing any discourse save white supremacy, has brought back to life the hermetic plantation world that Douglass experienced as a boy on the eastern shore of Maryland. Consider this passage from *Life and Times* and substitute "racism" for "slavery":

> There were certain . . . places, even in the state of Maryland, fifty years ago, seldom visited by a single ray of healthy public sentiment, where slavery, wrapt in its own congenial darkness, could and did develop all its malign and shocking characteristics, where it could be indecent without shame, cruel without shuddering, and murderous without apprehension or fear of exposure or punishment. (485)

The "high-handed and atrocious" crimes committed on Colonel Lloyd's estate "with strange and shocking impunity" would prove no worse than the unpunished lynchings meant to rob blacks of their voice and rights after Reconstruction (487). If anything, the situation would worsen by 1893.

The proximity of the free states, with "their moral, religious, and humane sentiments," had acted as "a measurable restraint" on the slave system's worst trespasses (485). The postwar North's embrace of reunion on southern terms eliminated that check, and no external influence now exists to mitigate the barbarism of racial tyranny.

Douglass will not give in to coercion, and a continued emphasis on "talking back" is evident in much of *Life and Times*. The address on the West Indies, for example, points out that emancipation came to the islands "not by the sword, but by the word." Lawful agitation and "the still small voice of truth" gained the victory.[13] The precedent of peaceful change through suasion, the lesson of *The Columbian Orator*, preserves its relevance for the American scene twenty-five years after the Civil War: "faith in the truth and courage in the expression" can still carry the day against seemingly insuperable odds (926–27). Hence Douglass's decision to enlarge his memoir and carry it up to 1893 (two years after Melville put his final touches on *Billy Budd*, another text preoccupied with speech and silence). The third part begins with him presenting himself, yet again, as "an advocate for a people long dumb." He will write for his dark-skinned "brothers and sisters, who, though free, are yet oppressed and are in as much need of an advocate as before they were set free" (938–39). But estrangement rather than sanguinity sets the tone for Douglass's picture of the post-Reconstruction United States.

Significantly, he resuscitates the subtitle *Written by Himself* (originally restored in 1881). Douglass felt secure enough in his abilities to cut the words from *My Bondage and My Freedom*; three decades later, no colored man or woman was free from the imputation of incurable mental and moral disadvantage. His claim of literacy contradicts the derogatory picture of black people popularized in, among other detractors, the dialect stories of Joel Chandler Harris. *Uncle Remus: His Songs and His Sayings* had been published to acclaim in 1881, and the collection's contribution to the impression of the former slaves as comic darkies confined to the cage of orality can hardly be exaggerated. Douglass's whole struggle under slavery had been to break free of that confinement. Harris, who describes his "legends," fantastically, as a supplement to "Mrs. Stowe's wonderful defense of slavery," portrays black people, excluding the presumptuous "New Negro," as uneducated but resourceful entertainers gaily telling stories, singing songs, and minting aphorisms for the delectation of whites.[14] Charles W. Chesnutt's later writing of such tales, as a *black* author, reasserts the minority's right to the ruling caste's technology of literacy.

The battle for recognition of the ex-slaves' potential has proven as dispiriting in its results as the phalanx of laws and amendments passed under Reconstruction. Despite his allegiance to the necessity for protest, Douglass has no illusions about how Republican and northern failure of nerve has eviscerated "the national statute book" and turned hard-won rights into ciphers "on paper and parchment" (931). Having previously reprinted a warm eulogy for the assassinated President James A. Garfield, he candidly admits in the third part that the Ohioan "was not a stalwart" for the Negro. More than that, Garfield was the antithesis of Lincoln in his valuation of language. Although many trembled at southern vows to secede in 1861, Lincoln "had an oath in heaven" to support and defend the Constitution, and he would not "evade or violate that sacred oath." His entire being revolted at the thought of "his saying one thing when he meant another" (924; quotes from the 1876 oration in memory of Lincoln, included in the appendix to the second part). Garfield, professedly another "Abraham" (his middle name was Abram), had a very different understanding of the verbal. When, as a representative in Congress, he used the phrase "perjured traitors" to describe the rebels who had betrayed their oaths to the federal government, and a former slaveholder objected, Garfield lamely apologized by saying "that he did not make the dictionary." Words to him were mere notations in a book, not weapons to rebuke insolence or uphold the Union; and he further revealed his character when, as candidate for president, he said he would appoint Douglass United States Marshall for the District of Columbia and then reneged on his promise. Neither Garfield nor any of the leaders of the Republican Party still "considered a man's word his bond" (951–52). They felt no Lincoln-like obligation to fulfill their sacred oaths. In the 1880s, they systemically broke the promises that the country had made to the freedmen.

The turning point, for Douglass, came in 1883 with the Supreme Court's nullification of the 1875 Civil Rights Act, a decision the "future historian" will study for indisputable proof of "national deterioration" (966). Along with the administrations of Cleveland and Arthur, the ruling, from a Court with a Republican majority, raised "the spirit of slavery and rebellion" to ascendancy, as if, Appomattox notwithstanding, Jefferson Davis had conquered the capital (963 and 967). The Act had been the brainchild of Charles Sumner, who fought for it in the Senate until his death in 1874; it outlawed discrimination in public accommodations in the South and allowed redress in federal courts. Striking down the law as unconstitutional in *United States v. Stanley* (better known as the *Civil Rights Cases*), the Supreme Court held that the national government had no jurisdiction over private acts of discrimination and that the freedmen could no longer "be the special favorite of the laws." Southern states proceeded to override the Fourteenth and Fifteenth Amendments by passing Jim Crow legislation and depriving blacks of the vote.[15]

To Douglass, the Court's decision stirred memories of the Kansas-Nebraska Act and the *Dred Scott* decision, comparable blows from the 1850s. But whereas those miscarriages provoked Lincoln and the antislavery alliance to determined opposition, the current tone in Washington was one of surrender. True, Douglass acknowledges, with the removal of troops from the South, Sumner's statutory legacy was "a dead letter and could not be enforced." But even from the grave, the law spoke:

> There are tongues in trees, sermons in stones, and books in running brooks. This law, though dead, did speak. It expressed the sentiment of justice and fair play common to every honest heart. Its voice was against popular prejudice and meanness. . . . It told the American people that they were all equal before the law; that they belonged to a common country and were equal citizens. (978)

Douglass goes on to equate the 1875 Act with the Declaration and the Sermon on the Mount; all proclaim "the golden rule" that people should treat others as they wish to be treated themselves (979). The Court's opinion in the *Civil Rights Cases* voided and silenced them all.

Douglass has two dissimilar reactions to the ruling. First, he observes that pressures for ideological conformity on issues of race have grown so intense in the country that no less a dissenter than Justice John Harlan can expect to be subjected to "an amount of criticism from which even the bravest man might shrink" (968). Blacks, more vulnerable, see their dissent distorted by the newspapers into a near-seditious condemnation of the court itself; they are "thus put in the attitude of bad citizens," and the disregard of their rights is justified (978). Douglass appeals to his people not to succumb to this renewed assault on "free speech" and "honest expression of opinion" (969). But second, the Court's decision, and the assent with which it has been widely received, staggers Douglass with the depths of American race prejudice and leaves him wondering, as he did under slavery, if "a still tongue" might not be the best defense against oppression. We have "been wounded in the house of our friends," he writes, and the wound is "too painful for ordinary and measured speech." Since attacks would only excite charges of disloyalty, the wisest course is to say nothing: "It may be, after all, that the hour calls more loudly for silence than for speech" (968). Or as Douglass puts it in *My Bondage and My Free-*

dom, "where slavery is powerful, and liberty is weak, the latter is driven to concealment or to destruction" (309–10).

The climax of this apparently acquiescent strain in *Life and Times* arrives some thirty pages later, when Douglass describes his visit to the Suez Canal and the pyramids. What quickly becomes clear is that the black leader's revived attraction to soundlessness is anything *but* backward looking: rather, it undergirds his ongoing commitment to the prophetic. Although the sandy wastes of Egypt might seem like the last place for an American traveler to experience renewal, the Israel-in-bondage trope is never far from Douglass's mind. The town of Suez immediately brings back his native realm. The Arabs who unload ships along the docks sing while they work, and he embraces them as "half brothers to the negro." As his own ship moves "noiselessly" through the canal, Douglass has an overwhelming "sense of unearthly silence" (1007–8). Entering the domain of the pharaohs, he observes a long line of camels moving across the desert, a sight unchanged since "the days of Abraham and Moses" (1009); the beasts with their heavy burdens remind him of a coffle of slaves in chains.

The meaning of the desert reveals itself to Douglass when he reaches the pyramids. Imagination, he realizes, flourishes in uninhabited spaces; the soul hears with greater acuity.

> The song of the angels could be better heard by the shepherds on the plains of Bethlehem than by the jostling crowds in the busy streets of Jerusalem. John the Baptist could preach better in the wilderness than in the busy marts of men. Jesus said his best word to the world when on the Mount of Olives. Moses learned more of the laws of God when in the mountains than when down among the people. The Hebrew prophets frequented dens and caves and desert places. . . . No wonder that Moses wandering in the vast and silent desert, after killing an Egyptian and brooding over the oppressed condition of his people, should hear the voice of Jehovah saying, "I have seen the affliction of my people." (1009–10)

The silence of the Egyptian landscape affords an apt parallel to the United States in the waning years of the nineteenth century. In the slave past, a chorus of voices arose out of the stillness to broadcast the message of freedom. America overflowed with prophet-liberators, and there was no shortage of candidates for the role of Moses. Douglass specifically compares Garrison and Lincoln to the leader of the Hebrews, and he remarks that he himself has devoted the Mosaic term of "forty years" to the cause of his people (914). But the writer of this final autobiography is too old to lead now, and no white men of stature have stepped forward to assume the charge. Still, Douglass does not doubt that the silence enveloping America will quicken the hearing of a prophet. Though the times look bleak, "there is a better day coming" for the long-suffering freedmen (934). A new Moses, catching the divine Word, will summon them out of captivity to the promised land. They may or may not have to flee the Egypt of American racism to find redemption. If Douglass is any model, many will already have withdrawn their affections from the nation that enslaved and then betrayed them. They will be symbolic expatriates pining for Jerusalem while they languish in Babylon.

In the last three chapters of *Life and Times*, Douglass describes his appointment (by President Benjamin Harrison) as minister to Haiti and his travails representing the United States in the world's first black republic.[16] The press denounced the selection on racist grounds—Douglass's color "was a shade too dark for American taste" (1023)—and while in Port-au-Prince he was under constant pressure to extract concessions from the Haitian government for an American naval station at Môle St. Nicolas. The Haitians, all too aware of Yankee bigotry, refused to alienate their territory, and the negotiations ended in failure. Douglass was blamed for sympathizing more with his black confreres than with the nation to which he owed his allegiance.

And he must have preferred the Haitians to the racist, often southern, politicians and businessmen who hounded him with their demands. It is telling that the last words he wrote about his life refer to the signal honor he received when Florvil Hyppolite, Haiti's president, asked him to represent that country at the World's Columbian Exposition in Chicago in 1893. The "White City," as the fairgrounds were known, proved to be a case study in the nationalizing of white supremacy, and President Harrison was thoroughly complicit in this development. He failed to name a single African American to the commission that planned the exposition; it took sustained protest to a get a colored school principal added as an alternate. Blacks saw their achievements crowded into segregated displays, all part of a "deliberate and cowardly tribute to the Southern demand 'to keep the Negro in his place.'" "A foreign power," Haiti, not the United States, conferred recognition on the greatest African American of the century.[17] No surprise there: as George L. Ruffin noted in his introduction to *Life and Times*, "our most celebrated colored man" should be mentioned in the same breath with Toussaint L'Ouverture, the Haitian warrior-hero whom white Americans almost universally reviled as a symbol of black savagery (473).

Douglass would stop short of advocating emigration, but his disgust with plantation America is palpable and little abated from the despairing mood of 1883. In his chapter on the *Civil Rights Cases*, he warned his compatriots that such a decision, by placing a whole people outside the government's protection, runs the danger of destroying "that love of country, which in the day of trouble is needful to the nation's defense" (974). The Court's ruling roused Douglass to a prophecy of vengeance redolent of the slaveholding past, and we might fittingly conclude with those words, knowing as we do what the next eighty years held in store for blacks, and what that moral and political calamity cost America. A ruling so patently unfair, according to Douglass, must eventually impact all citizens, not simply those to whom the wrong is done. The day of reckoning may be postponed, "but so sure as there is a moral government of the universe, so sure as there is a God of the universe, so sure will the harvest of evil come" (973).

Whitman: From Sayer-Doer to Sayer-Copyist

In 1848 Walt Whitman attended the convention in Buffalo, New York, that created the Free Soil Party, whose goal was to exclude slavery from the lands acquired from Mexico. Free Soilers had no illusions about the Slave Power's designs. They were convinced that the planter class intended not simply to spread its domestic institution westward, but also to insulate slavery from criticism by snuffing out open discussion in the North. Thwarting expansionism into the territories could not be separated from preserving civil liberties in the states. This insight seemed more relevant than ever six years later, when Congress passed the Kansas-Nebraska Act opening the entire West to slavery. Whitman, seething with anger at doughfaces, began work on his poetic masterpiece, and the battle over free speech was a key ingredient in the making of the 1855 edition of *Leaves of Grass*. Some of the most distinctive features of that most American of all poems, "Song of Myself," including the poet's strategies of articulation and reception, can be traced to the growing concern among opponents of slavery that all discourse would be regulated. A reawakened belief in the might of words informs Whitman's outpouring, which simultaneously prophesies and brings into textual being its vision of an egalitarian republic.[1]

But despite the imaginative inclusiveness of 1855, Whitman, no abolitionist, harbored misgivings about agitation that ultimately resurfaced, and his conception of song as action did not outlast the Civil War. His ideological retreat—he evolved into a foe of black rights and a supporter of Andrew Johnson—played itself out on the level of language, subtly in *Leaves of Grass*, more obviously in prose pieces written during and after Reconstruction. Whitman's frequently delivered oration on the death of Lincoln (1879) exemplifies his revisionary posture: it shows the disciple of Emersonian activism evolving into a retrospective celebrant of "the sepulchers of the fathers."[2] More surprising, *Democratic Vistas* (1871) traces a similar retrenchment. This apparent exercise in prophecy in fact proclaims the demise of effective speech. Disillusioned with both politics and language's benignity, Whitman pries apart the union of word and deed and relegates prophetic fulfillment to a future as distant and unattainable as the past.

Free soil, free speech, free verse: though *Leaves of Grass* appeared under the shadow of the Kansas-Nebraska Act, the legislation that returned Lincoln to politics and Thoreau to public polemic, an earlier public document may have been as important for the book's gestation. Published on July 4, which also happens to be the only specific date mentioned in "Song of Myself" (39), Whitman's epic in twelve parts joined an array of freedom's advocates in affirming the relevance of the nation's foundational document to the nineteenth-century present. Lincoln rushed to the Declaration's defense as slavery's supporters mocked it; Emerson, disgusted by the rendition of runaways, told an audience in New York, "You must be citadels and warriors, yourselves Declarations of Independence."[3] Works hymning equality and revolutionary speech at a time (according to Whitman's preface) when "tyrants and traitors" rule and "the cause is asleep" (16),[4] could not fail to invoke the Jeffersonian template, and its inspirational presence can be felt throughout *Leaves of Grass*.

According to Whitman, the end of poetry "is to cheer up slaves and horrify despots" (15). That objective, imperative in 1776 when Jefferson penned his manifesto, had equal urgency in 1855. The poet explicitly compares his own era to the Revolutionary past in "A Boston Ballad," which imagines the skeleton of George III resuming his throne in the city that sent the fugitive slave Anthony Burns back to bondage. Another poem on the Revolutions of 1848–49, "Europe: The 72d and 73d Years of These States," identifies the republic's beginnings with Jefferson's summons to nationhood rather than the Constitution (Lincoln would do the same thing in the Gettysburg Address). The poet's aesthetic of equivalence, his assertion of a common human core overriding differences of status, wealth, gender, and race, can be read as an explication and commentary on "all men are created equal."[5] *Leaves of Grass* thus answers the proslavery scoffers who wondered aloud what the Jeffersonian sentiment could possibly mean. Even Whitman's catalogs may owe something to the Declaration, which submits a long list of abuses by the Crown (i.e., George III) to the judgment of "a candid world." Nor should we forget that the man who authored the Declaration also, and in the same spirit, composed an essay,

Thoughts on English Prosody (1789?), which practically foreshadows Whitman in its exalting of blank verse and dismissal of rhyme as a violation of poetic liberty. The most telling example of Jefferson's influence, though, comes in Whitman's embrace of speech's agency. His verses seek to match the Declaration's revolutionary intervention in history. His book defies repression and foregrounds utterance as the "mightiest of the sciences" (144), the single force capable of righting America's course.

The preamble to *Leaves of Grass* introduces the poet as the bane of censors and the voice of liberty. Whitman refers to "slavery and the tremulous spreading of hands to protect it, and the stern opposition to it which shall never cease until it ceases or the speaking of tongues and the moving of lips cease" (8). The "tremulous" hands suggest a fearful awareness, on the part of the institution's defenders, that slavery is immoral and doomed, but the tongues and lips that would dismantle it have been rendered useless: "the strong throats are choked with their own blood" (8). The poet steps forth to assume the burden of speech, confident that his periods will have the impact of events. "In war he is the most deadly force of war. . . . he can make every word he speaks draw blood" (8). Supplanting politicians, *Leaves of Grass* will resurrect freedom and "set slavery at naught" (16 and 23). Whitman's preface heralds his coming as the poet/legislator whose verses will realize the promise of democratic equality. The subsequent poems prove that the "signs are effectual" (24) by making the imagined utopia tangible in words, and they reveal their protean author to be the Sayer as Doer called for by Emerson in "The Poet."

Whitman's verses, especially "Song of Myself," are unprecedented in their self-reference to the act of speech. Against the culture's demand for muteness, they never let us lose sight of the fact that someone is talking to us. (The affinity with Thoreau is evident.) We do not simply hear Whitman's voice. We hear his voice telling us that we are hearing his voice, and that he is speaking for us as well as himself, giving outlet to all those persons in antebellum America who are denied the means and opportunity of expression: runaway slaves, Indians, prostitutes, boatmen, drovers, trappers, opium eaters, and so forth. The pattern begins with the first lines of "Song of Myself": "I celebrate myself, / And what I assume you shall assume, / For every atom belonging to me as good belongs to you" (25). The Virgilian echo (made more emphatic by the later addition, "and sing myself") announces the text's epic pretensions while calling attention to the declaiming artist; and that voluble speaker does not leave us over the thirteen hundred lines to follow.

Consider, for instance, the poet's habit of preceding his statements with the words, "I say": "And I say it is as great to be a woman as to be a man, / And I say there is nothing greater than the mother of men" (44). Variations include "I step up to say" (46), "I do not say these things for a dollar" (81), and "I have said" (82). Another Whitman signature is "I tell": "This hour I tell things in confidence, / I might not tell everyone but I will tell you" (43). Still other speech-flagging mannerisms include "I speak" (48), "I translate" (44), "I call" (45 and 83), "I answer" (80), "I swear" (82), "I contradict" (85), "I sound" (85), and "It is time to explain myself" (76). Whitman refers constantly to his tongue and voice: "My voice goes after what my eyes cannot reach, / With the twirl of my tongue I encompass worlds and volumes of worlds" (50). His Deity is not a silent absence (or wordless presence) but a being much like himself, an irrepressible communicator who drops "letters" in the street, "and every one is signed by God's name" (83). Hawthorne, foe of agitation, had Roger Chillingworth swipe his finger across his lips in a gesture that summed up the censor's calling. Whitman tirelessly proclaims his difference: "I do not press my finger across my mouth" (48).

But it is not merely "Walt Whitman, an American, one of the roughs" (48), who talks in "Song of Myself." A cacophony of voices fills the text, and inanimate objects, animals, and parts of the body add their clamor to the din. Many sections begin with the sound of someone singing or speaking: "A child said, What is the grass? . . ." (chant 6, 29); "The pure contralto sings in the organloft" (chant 15, 37); ". . . . A call in the midst of a crowd" (chant 42, 73). The poet declares his love for the "human voice" (51), and just as he assumes the identity of others in a paroxysm of fungibility, becoming a fugitive slave, or an injured fireman, or a bride on her wedding night, so in his poem "many long dumb voices," are able to achieve utterance by an interchangeability with his own voice (48). At times these people speak through Whitman, who acts as the tongue that "was tied in your mouth" (82), but at other moments they enjoy a textual parity with him by being allowed to enter the poem and state their thoughts themselves. The poet's voice mutates into "the wife's voice" as she keens over the body of her drowned husband (61). It becomes that of a dying general who "gasps through the clot. . . . Mind me not . . . mind. . . . the entrenchments" (64). The famous lines of John Paul Jones while commanding the *Bon Homme Richard* are spoken anew in the captain's own voice: "We have not struck, he composedly cried, We have just begun our part of the fighting" (66). Perhaps the most memorable voice is that of the child asking Whitman about the grass, and like the other quoted statements, the child's question is in fact *not* quoted in the 1855 edition: it appears without punctuation marks and is typographically indistinguishable from the poet's words. This would change in later editions of *Leaves of Grass*; but here all voices are equal and claim equal ownership with Whitman in "Song of Myself."

There are also eruptions of unidentified and inarticulate speech. Fire fighters shout and soldiers roar; mobs emit the sounds of fury; the "overfed or half-starved" fall to the flagstones and groan (32). Lover of New York, Whitman puts into his poem the "living and buried speech" of the metropolis (32). He records the "ring of alarm-bells. . . . the cry of fire" (51), and he celebrates the pandemonium of urban existence:

> The blab of the pave. . . . The tires of carts and sluff of bootsoles and talk
>   of the promenaders,
> The heavy omnibus, the driver with his interrogating thumb, the clank
>   of the shod horses on the granite floor,
> The carnival of sleighs, the clinking and shouted jokes and pelts of
>   snowballs;
> The hurrahs for popular favorites. . . . (31–32)

Vying with this human uproar is the discourse of nature. Ganders "Yahonk"; sows grunt; a hawk "complains of my gab and my loitering" (36 and 85). "Speech is the twin of my vision," the poet says, and speech itself breaks into speech in *Leaves of Grass*, urging him to turn up the volume: "It says sarcastically, Walt, you understand enough. . . . why don't you let it out then?" (51). Exuberant with sounds, "Song of Myself" may be the most talkative poem written in English during the nineteenth century.

Whitman's determination to "say" in his verses, to flaunt utterance in the face of its critics, grew if anything more intense as sectional warfare approached. His self-referential insistence on the speaking subject attains a kind of apogee in the 1860 edition of *Leaves of Grass*, to which he added an eight-part section entitled "Says." Numbers 1 through 6 begin with "I say"; number 7 uses "I have said" as its opening; and "I say" returns in the final line of the eighth and concluding part (689–90).[6] Dedicated to "the good old cause" that catalyzed the 1855 preface, "Says" squarely ties Whitman's garrulousness to slavery's attempt to strangle the voice of liberty. Section 6, which the poet excised in 1867, warrants quotation in its entirety for the bluntness of its defiance:

> I say the word of lands fearing nothing—I will have no other land;
> I say discuss all and expose all—I am for every topic openly;

I say there can be no salvation for These States without innovators—
   without free tongues, and ears willing to hear the tongues;
And I announce as a glory of These States, that they respectfully listen to
   propositions, reforms, fresh views and doctrines, from successions of
   men and women,
Each age with its own growth.

An important theme in this "Say," one that also holds a central place in "Song of Myself," is the necessity for an audience, or an America, capable of hearing and appreciating the "free tongues" of dissent. The bard, Whitman avers in his 1855 preface, must be "commensurate" with the people (6); his country must absorb him "as affectionately as he has absorbed it" (24). With those in power doing their utmost to halt the spread of "incendiary" discourse, this self-exhortation in practice means that the poet must devise some way to ensure the unimpeded circulation of his words. He has to make his poems as immediately present and accessible as possible in order to circumvent censorship. Whitman aims to speak *to* in addition to speaking *for*; he even sets himself the task of reaching "the illiterate person," whom he praises for an "unconsciousness" that humbles "the noblest expressive genius" (9). Whitman's solution to these challenges is of course figurative, and his strategy is prefigurative too. *Leaves of Grass* has attracted widespread attention as a forerunner of the cinema from writers and directors such as D. W. Griffith, Vachel Lindsay, and Sergei Eisenstein.

The desire for accessibility immediately manifests itself in the frontispiece to *Leaves of Grass*, where the poet's daguerreotype appears without caption, and it continues through the preface and the poems. The sequence itself is revealing. It suggests that Whitman is gently guiding us through his book, from the most effortlessly digested art, a picture—which even the illiterate person can comprehend—through the most familiar form of written composition, prose—to the more rarefied domain of poetry. In Whitman's hands, moreover, poetry resembles its more commonplace sibling: laid out on the page, the unrhymed verses look like prose and promise a comparable ease of consumption.[7] *Leaves of Grass* strives to extend and enhance through language the availability of the introductory daguerreotype. Pictures, the poet's word for his catalogues, defy time by providing the viewer with an eternal present, and in Whitman's aesthetic, the ontology of the image coalesces with the Emersonian injunction to inhabit the moment. "What is past is past," the poet says (9), and he endeavors to create an almost endless now by relying on the present tense and making

repeated use of the present participle. We experience the events being described as ongoing because Whitman, our escort, participates in them as
he addresses us. "All these I feel or am," he insists of the "hounded slave,"
the bereft wife, even John Paul Jones (62). His forays into history slip into
the past tense on occasion but have an immediacy in spite of that fact:
we are there with him, and his credo, "I am the man. . . . I suffered. . . . I
was there" (62), tends to obliterate the distinction between then and now.
The poem's ending beautifully captures the perpetuity of the moment
by condensing into three lines the nineteenth-century poet, the present
reader, and the reader of the future: "Failing to fetch me at first keep encouraged, / Missing me one place search another, / I stop some where waiting for you" (86).

Whitman's kinetic catalogues heighten the impression of his poetry's
image-like accessibility and presence; they make clear why Eisenstein
could take pride in film having "a pedigree" in the "enormous cultured
past."[8] The scenes reeled out before us in "Song of Myself" are not static
but in constant motion, anticipations of the technologically produced
moving pictures. In chant 15, the poet's eye, like a camera, sweeps from
the "quadroon girl" on the auction block to "newly-come immigrants,"
from the "Wolverine" in the wilderness to the "cleanhaired Yankee girl"
at her sewing-machine (37–38). The pace quickens in chant 33: announcing, "I am afoot with my vision" (57), Whitman overleaps space and time
to record images from across the globe and throughout history. We get
rapid shifts of scene and abrupt juxtapositions of past and present; we zero
in on small details and pull back for panoramic vistas. Whitman's commitment to overcoming censorship and reaching as large an audience as
possible led him into experiments that would be consummated outside
literature, in the close-ups, tracking shots, and montage perfected as a cinematic syntax. His resolve to be heard inspired him to approximate in his
verses the most popular and American of all art forms, exactly sixty years
before Griffith would release his epic on celluloid and displace the poet's
egalitarian message with the anti-black *Birth of a Nation*.

Leaves of Grass could not overcome the limitations of its written medium and translate its prophecies into reality. It could not entice a mass
audience. As Vachel Lindsay observed in *The Art of the Moving Picture*
(1915), Whitman could "not persuade the democracy itself to read his democratic poems." It took the kinetoscope to vanquish aesthetic elitism and
penetrate "to the haunts of the wildest or the dullest." But the story of
Whitman and the movies would not end there, according to Lindsay, who
believed that the poet's legacy would be more positive than Griffith's ex-

ample suggests. "Sooner or later" the still primitive photoplay would rise to the level of the highest art and, taking "Whitmanesque scenarios" as its model, teach ordinary Americans the true meaning of their country. It would bring "the equality idea to the people who are so crassly equal."[9]

Whitman himself would move in a different direction once Appomattox settled the slavery issue. He may well have agreed with *The Birth of a Nation* had he lived to see it. His recoil seems almost inevitable given the ambitions of *Leaves of Grass*, and it has a parallel in the suspicion of language that Lincoln acknowledged in the Gettysburg Address. Like the president, Whitman had good reasons to feel uneasy about verbal grandiosity, having foretold cataclysmic change in the polity and joined his visions of parity with explosions of wrath. He had heaped curses on the United States, usually against slaveholders, that he judged too fierce for inclusion in the so-called "deathbed edition" of 1892. (Examples are the slave's "Damn him!" from "The Sleepers" [111] and the final lines of the original "I Sing the Body Electric": "Who degrades or defiles the living human body is cursed, / Who degrades or defiles the body of the dead is not more cursed" [123].) Writers, Whitman had said in the letter to Emerson that he substituted for the preface in 1856, must be revolutionists; the tensions of the present were the perfect "conditions for wording the future with undissuadable words" (1359). His outspokenness may have climaxed in *The Eighteenth Presidency!* (1856), a pamphlet so blistering in its portrait of political pusillanimity that Whitman could not secure a publisher and had to print it himself. The work teems with portents and prophecies. Whitman warns of "historic denouements" as the masses prepare for "some better era, some divine war. No man knows what will happen next, but all know that such things are to happen as mark the greatest moral convulsions of the earth" (1359). The author of such rhetoric could be excused for thinking that his words had contributed to the bloodshed of 1861–65.

The United States may not have absorbed Whitman as its poet-lawgiver, but the leader it did embrace, and who steered the country through war, had an oracular preexistence in the poet's antislavery passion. *The Eighteenth Presidency!* envisions the long-awaited figure who will terminate the reign of "slave-catchers" and "body-snatchers" headed by Pierce and Buchanan (1337). Whitman's redeemer president uncannily foreshadows the Illinois Republican who would win his party's nomination four years later. The poet describes him as a "middle-aged, beard-faced American blacksmith or boatman come down from the West across the Alleghanies," who will walk into the White House "dressed in a clean

suit of working attire, and with the tan all over his face, breast, and arms"
(1332). Prophecies that come true can have dire consequences: upon taking
office, Lincoln presided over the bloodiest military confrontation in history, and Whitman had firsthand experience of the carnage as a visitor and
wound dresser in Washington's military hospitals.[10] When the horrors of
war ended, the Radical Republicans passed what Whitman considered to
be the travesty of black suffrage, and American society degenerated from a
culture of sacrifice into a spectacle of money getting.

Democratic Vistas, which decries these aspects of postbellum America, reads at first like an updating of the 1855 preface or The Eighteenth
Presidency![11] The little book is Whitman's "Gilded Age." Arraigning the
nation's political leadership as morally rudderless—Grant was president—
it inveighs against the "unprecedented materialistic advancement" that
has plunged the restored union into an orgy of "robbery and scoundrelism"
(961). The United States suffers from "more hollowness of heart" than any
other land, the poet says, and because the republic is a synonym for democracy, for the people's rule, it must either reform itself "or else prove
the most tremendous failure of time" (961 and 954). Here again, as in 1855–
56, Whitman puts his faith in the "results to come" (953) and in a heralded
class of writer-heroes (or literatuses, as he calls them) who will usher in
that better future. A genuine "prophetic literature" does not merely "copy
and reflect existing surfaces" (1008 and 964). It brings to pass the possibilities it imagines and has a greater impact on society than "all its Constitu-
tions," wars, and riches (959).

The resemblance of Democratic Vistas to the aesthetic utopianism of
Whitman's previous work is more than misleading: the text actually erases
the literary past, and the bard's part in it, and translates the era's growing
amnesia about the causes of the Civil War into an analogous forgetfulness
about the word-as-deed paradigm of antebellum romanticism. Whitman
paraphrases figures who called for a literature of consequence twenty to
thirty years earlier and, amazingly, writes as though not only they, but he
too, never existed and never raised a voice against the Slave Power's war
on words. Echoing Emerson's "American Scholar"—"we have listened too
long to the courtly muses of Europe"—the poet protests, "Long enough
have the People been listening to poems in which common humanity, def-
erential, bends low, humiliated, acknowledging superiors" (1004). He reaffirms Thoreau's idea of engaged reading: "the process of reading is not a
half sleep, but, in the highest sense, an exercise, a gymnast's struggle"
(1016). Yet no one would guess from Democratic Vistas that Essays: First
Series, Walden and "Civil Disobedience," and Leaves of Grass, for that

matter, had reanimated language's authority in the 1840s and 1850s and established an indigenous renaissance. The native imagination is *still* secondhand, according to Whitman, still in thrall to foreign lands, and "America has yet morally and artistically originated nothing" (985). It has not produced "a single writer, artist, lecturer, or what not" who has put the common people into art (979). These retroactive deletions suggest an uneasiness with literature's culpability in history, and they point to a similar discomfort with powerful speech in the present. For just as linguistic agency disappears from the past in Whitman's revision, so prophetic consummation vanishes into an imperceptible future.

In contrast to the 1855 preface, where the "effectual signs" are fulfilled in the ensuing poems, the omens in *Democratic Vistas* are hedged with qualifiers. The poet, Whitman had said, is the deadliest force of war; we now read that the expected literatus "may . . . cause changes" to rival the results of armed conflict, but then again such breakthroughs "may not be realized" (958). If that transformative poetry or prose does appear, it will do so in "a long period to come," an epoch so far removed from the current crisis that it will leave extant society completely unaltered (959). The present tense of "Song of Myself" yields to a focus on future restitution, and the word that once made things happen becomes an instrument of indefinite postponement. "Far, far, indeed, stretch, in distance, our Vistas!" (980), Whitman exclaims, and the closest he comes to naming a specific date for "the prophetic literature of these States" to materialize is the second centennial, 1976, more than a "hundred years ahead" from his writing (1008 and 1002). The reader is reminded of Hester's prophecy, at the end of *The Scarlet Letter*, that "a new truth" about relations between the sexes would be revealed "at some brighter period, . . . in Heaven's own time." In a phrase underlining his similar lack of urgency, the poet predicts that the longed-for "new order," with its attendant convulsions, will arrive in "the coming *unsped* days" (1016; italics added), and he acknowledges that no more than Hester will he be the agent or witness of its actualization. Not for him "the joy of entering at the last the conquer'd city—not ours the chance ever to see with our own eyes the peerless power and splendid *éclat* of the democratic principle, arriv'd at meridian" (981). In *The Eighteenth Presidency!*, at the height of his oracular enthusiasm, Whitman both foretold and expected "to see" the Lincoln-like reformer (1332). No longer Moses-like, he is content not to behold what his literatuses will create.

Deferral is the leitmotif of 1871, and the immediacy of the original *Leaves* has dwindled into absence and withholding. Whitman's shift, coming well before Reconstruction's burial, prefigures the whole late nineteenth-century retreat from the performative language/proximity dyad. Examples of relinquished presence and speech are legion, among them the many unreported exchanges in *Billy Budd*, most notably, perhaps, the interview where Vere tells Billy the sentence of the court. One could include Verena's silence at the Music Hall, the nontranscription of Olive Chancellor's replacement speech, Tom Driscoll's nonconfession in his courtroom faint, and Twain's own nonstatement that Jim is a free man. Douglass's revaluation of silence would qualify, as would the failures or refusals of Dr. Miller and Colonel French to confront their communities after the deaths of their sons. And, on the side of reaction, indicating the redeemer takeover of the prophetic lexicon, there is the "electric" defense of white supremacy that Charles Gaston proclaims before a cheering audience of Red Shirts in *The Leopard's Spots*.

Eight years after his own linguistic recession in *Democratic Vistas*, Whitman delivered the oration on Lincoln's death that proved to be his most popular lecture. Performed after federal troops had vacated the former Confederacy, the lecture struck a chord for post-Reconstruction Americans fed up with moral strenuousness on behalf of the freedmen. They were more than ready, as was Whitman, to join forces with white Southerners. His lecture, he emphasizes, is "no narrow or sectional reminiscence" (1061). As one might expect from a New Yorker, the poet has praise for the erring but now reunited Rebels; the city's political ties to the region had strengthened since the war, and the Empire State's governor, Grover Cleveland, would capture the presidency in 1884 with Dixie's backing. In reviewing the causes of the war, Whitman apportions blame to both sides. He mentions the "hot passions of the South," the "inertia" of the North, and "the incendiarism of the abolitionists," expressing the growing consensus that overheated rhetoric, and not the expansionism of slavery, had pushed the nation over the brink. He goes so far as to declare that Lincoln, though raised in the West, "is essentially, in personnel and character, a Southern contribution" (1061). And he proceeds to evacuate the role of the "eighteenth" president's language in causing the war by representing Lincoln, who had passed through New York City on the way to his inauguration, as a wordless apparition.

Whitman recalls his first sighting of the newly elected leader in 1861 on the steps of the Astor House. An enormous mass of people, perhaps as many as forty thousand, had assembled in the streets to catch a glimpse of Lincoln, and some felt anxiety for his safety, "for he possess'd no personal popularity at all in New York city, and very little political." The crowd was utterly still: "There were no speeches—no compliments—no welcome—as far as I could hear, not a word was said." The president-elect turned to face the gathering and matched its quiet with a reticence of his own—an act of misremembering by Whitman that nevertheless catches something of Lincoln's reserve on that day. (He spoke very briefly, having "nothing just now worth your hearing," as he put it.)[12] Having taken a moment to inspect the crowd in silence, according to the poet, the tall figure dressed in black mounted the portico steps and disappeared inside, "and the dumb-show ended" (1062–63).

This mistaken memory of a speechless Lincoln, the politician whose debates and addresses had so maddened Southerners that they dissolved the Union upon his election, can stand as emblematic of the postbellum erasure of the political efficacy of language. It is Whitman's latest repudiation of the pioneering literary movement that he himself, the literatus of 1855, had helped to make. Whitman the eulogist of Lincoln has inverted the agenda that precipitated the American Renaissance: he has forsaken the performative discourse of prophecy to write "biographies, histories, and criticism." Dismissing "prospects," except those that recede into the distant future, the poet welcomes the new age of "retrospection" with open arms. He reconceives literature as commemorative and secondary, with no power to spark action.

Indeed, Whitman's basic idea in the "Death of Abraham Lincoln" is the weightlessness of utterance, or of any representation, when compared to the overwhelming reality of events. This attitude, the other side of the postwar backlash—not the verbal's guilt, now, but its impotence—emerges in the opening paragraph, and we are not allowed to forget that climactic historical moments, such as the president's assassination, always dwarf the attempt to render them in art. Why, the poet wonders in introducing his eulogy, "is statement so idle" for dealing with "truly profound themes, . . . why does the right phrase never offer?" (1060). The answer, we learn, lies in the discrepancy between what is said or written and what is done, and the setting of Lincoln's martyrdom, during a production of *Our American Cousin* at Ford's Theatre in Washington, spotlights the difference. At the popular drama's midpoint "the actual murder" occurred, heaping mockery on the "poor mimes" on the stage; an instant later, John Wilkes Booth—the famous thespian turned murderer—sprang into view, pronounced the words, *"Sic temper tyrannis,"* and disappeared. This "terrible scene," Whitman says, made "the mimic ones preposterous." In the pandemonium that followed, soldiers with fixed bayonets stormed the house, dispersing the performers, with their "play-costumes and painted faces," and the "one simple, fierce deed" that changed the nation's destiny completed the rout of make-believe by fact (1066–69).

As Whitman's language implies, his 1879 lecture transfers the act of artistic creation from human beings to a world spirit or "Muse" that works through nations. The murder is a "scene" (1067), a "tragedy" (1068), and a "denouement" (1069), and Lincoln himself is "the leading actor in the stormiest drama known to real history's stage through centuries" (1065). Instead of speech instigating reality, events assume an aesthetic or literary form that reduces man-made productions to insignificance. The blood oozing in "little bubbles" from the dying leader's lips overshadows any words he may have spoken (1068). In a burst of German-inspired idealism,[13] Whitman says that Lincoln's martyrdom "illustrates one of those climax moments on the stage of Universal Time" that condense and crystallize a people. His death, greater than any imagined by Homer or Aeschylus, constitutes his nation's most valuable legacy and trumps "its literature and art." Adds the poet in a parenthetical statement that caps his inversion of priorities: "(as the hero is beyond his finest portrait, and the battle itself beyond its choicest epic or song)" (1070). Whitman does not even offer his own eulogy as an installment on the small efforts of which humans are capable. Those histories and dramas, he insists, cannot be written so soon after the extraordinary occurrence; they belong to the faraway future, not the present. In *Democratic Vistas*, Whitman deferred the arrival of the prophecy-bearing literatuses until 1976. In the Lincoln oration, the time span has lengthened. The backward-looking poet who will build the sepulchers of the fathers will not appear until many centuries have elapsed.

Two years after honoring the fallen president, Whitman made his final revisions in "Song of Myself," and he added poems to the 1888 and 1892 editions of *Leaves of Grass*. On the issue of speech, these last versions of his work continue the emphases of the "Death of Abraham Lincoln." For the 1888 edition, the poet composed a "Note at Beginning" and a "Note at End" in which he intimates (not quite accurately) that he has left his verses unchanged so that they can serve as a faithful record of "Abraham Lincoln's fateful age" (1364). He says that "tally-stamp" impressions of an era, such as those recorded in his verses, may preserve "at second or third hand" aspects of the past that elude the "the historian of matter-of-fact," and he presents himself as providing a "sort of History of America" that does not compete with but rather complements the work of professionals (1362–63).

This demotion or contraction of language, from agency to scrivener-like copying, takes a somewhat different shape in the 1881 "Song of Myself." The original paean to equal voices and unbridled discourse modulates ever so slightly into a more restrictive singing. The 1855 version of the first canto ends with the words, "I lean and loafe at my ease. . . . observing a spear of summer grass" (25); in its final form, the canto has an additional eight lines, including, as the second half of the seventh, this curious clause: "I permit to speak at every hazard" (188). The phrasing arrests one's attention. Is Whitman assenting to his own speaking, as in the sense of "I give myself permission to speak"? Or should we gloss the statement to mean, "I am permitted to speak"—that is, someone else allows him to speak? In any case, yoking the two terms, permission and speech, indicates a conjunction alien to the Free Soil ideology of the antebellum period. As he did previously, Whitman acknowledges that utterance is potentially dangerous—"at every hazard"—but he implies here that it must be authorized in advance, if only by oneself.

Giving permission, moreover, seems to loom in the background of an apparently minor typographical change in "Song of Myself." We have seen that Whitman includes other speakers in 1855 without foregrounding their otherness through punctuation (except by the use of commas, which are common in the poem). The child's words and the poet's have parity on the page (although the poet has a lot more to say). In 1881, the non-Whitman voices are italicized, differentiated from the rest of the poem, and the distinction jumps off the page as one scans it. It is as though the poet is granting various individuals permission to speak while employing the most conspicuous punctuation possible to set them apart as visitors or interlopers on the imaginative terrain he possesses. Utterance, on this understanding, requires consent, and the other voices are there in Whitman's poem on his sufferance. The italicized words undergo a subtle reduction in proximity, in that the quoted speaker no longer inhabits the poet's voice. This change effectively reverses the strategies of Fuller and Stowe, whose transcriptions are meant to retain the presence and vibrancy of the original.

But there is one problem with the timing: many of the revisions I have summarized first appeared not in 1881, but on the threshold of national rupture, in the 1860 edition of *Leaves of Grass*.[14] The radical collection of "Says" that Whitman incorporated in 1860 tells only half the story of his thinking as the South's secession began to look inevitable. Cherishing the Union, the poet had always feared the consequences of partisan rhetoric, and the new edition reflects the depth of his unhappiness with the likelihood of dissolution. In "Starting from Paumanok" (called "Proto-Leaf" in 1860), he vows to "make a song for these States that no one State may / under any circumstances be subjected to another State, / And I will make a song that there shall be comity by day / and by night between all the States, and between any / two of them." These were precisely the kind of assurances with which moderates tried to calm southern apprehensions on the eve of Lincoln's election. Whitman still hopes for the survival of "the One form'd out of all," but he warns of "weapons with menacing points" and the "countless dissatisfied faces" watching the preparations for war (179).

The bard's dismay with what speech was doing to his beloved America produced a round of retractive alterations in *Leaves of Grass*. In the year of Lincoln's election, he introduced italics into "Song of Myself,"[15] and he composed the eight-line section for "Proto-Leaf" that includes "I permit to speak." Later, in 1881, he moved these lines to "Song of Myself." The initial dating of the changes, and Whitman's alarm over the unraveling republic, remind us that as early as 1855–56 (the first and second editions) he put limits on what he was willing to say and what he would permit as speech, and he firmly asserted ownership of his verses. Untitled in 1855, "Song of Myself" became "Poem of Walt Whitman, an American" in 1856 and "Walt Whitman" four years later. Even in 1855 Whitman imposed restrictions. Although he supported antislavery politics, like most Free Soilers he despised abolitionism and had no great love for African Americans. The United States, he believed, was a white man's country, and his lack of sympathy for the freedmen after the Union victory had its origins in his prewar prejudice. Whitman's poem welcomes a runaway slave and describes a Negro driver in terms suggesting his own daguerreotype (chant 13), but he stops short of affirming verbal equality among the races. A child asks a question, and we hear a host of other voices. We hear speech talking. But no black person utters a word in "Song of Myself."

Slit Throats in Melville

Melville's active career as a novelist spanned the run-up to Civil War, during which time his chosen medium, language, came to be seen as a threat to the republic's future. His first book, *Typee* (1846), appeared when the Mexican-American War began and as the slavery issue was moving to the forefront of national politics. The last novel he completed, *The Confidence-Man* (1857), coincided with the *Dred Scott* decision and with President Buchanan's support of the proslavery Lecompton constitution in Kansas, which split the Democratic Party and led to Lincoln's election in 1860. And Melville's masterpiece, *Moby-Dick* (1851), took shape as Congress was staving off disunion by cobbling together the Compromise of 1850 and calling on all patriotic Americans to oppose criticism of its provisions.

Melville came from a mercantile New York City milieu, with strong ties to the South. Moderate and conservative New Yorkers were in the vanguard of those who sought to suppress debate about the peculiar institution.[1] As we know from *Mardi* (1849), Melville shared his natal city's apprehension about antislavery agitation; *Mardi* also makes clear that he hated slavery as a sin and a disgrace to American democracy. The tension between pressure on free speech, a position he reluctantly endorsed, and passionate belief produced an array of responses in the novelist, from the self-expurgation of *Typee* through the linguistic defiance of *Moby-Dick* to the epidemic of silencing in "Benito Cereno" (1855) and the picture of a verbally evasive society of "No Trust" in *The Confidence-Man*.[2] Just one of these fictions deals with African bondage, and that one, "Benito Cereno," takes place a half century before the crisis of the Union. Yet slavery and its corollary, the sign of the censor, stalk everything Melville wrote in this period; they form the self-conscious subtext of his work as well as the animating context for his genius.

Typee, Melville's adventure tale about his encounter with cannibals in the South Seas Islands, is an investigation into cultural difference, framed in important respects as a gulf in access to language. The book's preface draws a distinction between the "published narratives" about the Marquesas by white visitors and the "vocal sounds" of the natives (vii–viii).[3] This difference calls to mind the analogous split between master class literacy and black orality in Douglass's *Narrative*, published a year earlier. Although *Typee* is not about slavery or even the United States, there are a number of striking connections between the two works—both author-protagonists are captives among racial others, both are bereft of "mother" and "home" (275), and so on—and the language theme highlights Melville's simultaneous acceptance and repudiation of the slave narrative's imperative: to speak for a racial minority that has no linguistic agency in the public domain. The novel could be described as a trial in benign ventriloquism, except that the empathetic voice confronts impediments, many of its own creation, that squander its message. Some of the difficulties stem from simple incomprehension, for Melville's narrator, Tommo, often cannot fathom what he observes; others are attributable to the resistance of American publishers and readers to unwelcome revelations. Or, to be more exact, a part of Melville's problem in voicing the other has roots in his literary ambitions—his own unwillingness to persist in articulating truths about dark-skinned people that could offend the market and jeopardize his professional prospects. Unlike Douglass or, somewhat later, Stowe in *Uncle Tom's Cabin* (1852), Melville aborts his exercise in advocacy with acts of physical and literary violence that align him with forces of suppression.

The preface's division between printed texts and primitive "sounds" introduces us to the narrow scope of the islanders' communicative capacities and reveals their vulnerability to unanswered misrepresentation by outsiders. The Typees inhabit a culture of presence in which writing is unknown and speech and gesture, limited in reach to immediate auditors, are the sole means of conveying ideas. Tommo commends "the eloquence of their gestures" (92) but also emphasizes "the imperfections of their oral language" (164), and he portrays them as a linguistically handicapped people for whom a single word has to do the work of many, variations in meaning resting on the inflections and expression of the speaker. The Typees' idol-god, Moa Artua, is silent, as are the indigenous birds:

"the spell of dumbness is upon them all—there is not a single warbler in the valley!" (242). The natives themselves lack any idea of singing. They practice tattooing, which Tommo calls "penciling" (246), but the custom merely emphasizes the circumscribed nature of their communication: they can write on the body but nowhere else.

For much of the novel, Melville presents himself as that rare foreigner who will give the Typees' side of the story and whose writing will correct the distorted accounts that have unfairly denigrated them and exalted their despoilers. Time and again he assails the "extravagant fictions" (231) circulated by colonialists and their missionary allies. These fabrications exaggerate the ferocity of the natives' cultural practices, "denominate" them savages, and suppress the "horrible cruelties" visited upon them by whites (40–41). The books published by the clergy to raise money for their missions, invariably "glowing," celebrate the bringing of Christianity to the heathen but manage to omit any mention of the ravages of "civilization": class divisions, impoverishment, starvation, drunkenness, and so on (222). An international audience consumes the narratives, and the illiterate islanders have no possibility of rebuttal. The enormities committed against them occur outside the purview of the metropole, and "there are none to reveal them" to the civilized world (40).

Until now. Also in the novel's preface, Melville promises that *his* published narrative will provide "the unvarnished truth" about the Marquesas (vii–viii). He pulls no punches on the colonizers and gives their abuse of the natives the detailed treatment missing from self-interested reports. Chapter after chapter is devoted to eyewitness descriptions of Polynesian customs, which, if often opaque, are never as barbarous as travelers assert. Eschewing the partiality of other sources, Tommo acknowledges that the Typees do engage in fearful behaviors such as cannibalism, but he insists that they do so only "to a certain moderate extent" and are in other respects "humane and virtuous" (232). Here, he adds in a key passage, "Truth, who loves to be centrally located, is again found between the two extremes" (231–32), and the formulation encapsulates the role he projects for himself as a mediator between the islanders and Western civilization. Lucky (or unlucky) enough to have lived among the cannibals, he is uniquely positioned to make a realistic case for them to readers in the United States and England. To dramatize the point, the text supplies an idealized facsimile for Melville the intermediary in the figure of Marnoo, the "taboo" native who can travel without hindrance from the civilized outposts to the villages of the Typees and the Happars. Marnoo can speak English as well as the aboriginal tongues, which gives him "a great ascendancy" over his verbally impoverished countrymen. He is welcome everywhere on the island, and his eloquence captivates the Typees: they attend to his words "as though they were listening to the inspired voice of a prophet" (160–62).

But Marnoo's appearance signals the beginning of Melville's retreat from activism. It turns out that the taboo rover enjoys his immunities because, and as long as, he flatters the prejudices of his auditors. He praises the Typees' courage in battle and heaps ridicule on their enemies, but the instant he takes Tommo's part, supporting his wish to return home, the downside of playing mediator between different cultures becomes all too manifest. The appeal encounters furious disapproval, with intimations of violence against both men, and when Tommo later asks the privileged stranger to speak for him again, Marnoo bluntly refuses: "Me no hear you talk anymore; by by Kannaka get mad, kill you and me too" (267). It is the most explicit statement in the text about the danger of telling the truth to a hostile audience, and it should be compared to the many passages in which Tommo reflects on the risks he takes by championing the islanders against their missionary "benefactors." His disclosures, he often observes, are likely to anger the friends of the missions and will not endear him to the civilized epicenters: "As wise a man as Shakespeare has said, that the bearer of evil tidings hath but a losing office; and so I suppose will it prove with me" (225). Regardless of what the biased "may say or write" against his narrative, Tommo adds, the "things which I have stated as facts will remain facts," and he will not cover them up because their dissemination might do some good for the Marquesans.

As it turns out, however, Melville was not true to his word. Marnoo's skittishness about speaking for the other betrays the novelist's own anxiety about discursive daring, and his vow of truthfulness yielded to a comparable discretion. *Typee*, initially published in England, was reissued in the United States by Wiley and Putnam of New York. The firm made a number of cuts in the book's off-color and antimissionary passages, to which Melville assented; and when these expurgations failed to satisfy religious reviewers, he set about revising and pruning extensively on his own. Many of the eliminated sections deal with the injustices suffered by the Typees; some, like the one quoted above on "facts," contain bold avowals, silently disregarded, of the writer's candor no matter what the consequences to himself. The pledge to tell the "unvarnished truth" appears in the last paragraph of the preface, but the previous two paragraphs were excised because they venture criticisms of the clergy and of Western imperialism. *Typee* thus marks the first, and the most visible, illustration of

Melville's lifelong sensitivity to the eye of the censor, internal as well as exterior, and it gives explicit form to the mutilations and prohibitions that are more typically hinted at than publicized in his later fictions. Throughout his career, Melville willingly regulated or obfuscated his speech to avoid alienating readers, offending relatives, or giving concrete utterance to sentiments he held only experimentally. *Typee* is dedicated to his future father-in-law, Lemuel Shaw, the conservative "Chief Justice of the Commonwealth of Massachusetts." Shaw had been a friend of Melville's late father, who died bankrupt, and it seems probable that the novelist saw his book as a way back into the social class from which he had been ejected. He was not about to let a handful of controversial paragraphs on behalf of an oppressed minority thwart that goal.

The presence of racial victims with whom he sympathized is the motive for reticence linking Melville the conflicted foe of imperialism with Melville the hampered critic of chattel bondage. *Typee* culminates in a lack of disguise about such muzzling that seems almost shocking. At the very outset of the narrative, Tommo humorously describes the near starvation of the *Dolly*'s crew after six months at sea, and he explains that the ship's captain will not steer for land until he has devoured the last chicken on board, a rooster named Pedro. "If putting a period to thy existence is to be the signal for our deliverance," Tommo cries, "why—truth to speak—I wish thy throat cut this very moment" (16). (That "truth to speak" is full of unintended irony.) At the end of the story, the incident is replayed for bigger stakes. The one-eyed chief Mow-Mow, armed with a tomahawk, tries to prevent Tommo from leaving the island in a whaleboat. To make good his flight, Tommo thrusts a boat hook at his pursuer, which "struck him just below the throat" (279). The wounded Typee is left flailing in the boat's wake.

In this instance, too, the blow is necessary to Tommo's "deliverance"; but its location, at the organ of both speech and breath, suggests that the escape is also literary. Melville's emergence into successful authorship required his silencing of the natives, his horrified ("I felt horror at the act I was about to commit") but necessary decision *not* to give unequivocal utterance to their grievances. He would cut their throats to save himself as a writer. It is noteworthy that not just Mow-Mow, who threatens violence, but Fayaway, the narrator's Polynesian lover, is deprived of voice in the concluding pages; clinging to Tommo and sobbing as he struggles to flee, she "seemed speechless with sorrow" (277). At this moment, Melville does not look very different from the missionaries and civilizers who effectively consign the native point of view to silence. He rehearses on the islanders the muting that he would shortly perform on the text itself, and readers familiar with his subsequent writings will realize how many of Melville's subsequent characters, white and black alike, experience a similar vocal repression, among them Ahab (strangulation), Babo (refusal to speak), and Billy Budd (stuttering). *Typee* is the novel that establishes the pattern for Melville's career: it announces the centrality of self-censorship to his work and points toward the convergence of his circumspection with the gathering storm over slavery.

Three years later, in the allegorical fantasy of *Mardi*, Melville's characters voyage to "the extreme South of Vivenza" (the United States) and, frustrated by the insolubility of the slavery problem, reach a Marnoo-like judgment about the peculiar institution: best not to talk about it. They take this position despite unanimously viewing the southern labor system as "a blot, foul as the crater-pool of hell." Upon their arrival in Dixie, the travelers are met by the imperious Nulli (John C. Calhoun), and when they insist on ascribing humanity to the slaves, he denounces them as "incendiaries" and "ranters." "The first blow struck for them [the bondmen]," swears the father of secession, "dissolves the union of Vivenza's vales"—more, "another word" on their behalf, and the visitors will be thrown into jail. These threats provoke not a cloudburst of protest but an anguished chorus of concession from the fictional personae, who "all but echo hardhearted Nulli" in their internalizing of repression. They agree that while it is easy "to stand afar and rail," continued attacks from the North will only stoke sectional enmity and possibly lead to race war. In sentences that verge on opacity, Melville's philosopher and proxy, Babbalanja, counsels a discipline of silence: "A thousand muscles wag our tongues; though our tongues were housed, that they might have a home. Whoso is free from crime, let him cross himself—but hold his cross upon his lips." Babbalanja further states, "All men are censors who have lungs." He means "censor" as faultfinder, but in context the sentence can be read as prescriptive: on the subject of slavery, all who have lungs should be censors, that is, expurgators, of themselves.[4]

Verbal restraint as the desideratum of a slaveholding republic was not the sole note Melville sounded at this turbulent period—the moment of the European revolutions and of the Free Soil Party. But Babbalanja's advice tended to be his *public* credo until the outpouring of *Moby-Dick*. Privately, he could be notably more defiant about censorship. Just before *Mardi* was published in the United States, he corresponded with Evert Duyckinck, a leading figure in the New York literary world and a proponent of Young

America, the stridently nationalist movement associated with the Democratic Party. Because Shakespeare lived in Elizabethan England, the novelist wrote, the bard wore "a muzzle" on his soul and "was not a frank man to the uttermost. And, indeed, who in this intolerant universe is, or can be?" But Americans, and the American writer, have an advantage over even Shakespeare, Melville continued: "the Declaration of Independence makes a difference."[5] Southern fire-eaters were already lacerating the Declaration as Jefferson's French-besotted radicalism; antislavery voices were rushing to its defense. Melville's mention of the founding document here, in relation to linguistic candor, suggests a lurking sympathy for the antislavery cause.

Southern reviewers, too vigilant to be satisfied by pledges of silence, would nose out these sentiments and pounce on them. The best-known such reviewer, William Gilmore Simms, a member of the Young America circle, decried Melville's treatment of his region in *Mardi* and cited as particularly objectionable "the loathsome picture of Mr. Calhoun, in the character of a slave driver, drawing mixed blood and tears at every stroke of the whip." This misrepresentation, Simms complained, "spoils everything to the Southern reader."[6] Once again, and despite having largely conceded the point, Melville faced criticism for defending nonwhites, and the condemnation had a distinct drawl from below the Mason-Dixon Line (with a trace of Duyckinck's New York accent in the background). It is surely significant, then, that when the novelist returned to the censorship issue, in his 1850 review of Hawthorne's *Mosses*, he adopted the pseudonym of "a Virginian Spending July in Vermont." No one knew better than a Southerner the danger of espousing unpopular opinions, and Melville's essay merges the ideological with the literary as it pictures "a world of lies" where "Truth is forced to fly like a scared white doe in the woodlands; and only by cunning glimpses will she reveal herself, as in Shakespeare and other masters of the Great Art of Telling the Truth—even though it be covertly, and by snatches." Profound literature is always an act of ventriloquism: the writer "craftily says, or sometimes insinuates" through the mouths of his characters the things that he dare not express in his own voice.[7]

The pose of Virginian would be prophetic for Melville, and, as tensions over slavery worsened, he would make more and more use of indirection and delegated speech. After the Civil War, in *Battle-Pieces* (1866), he would celebrate a real-life Virginian, the defeated Confederate general Robert E. Lee. But in 1850–51, the doctrine of obliqueness quickly gave way to something different, and far less cautious, in *Moby-Dick*. Ahab might be

Melville's mouthpiece or ventriloquist's "dummy," but the fiery whaling captain does not so much insinuate as broadcast his convictions, and he dismisses altogether the idea that truth should be disguised. "Who's over me?" he shouts to the *Pequod*'s crew. "Truth hath no confines!" (221).[8] This is the kind of unbridled rhetoric one expects from Free Soilers or, even worse, abolitionists, as in William Lloyd Garrison's declaration from the *Liberator* that "I *will be* harsh as truth, and as uncompromising as justice."[9] How did such pyrotechnics end up in the mouth of Melville's whaler, just months after the *Mosses* essay?

Geography is one answer, and the essay proved prophetic in this regard too, although in the opposite sense from identification with a Southerner (or with Hawthorne, in whose fictions Melville detected a Shakespearean, Virginian doubleness). Melville was in Massachusetts (not Vermont) when he wrote the review, and soon afterward he moved with his family from Manhattan to a farm in the Berkshires that he named Arrowhead. Although he had begun work on *Moby-Dick* in New York, he completed the bulk of the manuscript at his new residence in New England. It is customary to attribute the creative breakthrough of Melville's novel to his chance meeting with Hawthorne, but relocation to the Commonwealth may have been more influential. As Ishmael puts it, explaining his infatuation with Ahab's hunt for the white whale, "I gave myself up to the abandonment of the time and the place" (252). The time was that of the Compromise of 1850 and the Fugitive Slave Law and, despite establishment demands for silence, of widespread protest against the forced return of runaways. And few places in the Northeast were as unalike on the slavery question as New York City and western Massachusetts.

When Melville left New York, the metropolis was entering a long period of racial and political conservatism. As the commercial and financial hub of the country, New York had always had a policy of maintaining good relations with the South. A significant amount of cotton and tobacco passed through the city's port en route to Europe, and Manhattan factors and their agents furnished the credit that kept the plantation economy humming. The Compromise of 1850 brought a hardening of attitudes toward those who would put opposition to slavery ahead of sectional peace. Merchants, the financial community, and the mounting numbers of Irish immigrants, who saw free blacks as competitors for jobs, united to prevent further agitation. "We mean," one New Yorker told an antislavery clergyman, "to put you abolitionists down, by fair means if we can, by foul means if we must." Another said that if the nation's capital were "in Wall Street instead of Washington," no talk stirring up discord between the sections would be tolerated. Hostility toward antislavery persisted right up to the Civil War (and beyond, as we know from the worst mob violence in American history, the draft riots of 1863). Although the Empire State voted Republican in 1860, Lincoln lost the city where he had delivered his Cooper Institute speech; and when the Confederacy bolted the Union, Mayor Fernando Wood proposed that New York secede from the hinterlands and proclaim itself an independent republic.[10]

In Massachusetts, by way of contrast, disgust with the Fugitive Slave Law ran high. The Commonwealth had a tradition of Protestant reform and (relative) racial enlightenment, and though long represented in the Senate by the Cotton Whig Daniel Webster, in 1851 it sent the far more radical Free Soiler Charles Sumner to replace him in Washington. Prominent antislavery activity was centered in the state. Massachusetts was the residence of the famous abolitionists Theodore Parker, Wendell Phillips, and William Lloyd Garrison; Emerson and Thoreau, converts to the cause, lived and wrote in Concord. The *Liberator* was published in Boston, and, after the Compromise, numerous fugitives sought haven in the state. The slave known as Shadrach, taken into custody in early 1851, was freed by a mob in Boston; soon afterward, Chief Justice Shaw returned another slave, Thomas Sims, to Georgia, much to the dismay of Emerson and Thoreau (and, according to some critics, of Melville too).[11] Even before the Civil War, Massachusetts took the lead in overturning segregation in public transportation and schools. Once hostilities began, the Commonwealth pioneered in recruiting the first black regiment, the 54th Massachusetts Volunteer Infantry, commanded by Colonel Robert Shaw.[12]

In *Moby-Dick*, Ishmael makes a journey similar to that of his creator: he travels from Manhattan to the Massachusetts island of Nantucket, a center of the whaling industry, and adopts correspondingly progressive attitudes. He stays at the Spouter Inn in New Bedford, the community where Douglass found refuge after escaping from Maryland. On his first night, he meets and sleeps with a South Seas Islander, the harpooner Queequeg, and he forms a bond with his dark shipmate that figuratively saves his life. As the *Pequod* sets sail on its journey, Melville's narrator delivers an impassioned hymn, redolent of the Declaration, to "The Great God absolute! The centre and circumference of all democracy! His omnipresence, our divine equality!" (160).

Above all, "the time and the place" leave their imprint on *Moby-Dick* in the way that Melville/Ishmael falls under the sway of Ahab's electrifying oratory. The monomaniacal captain—and monomania was a condition routinely imputed to abolitionists by their opponents—is not, of course, an antislavery agitator, except in the metaphysical sense that he defies any superior authority. But Ahab's speeches, like the sermons of Arthur Dimmesdale, exemplify the dangerous capability of language to galvanize the masses, and such power was nowhere more on display in 1850–51 than among the Massachusetts activists and writers inflamed by the Fugitive Slave Law.[13] (Incited by the same piece of legislation, Stowe would shortly issue *Uncle Tom's Cabin* from a Boston publisher.) Ahab's rhetoric masters the crew and overwhelms their misgivings about changing the purpose of the voyage. They agree to follow him on his impractical, paranoid pursuit and to surrender their individual wills to his supreme obsession. "They were one man, not thirty," Ishmael says (700); Moby Dick becomes "as much their insufferable foe as his" (251). Ishmael insists that Ahab's search has a higher objective than revenge, and that his motivation, if mad, is absolutist and unselfish: "all evil, to crazy Ahab, were visibly personified, and made practically assailable in Moby Dick" (247). Ahab's pastoral double, Father Mapple, asserts the same kind of absolutist theology/philosophy, swearing to "preach the Truth to the face of Falsehood" and to root out sin from "under the robes of Senators and Judges" (279–80; such as Webster and Shaw?). In parallel fashion, the "sin" and "evil" of involuntary servitude ate at the souls of antislavery activists. Abolitionists on the platform and the pulpit ritualistically invoked the higher law of moral "Truth" to rid the world of slavery. Melville himself, in *Mardi*, associates the institution with sin and says that slaveholders will "die forever damned."[14]

But Melville's attraction to risk-laden eloquence had its limits, and the lessons of *Typee* and *Mardi* prove relevant for *Moby-Dick*. Ahab's "quenchless feud" (239) terminates in disaster for the American ship of state, just as one might have predicted from Nulli's threat to dissolve the Union. Ironically, Ahab in his imperiousness comes to resemble a despotic slave driver. He barks at the sailors, "Ye are not other men, but my arms and my legs; and so obey me" (716), and "his old Mogulship" (598) could be another Colonel Lloyd or Calhoun himself demanding conformity. The association reminds us of Melville's usual discomfort with both northern and southern extremists, here condensed into the single overwrought character of the one-legged captain. Melville's narrator, Ishmael, at first swept up by an unremitting discourse of Truth, similarly recoils from Ahab's lethal single-mindedness. He renounces his commander's mission in "A Squeeze of the Hand" and recalibrates his commitment to fraternal feelings and domestic images. "I forgot all about our horrible oath; in that inexpressible sperm, I washed my hands and heart of it" (532). The *Pequod* under

Ahab's command pushes on with the hunt until the ship is rammed by Moby Dick and sinks "to hell" under "the great shroud of the sea" (723). Having given free rein to language in his greatest novel, Melville ends by demonstrating how that license brings about not the eradication of evil, but the deaths of Ahab and all his crew save Ishmael. The hand of the censor is back in play, as the novelist reimposes wordlessness on the principal offender against verbal diffidence. Ahab flings his harpoon at Moby Dick; a moment later the flying line "caught him round the neck, and voicelessly as Turkish mutes bowstring their victim, he was shot out of the boat, ere the crew knew he was gone" (721–22).

The "voiceless" fate of the *Pequod*'s leader sheds retrospective light on the text's secondary but undeniable fixation with silence.[15] Queequeg will not speak during Ramadan and utters only a handful of sentences in broken English throughout the text. Ishmael extols the "pyramidical silence" of the sperm whale (448). No "profound being," claims Melville's narrator, has "anything to say to this world, unless forced to stammer out something by way of getting a living" (478). And it is tempting to read the novel's epilogue, in which Ishmael floats away from the shipwreck on Queequeg's coffin lifebuoy, as a reiteration of *Typee*'s native-silencing conclusion. The dark other has to die so that the author, distancing himself from controversial outspokenness, has a chance to live.

The difficulty of unfettered speech achieves thematic explicitness in "Benito Cereno," the elaborately ventriloquized story Melville published in 1855, a year after passage of the Kansas-Nebraska Act.[16] The Act's repeal of the Missouri Compromise convinced many, including Lincoln, that the South had designs for its peculiar institution on "every other part of the wide world."[17] "Benito Cereno" revolves around the insight that slavery is as silencing for whites as for blacks; this personal truth for Melville as a writer now assumed fresh urgency for the culture as a whole. The ship on which the action occurs, the *San Dominick*, becomes a figure for the polis under slavery, a society, like that depicted by George Orwell in *1984* (1949), where one is never free from surveillance and never able to speak without constraint. The text mirrors this verbal inhibition in its withholdings, impacted sentences, and convoluted syntax. Directly engaging with slavery and its consequences (though displaced to 1799, the epoch of the Haitian revolution) hinders Melville's speech even as he dissects, through his characters and plot, the mechanisms of ideological control. But that is to be expected: as "Benito Cereno" demonstrates, slavery replaces the heteroglossia of different perspectives with the monolith of a single voice.

Typee's resemblances to the slave narrative may have been fortuitous; in "Benito Cereno," the parallels have a transparency that invites us to read the tale as Douglass's *Narrative* in whiteface. The seizure of the *San Dominick* by the Africans installs a world-turned-upside-down of black mastership and white bondage, and the new dispensation replicates the dynamics of the old. The enslaved population, this time light-skinned Spanish mariners, can no more speak their minds honestly than could the slaves on Colonel Lloyd's plantation. Those Maryland bondsmen had to tell their master what he wanted to hear; if they contradicted him or found fault with his treatment of them, as in the case of the indiscreet field hand, they could be sold to a Georgia trader. In effect, they had to take dictation and repeat a "fictitious story" (248) in order to survive.[18] Don Benito, the *San Dominick*'s captain, is in the same position. Advised that he would be killed if he "uttered any word" about the true state of affairs aboard the ship (247) and not allowed out of the sight of Babo, "his constant attendant and companion" (222), he speaks in "a husky whisper," like a man "with lungs half gone" (169). His sentences are "brokenly" delivered (174), and he tells his interlocutor, Amassa Delano, that many of his experiences are so distressing as to be "past all speech" (209). The Spaniard is marked throughout by a "reserve" (170) that bewilders the American, Melville's latest avatar of a Massachusetts seaman.

No moment more chillingly condenses Cereno's linguistic plight than the shaving scene in the cuddy. The Spanish captain settles into a barber's chair that seems "a grotesque engine of torment," and his body servant proceeds to lather him "low under throat, all the rest being cultivated beard." Observing this operation, Delano cannot resist the whim "that in the black he saw a headsman, and in the white a man at the block." The steel blade, wielded by Babo, glints "nigh the throat," then draws several drops of blood as a warning to the Spaniard and a reminder to the reader of Melville's fiction of the fates of Mow-Mow and Captain Ahab (211–14). In the story's last paragraph, we discover that Babo, not Don Benito, is the one who suffers beheading, an actualization and inversion of Delano's vagary that suggests how slavery's violent silencing spreads from race to race.

Aphonia in "Benito Cereno" cannot be contained. The whites are ventriloquist's puppets for most of the narrative, and when the Americans retake the *San Dominick*, they return the blacks to slavery and to voicelessness. Babo and his followers are never permitted to express their point of view. But impeded speech is not limited to those in bondage. The mere existence of the institution, Melville suggests, acts as an obstruction to discourse, whether one is slave, master, or bystander. As he watches Babo and the Spaniard whispering to each other, Captain Delano finds himself falling silent as if "from contagion" (185). Often, oppressed by Cereno's reserve, he feels that "nothing more could be said" (222). As for the Spanish captain, his difficulty with language outlasts his rescue, when he leaps into Delano's whale boat and collapses in a "speechless faint" (232). Restored to the condition of master, Cereno seldom speaks again in his own voice. His legal deposition is in the form of a third-person account, not a quoted statement, and it is riddled with gaps and ellipses. At the trial, he "follows his leader," Babo, who refuses to utter a sound to the court. The Spanish captain is unwilling either to look at or to testify against his former slave: "Before the tribunal he refused. When pressed by the judges he fainted. On the testimony of the sailors alone rested the legal identity of Babo." Thereafter, Don Benito lapses into the ever-deepening quiet that ends with his death. Amassa Delano can only marvel at his continued incommunicativeness during the final scene. Cereno's reserve seems greater than ever, and the American's efforts to engage him in talk can barely coax him out of his "muteness." Melville's single-sentence paragraph sums up the failed exchange: "There was no more conversation that day" (258).

Can the Spaniard's deposition to the court at Lima, conveyed to us as an anthology of extracts, be trusted? His (white) version of events is the sole rendering the story provides, and Cereno, who until his deliverance has been little more than a mouthpiece for the insurrectionists, *dictates* his words to the Spanish officials. Few texts do as much as this one to discredit the reliability of dictated stories, so it should not surprise us that Melville encourages skepticism about the value of Cereno's recollections: "If the Deposition have served as the key to fit into the lock of the complications which precede it, then, as a vault whose door has been flung back, the *San Dominick*'s hull lies open today" (255). That "if" lingers because the whole point of the narrative has been that partial or one-sided accounts—the monopolistic sound of a single speaker—stifle other voices and preclude the possibility of truth. Recall that when Delano first boards the slave ship, "a clamorous throng of whites and blacks" surrounds him, and "in one language, and as with one voice, all poured out a common tale of suffering" (165). The elisions in that sentence are considerable, and they define the Spanish merchantman as an embryonic police state: the sufferings are not common, the voices have conflicting tales to tell, and the languages they speak are very different.

Melville repeatedly calls attention to the multiplicity of tongues on the *San Dominick*. We never learn the full number, because the story does not attempt a survey of the African dialects, but as many as four sepa-rate languages are spoken, and few characters can converse in more than one. Most of the slaves know Senagalese, which enables them to commu-nicate without being understood by the whites. Several, including Babo, command enough Spanish to have fabricated the fiction of heavy gales and to monitor conversations between the sailors and Amassa Delano. The captain of the *Bachelor's Delight* knows Spanish as well and speaks with Cereno in his native tongue. Delano's own language is actually spoken only twice in the narrative, once by his chief mate and once when the seaman with the knot mutters "in broken English—the first heard in the ship—something to this effect: 'Undo it, cut it, quick'" (202). And a Por-tuguese sailor in the whale boat shouts to the American—presumably in Portuguese?—to heed what Don Benito is saying, presumably in Spanish.

In short, there is a "hubbub of voices" (167) in the tale, but the fact of enslavement, first of whites, then of blacks, invariably reduces the ca-cophony to a monotone. "Benito Cereno" absorbs that flattening as a con-dition of its narration. Melville reprints an occasional Spanish phrase for which he furnishes a translation—the ship's chalked warning, *"Sequid vuestro jefe,"* is rendered, in parentheses, as "(follow your leader)"—but for the most part he silently goes about the business of putting into English, for the benefit of the American reader, the various languages heard aboard the ship (165). He also translates the deposition extracts, taken from "the official Spanish documents" (238). The reader thus experiences the tale as a monotone, and the lingual uniformity reinforces the persistent sense of excluded thoughts and opinions. Such, Melville implies, is the distorted nature of discourse in a slaveholding society, which stunts access even for those who are far removed from the institution. Something is always lost in translation when stories emerging out of the "clamorous throng" reach us in a single tongue.

Although Melville published "Benito Cereno" in *Putnam's,* a magazine with antislavery sympathies, the venue did not free him from his inclina-tion to caution. The possibility of race war and of savage vengeance haunts the story and struggles with Melville's loathing of slavery to produce often opaque writing that can be as daunting to make sense of as the myster-ies on the *San Dominick* are to Captain Delano. (A year and a half later, *The Confidence-Man* would significantly escalate the opacities.) Examples abound of proliferating qualifiers (the cataract of "buts" on 171, seven in the space of one paragraph), prolix sentences, and confusing shifts in point of view. Though told mostly from Delano's angle of vision, the narrative includes passages, among them those on blacks as happy-go-lucky "valets and hair-dressers" (212), whose source is elusive. Is the writer speaking here, or, much more likely in a tale where the black barber threatens to cut his master's throat, are we overhearing antebellum culture in 1855? If the latter, that would seem to make Melville himself a ventriloquist's dummy for American racism, a perverse variant on his decade-old hope of advocating for the Typees. Or should we think of "Benito Cereno" in its entirety as a ventriloquized "fictitious story," in which Melville, like the sailor with the rope, signals to the percipient reader (of the future?) antislavery sentiments he dare not state openly but must hide behind the historical Amassa Delano's *Narrative of Voyages and Travels in the Northern and Southern Hemispheres* (1817), the source from which he borrowed extensively?[19] If this is the case, then Melville has so embedded his truth telling that a critique of slavery and a defense of it seem almost identical. The unsaid in the story, though increasingly axiomatic in New England culture, is the injustice of racial bondage.

Melville can imagine no exit from the labyrinth of American slavery. He apportions blame to Northerners (himself included) as well as Southerners for the impasse and for the "ugly passions" the institution "breeds . . . in man" (218). Delano, the good American, and a New Englander to boot, does not hesitate to recapture the *San Dominick* and its human cargo once he understands what has happened. A slaveholder could do no more. An image that Melville may have gotten from antislavery literature dramatizes the nationwide extent of complicity. In his *Appeal to the Coloured Citizens of the World* (1829), the black abolitionist David Walker observed that white Americans "have their feet on our throats."[20] The sternpiece of the Spanish slaver in "Benito Cereno" features "a dark satyr in a mask, holding his foot on the prostrate neck of a writhing figure, likewise masked" (164). Melville reprises the tableau in the scene where Cereno jumps into the whale boat with his enraged body servant in pursuit. Captain Delano, his mind at last illuminated, strikes down Babo and with "his right foot, . . . ground the prostrate negro" (232). The masks are torn away, and the satyr crushing the throat of his dark-skinned victim stands revealed as a white American from Massachusetts.

The Confidence-Man, published when slavery's advance looked irresistible (*Dred Scott*, Lecompton in Kansas) and free speech faced physical violence in Congress (Sumner), carries verbal obstruction in Melville's work to its end point. Contemporaneous reviewers, with good reason, labeled

the novel unreadable.[21] The barber shop on the *Fidele* displays a sign reading "No Trust," and that principle, governing everybody's conduct on the
steamship, dovetails with Douglass's motto from his *Narrative*, "Trust no
man!" (6). Suspicion, for both writers, is essential to survival in a capitalist
society shadowed by slavery. We need not deny Melville's harsh portrayal
of market civilization to realize that the unfree labor system, the market's
apparent opposite, broods in the text's background, and sometimes in its
foreground, as an additional cause of mistrust and blockage.

Masking meaning and attenuating or occluding the sources of ideas
that might cause offense are the hallmarks of a censorship regime. *The
Confidence-Man*, subtitled *His Masquerade*, canvasses those protective
strategies in a primer of obscurantism. Melville deconstructs words by
festooning them with retractive prefixes—"unobserved," "unresented,"
"unlike," "unobnoxious," "unaffected,"—and by littering assertions with
strings of negatives: "not without," "not less," "not entirely," "not wholly."
He further complicates meaning by putting the stylistic tics together: "not
wholly unobnoxious" or "not unfrequently" (4–7).[22] A particularly un-
traceable brand of ventriloquism is rampant on the Mississippi voyage.[23]
Untrustworthy characters vouch or "speak for" other characters; dialogue
is given without a speaking subject; and stories are told at two or three
removes from the original source, replete with disavowals by the narrator.
As the cosmopolitan says after he relates the history of the Indian hater,
"There, I have done; having given you, not my story, mind, or my thoughts,
but another's" (177). More than half the novel's chapters (twenty-four out
of forty-five) open with quotations, with the identity of the speaker often
unclear, and numerous characters trail in the rear of their language, which
precedes them into the action.

The *Fidele* cruises from St. Louis in the border state of Missouri to the
slave states of the Deep South, with New Orleans as its final destination,
a trajectory that seemed to be the republic's in 1857. A nation with slavery permitted everywhere—one implication of *Dred Scott*—would drastically curtail the range of permissible utterance. But more than protective
disguise is at work in the obscurities of Melville's novel. The revulsion
or distancing from language evident throughout also seems connected to
the perception, gaining ground among moderates, that language had both
embittered sectional discord and proven ineffectual at calming it (a position Melville would explicitly endorse nine years later in *Battle-Pieces*).
Soured on an element so fraught with risk on all sides, Melville was already severing his ties to prose fiction. He did not examine the page proofs
for *The Confidence-Man*, and some ambiguity surrounds the source of the

words on the page: in their final form, are they his or the typesetter's? The first chapter of the novel augurs his extrication. The text begins with an unnamed deaf-mute writing on a slate, and that silent figure, recalling Mow-Mow and Ahab, Babo and Don Benito, would soon be Melville. He did not write fiction again for almost thirty years, until he began drafting *Billy Budd*.

"Speak, man!": *Billy Budd* in the Crucible of Reconstruction

*B*illy Budd, at once a relic and a recantation of American romanticism, is the hardest of all Melville's fictions to historicize. Most readers would probably agree with the judgment, from a recent guide to the
novelist's career, that "workable analogies between text and context" are
difficult to draw.[1] The tale distances itself by almost a century from the
postbellum United States, and its deliberately crafted web of mythological,
religious, and literary allusions seems to lift it out of its particular historical moment and invest it with timeless significance.

A new attentiveness to Melville's connection to Douglass has tried to
correct this erasure of the topical. Relevant studies reinstating the late
Melville into the world of Reconstruction fill out the picture of a writer
who affirms the desideratum of white kinship. In the wake of fraternal
slaughter, he also draws near to pragmatism, entertains a skeptical or
comparative patriotism, and nurtures suspicion of imperial designs. An
essay by Gregory Jay on *Billy Budd* in particular proposes the further idea
that the Handsome Sailor's fate reprises the lynching of black men in the
American fin de siècle.[2]

All these readings shed light on Melville's thinking, but more remains
to be said about what is, by critical consensus, a salient issue in the novella: the valences of language and silence. This concern, ostensibly ahis-
torical, has an unmistakable relationship to Melville's milieu in the late
1880s, when he resumed writing prose fiction. Although he himself said
little about contemporaneous issues, the language theme announces a
continuing preoccupation with the slavery controversy and its long aftermath: the Civil War, Reconstruction, and the abandonment of the freedmen to the exigence of national stability. Captain Vere's moral position in
the narrative, which turns on his speech to the drumhead court, reveals it-

self most sharply, and most ambiguously, through this nineteenth-century prism. When the undeniable linguistic emphasis is restored to history, it becomes possible to see Melville's work in a fresh way: as a participant in the paradigm shift that demoted language from potency to morally problematic irrelevance. *Billy Budd* not only enacts this change; it offers an explanation of why the cashiering came about. On this view, the saga of the *Bellipotent* proves to be a good deal more laden with Melville's social and political setting than we have imagined.

What caused the Civil War?

There is no shortage of answers: the aggression of the Slave Power in forcing its "peculiar institution" into the territories; the "irrepressible conflict" between two opposed labor systems; and the election of Lincoln in 1860, in defiance of southern vows to quit the Union if he won. Melville was among those who believed that language stoked sectional hatred and so bore a measure of responsibility for the bloodshed. The "incendiary" rhetoric of the abolitionists was as culpable as the provocative discourse of proslavery fire-eaters. Or as Melville reminded his readers in 1866, the "unfraternal denunciations, continued through years, and which at last flamed to deeds that ended in bloodshed, were reciprocal."[3] Most Democrats—and Melville's family had close ties to the Democratic Party—would have singled out the Republican coalition as leading verbal wrongdoers. The idea of an "irrepressible conflict" between free and slave labor (in the coinage of New York Senator William H. Seward) was a gauntlet thrown down to Southerners, a declaration of war against the plantation system. As for Lincoln's victory, it was the culmination of a decades-long campaign, waged in newspapers, books, and speeches, to discredit the way of life of half the states.

If language caused or even contributed in a nontrivial sense to internecine warfare, the war and its aftermath took revenge on language by disputing its claims to agency and precedence. In the eyes of many, the verbal was demoted to guilty impotence—"guilty" because antislavery agitation had produced more devastation than anyone could have imagined, and "impotent" because mere words seemed utterly inconsequential compared to the bloodshed and suffering that convulsed the nation from 1861 to 1865. A revulsion from language set in while the armies were still fighting, and Lincoln felt the impulse as strongly as anyone. His best-known addresses delivered before the war—the "House Divided" speech (1858), the performance at Cooper Institute (1860)—are detailed expositions that sharpened sectional antagonism. His most famous speeches of all, one coming at the war's midpoint, the Gettysburg Address (1863), and one, the Second Inaugural Address (1865), given as military confrontation drew to a close, are unmatched in eloquence but radically contracted in length, as though somehow disaffected from the medium in which they are composed. Neither fills a full page, and both seem charged with the conviction, explicit at Gettysburg, that utterance has a commemorative and secondary function and pales into nothingness before the reality of deeds.

To be sure, Reconstruction brought a renewal of linguistic agency, but in the end the nation's experiment in racial justice only completed the rout of words by actions. Reconstruction rested on the pillars of the Thirteenth, Fourteenth, and Fifteenth Amendments to the Constitution. Potentially transformative acts of writing, these three revisions of the national charter were rendered empty by the determined resistance of the South and the acquiescence of a weary North. The power of utterance had outlived its moment. Indeed, the verbal's puniness became one of realism's axioms, often in fictions directly or indirectly evoking the Civil War, such as Twain's *A Connecticut Yankee in King Arthur's Court*.

Melville had always put the necessity of preserving peace ahead of the plight of the bondsmen. The protracted aftermath of hostilities in Reconstruction and the undoing of Reconstruction heightened his conservative side and turned the fiery if fearful creator of Ahab into a proponent of stability and reserve. Scarcely had the Union been saved than he was warning of "enthusiasts" and "theorists" who would jeopardize peace with projects of "dubious constitutional rightfulness" (such as extending suffrage to blacks).[4] By the late 1880s, when he turned his energies to *Billy Budd*, Melville had long been an open skeptic about schemes for the world's betterment.

One aspect of this trajectory is especially relevant here: Melville's sympathy for the South, the section of the country least receptive to radical ideas, converged with his discomfort over language's subversive energies. His postbellum embrace of taciturn Southerners registered his alienation from Union triumphalism and, more generally, from modernity and its levelings. As the losers on the battlefield, Southerners had fresh reason to regret the linguistic impetuosity that had resulted in carnage. In "Lee in the Capitol," from *Battle-Pieces and Aspects of the War* (1866), Melville repeats the "censor's charge" that vocal "meddlers" on both sides "kindled the war's white heat." The poem portrays the great general ("Who looks at Lee must think of Washington") as reluctantly testifying before a Senate committee incapable of appreciating his appeal for magnanimity: twice Lee murmurs, "How shall I speak?" In a note, Melville observes that in fact Lee did *not* pronounce the words attributed to him: he chose silence and evasion when invited to elaborate by his victorious interlocutors. The author who spoke through dark-skinned South Sea islanders and common seamen now gives stuttering voice to a defender of the Confederacy. And in *Clarel* (1876), the Confederate veteran Ungar, who seldom speaks at all, has to be coaxed into articulating his creator's disgust with a United States degraded into an "Anglo-Saxon China" during "the Dark Ages of Democracy."[5] The distinguished chronicler of Redemption, C. Vann Woodward, labeled this sympathetic portrayal of an ex-Rebel renegade "A Southern Critique of the Gilded Age."[6]

Within a year of *Clarel*, the revolution in racial equality masterminded by the Republicans came to an official end. But Reconstruction was not quite defunct, and efforts to resurrect its provisions persisted right up to the time of Melville's death in 1891. This, and the fact that *Billy Budd* was composed at Melville's home in Manhattan (at East Twenty-sixth Street) after he stepped down from his position in the New York Custom House (one of many relevant affinities with Hawthorne), is the neglected context of the novella. Political turmoil over race and the vote swirled around the author as he wrote. The Republicans put protection of the freedmen's rights into their 1888 platform, and Benjamin Harrison was triumphant (narrowly) in the extremely divisive election that followed. The next year Representative Henry Cabot Lodge of Massachusetts, a disciple of Charles Sumner, sponsored an Enforcement Bill that would have reimposed federal supervision of southern elections. Democrats were in an uproar. They denounced the Republicans for reawakening discord between North and South and compared the proposed law to Louis Napoleon's monopolization of power in France. (France qualified as double bogeyman: the seedbed of revolution whose anarchical excesses led to tyranny, a pattern originating in the 1790s and seen as recurring in the Revolution of 1848 and in the 1871 Paris Commune and its aftermath.) Debate over the Lodge Force Bill gripped Congress until the Senate defeated the measure in 1891.[7]

The Empire State, Melville's birthplace and current residence, enjoyed a remarkably close relationship with the former Confederacy. Harrison's opponent in the 1888 presidential contest was Grover Cleveland, the latest in a string of New York candidates sympathetic to and, after the war, strongly backed by southern whites. Others included Horatio Seymour in 1868, Horace Greeley in 1872 (Greeley, a former abolitionist, had turned against Reconstruction), and Samuel Tilden in 1876. (General George B. McClellan, who ran from New York against Lincoln in 1864, might be added to the list.) Cleveland, a former governor, was nominated three times, in 1884, 1888, and 1892; he won twice. These men, all Democrats except Greeley, reflected the alliance between the cotton states and New York that sprang from the city's financial and commercial preeminence. Melville owed his appointment as inspector of customs to President Andrew Johnson, an adamant foe of radical Reconstruction and the bête noire of the Republicans. The novelist may have attended a massive rally in Union Square in support of Johnson, where banners proclaimed "Eternal Hostility to every Form of Tyranny."[8]

New Yorkers had their own unhappy experience with the supposed abuses of enforcement. The municipality, whose Tammany machine regularly tried to exclude blacks from the polls and to vote unregistered Irish immigrants, was the target of fully one-quarter of total federal expenditures for ensuring fair elections. The historian David Quigley, with pardonable hyperbole, uses the phrase "the reconstruction of New York City" to describe the entire twenty-year period of Melville's service in the Custom House. As late as 1893, when the reelected President Cleveland and the Democrats in Congress finally managed to repeal enforcement in the ex-Confederacy altogether, federal officers still descended on the city to oversee its balloting.[9]

Tying Reconstruction to the French Revolution, moreover, had a long pedigree in political controversy. Charles Sumner, in a provisional draft of the Thirteenth Amendment, proposed the phrase "equality before the law," a borrowing from the French Declaration of the Rights of Man. The Senate balked at this Gallic importation into the national compact, and after Appomattox Democrats from both sections automatically tagged proponents of political and civil equality as French-besotted "revolutionists." Albion Tourgée, himself of French Huguenot extraction, endured the epithets "Jacobin" and "sans-culotte" for his efforts on behalf of the ex-slaves. Thomas Dixon, in his apology for the Ku Klux Klan, The Clansman, applied the French formula to the whole postwar experience. He entitled his book 2, on the radicals' seizure of the government after Lincoln's assassination, "The Revolution," and his book 3, on the freedmen's rule over the prostrate South, "The Reign of Terror."[10]

A testament to the staying power of the anti-French perspective, The Clansman was a bellwether for early twentieth-century histories of Reconstruction. One of the classics of the genre, Claude G. Bowers's The Tragic Era: The Revolution after Lincoln (1929), in addition to paraphrasing Dixon in his subtitle, made a mantra of the French analogy. Bowers described the occupation of the South as a conspiracy hatched by hypocritical "philanthropists," dismissed Sumner as a "theorist," and trained

his ire on Thaddeus Stevens as the implacable leader of the House Republicans. He compared Stevens to "Marat in his tub" and observed that his
sense of humor had a "bitter Voltairian flavor." The diatribe concluded
with the thought that if Stevens "had lived in France in the days of the
Terror, he would . . . probably have died by the guillotine with a sardonic
smile upon his face."[11]

To critics, then, the Lodge Force Bill marked a resumption of ideological warfare in which the lessons of the Gallic prototype figured centrally.
The bill was virtually the last gasp, on the federal level, of the activist
tradition launched in the United States more than a half century earlier.
As it expired on the Senate floor, Melville was striving—crossing out, revising, amending, laboring painfully with words—to complete his story of
a maritime mutiny that never occurs. In this respect, *Billy Budd* is the opposite of "Benito Cereno," Melville's previous novella of a shipboard slave
revolt that does, however briefly, succeed. The older tale records the stran-
gulating effects of slavery on language and cautiously protests against this
verbal blockage.[12] In contrast, the story of Billy, Claggart, and Captain
Vere defects to the wariness about rhetoric endemic to the late nineteenth-
century social order.

What follows is a speculative reading of *Billy Budd* in light of the historical currents shaping the culture after Reconstruction. The interpretation can only be speculative because Melville goes to great lengths to
efface his own context, and because assertions of certainty would violate
the tale's investment in the unsaid and the provisional. Caution is further
enjoined by the absence of hard evidence about Melville's politics in this
period. About his thinking on the post-Reconstruction settlement, there
are hints but nothing definitive. Melville may have shared the revulsion
of his relatives at the "stolen" election of 1876–77, which denied the presidency to the pro-Bourbon Democrat Tilden and installed Rutherford B.
Hayes in the White House. He consoled himself with the thought that
life is too short to dwell on such disappointments: "Hayes' term is four
years, each of 365 days."[13] A poem from the very end of his life does reveal
an abiding concern with fratricide and guilt, central issues of the Civil
War. "Timoleon," published in 1891, just a few months after he set aside
his "Inside Narrative," retells a story from Plutarch about the ancient Co-
rinthian patriot who slew his tyrannical brother. Captain Vere is an avid
reader of Plutarch's *Lives*.

Although the caveats are indispensable, the historical matrix I have
sketched here has the merit of illuminating otherwise intractable features
of the novella. I offer this reading as a possibility in that heuristic spirit.

Melville, after all, wrote in a specific time and place, and he was seldom immune to the external political and social circumstances coeval with his acts of composition. Few readers would contend that *Moby-Dick* was untouched by the Compromise of 1850 and the protests that controversial legislative package catalyzed—although Ishmael's narrative makes no reference to those events. *Billy Budd* consummates a subtheme in the earlier book: the danger of unregulated discourse. Melville's fiction of an impressed seaman views speech as contaminated and its suppression as necessary to social order; it gestures at a space beyond politics as a refuge from "this world of lies."

On the surface, *Billy Budd* has nothing to connect it to the American scene. The action occurs during the Napoleonic Wars, in 1797, and the radicalism Melville deprecates is that unleashed by the French Revolution, not by abolitionism or Reconstruction. With the possible exception of Claggart, who has a slight accent hinting at foreign birth, all the principal characters are British. Even the dedicatee is "Jack Chase, Englishman." Melville mentions only two black characters, neither of whom has a significant role: a dark-skinned mariner introduces the Handsome Sailor motif and then abruptly vanishes, and a Baltimore Negro makes a cameo appearance. *Billy Budd* might thus be said to culminate the process of whitening or segregation in Melville's writing that began in earnest with the Civil War and *Battle-Pieces*. Finally, the text maintains a near-silence about the present, broken only by occasional jabs at the post-Darwinian disdain for religious faith.

One well-known American, long dead, does get a nod from Melville: Nathaniel Hawthorne, the friend and fellow romantic to whom he dedicated *Moby-Dick*. Hawthorne's name comes up in the second chapter, in a passage where Melville describes the vocal defect, a tendency to stutter, that mars Billy's otherwise faultless physical being. He compares the "one thing amiss" in his hero with the blemish on the cheek of "the beautiful woman in one of Hawthorne's minor tales," evidence that "the envious marplot of Eden" invariably "slip[s] in his little card, as much as to remind us—I too have a hand here" (302).[14] But this allusion to "The Birthmark" is not the only time that Melville invokes Hawthorne in *Billy Budd*, and the second moment similarly focuses on Billy's difficulty with speech. During the confrontation in the cabin, when the foretopman is unable to respond verbally to his accuser's charge of mutiny, Vere declares to him, "Speak, man! . . . Speak! Defend yourself!" (349). Although Melville does not mention Hawthorne by name here, he appears to have in mind the scene from

The Scarlet Letter (1850) where Hester Prynne stands on the scaffold while the Puritans harangue her to identify her secret lover. "Speak, woman!" cries an onlooker (Roger Chillingworth, as it happens); "speak; and give your child a father!"[15]

Neither allusion is casual. In "The Birthmark," Georgiana's slight disfiguration resembles a "bloody hand," and it costs her her life when her husband, Aylmer, seeks to remove it. Billy Budd, tongue-tied by his disability, strikes the blow with his fist that leads to his execution. The Hawthorne story, moreover, takes place in the late eighteenth century, at the same period as Melville's, and both authors rebuke the Enlightenment quest for perfectibility that drives the experimenting of Georgiana's husband, the scientist Aylmer, and the theorizing of the Jacobins. In the case of *The Scarlet Letter*, the theme of language supplies the important link. Hester and the minister, Arthur Dimmesdale, eerily prefigure Billy and Claggart in their relation to utterance: the heroine wraps herself in silence—on the scaffold, she shakes her head and exclaims, "I will not speak!"—and her pastor is an outwardly respectable, inwardly corrupt sinner whose hypocritical sermons dupe his congregants. Hawthorne himself reveals an abiding uneasiness with verbal fluency in his silences, unanswered questions, and withheld revelations. Melville tinkered endlessly with *Billy Budd*, which also abounds in reticences and mysteries, and because he never completed his manuscript, the text we read today is a product of editorial guesswork.

Hawthorne composed *The Scarlet Letter* at a high point of sectional tension, temporarily allayed by the Compromise of 1850, and he was allied with conservative Democrats, such as the president-to-be, Pierce, who wanted no further public debate about the slavery issue. It was just too dangerous to the republic's survival to be tolerated. Melville, looking back from the 1880s, may have sensed the renewed relevance of Hawthorne's attitude, for successful revival of the Radical Republican agenda would have jeopardized national reunion. No more than the author of *The Scarlet Letter*, of course, does Melville directly address the present; he operates through indirection and analogy. In *Billy Budd*, his agent of ideological fanaticism is the chaos across the Channel, and the threat of mutiny in the British fleet imposes the requirement of verbal reserve.

Censorship pervades every aspect of Melville's text. The disturbances at Spithead and the Nore, taking inspiration from events in France and fanned by the presence of so many impressed men in the king's navy, have created a state of constant vigilance that radiates out from the *Bellipotent* to the narrative voice. Claggart, the master-at-arms, is charged with "po-

lice surveillance of the crew" (344), and he has a network of spies to fer-
ret out seditious words and behavior. An underling's nickname, "Squeak,"
conveys the resulting constriction of voice. The master-at-arms is a virtuoso of equivocation who—until he accosts Vere on the quarterdeck—
never allows himself an unguarded expression. He always has a "pleasant"
word for his victims. The cunning Dansker is a man "of few words" who
similarly censors his real thoughts (318). The writers on whom Melville
relies for information about the Great Mutiny abridge their naval histories to avoid giving details about the outbreak. Even Captain Vere, praised
though he is for directness, participates in the regime of circumspection.
When Claggart is about to name a ship on which the bluejackets revolted,
Vere cuts him off with a peremptory, "Never mind that!" (343). The captain resorts to repeated acts of subterfuge and secrecy to avoid exciting
suspicion among the sailors, for example by ordering one of his subordi-
nates, "Contrive it that he [Billy] speaks to nobody. Keep him in talk yourself" (348). When he later addresses the crew about the sentence of death,
Vere pointedly refrains from uttering the word "mutiny," and he mentions
nothing about the importance of discipline. He believes, says Melville in a
revealing construction, that the consequence of Billy's infraction "should
be made to speak for itself" (368).

Billy Budd might almost be said to perfect the condition of verbal inhibition. Although Melville characterizes the Handsome Sailor's estrangement from language, his stutter, as the mark of Satan, it can be seen with
equal justification as the proof of his unworldliness or innocence. In addition to his vocal flaw, Billy is illiterate, and Melville frequently compares
him to a barbarian, once to a Tahitian (373). The description recalls the
murderous (i.e, cannibalistic) prelapsarian natives (an oxymoron, but one
that Melville encourages) of *Typee*. Billy often fails to understand what others, such as the Dansker, say to him; he can't begin to fathom the master-
at-arms, "the 'too fair-spoken man'" (338). He has an instinctive aversion
to the role of "a telltale" (335) or informer and twice refuses to report the
attempt, by one of Claggart's pawns, to entrap him into a mutiny. His fatal
blow when unable to speak—fatal to himself as well as the police chief—
underlines the hazards of Billy's linguistic dysfunction. But the tacit parallel to Hester Prynne is a reminder that like Hawthorne's heroine, the
Handsome Sailor stays outside the realm of duplicitous or destructive utterance exemplified by Dimmesdale and Claggart. Like the wearer of the
scarlet letter, he takes the penalty of silence upon himself.

If, in Billy's case, vocal difficulties are inseparable from goodness, evil
and the lethal misuse of language are united in the master-at-arms. The

usual claim that Claggart deals in indirection is only half right (and indirection is selectively true of Vere and Melville as well). What really sets the villain apart is his readiness to violate the code of verbal restraint necessitated by England's danger, a code he himself has responsibility for enforcing, and to traffic in inflammatory words that must result in death. To this end, he is surreptitious, but he can be blunt, too. His "confidential tongue" (339) spreads falsehoods about Billy, and he has his minions try to elicit treasonous statements or behavior from the foretopman. In the interview on the quarterdeck, he throws aside caution to level the charge of mutiny, answering "William Budd" without hesitation to Captain Vere's "Name him" (344)—a sharp contrast with the subsequent scene where Billy fails to answer the command to speak. Claggart makes the accusation even though he knows that he puts himself, and not just Billy, in mortal danger. "Heed what you speak," Vere warns him. "Just now, and in a case like this, there is a yardarm-end for the false witness" (346). Vere is wrong: Billy, not his accuser, ends up on the gallows. But the captain is also right: deploying speech to kill, Claggart instigates an act of retaliatory violence that dwarfs speech, and he perishes from the even more deadly, and instantaneous, rejoinder of a blow to the forehead.

Can we view the violence in Vere's cabin as analogous to or allegorical of the clash between North and South, with the two sections of the country represented by Claggart the possible immigrant and Billy the rustic innocent? Recall that in *Battle-Pieces*, Melville referred to "unfraternal denunciations" that "at last flamed to deeds that ended in bloodshed," and Billy fires out his fist at his defamer "quick as the flame from a discharged cannon at night" (350). Might Billy's tragic fate be meant to suggest the death of American innocence in the cauldron of internecine bloodletting? The Handsome Sailor, aged twenty-one in 1797, would have been born in the same year as the United States, and many intellectuals, perhaps Henry James most famously, regarded the war as spelling an end to American exceptionalism. Ungar, the ex-Confederate of *Clarel*, finds in the conflict and its aftermath "new confirmation of the fall / Of Adam."[16] Billy's harrowing encounter with "the diabolical incarnate and effective in some men" (371) seems a fictional counterpart to the nation's agony.

Some of these rather labile parallels (Billy as the South, Billy as the United States) have plausibility, and Melville's "Inside Narrative" is hardly shy of allegory. Rather than seeing the echoes of the nation's history as deliberate, it would be more accurate to say that they overlap and crisscross with the novella because they were in Melville's consciousness while he worked on it. They formed part of his cultural and political inheritance, like the writings of Hawthorne, and current headlines had revitalized their urgency. Other parallels are more evocative of postbellum history, and they resonate with contradictory meanings and racial identities, whose effect, as we shall see, is both to underscore the necessity for Billy's sacrifice and to soften the harshness of Melville's pessimism.

With Claggart's death or "lasting tongue-tie," as Melville terms it (359), the focus of interest rotates to Captain Vere, until now the least prominent of Melville's principal characters and one who does not speak at all in the text until the quarterdeck scene.[17] Roused out of silence by events, Vere makes his only half-willing entrance into Claggart's domain of fatal discourse. His words differ from the police chief's in that they are genuinely, not just nominally, meant to maintain discipline and avert mutiny, but they have a similar result. His address to the drumhead court brings about Billy's execution, and Melville does not minimize the doubts and difficulties that attend his role. Vere expects Billy to hang even before the court convenes; he serves as witness at one moment, prosecutor at the next; and he turns aside questions of motive or statement to concentrate exclusively on the foretopman's blow. Troubled by misgivings throughout, the members of the court yield to their commander less because he convinces them by argument than because they feel him to be "not less their superior in mind than in naval rank" (364). The responsibility for Billy's hanging is Vere's, almost Vere's alone, and his one sustained foray into speech entangles him in the tragedy of performative utterance. To return to the American context, the captain reprises the nation's course as it moved, during a war fought by words as much as by arms, into disenchanted maturity.

As the lingering doubts of the ship's lieutenants suggest, language does not emerge from this scene in a positive light. Ultimately, according to Melville, what wins over the court is Vere's closing reference to "the unconfirmed tone of the fleet at the time" (365)—a scare tactic identical to Claggart's talk of mutiny on the quarterdeck. Further, an ingrained suspicion of the verbal pervades the captain's performance, and he himself can barely hide his distaste for public speaking. Halfway into the trial we learn that Vere, being conscious of his intellectual superiority to his officers and obliged to restate what he believes is irrefutable, would prefer not to address them at all: "Similar impatience as to talking is perhaps one reason that deters some minds from addressing any popular assemblies" (360). The story hastens on from this rebuke of the rabble, as Vere overcomes his reluctance and assumes the role of "the speaker" (362), but it is not evident that the words attributed to him are actually his. Melville prefaces the captain's appeal to the court with the statement "What he said was to this effect" (361), implying that the passages to follow, though enclosed in quotation marks, are the indirect discourse of the narrator.

The trial chapter marks the apogee of language's tainted influence in the narrative, and the subsequent retreat from the verbal signals a shift in frame of reference from the Civil War to the Reconstruction era. (The valuation of music or poetry is another matter, to which I will return.) Captain Vere speaks directly only twice more, and briefly, in *Billy Budd*, once to praise "measured forms" (380) and once when he is dying. The celebrated and often-interpreted chapter 22, where he communicates the verdict to Billy, is perhaps most memorable for its unwillingness to quote him or to give the substance of what he says. The episode breathes contempt for "the gadding world," with language treated as a disreputable realm of speculation and uncertainty, unworthy to enter the "inviolable" sanctuary of the interview. Although the details of what transpired were "never known," according to the narrator, we are treated to a series of "conjectures," and the provisional note continues throughout the chapter. Given his nature, Vere "should . . . have concealed nothing"; "it is not improbable that such a confession"; "even more may have been"; Vere "may have developed the passion"; he "may in the end have caught Billy to his heart." And then Melville dismisses discourse altogether. Dropping a curtain of privacy and "holy oblivion" over the scene, he frankly acknowledges that "there is no telling" what went on between two such exceptional individuals as Billy and his commander (366–67). As at Gettysburg, silence or its approximation is the homage that writing pays to the hard fact of human suffering.

The cataloguing of language's disabilities in this chapter segues into a passage that introduces a new and corroborative dimension. Having dramatized the verbal's agency, Melville now suggests that words always have a supplementary or parasitic relationship to events. "Of a series of incidents with a brief term rapidly following each other," he remarks, "the adequate narration may take up a term less brief, especially if explanation or comment here and there seems requisite to the better understanding of such incidents" (367). The tone of the passage is neutral, but the implication seems clear. (Story)telling necessarily comes after the occurrences it seeks to describe and, afflicted with a kind of built-in verbosity, consumes more time to unfold than the occurrences themselves. It is secondary, not primary. But might Melville have believed with Hegel that the owl of Minerva flies at dusk, and that belatedness brings the boon of understanding? The story, with its silences and skepticism about certain knowledge, strongly indicates otherwise; and the circumstance that *Billy Budd* was never completed further upends the supposition of post facto wisdom. Indeed, Melville has nothing but contempt for the idea that those physically or temporally remote from an emergency, "when it is imperative promptly to act," can have a better grasp of the situation than the actors involved: "The greater the fog the more it imperils the steamer, and speed is put on though at the hazard of running somebody down. Little ween the snug card players in the cabin of the responsibilities of the sleepless man on the bridge" (365).

In the end, though, it is not action that supplants speech in Melville's narrative. It is the nation or the state, with its monopoly on legitimate violence and its essential role as the guarantor "of founded law and freedom defined" (303). Only the state—in this case, the English state, which Captain Vere refers to in shorthand as "the King"—possesses the moral authority and physical might to resist "those invading waters of novel opinion social, political, and otherwise" which endanger "the peace of the world and the true welfare of mankind" (312). As is palpable from this quotation, Melville portrays the French Revolution as a generalized threat that corrodes from within as well as attacking from outside. The mutineers put down at Spithead and the Nore, he writes, had caught the spirit of insurrection and transformed the British colors "into the enemy's red meteor of unbridled and unbounded revolt" (303). Melville singles out faith in nature's goodness, a variant of the idea that men are perfectible, as possibly the most insidious error of the regicides and their followers.[18] A Scottish admirer of Thomas Paine bestowed the name the *Rights-of-Man* on the ship from which Billy was impressed. But Paine's state of nature was "a rat-pit of quarrels" (295), and it took an act of violence, the Handsome Sailor's thrashing of Red Whiskers, to enforce peace. Vere, in his argument to the court-martial, says that allegiance to the king must prevail over the tug of nature, and subsequent events vindicate his preference for established institutions over the primeval. At the execution, the bluejackets echo Billy's blessing of the captain, but an instant later they revoke their words with an ominous murmur of protest that Melville compares to "the freshet-wave of a torrent suddenly swelled by pouring showers in tropical mountains" (378). With "Nature" on the verge of mutiny, the rituals of naval power are mobilized to disperse the men and restore discipline and order.

On just one occasion, Melville turns away from the English setting of his story and glances across the Atlantic, remarking that Napoleon's conquests filled even men who had fought at Bunker Hill with apprehension. But it is hard to miss the shadow of the present-day republic in his rallying to the nation-state, or to overlook how his criticism of Jacobinism dovetails with his dislike for the Radical Republicans. Reconstruction was another example of novel social and political theorizing that had shown itself "insusceptible of embodiment in lasting institutions" (312).[19] Melville apparently felt about America's "Second Revolution" (as many have called it) much as he did about France's first in this statement from the discarded preface to *Billy Budd*: "Straightaway the Revolution regency as righter of wrongs itself became a wrongdoer, one more oppressive than the Kings."[20] If allowed to return, Reconstruction would replace the slow reconciliation between the white people of the North and the South with sectional rancor. The peace and security of the United States would be the casualties. Twenty-five years before, in a poem on the New York City draft riots (or mutiny), Melville had applauded the state, "Wise Draco," for crushing the rebellion with artillery and disproving the Republic's adage "Which holds that Man is naturally good, / And—more—is Nature's Roman, never to be scourged."[21] He wanted no repetition of the civil unrest of 1863, even if the freedmen had to suffer. The conclusion of *Billy Budd* holds good for postbellum America (and recalls the conclusion of the Vivenza interlude in *Mardi*): the claims of justice have to yield to stability.

Many racists reached the same conclusion; but it is wrong to think of Melville, even the late Melville, as a racist. Like Captain Vere, his quarrel with radicalism was primarily philosophical, rooted in doubts about human nature and skepticism about implementing abstract political ideals. In the 1880s, such views were far less respectable than white supremacy, and Melville refers several times to the unpopularity of the biblical doctrine of the Fall. This sense of being out of step with the times helps to explain one aspect of Melville's self-reflexivity about language that we have not discussed yet: the fact that as author and narrator, he replicates or internalizes much of his plot's mistrust of words. The mistrust has a lineage in his fiction, but nowhere is the disavowal more constitutive than in *Billy Budd*.

Indeed, the story seems to operate under the same ban on verbal rashness that governs the *Bellipotent*, as though novelists, like seamen during the Great Mutiny, or historians of it, are required to exercise extreme caution about what they say. We have pointed out the provisionality of chapter 22, with its profusion of "may haves," but circuitousness and a reluctance to aver with certainty are common throughout the text. Melville commits the "literary sin" of wandering into byways (305). He explains Claggart's hatred of Billy "by indirection" (324) and then denies any hint of Holy Writ in his analysis, "for little will it recommend these pages to many a reader of today" (326). He regularly disavows his own thoughts by putting them into the mouths of others. The "honest scholar" of chapter 11, not Melville, extols the wisdom of the Hebrew prophets (324); "a writer whom few know" is the source for the passage (already quoted) critical of Monday-morning quarterbacking (365). And although Melville claims to have told the "Truth uncompromisingly" in a narrative "essentially having less to do with fable than with fact," it is exceedingly difficult to specify what that "truth" is, the elusiveness of *Billy Budd*'s meaning overshadowing its fearlessness (380–81). (Melville's very statement is disingenuous: few fictions draw more heavily on fable than this one.) Perhaps no work in all Melville's canon, with the possible exception of *The Confidence-Man* (1857), has generated so many conflicting interpretations. The unfinished condition of *Billy Budd* guarantees it a permanent and protective indeterminacy.

No language can wholly shed ambiguity, but poetry and music are by definition nearer to the indeterminate. They are emotive, suggestive, and, in the case of music, nonverbal. They rely for their effects on the rhymes and refrains produced by the iteration of sounds. *Billy Budd* ends with a ballad—the editors believe that the manuscript in fact began as a ballad—and scattered throughout are snatches of poetry and music that seem to belong to a separate generic constellation or (since many works of fiction incorporate verse and songs) to form a discrete sphere of value and expression within the prose of the story. A general movement from prose to poetry defines the late career of Melville, who changed genres around the time of the Civil War. He surely did so in part because of the waning audience for his novels, but he may also, as I suggested about Lincoln, have felt impatient with a medium whose consequences had been so devastating for the Union. Lincoln's turn toward concision modulated into something approaching poetry. No reader of the Gettysburg Address can fail to notice that oration's foregrounding of repetition, to the point where the three brief paragraphs, like the three stanzas of a poem, seem to proceed by linked patterns of sound: "conceived . . . and dedicated" (first paragraph); "conceived and so dedicated" (second paragraph); "cannot dedicate. . . . to be here dedicated" (third paragraph). The repetitions climax in the famous tricolon of the ending: "of the people, by the people, for the people."

Iteration proves similarly important in Melville's story, beginning with the disclosure that Billy has a stutter, the mark of that particular vocal impediment being a spasmodic, involuntary proneness to repeat. The second chapter identifies the Handsome Sailor with music and sets tone and sound apart from language as truthful indices to his unblemished character. Melville explains that though Billy could neither read nor write, he "could sing, and like the illiterate nightingale was sometimes the composer of his own song." Stress causes him to stammer and choke up, but his voice is otherwise said to be "singularly musical, as if expressive of the harmony within" (301–2).

These associations, allowed to lie dormant for much of the narrative, emerge as an antidote to the forces of disorder after the guilty verdict is announced to the crew. They move into the vacuum created by a flight from discourse. Direct speech almost disappears from *Billy Budd* after the trial scene, with the single sustained exception, a conversation between the purser and the surgeon, seeming to announce itself as a vulgar intrusion into the beauty and solemnity of the story. Utterance, having caused all the trouble, is no longer welcome in the text. The closeted interview between Billy and Vere, to which the reader is not privy, is the last exchange between them. The bluejackets listen to the sentence against their comrade "in a dumbness like that of a seated congregation in hell" (369). No one but the chaplain communicates with the Handsome Sailor, and that dialogue, too, is given in summary. The execution itself occurs in silence, "a silence but emphasized by the regular wash of the sea against the hull" (377). And chapter 26, which oddly jumps ahead to "some days afterwards," relates the conversation in which the purser, "more accurate as an accountant than profound as a philosopher," presses the surgeon about the singularity of Billy not ejaculating at the moment of death (376–77). The surgeon, plainly uncomfortable, finally manufactures an excuse and withdraws; many readers share his relief at being spared more of the discordant colloquy.

The silences cited above are broken not by discourse but by menacing eruptions of inarticulancy from the sailors, commotions that come closer to animal or natural noises than to human speech. The "murmurous indistinctness" emanating from the men after Billy's execution is "a sound not easily to be verbally rendered," the facsimile of a tropical torrent (378). At the foretopman's burial, the crew emits "a second strange human murmur" that blends "with another inarticulate sound" from seafowl as they swoop screaming to the spot where the body enters the water. Melville interprets the muttering as indicating "some capricious revulsion of thought or feeling such as mobs ashore are liable to" (379), perhaps recollecting the riots of 1863 that he wrote about in his poem "The House-Top."

Prosaic language, stigmatized by its sins, cannot calm these grumblings of discontent, and so Melville reactivates the musical and poetic iterations originally identified with the Handsome Sailor. Harmonious sounds displace raucous outcries. Billy's blessing of Captain Vere shows none of his liability to stutter—or rather, the bluejackets stutter for him. He pronounces the syllables "God bless Captain Vere!" in "the clear melody of a singing bird on the point of launching from the twig"; and the sailors, as though seized by "some vocal current electric," involuntarily repeat his words. "The silver whistles" of the officers dissipate the "sullen revocation" of the blessing, and it takes the drum "beating to quarters at an hour prior to the customary one" to disperse the crowd at the burial. Then the band plays "a sacred air," and the men, "toned by music," assume their allotted posts. Melville has the *Bellipotent*'s commander draw the moral: "'With mankind,' he would say, 'forms, measured forms, are everything; and this is the import couched in the story of Orpheus with his lyre spellbinding the wild denizens of the wood.' And this he once applied to the disruption of forms going on across the Channel and consequences thereof" (378–80). Music and poetry thus serve the British nation-state, an alliance reinforced in the early digression about Admiral Horatio Nelson, the savior of his country at Trafalgar. Nelson's heroism is championed through references to poetry. Melville quotes the well-known line from Tennyson's ode, "the greatest sailor since the world began," and he musters the grand "epics and dramas" in whose verse "the poet" glorifies warriors of Nelson's grandeur (307).

But *Billy Budd* never permits us to imagine that poetry or music is isomorphic with existing power. Though the two realms coalesce at times, they also diverge in ways that highlight the vulnerability of rhythmic art to the "disruption of forms," Vere's phrase for the lawlessness in France. The Empire perseveres, but music can be perverted or destroyed. The uprising at the Nore, Melville says, "converted into irony" the patriotic strains of Dibdin, "as a song-writer no mean auxiliary to the English government" (303–4). Claggart's manner during the quarterdeck scene reminds Captain Vere "of a bandsman, a perjurous witness in a capital case before a courtmartial ashore" (344). And Melville must expect us to remember that Orpheus's lyre stilled the bacchantes only temporarily. Their wild cries eventually overpowered his melody, and they dismembered him in a frenzy.

There is, then, a fragile and utopian quality to poetry and music, easily shattered but rich with possibility. At the end of Melville's story, the iterative genres gesture at a realm beyond politics,[22] a space where feeling and human brotherhood take precedence, however conditionally, over the exigencies of preserving order. Vere's idea of music as "measured forms" upholding established authority seems irrelevant to the final three chapters, whose "ragged edges" pointedly unsettle the "symmetry of form attainable in pure fiction" (381). The second of this last group of chapters reprints, "from an authorized weekly publication" of the navy, a distorted account portraying Billy as a vindictive killer and Claggart as a selfless patriot. Here is the "world of lies" in a nutshell, with language as its malignant facilitator. Chapters 28 and 30 provide poetic, and deeply moving, contrasts to this official fabrication. Fatally wounded during an engagement with the French, Captain Vere on his deathbed imitatively stutters in tribute to the man he sentenced to hang. His last words, delivered without remorse, are "Billy Budd, Billy Budd" (382). The concluding chapter describes how the bluejackets venerated the Handsome Sailor's memory and how one of them, gifted "with an artless *poetic* temperament" (Melville's italics), composed a ballad about him, "Billy in the Darbies." The inarticulate hero appears to speak (or rather recite) here, but the verses put in his mouth are not his; they are the invention of an unnamed shipmate.[23] Melville, in his old age, favored blank verse. But this poem of mariner communality is all rhymes and the repetition of sounds: "Bay," "pray," "look," "astray!," "nook," "day" (last words of the first six lines); "plank," "sink," "think," "sank," "pink," "deep," "asleep," "there," "wrist," "fair," "twist" (last eleven lines).[24] It is poetry as music, not poetry approximating prose, and it reaffirms the bond between the euphonious forms, as well as their capacity to engender emotional response.

Since the story of Billy Budd started out as a poem, the ballad marks a kind of formal iteration, a return to Melville's originary impulse. The fellowship of common seamen adoring their lost shipmate also sends us back to the beginning, this time to the first few paragraphs and to a recollection that seems obliquely related to the nineteenth-century American world. Introducing the figure of the Handsome Sailor, Melville describes an incident in Liverpool, "now half a century ago," that leaves the reader with a fleeting but indelible image of interracial brotherhood. The future author was strolling along the docks when he sighted a magnificent physical specimen, a mariner "so intensely black that he must needs have been a native African of the unadulterated blood of Ham." A company of shipmates surrounded this individual and reveled in his magnetism. They "were made up," Melville observes of the entourage, "of such an assortment of tribes and complexions as would have well fitted them to be marched by Anacharsis Cloots before the bar of the first French Assembly as Representatives of the Human Race" (291–92).

The black Handsome Sailor dissolves into Billy Budd and never appears again in the novella. But the opening, so quickly superseded by darker events, evokes the ideal of racial equality and fraternity associated with the French Revolution and formative as well in Melville's early work and in the American struggle to free the slaves and incorporate them into the polity. History undid those dreams: Cloots met his death on the guillotine, and Reconstruction, Melville believed, soured into oppression. Nevertheless, the image of the black cynosure, relic of a "less prosaic time," offhandedly accepting "the spontaneous homage of his shipmates," lingers in the mind. He shines with unfulfilled utopian promise, a poetic ray of hope in an otherwise tragic vision.[25]

Some concluding observations about the "race" of Billy Budd himself are in order. Does the African Handsome Sailor on the Liverpool docks melt into Melville's eponymous hero because Billy, too, should be thought of as black? Not literally, of course, but in the sense that the foretopman shares a myriad of traits with the freedmen of the century's final decades, when the republic entered the abyss of race relations. Until recently, historicist discussions of Billy's end tended to cite the hanging of the Haymarket anarchists,[26] but, as Gregory Jay suggests, a better comparison may be with the upsurge in lynching that occurred as Melville was writing. The number of lynchings jumped dramatically in 1889 and peaked in 1892, with 156 recorded deaths; coverage of the grisly phenomenon was national.[27] Like large numbers of blacks just twenty-five years removed from slavery, moreover, Billy is an illiterate without access to the ruling caste's technology of reading and writing. Melville describes him as childlike, primitive, and a barbarian (all terms routinely applied to the former slaves), and he identifies Billy generally with nature and the body as opposed to mind and culture. Finally, the Handsome Sailor's aptitude for music can connect him with black people, whose songs and spirituals under slavery and in freedom enjoyed international renown at this time. The Fisk Jubilee Singers, to cite but a single example, performed to acclaim in the North and throughout Europe.

Why might these filiations have entered Melville's mind, and what purpose could they have in a fiction upholding state power over justice? How might they mitigate his apparent indifference to the fate of the freedmen? No New Yorker with southern sympathies would have hesitated over such questions, for the answer was self-evident: the ex-slaves were as much the victims of Radical Republicanism as the defeated Confederates. Uneducated, ill-equipped for liberty, and swept up in thoughtless schemes of benevolence, the blacks had responsibilities and expectations thrust upon them under which they could only founder. Extremists in Washing-

ton, blind to southern realities, had passed "measures of a nature to provoke, among other of the last evils, exterminating hatred of race toward
race" (from the "Supplement" to *Battle-Pieces*). Blacks would benefit no
less than whites, and probably a good deal more, from a hiatus in the reck-
less imposition of voting and other rights. Persistence would only incite
retaliation from Southerners and further injure "the millions of ignorant
manumitted slaves in their midst."[28] From this perspective, Billy Budd,
the Christlike sufferer on the mainyard, exemplifies the regrettable but
necessary lot of the sacrificed freedmen. The logic may seem perverse to
today's readers, but it brings an additional grace note to Melville's melody
of Reconstruction.

Intertext: "Bartleby, the Scrivener"

"Bartleby, the Scrivener" forms a bridge between eras. It is an intertext connecting a minority viewpoint among antebellum writers, most of whom openly sided with antislavery, and the dominant condition of postwar authorship. Its reiterated demurral, "I would prefer not to," distills both Melville's refusal to speak out about slavery and American realism's aversion to explicit statement on race. Bartleby's echolalia, which infects his coworkers, also anticipates the hero's stutter in *Billy Budd*, Melville's own text that makes peace with the post-Reconstruction settlement. As an exercise in auto-censorship, the scrivener's mantra can be read as a displaced doctrine of aesthetic capitulation or accommodation.

True, "Bartleby" has nothing to say about slavery.[1] Equally true, one would like to construe its protagonist's odd behavior as a declaration of freedom of some kind, not a memorializing of constriction. Doesn't Bartleby practice "a passive resistance" against the forces of monotony and oppression (17)?[2] On this view, Melville's enigmatic narrative constitutes a classic text in what the Spanish novelist Enrique Vila-Matas calls "the literature of the No."[3] But let us consider the alternative possibility, that the scrivener's formula may be a version of compliance; Melville's subtitle would then assume an unexpected explanatory power. Recall that Wall Street, the setting for the lawyer-narrator's office, threw its enthusiastic support behind the Compromise of 1850 as the best guarantor of the Union's survival. "The merchants were alive," as one wrote, "to the vast interests New York City has in stopping agitation."[4] This position was Melville's desideratum in *Mardi*, and he had returned to it by 1853, two years after bridling Ahab.

The cadaverous clerk, to be sure, is an atypical denizen of Wall Street, but what precisely is the nature of his protest? His unknowability—he

would "prefer not to" tell the narrator anything about himself (25)—
problematizes his presumed dissent because it leaves that dissent enclosed
in mystery. Does he desist from copying because he will not regurgitate
other men's thoughts? Because the mid-nineteenth-century economic en-
vironment has become a dead end, a blank wall, for white-collar employ-
ees such as himself? Because he suffers from an incurable, metaphysical
malady? Or because a society predicated on the Declaration and the Bible,
but ruled over by slaveholders and their Wall Street allies, represents a
"dead letter" unworthy of his participation? No one can say which is the
right explanation, or even the right question. No one will ever be able to
say for sure.

While that is part of the story's charm, we have been too quick to en-
roll the copyist in the registry of the "No." His preferences and withholdings do not, in the end, pose much of a challenge to Wall Street. They
soften the narrator and enlarge his sensibilities to some degree, but they
do not change him very much. The lawyer retreats from his well-meant
resolutions because the rumors about Bartleby circulating among his colleagues threaten to scandalize his "professional reputation" (36). Eventually, unable to persuade his employee to leave the original Wall Street
building, and fearful of "being again hunted out by the incensed landlord
and his exasperated tenants" (41), he accepts as inevitable the more instrumental way of dealing with the copyist that removes him to the Tombs.
The news, he relates, "had a conflicting effect upon me. At first I was in-
dignant; but, at last, almost approved. The landlord's energetic, summary
disposition, had led him to adopt a procedure which I do not think I would
have decided upon myself; and yet, as a last resort, under such peculiar
circumstances, it seemed the only plan" (42). Many readers will incline
to sympathize with the narrator at this point, and to feel injured on his
behalf when, on a visit to Bartleby in the Tombs, he offers to assist his former clerk. That strange being declares—without looking at him—"I know
you, and I want nothing to say to you" (43). The recoil toward the lawyer-
narrator is slight and does not alter our fascination with Bartleby, but it
does tell us something about the efficacy of his "resistance."

The trajectory of Bartleby himself in the story only adds to the suspicion of inconsequence. From the moment he shows up at "No.___ Wall
Street" (4), the scrivener embodies the principle of immurement. Describing him as "a motionless young man," the lawyer proceeds to make good
on that characterization by figuratively enclosing his new worker behind
walls—the enormous walls that surround his office building, and the
"ground glass folding doors" and "high green folding screen" behind which

he places Bartleby (11–12). The copyist grows into the adjective "motion-less." He becomes "a fixture in my chamber," according to the lawyer, and, shedding his duties one by one, he spends all his time behind the green screen or "standing immovable in the middle of the room" (35). The nar-rator is forced to flee the building precisely because the scrivener refuses to budge from it. Bartleby sums up his preferred position by saying, "I like to be stationary" (41), and his end in the story, as an inmate at the Halls of Justice, seems a photographic negative of his beginning. In his "un-moving way," he "silently acquiesce[s]" to being conducted to prison (42), and the physical structure of the Tombs reproduces the Wall Street office where we first encountered him. Honeycombed with cells, the prison has walls of "amazing thickness" that "kept off all sounds behind them" (45). Bartleby, the scrivener, has made this much progress in the course of Melville's narrative: where his confinement was once voluntary, it is now compulsory, and where he once chose to wrap himself in solitary mute-ness, he now dies in silence, the yard where the lawyer finds his motion-less body being "entirely quiet" (45).

So there is logic to taking "I would prefer not to" as an act of submis-sion, a symbol of paralysis. The scrivener's immobility succinctly encap-sulates Melville's obstructed tongue on slavery and the no less stymied voices on race of leading realists. Like Bartleby, whose trademark is opac-ity, they would prefer not to reveal their innermost thoughts about the un-fulfilled promise of the century. They would rather take refuge in "strange peculiarities, privileges, and unheard of exemptions" (20). One cannot help but feel that, on some level, the loser was the country. "Ah, Bartleby! Ah, humanity! Ah, America!"

Before turning in detail to the post-Reconstruction writers, it might be ap-propriate to engage briefly with a question that has been implicit through-out this study. Why did clashes over slavery and race invariably steer into linguistic channels? What brought free speech to the foreground when Americans debated, or refused to debate, the place of bondage and equal-ity in their society? In some respects, the answer is obvious: telling the truth about slavery threatened its existence by exposing the falsehood of its justifications, and defenders had no choice but to oppose open discus-sion. A more speculative explanation has to do with the struggle over the founders' legacy—the written documents that created the republic and were passed down through the generations as the nation's scripture. As we have observed, the bond between slavery and utterance, or rather censor-ship, existed from the beginning, in the Declaration and the Constitution.

The compact of silence that banned the term from originary scrutiny and hedged it about with tacit protections allowed the institution to prosper by cementing the slave interest's control of the federal government for fifty years.

Naming and condemning slavery's wrongs would strip it of its privileged place in the polity, a fact Southerners were quick to recognize. The accelerating assault on their section's labor system spilled into a contest over the founders' intentions, and slaveholders sought to secure their position by converting the past's implied acceptance into explicit endorsement. In the *Dred Scott* decision, Justice Taney went so far as to claim, without apparently bothering to consult the document itself, that "the right of property in a slave is distinctly and expressly affirmed in the Constitution." Lincoln would have none of it: in his debates with Douglas and in the Cooper Institute speech, he bluntly dismissed Taney's pronouncement as a fabrication, "a mistaken statement of fact."[5] But Lincoln, too, came to understand that antislavery discourse implied a reinterpretation or rewriting of the federal compact. The Emancipation Proclamation, essential as a first step, would not be enough; the piece of parchment establishing the country's form of government would have to be changed to ensure freedom for the bondsmen. And of course this is what happened with the passage of the Thirteenth Amendment. Slavery was not simply ended; the national charter acquired new language pronouncing it null and void. Its fate was indivisible from linguistics.

The two subsequent amendments added during Radical Republican rule continued the imbrication of discourse with race. But the situation was very different now. Equality and suffrage had been scripted into the founders' text, and neutralizing those pledges required the emasculation and disparagement of constitutional statement. It would be necessary to deny or reinterpret the printed words, so that the mandate of reformation would lose its agency and legitimacy and slip into disrepute. Language would remain integral to the American dilemma, but, in a reversion to the polity's origins, it would operate more as its obverse, silence, than as an active player. And freedom of speech would effectively be redefined as an exercise in irrelevance, not to recoup its vitality on race until the agitation, court decisions, and legislation of the twentieth century.

PART IV

Postbellum

Tourgée: Margin and Center

We began our analysis of antebellum culture's revolt against slave-interest aphonia with Emerson, who occupies a central place in American literary history. His arguments galvanized a generation. Postwar culture's initiating dissenter against reunionist constriction, Albion W. Tourgée, holds a much less exalted rank in critical estimation. Even his admirers would hesitate to put him in the first tier of authors; *A Fool's Errand*, the novel he published in 1879 to protest Reconstruction's betrayal, had neither the staying power nor the influence of Emerson's pamphlet. Tourgée, the "bravest of the carpetbaggers," as W. E. B. Du Bois called him, may have been a beacon of racial enlightenment, but as a literary figure, he has never been anything but marginal.[1] In fact, he embraced marginality, criticizing the regnant realist aesthetic for dwelling on minutiae and asserting that only the romantic imagination could do justice to America's racial trauma. Some literary historians would add to this that Tourgée's challenges to late nineteenth-century ideological pacification inspired practically nothing. Despite his popular success with *A Fool's Errand* and, a year later, *Bricks without Straw*, the themes of his novels had few admitted followers among mainstream authors. And the practitioners of romance, such as Dixon, turned out to be "racial radicals" who sought to overturn everything he stood for.[2]

Yet Tourgée's supersession should not blind us to his importance for literature after Reconstruction.[3] His two best sellers explicitly conceptualize the clash between North and South as a battle over language, and in this respect he belongs at the very heart of his era, though worlds removed from better-known contemporaries in his directness. Among his unacknowledged heirs one might list James (*The Bostonians*), Twain (*Ad-*

ventures of Huckleberry Finn, A Connecticut Yankee in King Arthur's
Court, and The Tragedy of Pudd'nhead Wilson), and Crane (The Monster).
Chesnutt's The Colonel's Dream is also indebted to him. All these writers
expressed discontent in their work with the consensual pact that they, like
Tourgée, could not help being aware of, but none wanted his reputation a
a tiresome scold, not to mention his constantly declining sales. With the
exception of Chesnutt, none breached the parameters of "responsible" dis
course. If their circumspection, in contrast to his candor and obscurity,
made them more subtle and accomplished novelists, that obliqueness also
suggests the extent of the Gilded Age's growing orthodoxy on race. The ascendancy of reaction makes itself felt in A Fool's Errand, where it threatens to usurp the narrative voice; its near-conquest of the text foretells its
triumph in the culture. It would later pursue Tourgée to his faraway sanctuary in the French city of Bordeaux, and the disheartened former carpetbagger would surrender to its demand for silence.

A Fool's Errand is a cornucopia of lingual media. In an age of realism,
where the authorial hand tends to efface itself, Tourgée's book keeps foregrounding acts of writing and speaking, including his own. He incorporates newspaper clippings, legal testimony, and confessions. He quotes at
length from correspondence with southern foes and northern advisers, especially the "Wise Men" whose limited understanding of postwar realities doomed Reconstruction. In a chapter titled "A Thrice-Told Tale," he
provides three different accounts of the murder of the "Radical" John Walters, in three different forms: the first as stories from the local press, the
second as the testimony of a white man, and the last as a confidential conversation with a black hostler who eavesdropped on two of the killers.
Throughout, he highlights the salience of words in the sectional struggle
by using italics and quotation marks to flag conflicting interpretations of
terms such as "abolitionist," "scalawag," and "redemption."

Speech in the Reconstruction South had not lost the aura of danger
it possessed under the slave system. A Fool's Errand gives repeated instances of Southerners' intolerance toward those who disagree with them.
Comfort Servosse, Tourgée's protagonist and sometime proxy, is a Union
veteran from Michigan who migrates to Warrington, North Carolina, after the peace; when he gives in to local appeals for a speech, the natives
so resent his candor that they plot to assassinate him on his way home.
(He is saved by the warning of some Union men.) Other white "Radicals"
(the term is always in scare quotes) are beaten and killed, but what particularly galls people is independent speech by the freedmen. A self-reliant

blacksmith, Bob Martin, receives a whipping for the indiscretion of having "sed my say, and did my own voting, an' tole the other colored people
dey waz free" (185). Uncle Jerry Hunt, the black preacher who is prone to
apsodic trances, utters "burning words" describing how the KKK carried
it the murder of John Walters; his "terrible revelation" gets him lynched
,26–27).

Tourgée may be the first serious American writer to highlight the re-
emblance between antebellum and postwar suppression of dissidence.
The early part of the novel introduces a Warrington resident named Squire
Hyman, who is well-disposed toward Servosse and is not an extremist. Yet
before the war Hyman had condoned whipping abolitionist ministers from
the North, and even now he can't fathom why the colonel should regard his
actions as inexcusable. "We protected ourselves and our institutions," he
protests (95). Such attitudes originated in slavery, but they have obviously
not abated with the disappearance of African bondage: Hyman's defense is
the same pleaded by his neighbors against Reconstruction. "The terrible
suppressive power which slavery had exercised over liberty of thought and
speech had grown into a habit of mind," according to Tourgée, and the
ruling element still does not "allow people to differ from them peaceably
and quietly." One has to retire to "that refuge of free thought at the South,
the woods," in order to voice one's opinions (147–48). Squire Hyman learns
this lesson himself when his Republican son Jesse is seized and whipped
by the KKK. Education for blacks, anathema under slavery, remains an
object of hatred for the dominant caste, in part because it would enable the
freedmen to speak and write effectively against their oppression. The KKK
cuts out the tongue of one man before hanging him; accused of slandering
a white woman, his real offense was that he "could read and write" (193).

In Tourgée's telling, verbal contestation has been more important to
overturning the North's military triumph than extralegal force. The Civil
War, he says numerous times, "was a conflict between two divergent civilizations" (168); the conflict did not end with armed hostilities, and it is
now being fought out over the meanings of words and events. Tourgée has
an acute sense of the limitations or "imperfection" of language (244), and
he refers to the "elasticity of signification" that permits different under-
standings of the same locution. The epithet "abolitionist," for example,
had a relatively neutral meaning north of the Mason-Dixon Line, where
it signified someone favoring the emancipation of the slaves. South of the
line, it meant "one who was in favor of, and sought to promote, negro-
equality, miscegenation, rape, murder, arson, and anarchy" (178). Southerners still use the word pejoratively, but at least in the antebellum period

"abolitionist" had some honor, and many Northerners did not accept its disparaging connotations.

The idiom of Reconstruction cannot claim even sectional standing; it has been utterly routed on the front of language. A southern Unionist, Jehu Brown, has a point when he suggests that it was Grant's army that actually surrendered at Appomattox. Take the cognomen "carpetbagger," one of the critical terms in the lexicon of Reconstruction and "the lineal descendant" of "abolitionist." This word, though referring to many upright people who ventured southward in search of opportunity but also to help the freedmen, has no positive signification in either section. To Northerners, it means an adventurer without means or character, "a bummer." Former Confederates give it a much darker inflection: a carpetbagger is a man who preys on southern misfortune and incarnates "Northern hate, envy, spleen, greed, hypocrisy, and all uncleanness." It is the nearest American equivalent, all agree, to that term of opprobrium from the French Revolution, *sans-culotte*. The "conquering power" joins its supposedly vanquished foes in cursing the carpetbaggers and pouring contempt "upon the only class in the conquered territory who defended its acts, supported its policy, [and] promoted its aim" (177 and 179–80).

Tourgée routinely puts words like "carpetbagger" in quotes or italics to emphasize their disputed and provisional nature; the winning side in this new war over language will be the one to remove the punctuation marks and naturalize its interpretation. The number of embattled words is extensive and includes "nigger equality" (56), meaning, to Southerners, the elevation of the unfit, and to Northerners, the rights conferred on the freedmen by the Fourteenth and Fifteenth Amendments; "nigger supremacy" (248), same meanings; "N.T." or "Nigger Teacher" (54), the local insult for northern white women who instruct the ex-slaves; "Yankee-lovers" (148), those who sympathize with Servosse; "good society" (97), those who refuse to have anything to do with him; and the "great and holy aim" of restoring white supremacy (326), or the vitiation of black rights through KKK violence. What happens in the course of the text, as Washington hesitates and then refuses to impose its will and Reconstruction crumbles, is that the southern terminology prevails throughout the country, with the "Policy of Suppression" (326) achieving permanence as the enlightened will of the majority. Northern pusillanimity contributes mightily to this outcome, and the southern press, as Tourgée notes and Chesnutt would dramatize in *The Marrow of Tradition*, plays an essential role in spreading the gospel of Redemption. Northern newspapers, with their "usual subserviency," hasten to add their voices to the chorus of racial dogmatism (177).

The fate of the Ku Klux Klan encapsulates how perseverance in defeat pays off for the South. Outrage over the crimes of "The Invisible Empire," as the Klan calls itself (252), grows so clamorous that the Wise Men, having long stopped their ears to the freedmen's cries, have no choice but to appoint a congressional committee to investigate. (To Tourgée, the organization is "a band of Christian Thugs" [247].) Thirteen volumes of testimony ensue, federal legislation is passed, and steps are taken to break up the night riders. In the novel, a participant in the killing of Jerry Hunt, Ralph Kirkwood, reveals the details of what happened to Servosse and a local judge, and a spate of arrests decimates the Klan. But the laws composed in the capital prove no more efficacious than the new amendments to the Constitution; state intervention in the form of amnesty and pardons for the offenders nullifies the statutes, and within a year the whole business has been forgotten. Those who persist in bringing up the story are "greeted with the laughter-provoking cry of the 'bloody shirt'" (318)—yet another phrase in the suppressive arsenal of denigration.

Reflecting on this episode, the narrator concedes that "the triumph of the ancient South was incredibly grand" (258). The admiration is Tourgée's as well as his hero's, and a remarkable fact about A Fool's Errand is how close the region's philosophy and rhetoric come to taking control of the authorial viewpoint. The near-appropriation stands out distinctly because—in contrast to a more elusive text such as The Bostonians, which charts a similar course—Tourgée's politics are transparent, and no one can mistake his anger at the erosion of democratic liberties. Edmund Wilson commented on this aspect of the novel almost half a century ago in Patriotic Gore (1962), where, recognizing Tourgée's grudging respect for his adversaries, he spoke of the carpetbagger's "non-partisanship malgré lui."[4] In the linguistic competition between the sections, Tourgée often yields ground to the South. The malediction "carpetbagger," he admits, "was a stroke of genius," and it "was but natural" that a grieving people should excoriate the type (177 and 179). He strives for fairness in representing opposed perceptions of the postbellum situation, furnishing not only the northern and southern ideas, but also "The Northern Idea of the Southern Idea" and "The Southern Idea of the Northern Idea" (139). And Tourgée approaches effusiveness in his acknowledgment of the bold resolve that led to the creation of the KKK:

> It was a magnificent sentiment that underlay it all,—an unfaltering determination, an invincible defiance to all that had the seeming of compulsion or tyranny. One cannot but regard with pride and sympathy

the indomitable men, who, being conquered in war, yet resisted every
effort of the conqueror to change their laws, their customs, or even the
personnel of their ruling class; and this, too, not only with unyielding
stubbornness, but with success. (253)

Thomas Dixon could not have said it better. Southerners' attitudes may
be politically retrogressive and morally repugnant, but on the evidence of
A Fool's Errand, their superiority to Northerners in backbone is beyond a
doubt.

This divergence, too, is rooted in slavery, or rather in the antithetical economic systems adopted by the two sections. The habit of command bred by mastership has produced a people who think of themselves,
and are characterized by Tourgée, as "monarchical and kinglike" (382).
Though always a minority, they dominated government in the antebellum
period, and they have lost none of their imperiousness. On the contrary,
postemancipation arrangements—tenancy, convict lease labor, and the
like—have effectively reproduced the "serfdom" of bondage, and "the lords
of the soil are lords of the labor still," as Servosse complains (383). The
northern system prizes very different qualities. Based on the contractual
relations of the free market, it puts a premium on negotiation and compromise, and its practitioners, in a time of reconciliation, are no match for the
South's unbudging potentates.[5]

The discursive and political formation that encroaches on Tourgée's
voice eventually defeats his protagonist and brings about the kind of sectional marriage that became a benchmark of reunionist fiction.[6] Servosse
ends up as a tragic case study in northern demoralization. The colonel,
who both is and is not Tourgée, first shows signs of wavering during the
revelations about the Klan, when the complicity of the church and press
leaves him doubting his own notions of right and wrong. His accommodation with his neighbors grows after 1877, as the nation gives its "tacit
approval" to the subjugation of the freedmen (319). Although he does not
recant his principles, he submits "quietly to having them rendered inop-
erative and nugatory by the suppression of the will of the majority." The
community no longer takes offense "at his views, and he forbore to express
them." He ceases to show interest in the matters that originally drew him
southward, worries more about his comfort than the state of the country,
and feels thankful "that the struggle which the Wise Men had cast upon
his fellow-workers and himself was at an end" (339–40). By the concluding
chapters, Servosse has abandoned North Carolina for a business opportunity in Central America.

Meanwhile the narrative changes focus. The political plot, which thoroughly dominated the first two-thirds of the novel, recedes before the sexual blossoming of Lily Servosse, the carpetbagger's only child, and her courtship by the scion of a prominent Bourbon family, Melville Gurney. This reorientation starts immediately after the pardoning of the Klan, which ensures the downfall of both Reconstruction and Comfort's mission; the next chapter, "The Awakening," places Lily at the center of the action. Servosse, oblivious to his daughter's yearnings, is now excluded from secrets of the heart, not those concerning clandestine paramilitary orders. Tourgée transfers terms once applied to the ideological combat between North and South to the star-crossed wooing of the young woman: he titles the chapter in which Melville proposes against his parents' wishes "Unconditional Surrender." The political theme does not vanish completely. The senior Gurney and Servosse, who hold diametrically opposite opinions of Reconstruction, voice unhappiness with the match on the grounds of family history and sectional loyalty. Melville's parents refuse their approval, and Lily declares that she cannot accept her suitor's offer *"because I love my father!"* (361).

Yet the slackening of conviction and credibility in these passages of romantic byplay is palpable. Although Tourgée would later tout romance as a superior genre to realism, the unreality of a character such as John Burleson, Melville's best friend, seems discordant, at odds with the carefully documented truthfulness of the previous sections.

Burleson is a conspicuous anomaly in this novel of southern intolerance. A reluctant Confederate veteran and general skeptic about the tactics of Redemption, he fearlessly resists "the popular current" and suffers no harm for his defiance. Other characters with irregular views confine their thoughts to the woods; Burleson is "respected for his unshrinking bluntness, and feared for his terrible directness of thought, and explicitness of statement" (302–3). As Melville Gurney's confidant, he serves the important function of educating Lily's lover about Bourbon narrow-mindedness, but he exists under the sign of belief-suspending romance. In portraying Burleson, one suspects that Tourgée has allowed himself to fantasize about the reception of his own "explicitness of statement"—against all the evidence mustered by his text.

The last pages of *A Fool's Errand* complete the silencing of Servosse and carry the romantic story to the edge of fulfillment. They also make plain the separation of Tourgée from his protagonist. Comfort contracts yellow fever while passing through the Deep South on his way back to North Carolina; dying, he reaches out to his old enemies: "I was no doubt mistaken; perhaps I was too—too intense in my notions: but I hated no man" (397). "Good society," which once spurned him, gathers around his bedside, but the carpetbagger can no longer make his thoughts known: the only sounds "which his fevered lips uttered" are "rambling, half-incoherent words" (400). With her father gone, it seems certain that Lily will finally marry Melville; the elder Gurney gives his implied blessing by sending her a telegram urging her to return to Warrington. (She is in the North with her mother when Comfort falls ill.) Thus does an affair of the heart marked "for whites only," combined with the disappearance of "Radical" presence and speech, consummate one of the most forthright books written in the nineteenth century about the North's craven submission to racism.

But Tourgée, who would continue to write and speak against racial injustice, does not allow his novel to succumb without protest to the reunionist concordat. He has Servosse engage in a final discussion with a Wise Man, in which the hero reiterates his political ideals and ridicules "the State-Rights Moloch" that prevents the federal government from undertaking a massive education program in the South (389). The exchange even contains an intuition of the civil rights movement: describing African Americans as Israelites, Servosse predicts they will "have their forty years" in the wilderness until "a prophet" appears to guide them to freedom (384). The years would number more than eighty, but the idea of waiting for a Moses-like leader would become common among blacks: Frederick Douglass would intimate a similar hope at the end of his last autobiography. Moreover, we should remember that *A Fool's Errand* does *not* conclude with a wedding, which suggests that the ultimate blocking father may be the author himself. At an impasse in his own career after 1877, and eager for a success, Tourgée may have thought the North-South courtship would appeal to women readers; but the prospect of such an apolitical merger must have troubled him, and the book closes not with marriage vows but with the graveside reflections of a Southerner familiar with the hero's efforts. Servosse wanted this to be a free country "accordin' to Northern notions," the man says, but such ideas were not suited to this climate. "It mout hev been better for us, in the end," he adds, in the concluding sentence, "if they hed been" (404).

A Fool's Errand sold rapidly and well, eventually drawing as many as 200,000 readers and showing that a substantial audience supportive of the original Republican agenda still existed. The figures invite comparison to *Uncle Tom's Cabin*. Tourgée's novel was issued anonymously, and some critics speculated that Stowe was the author; building on the parallel, he issued a companion compilation of KKK atrocities, *The Invisible Empire* (1880), as his version of *A Key to Uncle Tom's Cabin*.[7] That factual "Part II" did not attract a readership, but another work of fiction, *Bricks without Straw* (1880), sold in the tens of thousands. The new novel recycles crucial themes from the first, including southern hatred for free speech and the linguistic warfare that the demand for conformity inevitably ignites, here represented as a struggle over the right of the former slaves to rename themselves. *Bricks without Straw* also dramatizes the lot of the Exodusters, blacks who immigrated to Kansas to escape their loss of freedoms in the South. Tourgée stumped for James A. Garfield in the 1880 presidential election, and his fiction may have helped the Ohioan to his razor-thin margin of victory. Republican campaign songs paraphrased the novelist's concerns and also echoed the slogans of the Free Soilers and 1860 Republicans: "Free schools, free speech, free thought, free press."[8]

Stowe's antislavery intervention arguably altered the path of history; Tourgée's novel definitely didn't. The differences in influence between the two books dwarf their similarities. Eight years after *Uncle Tom's Cabin*, Lincoln was elected president and slavery set on the course of ultimate extinction. Garfield, who knew and admired Tourgée, was assassinated shortly after taking office, and four years later the country put a Democrat with southern sympathies in the White House. The novelist's call for education reform and a reinvigoration of civil liberties went unheeded. It may be that for post-Reconstruction America, the most consequential part of *A Fool's Errand* was its treatment of the ex-Confederacy as a kingly and resolute society united in its opposition to an occupying power. Certainly that strain would prove to have the greater overt impact on literature.

Tourgée addressed the cultural situation in a piece published in 1888, "The South as a Field of Fiction." He starts by recalling a prediction he had made twenty years earlier: that slavery, its overthrow, and the color line would supply the richest material for future American novelists. By the 1880s the forecast has been realized: not only have writers gravitated to the southern type, giving Rebels leading roles and relegating Unionists to the periphery, but the nation's literature has become "distinctly Confederate in sympathy." A foreigner would have the impression that "the South was the seat of intellectual empire in America." As in the political arena, the cultural takeover has been spearheaded by southern absolutism scattering northern "doubt and uncertainty," the trademarks of teacup realism: "The Southern novelist has a vast advantage over his Northern contemporary. He never has any doubt. He loves the life he portrays and sincerely believes in its superlative excellence. He does not study it as a curiosity, but knows it by tuition. He never sneers at its imperfections, but worships even its defects."[9]

Two character types in particular are moving to center stage in this writing, according to Tourgée: the Negro and the poor white. The latter, evoking the Highlander of Scottish literature, is the only "interesting" nonblack element, while the African constitutes an unrivaled resource in his successive roles of "slave, freedman, and racial outcast."[10]

With his usual sensitivity to southern discourse, Tourgée has anticipated the arrival, more than a decade later, of Dixon's popular fictions, especially the first volume in the Reconstruction trilogy, *The Leopard's Spots*. (The only authors mentioned in the essay are Harris and Chesnutt.) Dixon was one of the "Confederate" novelists who drew upon and rewrote Tourgée's formula for success. His book includes KKK-Highlander militancy, degenerate black rapists, and a poor white veteran, one-legged Tom Camp; he adds a dashing young cavalier who ascends to the governor's mansion and weds "a daughter of the old fashioned South." Set, like *A Fool's Errand*, in North Carolina, *The Leopard's Spots* fetishizes Redemption's manly "citizen kings," and while Dixon took his title from the book of Jeremiah, he probably noted the passage in which Tourgée's Fool laments his naiveté in expecting that "the leopard *might* change his spots, while yet the Ethiopian retained his dusky skin" (339).[11] A number of people, among them the southern-born editor and publisher Walter Hines Page, were so struck by the affinities that they sent Tourgée copies of Dixon's book. He read one and, appalled by its falsehoods, threw the rest into the fireplace.[12]

Tourgée's essay ventured another speculation: the Negro himself would compose significant literature before the twentieth century. Chesnutt, Paul Dunbar, Frances Harper, and Pauline Hopkins would prove him right, but none of these writers would secure more than a small fraction of Dixon's readers, and the larger culture would not embrace an African American novelist until Richard Wright published *Native Son* in 1940. The nadir was about to begin. Tourgée would continue to swim against the historical tide, but with diminishing results. In 1894 a new and inexpensive edition of *A Fool's Errand* found no takers. Two years later, as lead counsel for the plaintiff in *Plessy v. Ferguson*, he devised the brief against segregated railroad cars that the Supreme Court rejected in upholding the doctrine of "separate but equal." By now, consensual intolerance for Tourgée's politics was national in scope. Although he campaigned for McKinley in 1900, the Republican Party regarded him as an embarrassment, and he was offered the consulate in Bordeaux on the understanding that he would cease agitating for African Americans. "I [am] determined to make no utterance," he promised the president-elect.[13] Shades of Comfort Servosse toward the end of his life in Warrington: Tourgée was welcome to his unfashionable ideas, as long as he said nothing about them in public.

Addendum on Tourgée, Jackson, and the Indian Question

Five years after *A Fool's Errand*, Helen Hunt Jackson published her romantic plea on behalf of displaced Native Americans and Mexicans, *Ramona* (1884). On the surface, few texts seem as remote from Reconstruction as Jackson's, which neither takes place in the South nor glances at the situation of the freedmen. *Ramona* dramatizes the Indian question at precisely the moment when concern over the plight of blacks was disappearing from the public square, replaced by a cultural shift of attention westward that would culminate, a decade later, in Frederick Jackson Turner's "frontier thesis."[14] Yet the novel invites our interest here because it reprises, in a different context, the theme of racial silencing. The verbal disenfranchisement of ex-slaves familiar from Comfort Servosse's story returns as the fate of mestizos and Indians in California, and Tourgée himself, in a review, points out the interlocking nature of the two species of oppression. Jackson's narrative is a case study in the cultural pervasiveness of the post-Reconstruction problematic that would shadow the American realists as an inhibitor of their own voices.

Jackson herself invoked Tourgée's novel as a model. As an agitator for the Indians, she was already famous, if largely ignored, for her polemical *A Century of Dishonor* (1881), which she made a point of sending to every member of Congress. She turned to fiction writing with the intent, as she put it, of "sugaring the pill" of her reform agenda and attracting the kind of readers who, allergic to a lengthy tract, had made blockbusters of *Uncle Tom's Cabin* and *A Fool's Errand*.[15] *Ramona* belongs in the line of "progressive" racial romances with a purpose, a tradition soon to be kidnapped for racist ends by the plantation school, and Jackson aimed to do for the Indians what Stowe had achieved for the slaves and Tourgée (far less successfully) for the freedmen. She would speak for a category of persons who had no say in the polity.

For Jackson, verbal dispossession is the corollary to physical conquest, and it spreads like a pestilence from one category of victim to the next. Seizing California under the banner of Manifest Destiny, the Americans have imposed their laws and their language on the Mexicans, who preceded them in colonizing the area, and on the Indians, the "original settlers of the soil" (a phrase favored by James Fenimore Cooper, another important influence on Jackson). The Americans brandish written documents to oust the Indians from their settlements and to claim lands which the natives hold by customary title. Jackson uses the words "law" and "papers" almost interchangeably to emphasize the lingual character of the usurpation. As the Mission Indian Alessandro observes after his people are driven out of Temecula, all our property "is theirs. That is the law. They're got all the papers to show it." Among his mostly illiterate tribesmen, "nobody had papers. The American law is different" (174). The Indians cannot appeal their evictions because they are not allowed to testify in court against a white man. In effect, they do not even exist unless their names are entered in English in the Indian agent's "book."

Mexicans, the first casualties of Yankee imperialism, fare little better. As Father Gaspara, brooding on American wrongs, concludes, "It is of no use; I will speak no word" (227). Señora Moreno essays another response to the takings: she internalizes the habit of domination and applies it to those weaker than herself. The señora turns language into a veiled instrument of manipulation. Having learned the necessity for subterfuge, she relies on devious words and indirection to get her way, although she is also capable of acts of violence. Jackson explains in the second paragraph of the novel that Moreno's voice gives a "mistaken impression" of self-effacement because she speaks with a calculated hesitancy that resembles "a stammer" (4). But like the Americans, she cannot tolerate other voices or viewpoints. Her subtle questions confuse and entrap her son, Felipe; with her niece and ward, the half Native American Ramona, she resorts to commands and force. "Silence!" she cries when she catches the girl in an embrace with Alessandro. "Speak not to me!" When Ramona opens her lips, the señora "struck the girl on the mouth, a cruel blow" (110–11). The stroke ricochets to Alessandro, whom the American Farrar will later kill by shooting in the cheek, a brutal literalizing of the voicelessness of the oppressed and a portent in redface of the lynchings of African Americans that would escalate in the late 1880s.

Alessandro, his fellow natives, and their allies are the text's principal targets of silencing, and all have devised versions of the slave's and the freedman's coping tactics. Douglass's precept, "Trust no man," returns here as Alessandro's "motto": "Not one unnecessary word" (290). Jackson adopts a convention of the western form stretching back to Cooper—Indian taciturnity—and she emphasizes the degree to which whites are complicit in, if not causative of, that reticence. If the Indians, as another character says to Felipe, "are as secret as the grave" (320), it is the whites who are bent on putting them there, and only by revealing as little as possible about themselves can they hope to postpone their deaths. Alessandro grows increasingly "chary of speech" (85) as the plot unfolds, reluctant to become entangled in the white-monopolized element, and a "monosyllable" of his, "nay, a look," seems more eloquent to Ramona than the "long sentences" of other men (204). He lets the Indian agent inscribe his name in the government's records in an attempt to save his child, but in doing so, he feels "as if he had put a chain around his neck" (289). The Americans, in any case, have no use for his locutions. Farrar shoots the hero before Alessandro can explain his error in taking the white man's horse, and "the blood was choking in his throat" as he falls to the ground dead without getting out a word (335).

In the end, what replaces language as *Ramona*'s preferred form of communication is that more emotive and universal medium, the lingua franca of the dispossessed, music or song. Jackson's novel thus echoes both the slave narratives and *The Last of the Mohicans*, an earlier tale of tribal extinction in which Uncas and Chingachgook, linguistically disinherited like Alessandro, say all they need to through the musical tones of their voices.[16] (The thematic progression from speech to song in turn foreshadows *Billy Budd*, another late nineteenth-century novel with no visible link to Reconstruction.) Music, distinguished from the transgressions of utterance, emerges as the text's nondestructive repository of value. The "notes" of the hero's singing voice precede him into the action and captivate Ramona (50). "What a voice that Alessandro has," she exclaims to Felipe. "We shall miss his music sorely when he goes, shall we not?" (86). Music solidifies the love affair between Moreno's niece and the handsome native: he calls her "Majella," the Indian name for dove, because "the wood-dove's voice is low like hers, and sweeter than any other sound on the earth" (191). After Alessandro's death, the "notes" of doves cooing to each other, their meaning "plain as if written on a page," always bring back to Ramona the memory of her Indian husband (122 and 353). So Jackson states in the penultimate paragraph; in the final one, her prose imitates the lovers and verges on music or poetry. She slips into a fuguelike string of repetitions and rhymes—"daughters," "daughters were all beautiful," "the most beautiful of them all," "the most beloved," "the eldest one," "the one who," "step-daughter"—ending with the words, "Ramona,—Ramona, daughter of Alessandro the Indian" (353).

Does more than analogy connect Jackson's vanishing Indians to the contemporaneous subjugation of the freedmen? Tourgée's review essay on

Ramona and H. H. Bancroft's *History of the Pacific States* in the *North American Review* leaves no doubt about the answer. According to the former carpetbagger, the two seemingly discrete loci of tyranny, the American South and the Southwest, are impossible to separate and have been intertwined for almost half a century, since the annexation of Texas and the Mexican-American War.

Tourgée's review rehearses a number of his inveterate themes, among them a passionate defense of romance as a fictional genre that addresses large subjects ripe with "the elements of pathos and tragedy."[17] He lodges his customary complaint against American arrogance and disregard for the rights of others. In California, as in other places, the Americans have shown themselves to be "a people who boast of religion and morality, yet are exceptional in the world's history as unscrupulous robbers of the poor and oppressors of the weak." Both books under review illuminate the distinctive character of Mexican civilization. Tourgée singles out as "especially worthy of consideration at this time" the tolerance of our continental neighbors for other races and admixtures, an acceptance rooted in Spanish efforts to convert the natives rather than to destroy them. Mexicans practice an imperfect but real racial harmony in which the mestizo and the mulatto, the Indian and the pure-blooded Creole, enjoy a rough "parity of right." The boasted liberalism of Anglo-Saxons, in contrast, "stumbles always at the color-line," and all who differ from the ruling caste, whether blacks, Indians, or conquered Mexicans, suffer from the denial of civil equality.[18]

So "race-prejudice," overriding the claims of "justice, humanity, or religion," is one area where the betrayal of southern freedmen converges with the conquest of California and New Mexico. But it is not the only area, says Tourgée. In American history, designs on Mexican territory have invariably furthered the oppression of black people, and lebensraum has revived under a Democratic president, Grover Cleveland, and his legions of supporters from below the Mason-Dixon Line. The South "has always been the home of the filibuster," and restless Southerners have always looked with eagerness on Mexico and Central America as targets of acquisition. Before the Civil War, the North often foiled these expansionist ambitions, correctly regarding them as a way to build up the strength of the peculiar institution. But now, continues Tourgée, the people of the North would find much to their own advantage in lands snatched from the Southwest. They would relish the prospects for wealth and imperial swagger, and the votes of enough Republicans in Congress would swing to the

Democrats to allow the Administration to carry out another "such piece of international robbery."[19]

Tourgée was mistaken, of course: Cleveland, unlike his Democratic predecessor in the White House, James K. Polk, did not incite a second war with Mexico. When war came, in 1898, it was under a Republican president, William McKinley, and against the virtually moribund Spanish empire; the fighting took place in Puerto Rico, Cuba, and the Philippines. But Tourgée got it right when he predicted that imperial expansionism, in fortifying national unity, would occur at the expense of American blacks. In his scenario, twelve years before the event, Southerners would rally to an attack outside American borders as a golden opportunity to deflect interest from "old political issues." Fresh plans were afoot to disenfranchise the freedmen, and the result would be a renewed "period of intense partisan conflict" unless the Redeemers could forestall it by directing attention elsewhere. The reviewer felt certain that they would succeed, if not immediately, then eventually, because unreconstructed white supremacists have always been "the boldest and most self-reliant" force in national politics. Tourgée felt certain, too, about the identity of the losers. They would be Mexicans, African Americans, and Indians like Alessandro and Ramona, who would "face hopeless degradation and inevitable extinction under the Anglo-Saxon democracy."[20] And while he did not mention it, another loser in that "Anglo-Saxon" pacification would be the unimpeded speech of all Americans, white as well as black, brown, and red. Tourgée's own voice would be included. It was McKinley, in his second term as president, who named him consul to Bordeaux in exchange for his pledge to maintain a public silence on race.

James and the Monotone of Reunion

The Bostonians (1886) may be the most astute "high cultural" medita-
tion that we have on the intellectual and literary costs of national
reconciliation. The book contains a degree of historical insight about the
aftermath of Reconstruction that was not matched by historians until the
revisionism of the 1960s and 1970s. *The Bostonians* is almost an allegory—
of reunion, of the suppression of language by a triumphant South, and of
the migration of cultural hegemony from the Boston-Cambridge-Concord
area to New York City. *Almost* an allegory: James is a realist, and his story
is a satire. Its targets include Boston reformers, the popular press, and the
emergent world of celebrity.[1] But the novelist's diagnosis of the era, and of
his quondam country—he had settled permanently in London in 1876, the
year Reconstruction unraveled—is so uncannily accurate that a reading
with some allegorical or symbolic flavoring doesn't seem altogether unwarranted. Though James cannot be described as a political writer, he had,
like any literary figure, a strong interest in imaginative freedom; and *The
Bostonians*, with its harsh portrait of the sectional takeover of speech, has
something to tell us about his trajectory as an author.

James's judgment on post-Reconstruction America is suffused with
ambiguity. While he clearly finds the views of Basil Ransom "narrow" and
"reactionary" (adjectives he uses more than once to describe them), his own
perspective is not always sharply differentiated from the ex-Confederate's,
and as the narrative unfolds, the silences and equivocations that envelop
Verena Tarrant and the other Boston women characters gradually master the
novelist himself.[2] This should be seen less as ideological concurrence than
as James's reasonable assessment of the limitations on utterance, and the
realities of the marketplace, in the last quarter of the nineteenth century.
The Bostonians was, after all, serialized in Richard Watson Gilder's *Cen-*

tury magazine, the culture's foremost sponsor of reunion; it ran simultaneously with the famous, and famously "non-partisan," series on *Battles and Leaders of the Civil War*. Gilder had already tipped his hand and ratified the North's newfound nostalgia for the slave plantation by publishing Thomas Nelson Page's story "Marse Chan," and James had spent a weekend with the editor before starting his fiction about New England's eclipse by the South.[3] James would have been obtuse not to grasp what was expected of him; moreover, dependent as always on his pen, he saw "no shame," as he wrote his sister Alice in 1884, "in offering my productions to the widest public, & in their being 'brought home,' as it were, to the great American people."[4] In the end, Jamesian ambiguity, capped by the final sentence informing us that Verena's tears "were not the last she was destined to shed," did not impress American readers (464).[5] It could not save the book from failure, and James became persuaded that Ransom's domineering tongue left no room for his own.

The novel focuses unsparingly on voice. No character in American fiction, with the possible exception (and model) of Arthur Dimmesdale, is so identified with mellifluous utterance as Verena Tarrant. The exclamation "A voice, a human voice, is what we want" (57), heralds her initial appearance in the narrative, at Miss Birdseye's apartment, where she delivers the first of multiple lectures on women's rights. Verena is variously ventriloquized—by her father, Selah, by Olive Chancellor, and ultimately by Basil Ransom, who keeps telling her what she really wants—and the coachings reveal the exhaustion of New England's prophetic idiom. But though James is often satirical about the heroine's opinions, the satire seldom extends to her vocal instrument. The voice "had magic in it" (390), and it casts a spell over everyone who hears her. She is "a vocalist of exquisite faculty"; the "notes of her voice" are "charming" (62); "she speechified as a bird sang" (232). Ransom, who can't abide her ideas, falls in love with Verena's voice and listens to it without attending to the sense. In a strikingly erotic phrase, the Mississippian is said to have "tasted her voice" when Verena addresses the Wednesday Club at the Burrages (275). Later he overhears her practicing her Music Hall speech at Marmion, the sound filling the night air "in ample periods and cadences," and he bursts out involuntarily, "Murder, what a lovely voice" (366).

Murder is of course what Ransom would like to do to the voice by restricting it to a single listener, himself, and eliminating its public message. One is tempted to say that Ransom, with some collusion from James, operates in *The Bostonians* much as Hawthorne did in *The Scarlet Letter*: as the opponent and censor of oratorical flights. James's study of Hawthorne was published in 1879, seven years before his novel. In Hawthorne's earlier tale of "the Bostonians," Dimmesdale possesses "a very peculiar voice," at once majestic and charged with pathos, that touches "a sensibility in every bosom."[6] The minister's voice magnetizes Hester when she listens at a distance to his election sermon; she can't make out the words, but, like Ransom, she is still able to appreciate the sound. Although James says little about Dimmesdale's eloquence in his Hawthorne study, he does note the romancer's antipathy, in *The Life of Franklin Pierce*, to antislavery agitation. Hawthorne regarded that speech as so much airy if dangerous "philanthropic theory," and he complained, in a passage quoted by James, of the "convulsion" it wrought in the polity. Such thoughts could indeed be Ransom's, who parrots a common postwar lament by laying the blame for disunion on abolitionism. "I regard Eliza [Eliza P. Mosely, James's fictionalized Harriet Beecher Stowe] as the cause of the biggest war of which history preserves the record," huffs the Southerner (92). James disagrees with both his character and his predecessor as Boston's chronicler. It was slavery, he insists in *Hawthorne*, and not "humanitarian 'mistiness,'" that plunged the nation into bloodshed, and the only people who suffered "social persecution" from abolitionist speech were the abolitionists themselves.[7]

Ransom updates the crusade against New England radicalism, now much diminished in the person of Miss Tarrant. The Mississippian's desire to woo Verena cannot be separated from his determination to silence her; the two objectives are synonymous. From the instant he sets eyes on "the little prophetess" (228), he "knows a way to strike her dumb" (329): that is, wedlock. This could be read as a feminist critique of nineteenth-century marriage, not surprising from the author of *The Portrait of a Lady* (1881); but no less significant is James's vision of reunion as linguistic bridling. Ransom comes from the "old slave-holding oligarchy" (12), and though like most Southerners he now regrets slavery, he endorses his class's attitude toward the modern world, especially its antipathy to free thought and discussion. His "Southern idea of chivalry," which has, according to James, "a thread of moral tinsel" in it, means forbidding the weaker sex from entertaining opinions different from his own (328). He tells Verena that her feminist sentiments are humbug and that she mustn't continue holding them. An editor to whom he sends a paper on "the rights of minorities" pronounces his thinking more compatible with feudalism than the nineteenth century: "This gentleman pointed out that his doctrines were about three hundred years behind the age; doubtless some magazine of the sixteenth century would have been very happy to print them" (193).

The editor's criticism revives the familiar charge of southern backwardness, an obsolescence typically stigmatized, as in *A Connecticut Yankee in King Arthur's Court*, as medieval. Whatever else James may think of Ransom's tirades against feminization and modern cant, he recognizes their provenance, in the hero's case, in his birthplace's long history of disaffection from democracy. The novelist regularly pokes holes in Ransom's sectional prejudices. The Mississippian can still sound a lot like a slavocrat—he astonishes Miss Birdseye by declaring that secession was "a good cause" (221)—but more often he strikes a Redeemer note in his dismissive contempt for carpetbaggers and everything they sought to accomplish. In his outburst in New York's Central Park, he denounces "those who wanted an extension" of freedom and heaps scorn on "the spread of education" as "a gigantic fraud" (336). Earlier, when he meets Verena's father for the first time, Ransom immediately identifies him with the Northerners who descended on the South during "the horrible period of reconstruction." He fondly remembers having "whipped" such figures "at political meetings," and James leaves it uncertain whether the whippings were purely verbal or physical as well (58). Although this ferocity may constitute an understandable response to the repellent Selah Tarrant, James keeps a marked distance from its ideological coordinates. In the park scene, Verena experiences Ransom's "bitterness" toward modern reforms as "aggressive and merciless," and she has to struggle "to forgive him for so much contempt and brutality" (336). Here the novelist appears to side with his heroine; certainly he would have had a much more nuanced perspective on Reconstruction. Two of his brothers served in the Civil War with black regiments—one, Wilky, with Colonel Shaw's celebrated Massachusetts 54th—and both returned to the South to try to improve the lot of the freedmen.[8]

Ransom can be regarded as a carpetbagger in reverse, an unreconstructed Southerner who ventures into the North to make his fortune and strike down unwelcome utterance at its source. He succeeds where Comfort Servosse fails. The vestige of Boston's greatness, Miss Birdseye, misconceives his presence altogether. She believes Ransom will be taken in hand by Verena, "a daughter of New England trained in the right school," and brought around to enlightened attitudes (378). That outcome would repeat the Union's victory on the battlefield, but the opposite occurs, and James subtly portrays the reversal as a second military confrontation between the sections, with the South coming out on top this time. As she begins to realize her danger, the novelist says, Verena "had taken up her weapons, she had told Olive she was exposed, she had asked *her* to be her defense" (386). Though the heroine promises not to "sleep at her post,"

Ransom proves too superior an adversary; defecting to the enemy, Verena consents "to drag her former standard in the dust" (387 and 399). James may have spent much of the previous decade in England, but an ocean's distance from the United States did not blind him to his own section's decline in toughness and moral fiber. He is not Tourgée raging at the feckless Wise Men, but the two authors share an insight into northern complicity with the forces of reaction. Verena's "nature [is] to be easily submissive, to like being overborne" (337). She recognizes all along that her suitor wants her "never to give another address, to open my mouth in public" (384), but the awareness fails to cure her infatuation. Reprising the post-Reconstruction North, she is an active (or rather passive) accomplice in her own gagging.

Miss Tarrant is not the only character whom Ransom deprives of speech. His first casualty, surprisingly, is Miss Birdseye, who allows herself to be manipulated by his calculated self-description as "a possible convert" (226). The "frumpy little missionary," a link to "the heroic age of New England life" (183), has had direct encounters with slaveholder intolerance. As she explains many times to Ransom, she was routinely harassed for speaking and distributing Bibles to black people in the antebellum South. Now, in the epicenter of agitation, repression tracks her down again, and she agrees, at Ransom's importuning, not to apprise Olive about his being in Boston: "I won't say anything" (226). Ransom extracts a similar promise of silence from Dr. Prance when he bumps into her on a night walk at Marmion. As for Verena, long before she gives up public speaking, the feminist oracle acquires the habit of self-censorship by keeping her meetings with Ransom a secret from Olive. She says nothing about his outing with her in Cambridge; she has "been covering up for ever so many weeks" their talks in New York (300). Eventually Verena repents her "perfidious silence" (394), but her pursuer's intervention at Cape Cod has the effect of stilling not just her voice but Miss Chancellor's as well. On their last night at Marmion, the two women sit mournfully in Olive's house without exchanging a word. Verena "was unwilling to speak. . . . she appeared not even to wish to hear the sound of her own voice. Her silence itself was an appeal—an appeal to Olive to ask no questions. . . . Olive understood. . . . and for an hour, as nightfall settled in the room, neither of the young women spoke" (425). The contagion of aphonia culminates at the Music Hall, where Ransom spirits Verena away from the waiting audience.

There can be no doubt that force, sometimes soft and sometimes coercive, hastens Verena's capitulation. She may consent to Ransom's attentions,

but—as the invocation of Miss Birdseye's southern experience suggests—
violence is never far from his actions. James compares his heroine to the
most notorious victim of slaveholder aggression, the runaway slave. Ransom, whose instinct is "to press, to press, always to press" (399), arrives
at Marmion determined "to take possession of Verena Tarrant" (359). Prepared to resort to "kidnapping" if necessary (405), he seizes her arm and
compels her to walk with him when she protests. Nor does he respect Verena's pleas for a reprieve at the Music Hall; continuing the ownership motif, he tells her, "You are mine, you are not theirs" (455). Ransom imagines
himself during this episode as "a young man" resolved "to discharge a pistol at the king or the president" (442), and the implied analogy to John Wilkes Booth and the assassination of Lincoln allies his campaign with southern vengeance against the North.[9] Verena's seizure is a rendition, in the
city from which Anthony Burns was returned to bondage, and Ransom's
foray northward, from this perspective, resembles the successful incursion
of a slave catcher. Verena's final mutation seems almost inevitable: in the
concluding paragraph, her muffling evokes the plight of the freedmen after
Reconstruction. Ransom throws the hood of her cape over Verena's head
"to conceal her face and her identity," and he pulls her through the mill-
ing crowd without anyone recognizing her (464). Like Henry Johnson of
Crane's *The Monster* and like the "black folk" of W. E. B. Du Bois, the
heroine is speechless and invisible behind the veil.

As Verena falls silent in *The Bostonians*, Ransom asserts his monopoly
over language. He is the seeker of her hand and the rival of her voice. The
first two-thirds or so of the novel dwell on Verena's verbal facility. In book 1,
at Miss Birdseye's, she delivers the half-hour address that galvanizes Olive and arouses Ransom's romantic interest; James provides several pages
of quotation and summary. (Ransom is captivated by her appearance and
tone, not "the inanities she uttered" [62].) Book 2 finds her lecturing at
the Burrage home before an assemblage of well-to-do and influential New
Yorkers. Ransom, listening from the back of the room, feels that Verena's
voice "had developed; he had forgotten how beautiful it could be when she
raised it to its full capacity" (270). James again includes a synopsis and a
few quoted passages, but the tide of discourse has begun to shift in the
Southerner's favor, and the novelist "does not deem it necessary to give a
larger specimen of Verena's eloquence" (274). Thereafter, and especially in
book 3 (the last book), Ransom's speaking part expands, while the heroine's radically contracts.

It has always been the Mississippian's ambition to educate the age,
substituting his own "narrow notions" (343) for the "third-rate palaver" of

women reformers (328). Toward the end of book 2, resolved "to take possession of Verena" for a day (327), he brings her to Central Park and gives his
impassioned speech assailing the "damnable feminization" of the present.
Although the rejection of this screed "by leading periodicals was certainly
not a matter for surprise" (343), according to James, the novelist proves
unable to keep his reactionary's opinions from taking command of *The
Bostonians*. Ransom makes his debut as an author in book 3, getting an
article accepted by the *Rational Review*, and the good news persuades him
to propose to Verena. "He speaks with the pen," she proudly tells Miss
Birdseye (380), and Ransom now feels confident that he can earn a living
from his writing. But as Verena knows better than anyone, Ransom also
speaks, and does so successfully, with his mouth. The "atrocious spell" he
has over her (420)—the phrase is Olive's—has been created, as spells usually are, by endless talking, arguing, haranguing, discussing, and plead-
ing. After Ransom says that matrimony is Verena's true vocation, James
observes that "these words, the most effective and penetrating he had uttered, had sunk into her soul and worked and fermented there. She had
come at last to believe them, and that was the alteration, the transformation" (396). At Marmion, his siege of her is mainly verbal: he makes her
promise to spend an hour a day with him for three weeks, "and what had
Verena done for the past three weeks but listen?" (415). She will do little
else for the rest of her life. The young woman who renounces her extraordinary voice will spend her marriage entertained and constrained by Basil
Ransom's confabulations.

The couple will make their residence, appropriately, in New York, that
state with a record of sympathy for the South and an important electoral
catalyst in the forging of reunion. In 1884, just after James returned to
London, Grover Cleveland, ex-governor of the Empire State, captured the
executive branch with Bourbon backing. New York City was home to
the *Century* and, increasingly, the publishing industry; the metropolis's
newspapers and magazines attracted readers across the country, and authors wishing to reach the mass public had to place their work there. (One
assumes that the *Rational Review* has its office in Manhattan.) Portions
of Howells's *The Rise of Silas Lapham* (1885) and Twain's *Adventures of
Huckleberry Finn* (1885) overlapped with *The Bostonians* in the *Century*;
Howells, long affiliated with New England and the *Atlantic*, recognized
the change in cultural preeminence by agreeing, in 1886, to contribute
a monthly column to *Harper's Monthly*. James, in constant negotiations
with publishers and editors and worried over the fluctuating market for his
fiction, knew the score when it came to the new literary terrain. If he had

any doubts, they were dispelled by the bankruptcy of his American publisher, James R. Osgood of Boston, while his novel was being serialized.[10] In the "indivisible political organism" (13) that was now the United States, media leadership belonged to New York, and New York had had enough of social revolutions—or, as Ransom puts it, of "an age of hollow phrases and false delicacy and exaggerated solicitudes and coddled sensibilities" (343). The Southerner's words will drown out Verena's in the reunified republic's cultural capital.

This turn of events appears to intimidate Verena's creator too, or at least to leave James with a sense that the narrowed range of thinking in his homeland set limits on what he could say in his fiction. At times he veers close to the ideology of conciliation, which celebrated the war as collective sacrifice but ignored the values for which the Union fought. During Ransom's visit with Verena to Harvard's Memorial Hall, the novelist describes the high chamber, its walls lined with tablets to the dead, as a "temple to youth, manhood, generosity." The hero forgets "the whole question of sides and parties" to admire the room that arches impartially over "friends as well as enemies, the victims of defeat as well as the sons of triumph" (248). Are the sentiments James's, or are they a concession to "the great American people" he was trying to court? Are they both? What we can say with assurance is that the novelist grows more taciturn as Ransom sights victory. For most of the narrative, James freely enters his characters' minds and relates their thoughts. He editorializes, he criticizes, he tells us that his ex-Confederate's view of women would have incurred the contempt of "superior minds" (328). But as the novel nears its close, he repeatedly withholds information and foregrounds his silences. The scene at Marmion, where Olive and Miss Tarrant sit soundlessly in the dark, is illustrative. Within the space of a single paragraph, James pleads "his incompetence to give an answer," alludes to "mysteries into which I shall not attempt to enter," and disavows "speculations with which I have no concern" (422–23). The process climaxes as the story does, with Verena's abduction from the Music Hall. When Ransom, "palpitating with his victory," hurries the veiled heroine into the street, denying the public her voice, James seems overborne himself (464). He leaves the reader in the dark by not reporting Olive's improvised speech.

Twenty years after he created Basil Ransom, James returned to the theme of the silencing South in *The American Scene* (1907), an account of a tour of his transformed, money-obsessed country. He had last visited the United States in 1883, gathering impressions for *The Bostonians*; he did not make another trip until the one that inspired the new book, in 1904–5. A motive for the long hiatus might have been his suspicion, implicit in the novel, that his natal land was not receptive to independent reflections. His experience with *The American Scene* would prove the accuracy of that perception.

A good portion of the book is devoted to travels in Maryland, Virginia, South Carolina, and Florida, and James finds some things unchanged from the antebellum era. He claims that "the old Southern idea," the project of "a vast Slave State" isolated from the modern world, has left indelible traces on the region, despite slavery's having been extinct for forty years. The intellectual blockade of the South, he continues in the chapter "Richmond," meant "a general and a permanent quarantine; meant the eternal bowdlerization of books and journals; meant in fine all literature and all art on an expurgatory index. It meant, still further, an active and ardent propaganda; the reorganization of the school, the college, the university, in the interest of the new criticism." The war did not abolish "the prison of the Southern spirit," and race—"the intimate presence of the negro"— has replaced bondage as the cause of censorship. "Preaching" against this bigotry would be salutary, James feels, but he hastens to add that candor "would never prove oil upon the waters." The mechanisms of repression reach the author of *The American Scene*: "The lips of the non-resident were, at all events, not the lips to utter this wisdom; the non-residents might well feel themselves indeed, after a while, appointed to silence, and, with any delicacy, see their duty quite elsewhere." One must tread "on tip-toe," James concludes, and he takes his own advice to heart and says nothing when he meets a handsome Virginian—shades of Basil Ransom!—who describes how his father killed a Union soldier. The young man, "all fair, engaging, smiling" would not, in 1905, hurt "a Northern fly." Yet that does not stop him from regaling James with grisly details of what "he would have done to a Southern negro."[11]

It almost reads like a gloss on *The Bostonians*, and just as that novel ends with a southern-dominated reunion, so *The American Scene* concludes with James's journey to the former Confederacy; the South is the last we see of the United States. Are the two geographical entities, one locked in a tawdry past, one the cutting edge of the equally crude future, somehow cognate in James's vision? In one respect, they would seem to be. When the book of travels and reflections appeared from Harper's in New York—a city, James says, consecrated to "the commercial at any cost"—it was missing the famous peroration (from the chapter "Florida") on the United States as "the triumph of the superficial and the apotheosis of the raw." The passage was included in the British edition, and Leon Edel speculates that the American publishers excised it to spare the sensibilities of native readers. James himself apparently did not review the Harper's proofs.[12]

The forced truncating, if that is what happened, would have confirmed that James's entire homeland was no more hospitable to unflattering ideas than the backward-looking South. In the preface to the New York edition of his works that he prepared for Scribner's in 1907, the novelist professed to see little difference between the sections. Rereading his book, he found it "as difficult . . . to trace the dividing-line between the real and the romantic as to plant a milestone between north and south."[13] The New York edition was planned to generate some needed income for the author, and James made a point of omitting *The Bostonians*, indisputably one of his major novels, from the collected volumes. His reasons are unknown, but his discomfort with the United States as a field of fiction is a biographical fact. After inventing the plot and characters of *The Bostonians*, Henry James never completed another novel whose action takes place in America. He attempted one such work, *The Ivory Tower*, but his progress on it was uneven, and it exists only as a fragment.[14] He appears to have felt that the creative latitude necessary for a full-length novel was simply not available to him on American soil, whether that soil was actual or imaginary. James was as much a nonresident of his birthplace as he was of Richmond or Charleston, and he must have decided, as he did in the presence of the murderous Virginian, that discretion was preferable to provocation.

Was Twain Black?

Mark Twain was a racial progressive who was also a celebrity, in love with his fame and chronically desirous of money, and the combination ensured that the culture's contraction of acceptable discourse about race would limit his choices as a writer. The most popular and successful author of his era had to exercise an inveterate circumspection about who he was and what he thought. Twain both accepted and loathed this state of affairs as a condition of his renown, and he turned it into a central theme of his fictions. The best of them—*Adventures of Huckleberry Finn* (1885) and *Pudd'nhead Wilson* (1894)—dwell obsessively on the risk of verbal indiscretion and the fear of being found out. Huck Finn, Jim, Roxy, Tom Driscoll, and—until the climactic trial scene that establishes him as "a made man for good"—Pudd'nhead Wilson (165) all have to dissemble to survive.[1] The particular survival strategy—concealing one's true nature behind a veil, shuffling (i.e., being accommodating) to disarm attack—had of course prevailed under slavery and became second nature to the freedmen once again under the racist regime that followed Reconstruction. Three of the characters cited above are black; a fourth, Huck, has been conjectured to have a black source; and the fifth, Wilson, emerges as an object lesson in the cost of popularity. Samuel Langhorne Clemens may have been white, but the question seems inevitable about his double, the public persona who was censored and censored himself in his art: was "Mark Twain" black?[2]

A "jackleg" novelist (169), as he describes himself in his author's note to *Those Extraordinary Twins* (1894), Twain wrote a total of just seven novels. One, *The Gilded Age* (1873), he coauthored with Charles Dudley Warner; the remaining six appeared between 1876 (*Tom Sawyer*) and 1894 (*Pudd'nhead Wilson*, his last completed novel). His career as an independent novelist

224

covered the dissolution of the nation's experiment in racial justice, beginning as Reconstruction crumbled and ending two years before its epitaph in *Plessy v. Ferguson*. Not one of his fictions announces itself as a story about race after Reconstruction; rather, with the exception of the weak *American Claimant* (1892), they deal with the slaveholding past or with medieval England (*The Prince and the Pauper* [1882] and *A Connecticut Yankee in King Arthur's Court* [1889]). This says less about Twain's interests than about his internalized checks on directly addressing the explosive subject before a national, and increasingly "southernized," audience.

In fact, all the novels arguably do address that concern, the slavery fictions most obviously but the feudal narratives, in their aspiration to counter or rewrite Sir Walter Scott, only slightly less so. Twain laid into Scott in *Life on the Mississippi*, the travel book he published two years before *Huckleberry Finn*. There he famously charged the romancer with being "responsible" for the Civil War. The addiction to unreality fostered by Scott's "Middle Age sham civilization," according to Twain, continues to obstruct progress in the postwar South, where "reverence for rank and caste" has outlasted Appomattox. The principal culprit is *Ivanhoe*, proof "of the power of a single book for good or harm." As an example of literature's constructive influence, Twain cites Cervantes's *Don Quixote*, a tale that debunked "chivalry-silliness" but is now "pretty much a dead letter, so effectually has Scott's pernicious work undermined it."[3] In *Huckleberry Finn*, Tom Sawyer still cherishes *Don Quixote*, but, being a conventional Southerner, he completely misinterprets the novel as a defense of "enchantment" (16).[4] Twain's English romances are Cervantes-like efforts at reconstructing the medieval South, displaced reenactments in fiction of the revolution carried out by the Radical Republicans. He doubtless supposed that the novels would have some modest power for good among readers infatuated with Scott; but he had abandoned any such hopes by 1889 and *A Connecticut Yankee*. The story of Hank Morgan retells the collapse of Reconstruction and makes almost if not quite explicit Twain's disgust with southern recalcitrance. It is also a requiem for the verbal's efficacy, and it forms the necessary bridge between *Huckleberry Finn* and the darkening vision and self-criticism of *Pudd'nhead Wilson*.

Twain could have mentioned his Hartford neighbor Harriet Beecher Stowe and *Uncle Tom's Cabin* as a more recent instance of fiction's activism; but however much he would have relished Stowe's sales, he coveted popular adulation too avidly to emulate her forthrightness. Aiming at a mainly regional (northern) audience, the antebellum Stowe did not worry about gratifying the millions. Twain's reputation and financial well-being depended on his reaching a mass readership, and he had an unusually direct investment in how his books were received. All his writings were issued by subscription publishers, houses that sold their merchandise door to door through canvassers carrying sample chapters and illustrations. Bookstores did not stock subscription volumes, which targeted rural households and were not produced in advance; the canvassers had to line up sufficient purchasers for the printing to begin.[5] This intimate involvement with the consumer was magnified, in Twain's case, by his having founded his own subscription firm, Charles L. Webster and Company, to market his fiction, starting with *Huckleberry Finn*. He had, then, a double reason to be cautious about his speech: a book of his that failed could send the publishing business he owned into bankruptcy.

So not only was Twain a public performer of his stories, in constant contact with live audiences, but his very method of selling his works brought him into close proximity with the likes and dislikes, the tolerances and intolerances, of the American public. That mass readership, its sights on reunion, its sympathies more "Johnny Reb" by the day, had decreasing patience for schemes of racial equality. In the decade between *Huckleberry Finn* and *Pudd'nhead Wilson*, subscription lists were dominated by histories of the Civil War and memoirs and biographies of its heroes. (Twain himself obtained Grant's *Memoirs* [1885] for Webster and Company.) These books exalted common sacrifice over ideological difference, and no other genre could rival their appeal to the public.[6] Twain's decidedly deflationary "The Private History of a Campaign That Failed" (1885), which recounts his desertion from the Confederate army, gives some sense of his distance from this trend, even as the piece's appearance in Gilder's *Century* alongside more heroic recollections shows how readily he allowed the distinction to be lost. *Huckleberry Finn*, published the same year, was excerpted by Gilder for his magazine and read aloud to enthusiastic gatherings of up to a thousand on the platform tour that Twain undertook with George Washington Cable. The novel brilliantly incorporates oral storytelling techniques into prose fiction. It is narrated by its boy protagonist, but Huck's sense of being continually monitored, and of having to adjust his words accordingly, owes a good deal to the situation of his creator. Neither Twain nor his fable-making character could escape the ordeal of immediate reception by auditors.

No reader of *Huckleberry Finn* can miss the atmosphere of surveillance. Huck is watched and/or regulated by Miss Watson and the Widow Douglas, representatives of respectable society; by his father Pap, an embodi-

ment of herrenvolk democracy; and by Tom Sawyer, who recruits him for
his gang of robbers and, anticipating the Duke and the King, imposes on
him a Walter Scott–like regime of make-believe, secrecy, and silence. In
all these instances, language emerges as a primary object of control. When
Huck expresses a preference to go to hell (foreshadowing his celebrated
decision in chapter 31), Miss Watson tells him, "it was wicked to say what
I said." He doesn't mention the subject again "because it would only make
trouble, and wouldn't do no good" (8). Tom, too, disciplines his friend's
tongue. He requires Huck to take an oath swearing allegiance to his band
and promising never to reveal its secrets; anyone who does so "must have
his throat cut" (12). As for Pap, he becomes incensed at Huck's going to
school and vows to thrash him for learning to read and write.

Practically everything Huck experiences after fleeing home reinforces
the lesson that careless or unauthorized words can be dangerous. On the
wreck of the *Walter Scott*, an actual gang of robbers literalizes Tom's rules:
they plan to murder one of their members because "he's said he'll tell, and
he will" (59). In a ramshackle Arkansas town, impolitic speech leads to a
killing in broad daylight before a crowd of hundreds. The drunken Boggs
infuriates Colonel Sherburn by calling him "everything he could lay his
tongue to," and when the foolish man ignores a warning not to "open [his]
mouth" again after one o'clock, the Colonel shoots him dead (114–15).

Huck himself proves remarkably adept at managing his own speech
so as not to affront his culture's restrictions on utterance. He keeps his
mouth shut with Miss Watson, with his father, and with the Duke and
the King. Realizing that the last two are charlatans, he "never said nothing, never let on; kept it to myself; it's the best way, then you don't have
no quarrels, and don't get into no trouble" (102). Huck also practices lying, selective withholding, impersonation (of a girl, of an English valet, of
Tom Sawyer), and the fabrication of extended stories. Some of the stories
he acts out. He stages his own death in order to get free from Pap, but more
often he elaborately vocalizes his yarns, with trumped-up details about
his family history or Jim's identity. "I told them how . . ." (82), he charac-
teristically begins a narration at the Grangerfords', where he morphs into
"George Jackson" from Arkansas, and he has to devise one "stretcher"
(139) after another at the Wilkses to allay suspicion about his ignorance
of England. Although Huck is not unique in his storytelling—the phony
royals deploy endless falsehoods to exploit others—his own fictions and
self-censorship have the goal of protecting himself and others. In this respect, he *is* unique, or rather, he resembles the white Southerners far less
than the black ones.

Start with the simple fact that Huck is a runaway who allies himself with a runaway slave. At critical moments, the two characters converge, as when Huck shouts upon his return to Jackson's Island, "Git up and hump yourself, Jim! There ain't a minute to lose. They're after us!" (54). The "us" here has roots in the white youngster's experience; he is accustomed to being whipped like a slave by his father—"I was all over welts," he complains (24)—and, to keep him from running off, Pap locks him in his cabin, just as Jim will later be imprisoned at the Phelpses. All the slaves in the novel appreciate the value of playacting and holding their tongues. Jack, Huck's slave-on-loan at the Grangerfords', does not reveal that Jim is nearby; instead, he offers to show Huck a nest of water moccasins: "If anything happens, *he* ain't mixed up in it. He can say he never seen us together, and it'll be the truth" (93). As an escaped slave, Jim has to take special care to guard against indiscriminate speech. Like the runaways in countless slave autobiographies, he and Huck swear not to disclose each other's secrets:

> "But mind, you said you wouldn't tell—you know you said you wouldn't tell, Huck."
> "Well, I did. I said I wouldn't, and I'll stick to it. . . . People would call me a low down Abolitionist and despise me for keeping mum—but that don't make no difference. I ain't agoing to tell . . ." (39)

And Huck does stick to it, even though sorely tempted by conscience in chapter 31 to betray Jim and violate his fugitive's vow of silence. Only when the two are alone on the raft, safe from the supervision of shore society, can they speak without impediment: "I told Jim everything" (165).

Twain did not live on a raft, and he did not have the luxury of silence (strategic silence was another matter) when in the presence of a paying audience. But he knew perfectly well, as Huck puts it, that a person telling the truth "when he is in a tight spot, is taking considerable many resks" (148). To cope with potentially hostile readers and listeners, the novelist adopted his protagonist's (black) subterfuge of accommodation: "If I never learnt nothing else out of pap, I learnt that the best way to get along with his kind of people is to let them have their own way" (102). Not unexpectedly, audiences did not come out of such encounters in a flattering light, at least to judge from *Huckleberry Finn*. There are few novels in the nineteenth-century American canon that present such a relentlessly negative picture of the public for entertainment. The heartless audience at the circus, laughing at the putative drunk's wild horseback ride (which Huck watches fearfully, "all of a tremble to see his danger" [120]), is typical, as are the people at *The Royal Nonesuch,* who, feeling "badly sold" (122), plan to tar and feather the performers. Spectators, or, better yet, mobs, for real-life performances belong in the same category. When the unarmed Boggs, mortally wounded, drops to the ground, the crowd "shouldered and jammed one another, with their necks stretched, trying to see" (116). Huck and the two frauds are able to make their escape from the Wilkses because the townspeople, finding a bag of gold in Peter's coffin, forget about them in their scramble to get a look.

Twain's treatment of the spectacle-spectator phenomenon contains an unmistakable element of self-criticism. Entertainers in the narrative don't fare much better than their publics. This is especially true of the Duke and the King, who possess an acute understanding of the popular temperament and, like their creator, are experienced hands at attracting and amusing customers. The Duke boasts that "he could size up their style," which is for "something ruther worse then low comedy," and he promotes *The Royal Nonesuch* by advertising it as off-limits for women and children. "There," he says, "if that line don't fetch them, I don't know Arkansaw!" (121). (It is a truism that Twain excelled at "low comedy"—and was defensive about it.) Although the staging of the "play" reeks of fraud, the impostors are genuinely talented performers. The King makes a killing at the Pokeville revival meeting by passing himself off as a reformed pirate, and at *The Royal Nonesuch* he has the audience in stitches with his obscene prancing. An impressed Huck observes, "Well, it would make a cow laugh to see the shines that old idiot cut" (122).

It should not surprise us that Huck can appreciate the King's gift; in certain respects, they resemble each other. They have in common a quick-witted resourcefulness, on evidence when the inventive faker, "in a tight spot" indeed, thinks up the blue arrow tattoo on Peter's breast, or when Huck, approaching the Phelps place, trusts "to Providence to put the right words in my mouth" (173). The point is not that Twain conflates the two characters, but that he recognizes how easily Huck's, or rather his own, masquerade can slide into something conscienceless. Unlike his hero, but very much like the King, the author of *Huckleberry Finn* does his storytelling and performing for money.

Which brings us to the evasion. Critical opinion has long split on the merits of the last quarter of the novel, where Tom Sawyer reappears and subjects Huck and Jim to a protracted charade "to set a free nigger free" (227). The critical division has been encapsulated by the title of a valuable collection of essays, *Satire or Evasion?*[7] But the choice is a false one: the ending should be seen as both satire and evasion, an inseparable mixture of self-conscious critique and betrayal. Tom humiliates Jim, and Huck as well, and Twain, always aware of what would appeal to audiences, was complicit in that demeaning. Like Tom, he loved fame and savored the admiration he garnered for staging Jim's escape "slick" and "elegant" (216). He made the ending a regular feature of his lucrative reading tour with Cable (and of later tours), reenacting the scenes with flair and delighting in the applause and laughter that his showmanship generated. But Twain could also recoil in self-disgust from his performance of the evasion. The reasons for this abound in the ending's subtext, which concerns the Bourbon overthrow of Reconstruction and the devastating consequences for the freedmen.[8]

Twain had stopped work on *Huckleberry Finn* during the Compromise of 1876–77, which led to the removal of federal troops from the South. When he took up the manuscript again, he added material reflecting his pessimism about the region's future. Textual traces of the new old order include Pap's outrage at free blacks voting and the attempted hanging of Colonel Sherburn, who assails lynchers for wearing masks and operating in the dark. (For good measure, Sherburn takes a verbal shot at northern cowardice.) Behind these episodes lie widespread attacks on black suffrage and the marauding of the KKK and other terrorist organizations. Most relevant for the evasion are the multiple affinities between Tom, who dominates the final pages, and the Duke and the King, who occupy much of the middle section.[9] As their bogus titles suggest, the two "royals" have their sources in both the medievalism of Sir Walter Scott and the contemporaneous dismantling of racial gains.

The "Bourbons," the name given to those "redeeming" the ex-Confederacy—that is, the old planter class, determined to recoup its power—was meant to evoke European royalty, fit rulers for a society still clinging, as Twain put it in discussing Scott, to the "absurd" past's worship of "rank and caste." In *Huckleberry Finn*, Huck and Jim discover a cache of books on the wreck of the *Walter Scott*, and soon enough the two frauds turn up, as though summoned straight out of the pages of the romancer. One declares that he is the lineal descendant of "the rightful Duke of Bridgewater"; the second claims to be "the pore disappeared Dauphin, Looy the Seventeenth, son of Looy the Sixteen and Marry Antonette," and thus "the rightful King of France" (100–101). (His supposed parents perished on the guillotine; in the same chapter from *Life on the Mississippi* where he dissected Scott and his poisonous influence below the Mason-Dixon Line, Twain defended the French uprising that exacted the heads of Marie Antoinette and her spouse. The Revolution, he said, "broke the chains of the *ancien régime*" and "made of a nation of abject slaves a nation of freemen."[10] Previewing Tom, and modeling post-Reconstruction realities, the pair of mountebanks lord it over Huck and Jim and sell the runaway slave back into bondage for forty dollars.

Tom, for his part, materializes at the very moment the King and the Duke evacuate the text, in the chapter where we last see them on a rail daubed in tar and feathers. Successor to the Scott-like twosome, Sawyer has learned his cruel rigmarole from the same kind of books out of which they emerged, including Dumas's *The Count of Monte Cristo* and Carlyle's *The French Revolution*; and in contrast to Twain, who grew more enthusiastic about the French Revolution as Bourbonism tightened its grip on the South, Tom wishes he could have been there to save Louis XVI, the King's father, by rushing him "over the *border*" (216). Huck's friend is a junior-league Redeemer, spouting the high-minded and "inflated speech" characteristic of that group.[11] He is "full of principle" (194) and talks endlessly about honor and morality. Tom restores things to the status quo ante, freeing "a free nigger" precisely because he would never have emancipated an enslaved one. Like the historical Redeemers, he may try to delude us (and himself) by pretending that Jim is now, in 1885, "as free as any cretur that walks this earth" (226). But we and Mark Twain know better. Nor does Twain's audience escape critical judgment. The burlesque ending implicitly skewers them, too, for their moral smugness in embracing antislavery two decades after the institution was abolished.[12]

It is all so tacit and, well, "private"—rather like Twain's unpublicized acts of support for blacks or Booker T. Washington's backstage lobbying against legal discrimination. Exactly: an overt attack on white supremacy would have destroyed Twain's reputation as America's humorist, the Lincoln of our literature, as William Dean Howells called him (at a time when Southerners, and many Northerners, too, were portraying Lincoln as a dyed-in-the-wool racist who would never have endorsed the Fourteenth and Fifteenth Amendments). A muteness, the silence of external repression and internalized policing, suffuses the text structurally as well as thematically, which may help to account for Twain's fascination with deaf-and-dumb characters, such as Jim's daughter Elizabeth and William Wilkes. The auto-censorship makes it all the more ironic that *Huckleberry Finn* has been the target in this century of various campaigns to ban or bowdlerize the book, on the grounds that it degrades Jim and confers legitimacy on the word "nigger." In 1957 the National Association for the Advancement of Colored People charged the novel with racism, and since the 1980s it has been proscribed or boycotted in Illinois, Virginia, Oklahoma, and New Jersey. I think these efforts misguided; more important, I think they overlook the extent to which the text telegraphs its own muzzling and implicitly denounces the insouciance about racist behavior that its author and characters (and audience) are guilty of.

Twain's next novel, *A Connecticut Yankee in King Arthur's Court*, takes his anger about southern recidivism a step closer to the surface. There is the usual evasion or evasiveness: the action, in which ingrained habits of thought vanquish "progress," is transferred thirteen centuries into the past. Twain had no intention of being lumped together with Cable or Tourgée, politically fearless writers on the postbellum retreat who went more and more unread as tedious scolds.[13] The reference to Tourgée is deliberate. If Twain's antiromance is in one respect an attempt to Americanize Cervantes, in another it can be read as an early medieval reworking of *A Fool's Errand*, with Hank Morgan in the role of the idealistic stranger ignorant of feudalism's staying power. Twain's fiction far outstrips its predecessors in its appetite for retributive bloodletting, but by 1889 he couldn't believe that even a wholesale extermination of the ruling class would wean the ex-Confederacy from its culture of injustice.

In the four years since *Huckleberry Finn*, the situation in the South, after appearing to stabilize, had rapidly deteriorated. Grover Cleveland of New York, the first Democratic president since James Buchanan, had been elected in 1884 with the backing of reform-minded mugwumps such as Twain. Although Cleveland had promised to protect voting rights, it quickly emerged that the southern oligarchs to whom he owed his victory had different ideas. By the mid- to late 1880s, lynching was on the rise, and violent or fraudulent disenfranchisement of the freedmen had become commonplace. Henry Lodge of Massachusetts, sponsor of a reinvigorated enforcement bill, warned (in an unconscious echo of Twain on Cervantes) against the systematic reduction of the Fifteenth Amendment to "a dead letter."[14]

Twain's response to these developments can be traced in his growing appreciation, not just for the French Revolution, always associated in his mind with the overthrow of the slavocracy, but with the most ruthless phase of that upheaval, the Reign of Terror. While composing *A Connecticut Yankee*, he paused in his labors at least twice to reread Carlyle's *The French Revolution*, one of Tom Sawyer's favorite "authorities," and he turned more radical with each revisiting of his source. Twain observed in 1887 that when he had first finished the Carlyle, he was a Girondin; "now I lay the book down once more, and recognize that I am a Sansculotte!—

And not a pale, characterless Sansculotte, but a Marat." (Recall that according to Tourgée, the nearest American equivalent for *sans-culotte* was "carpetbagger.") Another rereading, and Twain justified the "blood, and terror, and various suffering" of the Revolution as an unavoidable stage in human emancipation. The "sublime result," French liberty, was worth the price.[15] Around this time Twain inserted into *A Connecticut Yankee* a passage arguing that France had experienced "two Reigns of Terror," the one lasting a few months and costing ten thousand lives, the other abiding for centuries and claiming a hundred million victims. We "have all been so diligently taught" to abhor the first Terror, he wrote, but the "real Terror" is the earlier tyranny, "that unspeakably bitter and awful Terror which none of us has been taught to see in its vastness or pity as it deserves" (86–87).[16]

Twain's emphasis in this statement on education or training spotlights the continuity between his book and *A Fool's Errand*; it also points to the difficulty facing anyone, whether Hank Morgan, Comfort Servosse, or the novelist himself, for that matter, who would overturn "inherited ideas." As we have seen, Tourgée's hero migrates to postwar North Carolina to seek opportunity and aid the freedmen. He comes to realize that the stranglehold of custom and upbringing dooms his plans and the whole Radical Republican project. *A Connecticut Yankee* charts a similar course for Hank, Twain's equally naive protagonist, whose idealism, encountering the obstinacy of Arthurian tradition, sours into disillusioned fury.

The American correlates of Twain's tale are manifest if also highly unstable, especially in chronology: at one moment we are reminded of the slaveholding South, at the next of the promise and subsequent undoing of Reconstruction. The unavoidable conclusion is that little separates the two periods. (Tourgée frequently makes the same point.) Camelot is not North Carolina, but it could well be the neighboring state of South Carolina, instigator of secession. Hank initially suspects that he has wandered into an asylum, and South Carolina had a well-deserved reputation for "eccentricities and heresies" (Lincoln's words); a state legislator once remarked that it "is too large to be a lunatic asylum and too small to be a republic."[17] Like the antebellum South, sixth-century England is divided into three tiers, aristocrats, slaves, and impoverished freemen, with the last, twins of "the 'poor whites' of our South," regularly siding with the "slave-lords" who oppress them (229). The slaves are themselves white, and Hank and the king endure the humiliation of being sold at auction. But the civilizing of Camelot through external intervention brings us abruptly up to carpetbagger rule. After he awes the natives and acquires his title as "the Boss," Hank sets about transforming Arthur's kingdom into a democratic nation: he establishes schools, builds factories, puts the nobility to work, and introduces improvements such as the newspaper and the telephone. The land of the Round Table seems well on the way to joining the nineteenth century.

It doesn't last. In a moment of doubt, Twain's Yankee speculates that any successful revolution "must *begin* in blood," and that petrified beliefs will have to be eradicated through "a reign of Terror and a guillotine" (135). The prophecy comes back to haunt the narrative. While Hank is away on a visit to France, the proponents of caste conspire with the "slave pen" of established religion (135) to reassert hegemony and liquidate all evidence of progress. The reversal comes with startling speed, through an interdict handed down by the church, and its completeness feeds the tormented mood of the final pages, where a mere fifty-two boys, those young enough to have had the superstition educated out of them, refuse to turn against the republic. They alone are faithful to the Reconstruction-like dream of *"LIBERTY AND EQUALITY"* (232). All the other inhabitants of England, from the nobles to the gentry to the common people, desert to restoration, now blazoned forth, in familiar Redeemer rhetoric, as the "righteous cause" of England (328). Armed with Gatling guns and seemingly secure behind an electrified fence, Hank and his tiny army unloose a "red terror" (233) that annihilates thirty thousand knights.

The Battle of the Sand Belt is not an allegory of the Civil War: it erupts after, not before, the Yankee spreads enlightenment to Camelot. Symbolically brought back with him from France, the mechanized violence represents the bloody French Revolution that the postwar South never had, a liquidation of the Bourbons who were rolling back the last vestiges of reform. This horrific outcome may have satisfied a wish to punish wrongdoers, but it is self-defeating, a cry of impotence on Twain's part. The Boss falls wounded, and he and his fifty-two assistants are trapped behind their defenses while thousands of rotting corpses lie outside, emitting the deadly gas that will kill them all. Merlin, the sorcerer and chief adversary of the Yankee, is trapped with them; he dies, too, but in a state of exultation at the republic's demise and with his mouth stretched wide open in a grin. Morgan, who wakes up again in the American present, has no more to show for his years of effort than did Tourgée's carpetbagger, Comfort Servosse.

What *A Connecticut Yankee* makes clear is how much Reconstruction's failure contributed to the late nineteenth-century devaluation of linguistic agency. Tourgée labeled the new amendments to the Constitution "paper rights,"[18] and Twain sees egalitarian pronouncements as so many useless words when set against the immobility of prejudice and birth. As Hank puts it, "Arguments have no chance against petrified training; they wear it as little as the waves wear a cliff" (114). Resignation to the verbal's fecklessness pervades the story. According to the hero, "goody-goody talk and moral suasion" have never yet won any people to freedom (135). Events, not words, accomplish such world-changing reforms; to think otherwise is to mistake cause for effect and surrender to the superstition of sorcery. "Words realize nothing," the Yankee states elsewhere (213); they "are only painted fire," not the actual flames, and can "vivify nothing to you" without the thing itself (275). The lesson Mark Twain drew from the reinstatement of racial caste was the antiromantic and politically disaffected one of the emptiness of written or spoken promises.

But Twain knew the South, and the nineteenth-century publishing scene, too well to leave it at that. His novel contains the historically accurate recognition that postwar Southerners held a diametrically opposed view of utterance, one much closer in spirit to that of antislavery romantics like Emerson and Stowe. The characters in *A Connecticut Yankee* who believe in the verbal's power are the residents of Camelot. Sandy holds forth in interminable monologues, to the Boss's irritated bemusement, and the entire population of sixth-century England has a deep reverence for spells. No miracle concocted by Merlin can have its maximum effect without the requisite mumbo-jumbo, and Hank has to imitate the magician's patter to consolidate his own authority. When the Yankee speaks disparagingly to Clarence of Merlin's prestidigitation, his young ally sinks to his knees in fright: "Oh, beware! These are awful words. Any moment these walls may crumble upon us if you say such things" (34). Despite all the apparent good he accomplishes, a mere piece of writing, the church's interdict, causes the hero's downfall, so firm is the hammerlock of priestly speech on the imaginations of the natives.

This understanding of language's potency may or may not have been true of Arthurian England, but it certainly applied below the Mason-Dixon line. Burned by abolitionist agitation and now threatened again by the war amendments, Southerners felt that discourse had destroyed their way of life, and they were resolved to combat it in any way possible, from outright acts of violence to stories, biographies, and histories espousing their point of view. The plantation and anti-Reconstruction schools of romance found a ready following for their paeans to the Lost Cause and white supremacy, Dixie's homegrown version of Sir Walter Scott's make-believe and a textbook illustration of literature "for . . . harm." The magazine and book outlets were based in the North, mostly in New York; the readers and platform audiences were northern, too, and rhapsodized over the glowing accounts of slavery. As the fortunes of Twain's publishing house sagged and the country entered the nadir of race relations, he furnished, in *Pudd'nhead Wilson*, a scathing (if oblique, as always) judgment on popular performance, including his own, and an indictment of northern complicity through his eponymous "hero," the modern magician David Wilson, an emigrant to Dawson's Landing from "the State of New York" (24).

The historical and personal matrix of the novel can be quickly sketched. Twain wrote the book abroad, in Florence, where he had moved with his family in 1892 to live more cheaply. Webster and Company was failing, and he had lost a fortune on his investment in the Paige machine, an invention for setting type automatically. In 1895, after both businesses collapsed, Twain was forced to declare bankruptcy. His need for a financial success with his new fiction had never been greater, but at the same time his estrangement from his country's ideological values, as suggested by his relocation to Europe, had worsened. Cleveland was elected president for a second time in 1892, in good measure because of popular revulsion from the Republicans, who had tried (and failed) to save the black franchise in an effort widely perceived as a backward-looking threat to reunion. In 1893 a Democratic Congress passed legislation repealing the enforcement acts, and a compliant Cleveland signed the measure into law. Southern democracy, with an assist from the North, had expired, and three years later a northern-controlled Supreme Court would bestow the federal government's imprimatur on the ex-Confederacy's latest peculiar institution, racial segregation.[19]

Background issues press their way into the text most obviously as a questioning of American apartheid and a metafictional obsession with authorship and printing. Forcible separation of the races preceded *Plessy*'s formalization, and Twain exposes the practice's folly in his story of near-doubles, the white heir to the Driscolls on the one side, and Roxy's son, who is 1/32 black, on the other. Roxy switches the two infants to secure a better life for her child; their paths as Tom Driscoll and the slave Chambers sharply diverge, but in the end their fates prove inextricable. (*Those Extraordinary Twins*, to which we will return, iterates this conclusion with both more and less disguise.) The metafictional or self-reflective aspect of the tale centers on the prominent roles of doubling, fingerprinting, and palmistry, all of which direct attention to the mechanical reproduction of writing. The Italian twins, Luigi and Angelo, are "exact duplicates" (51), and duplication or multiplication is the quintessence of the printing process. Fingerprinting is another technology of replication: a given individual's print, or "natal signature" (160), as Wilson calls it, is absolutely unique and always the same. Ditto a person's palm print. One can detect in these details the traces of Twain's careers as a journeyman printer and a subscription publisher, as well as his involvement with the Paige typesetter, the intricate duplicating machine that bankrupted him.

The emphasis on print also points us to Twain the writer. The twins, experts at palmistry, assure a skeptical Tom Driscoll that the lines on one's hand are an infallible index to character: "four years ago we had our hands read out to us as if our palms had been covered with print" (82). From reading the "print" on Luigi's palm, Wilson correctly deduces that the Italian once killed a man during an attempted robbery, just as he later determines the identity of Judge Driscoll's murderer from reading a set of fingerprints. The theme of ferreting out secrets from the hand or finger should remind us of Huck Finn's incessant worries about saying the wrong thing and getting caught. Authors write with the hand, after all, as Twain himself indicates in the second paragraph of his preface, which begins "Given under my hand . . ." (xx). The sensibility and beliefs of the artist, in Twain's case a writer *and* a performer, can, like the identity of a murderer or a thief, be "read out" from his handiwork or utterances. "Heedless speech" (95) is as much a source of danger as it was in the earlier fiction, and characters in *Pudd'nhead Wilson* have to watch what they say as closely as what they do.

The person who first runs afoul of majoritarian sentiment is David Wilson, who gains his nickname "Pudd'nhead" because of an ironical statement he makes about wishing to kill half of a disagreeable dog. The community can make no sense of his words, with serious consequences: the "deadly remark" ruins Wilson's chances as a lawyer in Dawson's Landing. "No clients came," and the newcomer is obliged to revise the sign announcing his profession, crossing out the legal aspect and offering his services exclusively as land surveyor and accountant (27). Twenty-three years later, he's "still toiling in obscurity," and when he recklessly shares his equally ironical calendar with the townspeople, they feel confirmed in their conviction that he's an utter fool (48). But if Wilson's verbal indiscretions lead to financial hardship and loss of reputation, Tom Driscoll's put his very identity at risk. They imperil his masquerade as a master and could turn him back into a slave. He has to guard his speech around Roxy and rein in her speech, too: angered by his harsh words and treatment of her, his mother/slave threatens to tell the truth about him to Judge Driscoll. (He subsequently sells Roxy down the river to ensure her silence.) A bit like Wilson, but rather more like Twain himself—since the erstwhile lawyer's irony is anything but stealthy—Tom is said to be "furtively, and sometimes openly, ironical of speech, and given to gently touching people on the raw" (47). Particularly after he begins stealing money and valuables, Tom becomes less restrained about his wisecracks and goes after the two characters with the most reason to catch him. He injudiciously taunts Wilson about his law practice and mocks Constable Blake for his tardiness in apprehending the old woman who is suspected as the criminal. His verbal indiscretions will cost him dearly.

The hinted affiliation between Tom and his creator, Mark Twain, reopens the matter of the writer's blackness. The need to be cautious about utterance applies to him as well, and the resulting constriction is evident from the novel's first page: the preface bears the title "A Whisper to the Reader." This hushing or verbal obstruction has an analog in Tom's humbled speech after he learns that he is a "nigger" and begins to lapse into "the wheedling and supplicating servilities . . . of the born slave" (75 and 64). Scripted into the text are repeated gestures at the novelist's own trials in literary mastership and slavery, darling of the reading public and/or toady to the market. The categories are fungible, and Twain constantly plays with their fluidity, a pattern of instability set in motion by Roxy's switching of the babies. She herself calls the grown-up Chambers an "imitation nigger" (62), while Twain adds the epithet "pure-white slave" (64).

Nor does the enslavement of a white person have to stem from an act of deception. The twins, who are described as musical prodigies, observe of their youthful experience being exhibited "as a show" that they "escaped from that slavery at twelve years of age" (53). Twain was familiar with the bondage of showmanship, but in this novel the category of slavery is no more stable than that of race: when the twins perform for the townspeople, the latter "realized that for once in their lives they were hearing masters" (56). The brothers experience both these antipodal conditions in Dawson's Landing, going from venerated exotics to jailed assassins to rehabilitated "heroes of romance" (165). Moreover, Tom and Chambers will switch places a second time, with the white master becoming a black slave, and the black slave a white master. Twain gives a European twist to these reversals and slippages. The striped pole signifying nobility in Venice "indicated merely the humble barbershop" in Dawson's Landing (22), and when the judge is found dead, the local papers name the assassin as "a profligate Italian nobleman or barber" (143). In *Pudd'nhead Wilson*, a count can be a common barber, and vice versa, and a master and white heir can be a slave and penniless black. Vice versa again.

Twain is not a master of his chosen genre; as already noted, he is a jackleg who was "not born with the novel writing gift" (168). This deficiency makes him a "slave" to his medium. He explains (in the note to *Those Extraordinary Twins*) that his manuscript took on an existence of its own and reduced him to a kind of helpless subordinate, a state very like that experienced by Roxy once Tom, her creation and "imitation-master," starts to lord it over her (41). We can also think of Twain as being in bondage to his fiction because, as he was keenly conscious in 1894, he had to cater to the popular audience or jeopardize his reputation and sales. (*Pudd'nhead Wilson* was serialized in the *Century*.) Anxiety about having his secrets exposed troubles him as much as it weighs on the false white master (in reality a black slave), Tom Driscoll.[20] Tom resolves to exercise greater precaution, but, writes Twain, "that was because he did not know himself," and he quickly reverts to his improvident ways (76). Twain did know himself, and in the ending of the book, with more candor than at the ending of *Huckleberry Finn*, he arraigns public performance as surrender to racism and intimates his liberation from the novel form that enslaved him.

The climactic trial scene is staged like one of those public spectacles plentiful in Huck's narrative, or like an exhibition by that virtuoso of the platform circuit, Mark Twain. The episode includes audience reactions in brackets (applause, murmurs, muttered ejaculations, laughter), and Wilson, on the verge of consolidating his celebrity, manipulates his listeners masterfully. His showmanship builds to the revelation of Tom's guilt; the fake heir has given himself away by rashly visiting Wilson the night before the trial to "goad him with an exasperating word or two" (151), and he leaves a telltale fingerprint on a glass strip. It is almost as though he wants his true nature to be discovered; Twain, more consciously, is taking the same chance. At the moment of Tom's exposure, Wilson condemns him as a "Negro and slave" (163), drawing an equation between race and bondage that postbellum Southerners were finding too comfortable to surrender. Wanting to see Tom hanged—or is it lynched?—Wilson commands him to "make upon the window the fingerprints that will hang you." But the slavocracy, not wanting to lose valuable property, sells the "imitation-master" down the river.

Wilson's ascent mirrors Tom's fall, and the temptation is strong to see in this denouement Twain's judgment on the moral compromises of public success in the 1890s, his own in particular; the novel's full title is *The Tragedy of Pudd'nhead Wilson*.[21] The reversal in fortune between the two characters picks up on the theme of theft. In chapter 2, a slave of

Judge Driscoll's steals a small sum of money; but should slaveholders or their human property be considered thieves in the prewar South? According to Twain, possibly influenced by Frederick Douglass,[22] the black has taken but a "trifle from the man who daily robbed him of an inestimable treasure—his liberty." Wilson succeeds by imitating the master class and stealing a black man's freedom, a theft that completes the lawyer-sorcerer's transformation into a full-fledged Southerner. Wilson has steadily ingratiated himself with the culture of slavery. He begins to repair his reputation well before the trial when he agrees to serve as Luigi's double in the duel with Judge Driscoll. Dueling being "the summit of human honor" to Southerners, Wilson awakes to find himself "a made man and his success assured" (114). His stature only increases as his independence diminishes. When he unmasks Tom as a "Negro and slave," Wilson is serenaded by "gangs of enthusiasts," and the crowd roars "over every sentence that fell from his lips—for all his sentences were golden, now, all were marvelous. His long fight against hard luck and prejudice was ended" (165). Was Twain recalling here how he secured his own success in *Huckleberry Finn* at the expense of Jim, whose freedom Tom Sawyer stole while pretending to set him free? He is certainly passing judgment on the adoring audience for his own and Wilson's stagecraft.[23]

In contrast to Wilson, Twain's fight against prejudice and racism was about to intensify and to shed many of its disguises. As the decade wore on, his writing grew more controversial and more open about attacking imperialism and the racist abuse of native peoples: witness *Following the Equator* (1897), or the devastating "King Leopold's Soliloquy" (1905). The writers and politicians whose words carried greater weight with the American public in this period were composers of romances "of the white man's burden" such as Dixon and northern turncoats such as President Cleveland, whom Pudd'nhead Wilson strikingly resembles. Cleveland, a fellow New Yorker, was trained as a lawyer and got his political start as the mayor of Buffalo; in his second term in the White House, he acted as a reliable ally of the southern ruling class. Wilson's redemption in Dawson's Landing leads to his being asked by the local Democratic Party to run for mayor and handily winning the election, so completely has he been absorbed into the system of white supremacy. And Twain's implied critique of the New Yorker as Bourbon is a self-critique: he had been seduced by Cleveland's appeal as a post-Copperhead Democratic reformer.

Pudd'nhead Wilson concludes with an echo of "Benito Cereno," an earlier text about slavery and race in which "whispering" also plays a part. In the Lima courthouse, Don Benito—another master who became a slave—faints on the stand and cannot give testimony against the rebel Babo, who refuses to testify in his turn. In Twain's Missouri courtroom, Tom Driscoll "slides limp and lifeless to the floor" without answering the charges against him (163), and Roxy, shattered by her son's cruel fate, falls silent as well: "the sound of her laughter ceased in the land" (166). One more black-white, master-slave figure felt the attraction of silence: Mark Twain. Although he continued to publish nonfiction, stories, and polemics, he never completed another novel. But he did extract from *Pudd'nhead Wilson* the novella that was published with it as *The Comedy of Those Extraordinary Twins*.

The two works, like Tom and Chambers, have different racial compositions: there are no central black characters in *Those Extraordinary Twins*. Grounds enough, perhaps, for a comedy, yet the novella has a secret or hidden side that comments obliquely on the self-destructiveness of segregation. This time Twain portrays the Italian brothers as Siamese twins. Luigi is dark, while Angelo is blonde, and their physical indivisibility underlines both their mutual dependence and their mutual danger. No individual action by either twin can fail to impact the other, and to the modern reader the pair seems clearly intended as a trope for the imbrication of whites and blacks in the post-Reconstruction South, a relationship that can be painful and risky at times but that can, or should, foster affection and support. Dawson's Landing, however, refuses to accept this lesson and, insisting that the brothers be separated, will not allow them to sit together on the board of aldermen. The city government, brought to a halt, falls into "rack and ruin," and the enraged citizens decide to hang Luigi, and Luigi alone, convinced that the killing will not harm the fair Angelo, who of course perishes with his brother: "And so ends the history of 'Those Extraordinary Twins'" (184).

One might say, then, that like Tom Driscoll, the "separated at birth" all-white narrative has a black subtext that causes it to end unhappily. In order of composition, the two tales correspond to the two halves of the century, which I have described, following Aristotle, as comic and tragic. The novel began as "The Suppressed Farce," in Twain's words, acquired a series of uninvited characters ("a stranger named Pudd'nhead Wilson, and a woman named Roxana, . . . and a young fellow named Tom Driscoll, whose proper place was away in the obscure background" [136]) and mutated without his volition into *Pudd'nhead Wilson*. The tragedy rapidly engulfed the comedy. It even cast its shadow on the predecessor story, which in its printed form abruptly runs out of humor with the hanging/ lynching of the "dark-skinned" Luigi (132). The historical tragedy of the

separate-but-equal doctrine, KKK terror, and minority disenfranchisement had much the same effect: it spoiled the comedy of emancipation
by consigning black people to a condition little removed from involuntary
servitude.

So the answer to the question with which we began is yes, Twain was
black, but he was black like Booker T. Washington, not like the outspo-
ken Ida B. Wells. Even in *Pudd'nhead Wilson*, he pulls his punches and
leaves it indeterminate whether Tom's crimes are the result of his drop of
black blood or his spoiled upbringing as a white aristocrat.[24] Some masks
he did not discard. The relevance of bringing up the activist Wells should
be apparent: she campaigned in public, at considerable risk to her welfare,
against the surge in lynching that Twain and Washington deplored but
were far more circumspect about condemning. Moreover, Wells paid for
that verbal transgression in poverty and obscurity; her investigative volumes found few takers among the white population whose tastes governed
the marketplace. Twain and Washington, in contrast, were well rewarded
for their reserve, and the two men seem to have felt a certain affinity; we
know, at any rate, that Twain spoke at a Carnegie Hall fund-raiser for the
Tuskegee Institute.[25]

Louis R. Harlan has described Washington as the "wizard of Tuskegee" because, like the Wizard of Oz, he worked behind the scenes against
the segregation of sleeping cars, lynching, and other racial injustices.[26] De-
nunciation without the whisper was another matter. Like that other wizard, Twain, Washington seldom raised his dissenting voice in public: there
were too "many resks" in telling the truth, and he could not afford to offend the white patrons he needed for his school. A southern farmer warned
him when he was about to deliver his famous Atlanta Exposition Address,
"You have got yourself into a tight place."[27] The line could serve as the
motto under which he strove to propitiate whites without sacrificing black
interests. It was Huck Finn's, and Mark Twain's, motto as well.

Twain did voice a last outcry against lynching in a piece from 1901 that
is noteworthy for both its bluntness and its insight into the writer's, and
the culture's, self-repression. The essay, "The United States of Lyncherdom," does not maintain the usual distinction between North and South.
Lynchings have spilled beyond their section of origin and reached states
as remote as California and Colorado, according to Twain, who says that
he "may live to see a negro burned in Union Square, New York, with fifty
thousand people present." The reason for the epidemic is simple: moral
cowardice. Individuals who privately abhor the appalling spectacle keep

their own counsel because "it would be unpopular" to speak out, and "each man is afraid of his neighbor's disapproval." Public sentiment, in the supposedly democratic and enlightened republic, is "more dreaded than wounds and death."[28] Is it necessary to add that the best-selling author of *Huckleberry Finn*, *A Connecticut Yankee*, and *Pudd'nhead Wilson* knew the truth of these statements on his pulses? Twain never dared to publish "The United States of Lyncherdom," instead suppressing it because it would have alienated his adoring readers. And when Albert Paine Bigelow discovered the manuscript and brought it to light, he made cuts and added language of his own to tone down Twain's blistering attack on the lynchers as "assassins" who deserved to be executed. The date of publication was 1923, a year before the National Origins Quota Act reducing access to the United States for non-Anglo-Saxon immigrants, legislative testimony to the longevity of the exclusionary cultural formation that sanctioned lynching in the first place.[29]

Crane and the Tyranny of Twelve

The Red Badge of Courage and *The Monster* were both products of the post-Reconstruction depths, a temporal congruity too often overlooked in their usual isolation as narratives about, respectively, the Civil War and small-town parochialism. Crane, born in 1871, wrote his novel of a young man's initiation into combat almost thirty years after hostilities ended. With one significant change, the social atmosphere depicted in *The Monster* (1899) was also the context for his reimagining of the clash between North and South. The tale about the ostracizing of a physician for his allegiance to a damaged black stable hand is our strongest evidence for Crane's alienation from his culture's ideological rigidities. It may be our only evidence. About Crane's life relatively little is known for certain; about his politics, almost nothing. Clearly he often took positions that went against his era's conventional beliefs, such as his attraction to fallen women or his doubts about survival of the fittest. We know that in 1892 his brother William tried to stop the lynching of a black man in Port Jervis, New York, the town that served as a model for the imaginary Whilomville. We also know that like so many late nineteenth-century American novelists—most notably, his seniors Twain and James—he fled the United States during the 1890s, settling outside London with his "wife," the ex-madam Cora Taylor, and eventually dying in a sanatorium in the Black Forest.[1] Yet we can only speculate about whether, and to what extent, his relocation abroad was motivated by discontent with his society's growing intolerance. The grim picture of majoritarian pressure painted in *The Monster*, which was composed in England in 1897, lends support to that idea; the story of Henry Fleming, which preceded Crane's uprooting and shows the hero and his comrade Wilson defying a slur on their valor, seems considerably more ambiguous.

How, then, might we describe the relationship between the two fictions in a way that would shed light on Crane's perception of the fin-de-siècle United States? Ralph Ellison, in an essay published in 1960, suggested that "the line between civil war and civil peace" had become blurred in the late nineteenth century, and that the struggles of Crane's characters to find "moral and physical courage" were "symbolic equivalents" for their culture's efforts to face the truth about its betrayals. *The Monster* dispels any doubt "as to the Negro's part" in this process, according to Ellison, and he saw Crane, along with Twain and James, as laboring to enlighten a society whose vaunted freedom masked a thoroughgoing aversion to dissent. The author of *Invisible Man* (1952), who imagined a whole people in the situation of Henry Johnson, *The Monster's* hostler without a face, declared of the climate in which the three realists worked, "It was as though a rigid national censorship had been imposed—not by an apparatus set up in Washington, but within the center of the American mind."[2]

Recast ever so slightly, Ellison's insights provide the answer to our question: it takes the presence of the Negro to make the censor's "apparatus" palpable in Crane's work. The sole nonwhite character in *The Red Badge of Courage* is dispatched on the first page, and what demarcates Crane's martial novel, composed in 1893–94, from its successor is that, however shot through with irony, the former still entertains the possibility of resistance to supervisory intimidation. Indeed, the irony confirms the possibility of cognitive distancing, whereas in *The Monster* no such aloofness or opposition seems possible, even by the author himself. The difference is precisely Henry Johnson, the Trescotts' colored servant. *Plessy v. Ferguson* (1896), which intervened between the two works, and to which Crane seems to allude in the novella, may have contributed to his change in outlook. *The Monster*, with its racial fungibilities, subtly interrogates the segregationist logic of Jim Crow, but unlike *The Red Badge of Courage*, it allows no successful struggle against the falsifications of postbellum speech.

Billy Budd, oddly enough, offers us an entry to *The Red Badge of Courage's* topicality. Besides their shared subject, war, the novels—two of the most iconic American fictions of the 1890s—have an array of resemblances. Each begins with a black man who vanishes to make way for a white one: Billy supplants the ebony Handsome Sailor, and a "negro teamster" dancing to entertain the troops is replaced by Henry Fleming (3).[3] Each features an innocent hero who is changed through his encounter with harsh reality; each strives for an aura of timelessness or universality, in Crane's case by omitting any reference to actual places, battles, or regiments. But the most relevant affinity may be a common distrust of language. The brevity of the stories hints at this—they must also rank among the shortest novels of the decade—and the fraught relation of the two protagonists to speech, right down to the detail of a vocal blockage, thematizes the skepticism. Like Melville's foretopman, who cannot answer when Claggart accuses him of mutiny, Fleming stammers at a critical juncture in the action. In chapter 12, at the narrative's midpoint, he tries to question some retreating infantrymen and keeps repeating "Why—why—" while "struggling with his balking tongue" (62). Each scene culminates in a blow, and though the results radically diverge—Billy's hanging versus Henry's transformative wound—each dramatizes the supersession of words by deeds. The two works, moreover, come down to us in a state of indeterminacy, as if they were themselves afflicted with a "balking tongue." Neither writer left a definitive text; Crane did not die while working on his book as Melville did, but he professed no interest in seeing page proofs, and the surviving manuscript of *The Red Badge of Courage* incorporates revisions by several hands.[4]

The difficulties with utterance can be read in multiple and sometimes contradictory ways. One theme that stands out in both books, discussed elsewhere in this study, is the inadequacy of the verbal in the presence of violence, a widely drawn lesson from the Civil War.[5] But Melville and Crane also convey an impression of language as an adversary or danger, an agent capable of misleading, distorting, and inflicting injury. The captain of the *Bellipotent*, nervous about mutiny, bars inflammatory talk, and Claggart violates that prohibition with fatal consequences. There is no master-at-arms in *The Red Badge of Courage*, but the heedless sentences of a general play an essential part in Henry's "growth" as a character. The novel's subtitle is "An Episode of the American Civil War." Whatever else war may be, to Crane it is a discursive phenomenon, and discourse can be almost as destructive as skirmishing with cannon.

Indeed, the trademark of war in Henry Fleming's world is that it surrounds one with incessant tongues. Crane calls the battlefield "the place of noises" (39), but it could just as accurately be described as the place of words or of voices. The opening scene composes the Union soldiers into an "attentive audience" ingesting rumors and tales of imminent maneuvers (3), and the cacophony escalates once Henry and his friends experience the fighting directly. Officers rant and bellow. In combat, the men emit "a wild, barbaric song" comprising "cheers, snarls, imprecations,

[and] prayers" (32). The insistent questions of the "tattered man" (55) taunt Henry with the memory of his cowardice, and he suspects that his comrades are making derisive remarks about him behind his back: "He was a slang phrase" (61). As this last example indicates, the voices are internal as well as external. Henry, debating the great "Question" (22) of whether he will run away, has "visions of a thousand-tongued fear that would babble at his back and cause him to flee" (18). Writing no less than speech permeates the site of belligerence. Wilson, expecting that his first engagement will be his last, presses a packet of letters on Henry, and the protagonist fears that the wounded men he passes on his flight can read "the letters of guilt he felt burned into his brow" (48).[6]

These overlaps of war and dialect bristle with misinformation and malignancy. The rumors of the first page are "'a thunderin' lie!'" (3). No more reliable are "the mental pamphlets" that Henry consults so assiduously; they fail to prepare him for the realities of battle (61). As marked as the unreliability of words is their association with weaponry and death. The tattered man's questions pierce Henry like "knife thrusts . . . They asserted a society that probes pitilessly at secrets until all is apparent" (55–56). Crane tends to trope the sounds of arms as acts of speaking. On a single page, Henry hears the "voices of cannon," "the courageous words of the infantry," and "the spiteful sentences of the musketry" (45). The lingual frame of reference is not unique to the author; it besets Fleming too, as when he scrambles into the woods "to get out of hearing of the crackling shots which were to him like voices" (41). The murderous metaphors conjure the ability of speech to cause irreparable damage.

An emphasis on surveillance dovetails with the oppressive atmosphere of discursive assault. (Here, again, Crane's tale seconds *Billy Budd*.) In the first chapter, upon learning of Henry's enlistment, his mother cautions him not to do anything "yeh would be 'shamed to let me know about. Jest think as if I was a-watchin' yeh" (7). The watching never ends, not even when Fleming becomes the watcher. Officers closely monitor the men to forestall straggling. The youth tries to escape observation by plunging into the woods, but there too he encounters eyes, those of a corpse: "The dead man and the living man exchanged a long look" (43). As color bearer, he is at once "deeply absorbed as a spectator" (108) and the highly visible moving point both armies keep in sight. The text's conjunctures of optical and verbal policing reinforce the sense, which Henry feels under the tattered soldier's questions, of belonging to "a society" where nothing can be hidden, nothing can be separate from the mass. They are the war novel's version of *The Monster*'s regime of "everybody says," and they establish the clearest continuity between the corpse-strewn battlefield and the ostensibly irenic setting of Whilomville.

Yet in *The Red Badge of Courage*, Henry escapes the defeat of Dr. Trescott—and so does Stephen Crane. The hero's ironized acts of heroism do not only suggest that language's harmful power can be broken in the absence of African Americans. They also imply a point of view from outside the narrative, a perspective that is not identical with the world of the battlefield. Henry and his comrade Wilson mature into a laconicism that confers a measure of autonomy and apartness, but that character development is never quite free of mockery, and Crane's gently parodic rendering of it constitutes an aesthetic equivalent to the two soldiers' evolution. It marks the text's own resistance to the coercive quotidian. In this, Crane's realist novella does differentiate itself from Melville's anachronistic romanticism. The laconic in *Billy Budd* modulates into tragedy and poetry; in Crane, it reprises the conventional gender conditioning of men at war and is swathed in irony. But the two classics remain kindred in their privileging of distance or absence as the only free space left in a society of linguistic corruption.

The about-face for Henry and Wilson begins after the hero's return to camp, when he falls asleep for a mythic "thousand years" (71). He awakes to find that his friend has abjured the braggadocio of his earlier manner: "He [Wilson] seemed no more to be continually regarding the proportions of his personal prowess. He was not furious at small words that pricked his conceits. He was no more a loud young soldier" (73). Fleming responds with a similar vocal self-discipline: he refrains from tormenting Wilson with invidious comments when the erstwhile blusterer asks for his letters back. (Crane does not fail to note that Henry inwardly swells with pride at "the generous thing" he has done [78].) And unlike the rumormongers of the first chapter, the two show sufficient control not to alarm their comrades with the unnamed general's prediction of their slaughter.

At this point the objective changes, and the wish to confound an unjust and dismissive vocabulary, and not merely to ignore it, moves to center stage. Henry and Wilson become consumed with refuting their tormentor after they overhear the division commander speaking of the regiment as indifferently "as if he referred to a broom." Needing some troops to charge the enemy, the general and another officer decide to send the 304th to their almost-certain deaths because they "fight like a lot 'a mule drivers" and can be easily spared. "I don't believe many of your mule drivers will get back," the general says (89). No words in the novel resonate more potently for the hero. They stun him with their unfairness but also arouse a fierce resolve to prove them wrong, and the desire to repulse the general's false name for himself and the regiment and secure a true one motivates Henry throughout the final chapters. When the Union charge fails, the words ring in his ears with renewed reproach: "He had thought of a fine revenge upon the officer who had referred to him and his fellows as mule drivers. . . . And now the retreat of the mule drivers was a march of shame to him" (97). Though Crane lavishes irony on Henry's musings of revenge, he does not let the protagonist give in to the general's contemptuous characterization. Riveting his anger on the man who "dropped epithets unconcernedly down" (97), Fleming helps to rally the Union soldiers so that, "when on the verge of submission to those opinions" (100), they muster the courage to fight bravely and halt a Confederate counterattack.

Crane takes this dynamic of denigration and rebuttal seriously enough to repeat it a few pages later. The caustic general, having observed the troops' inability to overrun the enemy position, reappears to shower more abuse on the 304th, exclaiming to the regimental colonel, "What a lot of mud diggers you've got anyway!" (102). Once again, the unjustifiable censure stirs Henry's indignation, and it preys on his thoughts when he leads the assault that captures the Confederate colors: "In all the wild graspings of his mind for a unit responsible for his sufferings and commotions he always seized upon the man who had dubbed him wrongly" (108). But this time, the hero is not alone in his outrage. The regimental colonel and Lieutenant Hasbrouck protest that their soldiers fought well, and these better-informed witnesses think the categories of approbation and opprobrium need to be reversed. As Hasbrouck puts it, the general is "a damned fool" for disparaging the men, and Henry is a "jimhickey" (a fine fellow) for carrying the flag. The colonel adds his own words of praise, figuratively promoting Wilson and Fleming to the rank of the regiment's faultfinder: "'They deserve t' be major-generals,' he ses. 'They deserve t' be major-generals'" (105).

The element of satire here is undeniable, but so is the regiment's bravery in rebuffing the insult to their honor. And the same combination of perspectives is operative in the final chapter, where Henry, out of range of "the stentorian speeches of the artillery," silently reviews his past actions. He acknowledges his "error" in abandoning the tattered soldier and discovers that he now despises "the brass and bombast of his earlier gospels." The manhood he feels is said to be "quiet" and "unassertive," but the florid writing of the last page—"he was a man," "his soul changed," "scars faded as flowers"—complicates without discrediting the moment of triumph

(115–17). Crane's tone creates a rhetorical correlative to Fleming's refusal to submit to the powers that be, a stylistic detachment that matches the hero's overcoming of the general's misnomer. Even as it mocks Henry's maturation, the irony keeps alive the idea of an outside or antagonistic space (or opposite meaning, the dictionary definition of irony)—precisely what is missing from *The Monster*.

In that story, written three years later, the opinions of a town integrated into the national media through mails, telegraph, and newspapers cannot be circumvented; and the military novel's transvaluation of judgment, in which epithets have so large a role, returns as an unstated question about the true referent of the monstrous entity of the title. Whilomville is another zone of rumors and tales, but totalized now, a place where what people say about you determines your fate. *The Red Badge of Courage* can thus be seen as a kind of bridge or pivot, most familiarly between the realist aesthetic and modernism, but more unexpectedly between the residue of freedom still imaginable under wartime oversight and stereotyping and the near-disappearance of that possibility in the civilian formation regnant by the end of the decade. The latitude appears to dissolve for Crane too, even at the remove of an ocean.

Interestingly, not long after he finished *The Monster*, the novelist imagined himself occupying a position rather like that of Fleming and Wilson, buffeted by terms of abuse. He wrote to his brother William from England complaining of American reviewers who

> want to kill, bury and forget me purely out of unkindness and envy and—my own unworthiness, if you choose. . . . Now I want you to promise to never pay any attention to it, even in your thought. It is too immaterial and foolish. Your little brother is neither a braggart or a silent egotist but he knows that he is going on steadily to make his simple little place and he cant be stopped, he cant even be retarded. He is coming.[7]

The mixture of equanimity and defiance in this letter duplicates the two soldiers' behavior on the battlefield. But in writing *The Monster*, Crane could not altogether rid himself of the intrusive monitoring. He felt apprehensive about "the eye of your glorious public" tracking him, as he put it in a subsequent letter to William admitting that Port Jervis was on his mind when he composed the novella.[8] And this time, the hero's fight against destructive words and attitudes is much less effectual. It cannot rescue Whilomville's foremost physician from the marginalization that greeted anyone who allied himself with African Americans after *Plessy.*

The general's epithets, mule drivers and mud diggers, were routinely applied to freedmen in the postbellum period, but *The Red Badge of Courage* never acknowledges the association. The small-town fiction, in contrast, abounds in stereotypes for blacks, and it is unstinting about the use of clichés and tired, iterative language by whites.[9] Like Henry Fleming's narrative, *The Monster* consists of twenty-four chapters. Whereas the first work might be considered an anti-epic of war, the second constitutes an anti-epic of peacetime America, a society where every word and thought has been infiltrated by public opinion. Crane participates in the formulaic, but the notable contraction of his text suggests impatience with the discourse of unoriginality. The hundred-odd pages of *The Red Badge of Courage* shrink to half that number, and many chapters fill just a page or two.

Within the text itself, it more often seems that Fleming's stammer has taken over the town's speech. The first chapter spotlights the motif. Jimmie Trescott, playing at being a train, runs over a peony, much as he will inadvertently cause Henry Johnson's injury a few chapters later, and he tries to get his father's attention by repeating "Pa!" four times and "There!" five times (146–47). The make-believe train may be an invocation of *Plessy's* upholding of separate railroad cars for the two races, another damaging of black people; what is definite is that iteration, which Crane links to modern technologies of transportation and communication, impinges negatively on Henry and his protector. It reduces language to a carceral realm ruled by the mindless recycling of communal orthodoxy, often through stereotype, always with the effect of suppressing intellectual independence. Speech becomes "a cave of echoes" (158) in which deference to "what my father says" (165) or what "it was fashionable to say" (155) or what "everybody says" (196) ensures that no individual will stray from the "accustomed road of thought" (167). Rumor and gossip seize upon the banalities and give them the authority of a "solemn and terrible voice, speaking from the clouds" (157). Martha Goodwin, Whilomville's most fearsome gossip, sniffs that Dr. Trescott deserves "to lose all his patients" for his effrontery in contravening the will of the town (188). Crane compares her to Napoleon—the tyrant of the majority—and he says that the otherwise insignificant spinster is all the more formidable because she has no inkling of her power. But the recirculation of false or compulsory speech is hardly confined to women. The men at Reifsnyder's barbershop traffic endlessly in clichés, and the delegation of local eminences who try to pressure Dr. Trescott into abandoning Henry likewise quail before popular prejudice. They are no more capable than Martha of escaping the "mental tyranny" (196) of custom and consensus.

Racial caricature has a prominent place in this coercive majoritarianism. When Henry, dressed in lavender trousers, sets out for Bella Farragut's, the barbershop explodes in mockery of his minstrel airs. Those who first catch sight of the well-dressed "coon" are said to have "instantly telegraphed news of this extraordinary arrival" (152), and Crane shows an acute awareness of the dehumanizing images of blacks widely distributed throughout post-Reconstruction culture via telegraph, newspaper, and other media. Few white Americans doubted that Negro males, liberated from the wholesome constraints of slavery, were degenerating into "monsters" lusting after fair-skinned women. Another demeaning formulation had it that Africans fell so far below whites on the evolutionary scale that they constituted another order of being. A black man with the name of William Henry Johnson appeared in freak shows as an exhibit titled "What Is It?"[10] After Crane's Henry is badly burned in the fire, the narrative voice refers to him as "a thing" (163); and when he disrupts the party at the Pages', a mother asks her terrified daughter, "Was it a man? She didn't know. It was simply a thing, a dreadful thing" (183).

The Monster almost reads like a condensed review of the black experience in America since slavery, suggesting how integral that history of diminished possibility is to the erosion of free opinion. The fire in the Trescott home begins by destroying an engraving of the founders "Signing the Declaration," whose "proposition" of human equality (Lincoln at Gettysburg) inspired Congressional Reconstruction. Crane likens the droning of the flames to "fire-imps calling and calling, clan joining clan, gathering to the colors" (158), a probable reference to the Ku Klux Klan. When the hostler, plunging into the house to find Jimmie, despairs of success, we are told that he "was submitting, submitting because of his fathers, bending his mind in a most perfect slavery to this conflagration" (160). But Henry, a postemancipation black man, recovers his courage—a bit like the 304th regiment refusing "submission to those opinions"—and manages to save the boy.

Is the setting for the fire, the doctor's lab, another gesture at Reconstruction, frequently spoken of as a botched experiment in freedom, a social-engineering project gone awry? Judge Hagenthorpe, addicted like almost everyone else to "habitual oratory," invokes the Frankenstein myth by telling Trescott that Henry "will be your creation. . . . You are making him, and he will be a monster, and with no mind" (168–69).[11] The townspeople, incensed at this alien creature in their midst, foment a riot, "firing rocks" and chasing the stable hand like a lynch mob as he runs away (185). In sentences that could be applied to all African Americans in the nadir, the policeman observes about Henry, "Guess there isn't much of him to hurt anymore, is there? Guess he's been hurt up to the limit" (185). The chief urges Trescott to use a mask or veil to cover Johnson's face, advice the doctor follows; and thereafter every time Henry appears in the text, he does so "behind the veil," as Du Bois famously put it, or "wear[ing] the mask," in the refrain to Paul Dunbar's poem of 1896, "We Wear the Mask." And much of the town's musing about Henry's plight parrots social-Darwinist conclusions about the freedmen, especially the inevitability of the race's dying out because of its unfitness in the struggle for existence. Gossipers debate whether Dr. Trescott "should have let him die" (176), while Judge Hagenthorpe accuses the physician of "questionable charity" and "blunders of virtue" in preserving his life (168). The murderousness of this "white" discourse about blacks culminates seasonally, as it were, in the final chapter's revelation that it is now winter—Trescott "loudly stamped the snow from his feet" (200)—and in the fact that Crane gives the surname "Winter" to the principal alarmist about the disabled hostler. Father of the girl who glimpsed Henry at the party, Winter is also the community's most vituperative critic of his defender; he demands that Trescott himself be jailed.

Jake Winter's harassing of the protagonist reminds us of the corollary to black degradation: the denial to nonconforming whites of discursive and behavioral liberty. Whilomville monitors Trescott's every move, with Carrie Dungen eagerly relaying the details of his confrontation with Winter, and the doctor's determination to look after his son's savior so angers his patients that it costs him his practice. Trescott's cross-racial kindness drastically circumscribes his ability to speak or be listened to. Badgered by critics, he either declines to say anything (as when Winter rails at him) or slips into a stutterlike repetitiveness that leaves him unable adequately to explain himself. In the scene with Hagenthorpe, Trescott repeats five times, "What am I to do?" (169–70); in the meeting with the town delegation, his reasoning—"nobody can attend to him as I do myself" (199)—goes basically unheard. After Jimmie and his friends play a cruel game on Henry, the dismayed doctor takes his son aside and questions him sternly, only to relent when Jimmie bursts out crying. "Only I want to explain to you—" (194), he starts to tell his son; but Crane breaks off the conversation at this point, and the reader never learns the explanation.

One wonders at the elision. Beyond reaffirming Trescott's silencing, does it suggest Crane's own misgivings about expressing himself candidly in a story betraying sympathy for blacks? (The novella was first published in the United States, in *Harper's New Monthly Magazine*.) Although we cannot know for certain, surely it is relevant that the meddlesome delegation is headed by a man named John Twelve. Crane appears to have had no high hopes for fairness from the jury of his peers, the narrow-minded American public about which he had nothing good to say in letters to his brother. William Crane would have appreciated his brother's feelings. The members of the mob who had carried out the 1892 lynching in Port Jervis, though their identities were well-known, escaped punishment through community pressure. A coroner's jury reported that "Robert Lewis [the victim] came to his death in Port Jervis, June 2, by being hung by the neck by a person or persons unknown to this jury."[12]

Yet much in *The Monster* seems to reflect Crane's own racism. It would be easy enough to list examples: he names the street where the Farraguts live "Watermelon Alley," and he burlesques all the black characters, from Henry and Bella to Alek Williams. During the fire, he states that Johnson "ducked in the manner of his race in fights" (161). Again, one can't say for sure whether the novelist endorsed these stereotypes or included them as a concession to the democratic readership. Crane was in constant need of money, and given his familiarity with magazines like the *Century*, whose "Leaders and Battles of the Civil War" series he had researched for *The Red Badge of Courage*, he could not have misunderstood what the public expected from a best-selling fiction writer.[13] Caricatures were current, and he probably shared them to some extent. His protagonist indulges in them, too: when Alek Williams yells in horror upon first seeing the faceless stable hand, Crane writes of Dr. Trescott that he "seemed to be looking for epithets. Then he roared: 'You old black chump! You old black—Shut up! Shut up!'" (172). A stammer invades Crane's style, as though he were laboring under the same compulsion to repeat as the people of Whilomville. In the penultimate paragraph, he counts the empty cups at Mrs. Trescott's tea party: "There were fifteen of them." And he repeats himself verbatim in the novella's final line: "There were fifteen of them" (201). The conclusion appears unavoidable: the echo chamber of racial disparagement so enclosed fin-de-siècle American culture that not even Crane could escape it.

To be sure, irony exists in *The Monster*, as it does in all Crane's work, but the irony and parody seem directed as much at the black characters as at white attitudes toward them. On the topic of race, no contrary or alternative position emerges to challenge the dominant viewpoint. What critique of racism there is in the story is immanent: it depends on the reader's "outside," not an outside posited by the text and coterminous with it. The novelist's "submission" did not stop him from insinuating his disagreement with the post-*Plessy* hegemony of segregation. But his skepticism is implicit and formal and does not rise to the level of articulation.

The doctrine of "separate but equal" dictated social and spatial divisions among the races in the United States, and on the surface Crane's narrative could be seen as reproducing that structure. Discrete chapters deal with the white men at Reifsnyder's, or the women at Martha's, or the comic antics of the Williams family when they board "the monster." But the bonding of Henry with Jimmie, and later of Dr. Trescott with Henry, overrides the separations and points toward a recurrent textual pattern in which racial identities swap places. Many of the segregated chapters merge into each other. The white gossipers differ little from the Farraguts; the "habitual oratory" of the judge mutates into Henry's oft-repeated salutation to his fiancée: "Don' make no botheration, Miss Fa'gut. Don' make no botherations" (184). In his disfigured state, Henry regularly confounds racial boundaries, first disrupting a gathering at the Farraguts', then at the Pages', and then (in absentia) at the Trescotts'. The Frankenstein monster in Mary Shelley is white; in Crane, he is an African American; and in the course of the tale the epithet migrates from the broken hostler to the monstrous white community that stigmatizes him and his guardian. One might suggest that the term's referent gets transferred one last time, to the reading public. Visiting Trescott, Judge Hagenthorpe feels intensely uncomfortable under "the scrutiny of [Henry's] unwinking eye, at which he furtively glanced from time to time" (166). As noted, Crane confessed in his 1899 letter to William that he could not speak freely "if I thought the eye of your glorious public was upon me."

The literary world's reaction to *The Monster* bears out the wisdom of Crane's assessment. Though anything but an innocent about popular and editorial prejudices, he chose, like Dr. Trescott, to ignore them. He disregarded the advice of friends such as the American novelist Harold Frederic, who recommended that he shelve the work, and he submitted it to Gilder of the *Century*; that advocate of reconciliation on southern principles turned it down. Gilder is supposed to have objected, "Good heavens, we couldn't publish that thing with half the expectant mothers in America on our subscription list." The cultural gatekeeper's exclamation, reducing the story to its shock value, resonates deeply and ironically with the problematics of minority characterization: Crane's fiction about a monstrous black man in a culture fixated on interracial rape is a "thing" and unsuitable reading for America's "expectant mothers." *The Monster* did eventually make its way into print, but for a world-famous author with a bankable name, the search for a venue was unusually protracted. For reasons that have never been fully explained, the novella did not appear in *Harper's* until August 1898, almost a year after Crane finished writing it.[14]

The communal myopia with respect to *The Monster* had a sequel in the movies, and *The Red Badge of Courage*, though written before the novella, adumbrates the passing of the torch. When the 304th charges the Confederate position, Crane writes that his protagonist could see everything: "His mind took a mechanical but firm impression, so that afterward everything was pictured and explained to him, save why he himself was there" (92).

Because the two armies are not still, and because Fleming himself runs "madly" with the flag, the visual mechanism must be the kind of primitive motion-picture camera that supplied reels to Edison's kinetoscope, patented in 1891; Henry is filming the landscape as he dashes across it. At the conclusion of the novel, the fighting over, Crane returns—more atmospherically this time—to the cinematic motif. Rain falls, and "images of tranquil skies, fresh meadows, [and] cool brooks" pass before the eyes of the satisfied hero. The curtain drops—or the picture fades—on a single-sentence paragraph: "Over the river a golden ray of sun came through the hosts of leaden rain clouds" (117). Absent the irony, it makes for a Hollywood ending, worthy of Biograph's innovator, D. W. Griffith, and his white supremacist *Birth of a Nation*, the film that conscripted the cultural future for Whilomville's scapegoating of the Negro.

Choking in Chesnutt

In a plug for *The Marrow of Tradition* (1901) that he contributed to the *Cleveland World*, Charles W. Chesnutt stated that his book's title "fairly embodies the theme" of the viselike grip of the past on the present. Tradition crowned southern whites as masters and demoted blacks to slaves; though the "old order has passed away," regressive ways of thinking, "deeply implanted in the consciousness of the two races, still persist." Race prejudice has supplanted slavery as the country's enduring cause of oppression. Chesnutt claims that he examines without "pessimism" the intransigence of the old in the new, confident "that the forces of progress will in the end prevail."[1]

According to both *The Marrow of Tradition* and the novel that came after it, *The Colonel's Dream* (1905), the reconfiguration of slavery as race infiltrated almost all aspects of post-Reconstruction life, perhaps none more so than language. Chesnutt sees the South's dominance of the nation's print media and, in turn, northern opinion as the enabling condition for black debasement. Linguistic blockage invariably accompanies racial tyranny and manifests itself in the silencing that spreads like an illness throughout Chesnutt's work, assuming a thematic prominence reminiscent of the fiction of two other white writers, Melville from the antebellum period and Twain from the late nineteenth century. Yet again, the disempowering of black voices forms the prelude to the throttling of white ones; yet again, the process engulfs novelists as well as ordinary men and women. Repression silenced Chesnutt after *The Colonel's Dream*, and it caused his sponsor, William Dean Howells, to withdraw his support when the younger writer dared to tell the unwelcome truth about America's racial legacy.[2]

Chesnutt's sole nonfiction book was a biography of Frederick Douglass highlighting the great reformer's oratory as an indispensable weapon in the fight against slavery.[3] Douglass himself attached importance to utterance because he knew that the regimen of chattel bondage permitted just one voice to speak, that of the master. As Chesnutt shows in *The Marrow of Tradition*, a fictionalized account of the 1898 "race riot" (in actuality, white terrorism against blacks) in Wilmington, North Carolina, the "redeemed" South has endeavored to reproduce that monotone. Southerners refuse to listen to, or even tolerate, the point of view of the former slaves and create an ideological bunker mentality that compels skeptical whites to muffle their dissent. The "curse" of slavery abides "long after the actual physical bondage had terminated"; it incites the ruling caste to fury and then violence against what its members perceive as the "presumptuous freedom of speech and lack of deference" of their inferiors (276 and 291).[4]

The novel singles out one kind of minority discourse as particularly offensive to whites: that which questions the rationale for lynching by noting the prevalence of consensual sex between white women and black men. An editorial in the Wellington *Afro-American Banner* claims that "voluntary acts" lie behind many rape charges; this provides the ammunition that the three white conspirators, Major Carteret, General Belmont, and the one-eyed Captain McBane, use in their campaign against black voting rights. Although the assertion, Belmont concedes, has some "truth in it," McBane's response best captures (white) southern attitudes: "Truth or not, no damn nigger has any right to say it." All the plotters agree that such words from a black man constitute an inexcusable offense and that, as Carteret insists, "the paper should be suppressed immediately" (85–86). Later reprinted with inflammatory commentary in Carteret's *Morning Chronicle*, the editorial precipitates the pogrom that culminates in the disenfranchisement of the freedmen and the elimination of their voices from the civic sphere.

The significance of Carteret's white-supremacist newspaper in Chesnutt's narrative can hardly be exaggerated. The *Morning Chronicle* extinguishes black speech in the South and corrupts judgment in the North so that sympathy for the freedmen shrivels among their former allies. Its function in Wellington seems to be to mobilize the mob for acts of reprisal against imagined offenses: to quote General Belmont, "This is the age of crowds, and we must have the crowd with us" (81). Rioters destroy the offices of the *Afro-American Banner* and force its editor, Barber, to flee the state. The journalist's flight, modeled on the actual escape of a black Wilmington newspaperman named Manly, owes something as well to Ida B.

Wells's experience: owner-editor of the Memphis *Free Speech*, Wells was driven from Tennessee in 1892 by white papers demanding that she be lynched for her crimes of language.[5] In Chesnutt's novel, as in her ordeal, the potential incommensurability of the First Amendment's guarantees of free speech and a free press becomes apparent: the fourth estate crushes verbal liberty in the name of race mastery. As we shall see, no less a participant in this process than Major Carteret, the newspaper owner himself, gets caught in its toils.

Abuses by the *Morning Chronicle* also foment violence and lead to silencing in the aftermath of Polly Ochiltree's murder; the victims are both black and white. Carteret runs an article suggesting that Sandy Campbell, Mr. Delamere's erstwhile slave, now servant, raped Polly in addition to killing and robbing her, and the enraged citizens of Wellington prepare to lynch the accused man. Meanwhile, the Associated Press picks up the story of the crime and flashes the racial identity of its perpetrator "all over the United States." But although Sandy is finally exonerated, the truth can get no hearing. Carteret refuses to print the name of the real criminal, Tom Delamere, because exposing the scion of a distinguished white family would injure the reputation of the race. The country's papers bury news of Sandy's innocence in a brief paragraph on "an inside page," and the "facts of the case never came out at all" (233–34). White prestige prevails at the expense of justice for the slain woman's killer.

As Chesnutt emphasizes, the late nineteenth-century southern press owes its reach and influence to technological developments that have created an unprecedented ability to disseminate information. At the meeting of the plotters, Belmont expatiates at length on the decisive role played by the new media in constructing public opinion: "You, Carteret, represent the Associated Press. Through your hands passes all the news of the state. What more powerful medium for the propagation of an idea? The man who would govern a nation by writing its songs was a blethering idiot beside the fellow who can edit its news dispatches" (82–83). Thanks to the national wire services (plus the telegraph, telephone, linotype machine, and other communication advances), the *Morning Chronicle* and similar papers from below the Mason-Dixon line can define the Negro Question for the whole republic. They can broadcast distorted versions of the Wellington riot throughout the land and thus determine "the attitude of the great civilized world toward the events of the last ten hours" (313–14).[6] Chesnutt, to be sure, has no illusions about the North's complicity in eradicating unpopular—that is, unbiased—discourse. Whites from outside Dixie make easy dupes for the southern press because they have long since transferred their allegiance from the "Israel" of justice for the former slaves to the "new Pharaoh" of empire and racial subordination (238). They are content to take their views of African Americans "from the 'coon song' and the police reports," much like the party of northern visitors who are entertained at Wellington's best hotel in chapter 13, "The Cakewalk," and who never converse alone with any black person except a servant.

This dynamic, in which the quashing of minority perspectives fans outward to stifle the privileged race, gets endlessly recycled on the level of *The Marrow of Tradition*'s plot. Even the few "conscientious men" who disagree with the policy of wholesale disenfranchisement succumb: "Their objections were soon silenced by the all-powerful race argument" (239). The family drama concerning the half sisters Olivia Carteret, who is white, and Janet Miller, who is mulatto, revolves around acts of verbal suppression. The will and marriage certificate (to Janet's mother, Julia Brown) left behind by Sam Merkell, the father of both women, never sees the light of day because Polly intervenes to protect the family honor and steals the documents before Julia can retrieve them. When, after Polly's death, Olivia obtains the papers, she destroys them with the resolution that "the secret should remain buried forever in her own heart!" (270). Julia and Janet are the most obvious victims of these silencings and thefts; they lose their claim on Merkell's name and wealth. But the written instructions of the father are also disregarded, and Olivia violates her own conscience by expunging the truth about his second marriage. Sam Merkell himself provides one of the book's saddest examples of the way "race loyalty" operates to curb white speech. His letter to Mr. Delamere amounts to a litany of self-reproachful excuses for bowing to community pressure and not going public with his marriage: "I have never had the courage to acknowledge it openly," "the atmosphere I live in does not encourage moral heroism," "ask her [Janet] to forgive her father's weakness," and so on (260–63). The missive, intercepted by Polly and then Olivia, never reaches its intended recipient, and its full contents are never made known.

The experience of Mr. Delamere constitutes another textbook illustration of the perverting effects of white supremacy on language. Delamere rushes to his servant's defense when this "gentleman in ebony," as he likes to call Sandy (25), is imprisoned for Polly's murder. The white aristocrat "solemnly" affirms Sandy's innocence, but his "bare word" no longer carries weight in the post-Reconstruction climate of race hatred (211). It turns out that he can save his servant from lynching only by swearing under oath that Sandy was with him on the night of the crime. Already shaken by his grandson Tom's guilt, Delamere agrees to perjure himself in a scene that gives the final blow to his declining spirit. His "voice might have come from the tomb, so hollow and unnatural did it sound," Chesnutt writes, and to Ellis, who knows what really happened, the old man's sentences strike the ear "like clods dropping upon the coffin in an open grave" (231). The intimations of mortality prove prophetic: Delamere dies from the defiling of his word. He suffers a paralytic stroke shortly after Sandy's hearing and expires a few days later "without having in the meantime recovered the power of speech" (235). In a reprise of the Merkell subplot, his will bequeathing his estate to Dr. Adam Miller, Janet's light-skinned husband, never comes to light: General Belmont, Merkell's executor, suppresses the dead man's statement on the grounds that his property rightfully belongs to the white race.

Chesnutt was signifying upon Twain's Tom Driscoll, from *Pudd'nhead Wilson*, when he imagined Tom Delamere, substituting for a black villain disguised as a white man, a white villain disguised in blackface. Less often noted is how much Lee Ellis, Tom's rival for Carteret's half sister, Clara Pemberton, resembles Wilson himself. Like Twain's irreverent outsider, Ellis has to internalize local mores to make his way upward in the community; but whereas Wilson performs his ultimate defection at a public trial, Carteret's assistant editor learns to keep his mouth shut to advance himself and win Clara. (The love story has "a happy ending," as Chesnutt promised in the *Cleveland World*, but it pretty much disappears from the novel after the outbreak of the riot, overwhelmed by the political plot.) Cloning Wilson, Chesnutt gives Ellis Scotch ancestry, and the character differs from most Wellington whites in that his father was a Quaker and non-slaveholding Whig. Moreover, unlike Major Carteret, "he did not believe in lynch law" (216). But caution and ambition almost always trump Ellis's reservations about his white-supremacist employer and neighbors. He regularly stays mute during Carteret's racist diatribes (see especially chapter 16, "Ellis Takes a Trick"), and, though he realizes that Tom and not Sandy killed Polly Ochiltree, he elects not to speak out for fear of jeopardizing his standing with Clara. As he says to Mr. Delamere, he won't publicize the secret unless "absolutely necessary" (221), with the result that he waits too long to prevent the old gentleman from committing perjury.

Ellis's stature further decreases after the riot begins, and he remains unable to free his tongue from the shackle of race solidarity. He offers to ride with Miller to provide the doctor with white cover, but he cannot bring himself to condemn the attack on Wellington's black population "to a negro." Chesnutt's account of the two men's ride together bristles with silences: "Neither of them spoke"; "there was nothing for Ellis to say"; "hence he was silent." (291). Nor does Ellis object when his employer disavows responsibility for the riot's excesses, such as the burning of Miller's hospital. And when Carteret can't oversee the *Morning Chronicle*'s presentation of the murderous affair because of his son Dodie's croup and turns over the job to Ellis, we have to assume that the subeditor wrote what was expected of him. The conflagration passed into history as a black-led eruption of disorder, owing to the southern press's success in so portraying it.[7]

The flames that consume the hospital illuminate the hard fact that even Major Carteret can't escape the censorship of white bigotry. The text's primary agent of repression is silenced by his own voice. Having caused so much damage with his writings, Carteret reacts with horror when the townspeople start burning buildings and shooting women and children. He tries to restrain the rioters from attacking Miller's hospital, forgetting that they are merely implementing the message of the *Morning Chronicle*. As he pleads with the mob to desist, using the misnomer "Gentlemen!," which he would reserve for whites only, they recognize him as Wellington's leading editor and interpret his words as yet another tirade against "'nigger domination.'" "Their oracle had spoken," Chesnutt remarks, and the bloodthirsty audience cheers and understandably concludes that Carteret is offering encouragement. The "baffled orator" has no choice but to retire in defeat (305–6).

Yet the newspaperman's verbal obstruction, with all its ironies, pales beside the novel's most graphic evidence of racism's rebound effect: the difficulties, from birth, that attend Dodie Carteret's efforts to breathe. Early on in the narrative, Chesnutt notes that the color line forms a "veritable bed of Procrustes" for African Americans: "Those who grew above it must have their heads cut off, figuratively speaking,—must be forced back to the level assigned to their race; those who fell beneath the standard set had their necks stretched, literally enough, as the ghastly record in the daily papers gave conclusive evidence" (61). (There are no cases of beheading in the novel, but that punishment, crafty Babo's fate in "Benito Cereno," reminds us that the very existence of a highly educated black like Dr. Miller affronts Wellington's whites.)[8]

Dodie, heir to a prominent family whose patriarch publicly advocates lynch law, experiences as a white child the menace confronting all freedmen after Reconstruction. In the very first chapter, we learn that he has a mole under his left ear, suggesting to Mammy Jane that, were he black, he would surely "die by judicial strangulation" (10). She believes that the blemish, located "just at the point where the hangman's knot would strike," augurs grave misfortune (46), and the rest of the novel shows that she is correct. Dodie breathes "heavily, with a strange whistling sound" (45), after he swallows a piece of the rattle Polly gave him at his christening, and it becomes lodged in his throat; he is saved by Dr. Burns, who had traveled to Wellington from Philadelphia on the same train that carried Dr. Miller. Here, under pressure from Major Carteret, occurs the text's first case of lying for the race, a preview of Delamere's perjured testimony: Dr. Price, to prevent Miller from participating in the planned surgery, as Burns invited him to, denies the black man entrance by falsely stating that he has arrived too late. At the story's end, Dodie's implication through his father in the suppressing of black speech threatens his survival once again. During the riot, he develops the croup and, like the black victim of a lynching party, such as Wellington's citizens intended for Sandy, gasps and struggles for breath. Nothing short of a tracheotomy, "an operation to open the windpipe" (317), can prevent his strangling to death, and on the final page Miller agrees to perform the procedure that will preserve his life—and, one fears, enable him to carry on his father's racist crusade when he grows into an adult.

The cynical note is extratextual, as it were, for although Chesnutt said that his book eschewed pessimism, we know from history that Dixie's newspapers did not relent from their white-supremacist rhetoric for another seven decades. The text encourages the thought because of its own oscillations. The novelist seems to call for justice in The Marrow of Tradition, as indicated by the title of his penultimate chapter, "Fiat Justitia" (Let justice be done), but then he backpedals and opts for mercy by having Miller save his enemy's child. Chesnutt had wanted to win sympathy for southern blacks with his story, and he may have deliberately softened or censored his narrative in hopes of reaching a white audience. He often takes a practical, conciliatory line, as when he observes of the Afro-American Banner's rash editorial: "The right of free speech entitled Barber to publish it; a larger measure of common-sense would have made him withhold it" (278). The novelist also sides with Miller's caution over Josh Green's bravery, noting that whereas all who battled the rioters were dead, "those who had sought safety in flight or concealment were alive to tell the tale" (316). But the Job-like warning would have no purchase in 1901, any more than it did a half century earlier when Melville invoked it in the epilogue to Moby-Dick, another tale that shrinks from its own radicalism. For who would listen to Miller's words in turn-of-the-century America, where, as Chesnutt himself admits, "public opinion in matters of race" was "thoroughly diseased" (296)? In exercising his own "right of free speech," the novelist produced a volume that few white readers had any interest in, and he seems to have suspected its limited appeal. He reopened his legal stenography business at the same time that *The Marrow of Tradition* was published, hedging his bets about popular success with a book so critical of the New South.

Clearly William Dean Howells was on to something when he pronounced the novel "bitter, bitter" and concluded that it favored justice over mercy.[9] Though Chesnutt disputed this characterization, and though the text ends with Miller's rejection of vengeance, a prophetic undercurrent hints at retribution against the United States, the former Confederacy in particular. Prophecy had largely vanished from the work of white realists, but Chesnutt still believed in language's power, and he suggests more than once that just as slavery cursed the land and plunged it "into a bloody war" (92), so a nation forsaking Israel for the Pharaoh of racial caste will suffer punishment for its sins. "The South paid a fearful price for the wrong of slavery," the novelist warns; "in some form or other it will doubtless reap the fruits of this later iniquity" (241). Miller himself, "with prophetic instinct," foresees the distrust and hatred that will disquiet the region for years as a result of the Wellington riot (291).

As for Howells, after *The Marrow of Tradition* he wanted nothing more to do with this writer, "not entirely white,"[10] who drew such a bleak portrait of the reunited republic. In his review of the novel, Howells acknowledged the picture's accuracy and added that Chesnutt's power as an author was "a portent of the sort of negro equality against which no series of hangings and burnings will finally avail."[11] But in a private letter to the novelist Henry B. Fuller, he sounded a more fearful strain. Committed to the pacific policy espoused by Booker T. Washington, Howells recoiled from what he perceived as Chesnutt's militancy. "How such a negro must hate us!" he exclaimed. "And then think of the Filipinos and the Cubans and Puerto Ricans we have added to our happy family. But I am talking treason."[12] And so, rather like Ellis, unwilling to affiliate himself with treasonous discourse about the white race, Howells terminated his sponsorship of Chesnutt.

The disappointing reception of *The Marrow of Tradition* did not deter Chesnutt from returning to the novelistic fray in 1905. Like its predecessor, *The Colonel's Dream* aligns itself with "the forces of enlightenment" seeking to ameliorate conditions in the South (from the "Dedication," 3).[13] Again, and still more graphically this time, the "dead" past maintains its stranglehold on the present: the episode that breaks Colonel Henry

French's resolve to lift up his hometown is the desecration of a grave, caused by his attempt to desegregate the whites-only Oak Cemetery. The "spirit of slavery" (112) continues to embroil the people of Clarendon, North Carolina, reasserting itself in the systematic denial of basic rights to African Americans. "Negroes," summarizes Chesnutt, "must be taught that they need never look for any different state of things. New definitions were given to old words, new pictures set in old frames, new wine poured into old bottles" (182).

Chesnutt's reference to "enlightenment" in his "Dedication" clarifies his novel's lineage. It belongs on our list of postwar fictions casting the French revolution in a positive light and comparing the defeat of the South's slaveholding oligarchs to the Gallic overthrow of monarchical rule. The hero bears the surname "French," and, like Tourgée's Comfort Servosse, he journeys to the ex-Confederacy—in his case, it is a return—on a mission of reform. Another relevant comparison would be to the Connecticut Yankee, Hank Morgan, who wakes up in medieval Camelot and whose fate suggests the resilience of feudal ideas. French's antagonist, the son of an antebellum overseer who now controls Clarendon through his wealth and influence, has a no less symbolic last name, Fetters. He has made his fortune through a convict lease plantation, which effectively returns the freedmen to slavery, and a cotton mill, which, in the view of a local liveryman, does the same thing to white women and children.[14] Bill Fetters, who actively backs the drive to disenfranchise North Carolina's black population, represents the New South's failure to free itself from the manacles of the past. His machinations reactivate the pattern we have traced in *The Marrow of Tradition*: the fettering of southern mouths as well as minds, and the progress of voicelessness from blacks to whites.

Indeed, a key subplot in *The Colonel's Dream* foregrounds the act of silencing as a disability of blacks that directly, and adversely, impacts their fair-skinned oppressors. Old Malcolm Dudley has been searching for twenty-five years for a cache of gold left behind during the Civil War by his uncle Ralph. A single individual knows the location of the treasure, Malcolm's former slave and mistress, Viney, but she suffered a stroke and lost the power of speech after he had her whipped by an overseer. Having fallen on hard times since the war, like so many Southerners, Dudley repeatedly exhorts his housekeeper to divulge the money's hiding place; just as often, she points to her mouth and—like a person being lynched—emits "inarticulate" sounds while moving "her lips as though in speech" (131). Presumably Viney could reveal the treasure's whereabouts with "a few strokes of the pen" (165) . . . if only she could make use of a pen. But Viney was a slave, imprisoned in illiteracy, and not one of the lucky few, like Frederick Douglass, taught to read and write.

Not Malcolm Dudley alone, but the entire community of Clarendon, pays a heavy price for the muteness of African Americans such as Viney. At the end of the narrative, as Dudley lies on his deathbed, Viney recovers the capacity to speak and informs him, "strangely, slowly, thickly," that his uncle returned after an hour and retrieved the fifty thousand dollars in gold. "But I never told you," she cries. "I could have spoken at any time for twenty-five years, but I never told you!" (260). The mulatto woman, who dies moments after her quondam lover, kept the secret because she didn't wish to share it with a man who had mistreated her; and Chesnutt suggests that black aphasia and noncooperation will have similar consequences for the South. To the townspeople, the treasure hunter, digging frantically on his grounds, appears to be a lunatic; to the outsider, whites seem equally unbalanced in their obsession with race. Disregard for minority rights, says Chesnutt, "was bound to react, as slavery had done, upon the prosperity and progress of the State" (183). Certainly it has that effect in Clarendon. Colonel French becomes an object of opprobrium "as the protector of Negroes and the enemy of white men" (258). Worn down by popular resistance to his schemes for betterment and by the eruption of mob action that proscribes race mixing even after death, he follows the example of Uncle Ralph and takes away the treasure that he brought with him, the colorblind future that passes Clarendon by and leaves it sunk in backwardness for years to come.

Clarendon's whites are not spared their own approximation of Viney's vocal difficulties, and much of the obstruction, as with her, is self-imposed. For whites, though, fear and cowardice rather than anger provide the motivation for their refusal to speak. The town's "prominent citizens" listen to French's plea not to restrict suffrage, but, while partly agreeing with him, they "said no word" against the unfair proposal because "to take the Negro's side in any case where the race issue was raised, was to court social ostracism and political death" (182–83). And when Fetters's allies dump the coffin containing the body of Peter, French's family retainer, on the colonel's front porch, no one dares to raise a voice against the outrage. They are too cowed by the mobocratic spirit: "If there were those who reprobated the action they were silent" (268). As for the people of the North, they find it more expedient to say nothing. Colonel French writes to friends in Washington exposing the convict lease system, and his words create a sensation, but "owing to the exigencies of national politics it was not deemed wise, at that time, to do anything which seemed like an invasion of State rights or savored of sectionalism" (219).

Then there are Laura Treadwell, French's fiancée in Clarendon, and the colonel himself; they, too, enter the ranks of the silenced. Laura, whom French knew in his youth, exemplifies the best in the Old South. Kind, generous, and relatively free of race prejudice, she gives music lessons to the daughter of Nichols, the colored barber, and she admires French's ambitious ideas for his birthplace. But when she accepts his marriage proposal, Laura—with hardly any explanation—requests that the engagement be kept secret, and it repeats the fate of Sam Merkell's will and marriage certificate. The people of Clarendon never learn of the engagement, and, because Laura declines the colonel's offer to accompany him back to New York as his wife, she will take the secret with her to the grave, one more sacrifice to the undead past. As she tells French before he departs, she guessed all along that the town's bigotry would blight his plans. Foreseeing his disappointment and flight, she chose not to publicize the wedding because she suspected that it would never occur. French experiences an analogous divestment of speech: defeated by the ineradicable afterlife of slavery, he abandons Clarendon and with it his "dream of usefulness" (269). In a region where the "very word 'equality' was an offense" (250), there is little point, he realizes, in articulating his more enlightened attitudes: "He may as well have talked to the empty air" (265). Henceforth Colonel Henry French will do his talking in the North, where his words will have a chance of being heard.

From the perspective of this study, the colonel's vanquishing marks the end, not simply of Clarendon's prospects for joining modern life, but of a whole prophetic tradition in support of racial justice. We have explored how that American injunction, originating in the antebellum period, disintegrated after the Civil War, undone by a loss of faith in the verbal's efficacy. *The Colonel's Dream*, as its title hints, can be read as an ave atque vale to visions of national righteousness. Colonel French vows to get the better of Bill Fetters, much as he did as a schoolboy, but Fetters is the one who triumphs in the 1890s, and the hero's prediction comes to nothing. French has a literal dream the night that Peter's grave is desecrated, and his conscious or unconscious ideal furnishes the requiem for a now-moribund tradition. He imagines, writes Chesnutt in a sentence-long paragraph,

> a regenerated South, filled with thriving industries, and thronged with
> a prosperous and happy people, where every man, having enough for his
> needs, was willing that every other man should have the same; where

law and order should prevail unquestioned, and where every man could
enter, through the golden gate of hope, the field of opportunity, where
lay the prizes of life, which all might have an equal chance to win or
lose. (267)

The fact that French's son Phil dies in Clarendon, depriving the colonel of
an heir, underscores the perishability of this idyll; neither the man nor his
vision has any progeny.

In fairness, one must note that the colonel's squandered dream is not
Chesnutt's final statement on his country. Perhaps still seeking to attract
readers with his optimism, he tacked on two last paragraphs in which he
gestures at a "changed attitude of mind" that will someday enable liberty
and justice to "prevail throughout all our borders" (280–81). It is hard to
take the sentiments seriously. The realities of the narrative expose the de-
lusion of transcending the color line, and no reader who finishes the novel
can put it down without a sense of despair. In *The Colonel's Dream*, the
old ways prove too potent for scenarios of a better future; the past's loyal-
ists slam shut "the golden gate of hope." The publication date of Chesnutt's
novel, 1905, was also the year of Dixon's *The Clansman*, and Dixon would
abduct the prophetic voice to resurrect a dictatorship of racial caste as the
only American dream worth fighting for.

For Chesnutt's fictional South, the prognosis is grim; Fetters and his
ilk will control the region's destiny for the foreseeable future. Bud Johnson, the fugitive convict laborer who is subsequently lynched, shoots Bill's
son Barclay Fetters in an ambush, and the young ruffian suffers a loss of
vision from his wound. When he later recovers the use of one eye, Barclay is so embittered by his deformity that he devotes all his energies to
the "debasement" of "the whole Negro race" (278). Fetters's son is the second Chesnutt villain with a single eye; Captain McBane from *The Marrow of Tradition* is similarly disfigured. In portraying the two characters,
Chesnutt may have been signifying on "Pitchfork" Ben Tillman, the er-
satz South Carolina populist and scourge of nonwhites. Blind in one eye,
Tillman was known for "his fierce one-eyed glower."[15] Or Chesnutt may
have been thinking of a figure called the "Grand Cyclops," a local head of
the Ku Klux Klan. In the *Odyssey*, Odysseus and his companions flee the
cave of the Cyclops, a one-eyed monster who dines on humans. Governed
by blind and blinkered men like McBane, Fetters, and Tillman, the post-
Reconstruction South cannot be anything but a place for blacks to escape
from, as it was for Chesnutt, even though he could pass for white. The sec-

tion "has had its chance" (280), and thrown it away, and it would not soon have another opportunity to right its course.

Chesnutt had no better luck in his future as a novelist. The two outcomes were cognate: the South's cankerous racial views became entrenched in American culture as a whole, and the audience for books such as *The Colonel's Dream* evaporated with the new century. When the novel was published, southern newspapers implied that such gloomy and "libelous" fictions should be banned because they did more damage than good. As a reviewer from Nashville, Tennessee, put it, the "negro problem would likely be no problem, if it were possible to stop its discussion, and it is greatly aggravated by being made material for novels."[16] Partly enforced from without, partly prompted from within, Viney's reticence overtook her creator. Chesnutt's work was not literally proscribed after *The Colonel's Dream*, but the novel sold poorly, and he grew sufficiently discouraged that for the next decade and a half he channeled almost all his talent into his business career. When he resumed writing fiction in 1919, he went on to complete a collection of short stories and two novels. None could find a publisher until the 1990s, sixty years after Chesnutt's death.

Dixon and the Rebirth of Discursive Power

It is a minor scene, but characteristic in its obsessions with the related phenomena of white racial purity and organs of speech. Annie, the daughter of Tom Camp and "as plump and winsome a lassie, her Scotch mother declared, as the Lord ever made" (122),[1] is dragged from her home by a gang of colored troopers stationed in Hambright, North Carolina, to back up the Reconstruction governments. They are about to commit "The Unspoken Terror," as a later chapter title has it, of rape, and they muffle Annie's screams by sticking a gag in her mouth. A group of white mountaineers—urged on by Tom, for whom "there are things worse than death"—open fire on the blacks; five are hit, and in the midst of the heap of bodies "lay the unconscious girl gagged." Annie has been killed by a bullet in the temple "from which a scarlet stream was running down her white throat." The episode ends with Tom thanking and shaking the hands of the white men for having "saved" his child (125–26).

Rape, an extreme example of the outrage of black assertiveness, is designed to throttle utterance in addition to violating the body. The crime dramatically underscores the struggle between white Southerners and freedmen—or, more generally, between the opponents and advocates of Reconstruction—for the right to speak in the reunited republic. Victims are forcibly silenced, the horrific act cannot be spoken, and the sexually debased women invariably die, as Annie and her sister Flora do in *A Leopard's Spots*, and as Marion Lenoir does in *The Clansman*. The blood running down Annie's "white throat" parallels the broken necks of lynched rapists. In *The Leopard's Spots*, Tim Shelby, a former slave who had belonged to the Shelbys of *Uncle Tom's Cabin*, suffers that penalty when he dares to request a kiss from a white woman who has applied for a position as teacher. Tim holds the title of school commissioner, itself a travesty;

his other infamies include a "native eloquence" that enables him to rivet Negro audiences (88). But this time his abuse of language has gone too far, and irate Klansmen exact revenge. His corpse is discovered hanging from a tree; his "thick lips had been split with a knife," and a note between his teeth reaffirms white control over minority dialect: "*The answer of the Anglo-Saxon race to Negro lips that dare pollute with words the womanhood of the South*" (150).

By staging the vocal as a decisive arena of Reconstruction conflict, Dixon's romances follow the lead of *A Fool's Errand*, but the Southerner's goal is not simply to invert Tourgée's emphases by vindicating the defeated section's "story." Preacher turned novelist turned playwright turned screenwriter, Dixon seeks to overthrow the egalitarian narrative by seizing and transferring its agency in history to the longtime victims of its falsehoods, the white men and women of Dixie. In his account, the most fanatical elements in the North have held the rhetorical upper hand for half a century, from the abolitionists to the Republican architects of racial equality; at long last, an awakened South is finding its voice and speaking through heroic characters such as "Preacher" Durham (a self-portrait), Charles Gaston, and Dr. Cameron. Above all, the South expresses itself through Dixon's novels, and he self-consciously frames *The Leopard's Spots* as a linguistic battle between himself, on the one hand, and Stowe, Tourgée, and possibly Chesnutt, on the other. It is a feud in which the documentary armature of "radicalism"—activist fiction, the Declaration, the Bible—is mobilized on behalf of reunionist closure, destined to last, according to Gaston, for a thousand years; and a reinvigorated, transformed Slave Power finally achieves its ambition of stamping out dissent.

The Reverend John Durham, the novel's spokesman for race purity and the preceptor of Gaston, has a voice "full of a magnetic quality that gave him hypnotic power over an audience" (8). He could hold a church of slaves spellbound, but he has lost his dark-skinned parishioners to the distrust sown by Reconstruction. The preacher has a long string of confrontations with those characters, both white and black, who seek to advance the Republican program and are themselves often formidable if fraudulent speakers, from the carpetbagger Simon Legree through Tim Shelby to the scalawag Allan McLeod. Legree, who has hired a pronunciation and grammar teacher since *Uncle Tom's Cabin*, delivers tirades for the Union League, at which "negroes hang breathless on his every word as the inspired Gospel of God" (86). With former Rebels disenfranchised and blacks voting more than once, Uncle Tom's killer is elected to the state legislature and presides over an orgy of corruption as "Speaker of the House." McLeod has "an oily tongue" that "will carry you a long way in this world," as Durham tells him (174); the chapter in which the scalawag tries to entice Gaston over to the Republican side is titled "The Voice of the Tempter." These exchanges are not mere differences in point of view. They are clashes between lies and "the Truth" (40)—no northern isms for Dixon, including relativism—and one party is typically silenced, as when the KKK lynches Shelby or the preacher is thrown in jail for inciting insurrection and forbidden to speak or sing during his imprisonment.

Durham's incarceration and muzzling evoke the fate of the South. Declining a permanent invitation to head a congregation in Boston, he describes the tragedy of his region as well as his hopes for the future:

> The South has been voiceless in these later years, her voice has been drowned in a din of cat-calls from an army of cheap scribblers and demagogues. But when these children we are rearing down here grow, rocked in their cradles of poverty, nurtured in the fierce struggle to save the life of a mighty race, they will find speech, and their songs will fill the world with pathos and power. (334)

The motif of the former Confederacy's muteness or overborne speech fills the text, often in formulations that suggest, as with Annie Camp, a reverse lynching. Gaston refuses to defect to the Republicans because they have "tried to ram down our throats, Negro supremacy in politics" (194). Mrs. Durham, the preacher's wife, complains that the Negro's presence, grotesquely romanticized by "an ocean of maudlin sentimental fools," is "a grip of steel on the throat of the South" (262).

Mrs. Durham also draws our notice to the principal factor in the South's victimization, the power of literature, a phenomenon that Dixon strives to replicate in his epics of white supremacy. She points an accusing finger at *Uncle Tom's Cabin* as a devastating exercise of northern speech: "A little Yankee woman wrote a crude book. The single act of that woman's will caused the war, killed a million men, desolated and ruined the South, and changed the history of the world" (262). In 1902, no realist, and quite possibly no northern author, would have endorsed such extravagant claims for the aesthetic (or the unaesthetic, according to the preacher's wife); but the South, blaming the war on abolitionism and still smarting from the Reconstruction amendments, had never forgotten what writing could accomplish. A vulgar novel was the cause of it all. Dixon hijacks characters from *Uncle Tom's Cabin*—Legree, Shelby, George Harris, Eliza's son, and others—and uses them to discredit the antislavery narrative; he originally planned to call his novel "The Rise of Simon Legree." At the same time, he knows that the "speech" and "songs" of Southerners must capture the efficacy of the Stowe model. (Harris is a Harvard-educated mulatto and aspiring composer who reveals his depravity by seeking the hand of a white woman.) The language of Redemption, and the novels that deploy it, will then set history back on the right track. To paraphrase Lincoln at Cooper Institute, they will unsay what Stowe said, and undo what Stowe did.

Not all Dixon's sources can compete with Stowe in influence. Tourgée is another unwilling rhetorical collaborator, legitimating from the outside the idea of defiant Southerners as manly and medieval. The characterization becomes a refrain in *A Leopard's Spots*, where a typical passage compares the hoods of the Klansmen to "the mail helmets of ancient knights" (149). Tourgée's arraignments of the KKK are the photographic negative of Dixon's celebrations. The carpetbagger documented the marauders' crimes in *The Invisible Empire*; Dixon says in the prefatory "Note to the Reader" from *The Clansman* that he aims to provide "the true story" of KKK resistance. Dixon may also have had Chesnutt's *The Marrow of Tradition* in mind. Chesnutt narrates the African American view of the 1898 North Carolina "race riots" that led to the white coup d'état; Dixon defends the Redeemer side. Moreover, an incident central to Chesnutt's text reappears late in *The Leopard's Spots*, when Dixon interpolates the story of a black newspaper editor who defames "the virtue of the white women of the community." Local whites burn down the paper's office and march the offending Negro to the train depot "with a rope around his neck" (411–13).

Other writings conscripted by Dixon to the Redeemer cause rival or surpass even Stowe in the history of northern agitation. They include the scriptures, cited frequently by the preacher and evoked in the novel's title; the speeches of Abraham Lincoln, quoted on postwar reconciliation and Negro unfitness; the Declaration of Independence, invoked to justify secession; and the "higher law," a staple of abolitionist protest now mobilized on behalf of white restoration. (A late chapter is titled "The Higher Law.") *The Clansman* adds a further twist to these appropriations by portraying southern ruthlessness in blackface, as the aggression of the sufferers; what is coopted here is the possibility of any victimhood save that of southern whites. Black characters have the surnames "Lynch" and "Whipper," and Dixon inverts the racial referents of a famous sentence in the *Dred Scott* decision, turning it into the credo of Radical Republicanism: "A white man has no right a negro need respect."[2] The whole novel details the horrors of blacked-up tyranny, with the KKK revolting against the dictatorial regime established by erstwhile slaves called "Napoleon" (Whipper's Christian name) and "Augustus" (Gus, the rapist of Marion). Because it was the freedmen who in reality experienced caste oppression, one might compare Dixon's tales to the masquerades of whites like Tom Driscoll (of *Pudd'nhead Wilson*) and Tom Delamere (*The Marrow of Tradition*), who pass off their crimes as the misdeeds of blacks.

One additional source for Dixon requires mention. He had to dig back to the beginning of the nineteenth century for a literary predecessor he could mime wholeheartedly, and he found that figure in Mark Twain's nemesis and nominee for the South's bard of slavery, Sir Walter Scott. We have barely glanced at Dixon's idealizing of Covenanter blood, but this element, so integral to his worldview, suggests that he has as good a claim as James Fenimore Cooper to being Scott's American successor. His Reconstruction trilogy chronicles the wars between nativist Highlanders and enemies from without (northern carpetbaggers) and from within (the freedmen).[3] Dixon describes the Scots, "the backbone of the South," as a "race" with a glorious history of fighting for self-rule; the KKK on their missions to preserve the purity of white blood are "the reincarnated souls of the Clansmen of Old Scotland."[4] The novelist whose royalist avatars reduced Huck and Jim to silence on the raft was again in the cultural vanguard. His outmoded brand of romance, buried by Twain but reincarnated in Dixon, would best Stowe, Tourgée, and Chesnutt as the nation embraced the Jim Crow system of racial subordination.

The Leopard's Spots recounts the story of Gaston's rise to political authority and his successful courtship of Sallie Worth; through the young hero, Preacher Durham's vision of a South that has recovered its voice is realized. The dual plot lines have to be seen as one because Dixon, rejecting the pro-Reconstruction argument that social behavior can be disarticulated from political rights, the marriage bed from the voting booth, treats the two as inseparable.[5] And both plots require the vanquishing of false, that is, Republican, speech by the idiom of the absolute color line. The scalawag McLeod, for example, does not just oppose Gaston's ambitions for the governorship. He wants to marry Sallie, too, and the slanders he directs against the hero politically are paralleled by the lies he tells her father, General Worth, in an attempt to sabotage his rival's suit. McLeod also has political run-ins with the preacher, who accuses him of perjury and lying; and he embarks on a campaign to seduce Mrs. Durham with his "oily tongue" so that he can blacken her reputation and destroy her husband.

Gaston possesses "oratorical genius" (193), and he conquers Sallie's heart with an address commemorating the Confederate dead. But he needs to fully internalize the preacher's ideology of Anglo-Saxon domination to achieve his destiny as the New South's empowered voice.[6] Durham's various mantras—"one drop of Negro blood makes a negro" (242), "the Republic [will] be Mulatto or Anglo-Saxon" (97), and so on—fail to impress Gaston with the urgency of the danger of race mixing. Nor do they cure the protagonist of his friendship with Dick, the shiftless young freedman who flees Hambright after he is whipped for a prank (by a black man!) and who later returns for the sole purpose, it seems, of raping and murdering Tom Camp's second daughter, Flora. That act, the companion to Annie's violation, occurs in the chapter "The Unspoken Terror"; language is inadequate to such evil, as all whites understand except for Gaston. A crowd prepares to burn Dick alive in an "uncanny silence" that is broken only by the Negro's screams and the hero's misguided attempts to save him. It is the low point in Gaston's relation to the community: his pleas for a fair trial sound "strained and discordant," and the "voiceless mob" ignores him to carry out the lynching (377–79).

A subsequent scene involving the Yankee philanthropist Everett Lowell underlines the folly of Gaston's mistake. At Boston's Faneuil Hall and New York's Cooper Union, Lowell gives speeches denouncing the Hambright affair, which has stirred indignation across the North. George Harris, who works for him, is emboldened by Lowell's defense of equality and asks to marry his daughter Helen on the assumption, entirely legitimate in Dixon's view, that equal rights cannot be limited to politics. Lowell, however, is repelled by the mulatto's effrontery and glares at him like "a leopard or tiger . . . about to spring at his throat" (390). This time, the Negro is the one silenced, as Lowell refuses to allow Harris to propose to Helen and orders him from the house. Eliza's son predictably degenerates, and we last see him visiting ash heaps in "Colorado, Kansas, Indiana, and Ohio" (403), where other trespassers of the color line have been burned to death. As Mark Twain would observe a few years later, the North had begun to see eye to eye with the South on the proper punishment for being black.

The rape of Flora and Dick's lynching mark the turning point in Gaston's maturation. He grasps that the barrier between the races is insurmountable, and Preacher Durham's "fateful words," recollected and pondered in tranquility—"*You can not build in a Democracy a nation inside a nation of two antagonistic races. The future American must be an Anglo-Saxon or a Mulatto*" (382–83)—complete his conversion to white supremacy and Negro disenfranchisement. The political and romantic climax of the novel follows in a rush: under Gaston's leadership, whites seize control of the nearby town of Independence and issue "a second Declaration of Independence" from Negro rule (411). The hero and Sallie exchange marriage vows in jail, where he has been placed on fabricated charges of fraud. Gaston then delivers the oration that establishes Anglo-Saxon government—"Citizen kings, I call you to the consciousness of your kingship" (442)—and gains him the Democratic nomination for governor. His speech wins over General Worth, who gives his consent to the marriage; and McLeod, exposed as the slanderer of Mrs. Durham, is forced to write a recantation and flees to Boston.

Gaston's oration is the text's definitive answer to *Uncle Tom's Cabin*, the rhetorical performance in which the suddenly articulate South finally defeats its tormentors. It is "A Speech That Made History," as another portentous chapter title assures us, and its impact thus counters the great reach of Stowe's book, said by Mrs. Durham to have "changed the history of the world." But Gaston's triumph will outdo and outlast the radical successes of the past, because this time—and the time is 1898, year of the Spanish-American War—the two sections are in unison. The North, belatedly come to its senses, turns a deaf ear to the entreaties of blacks and Republican "Stalwarts"; sentimental humanitarianism has been ousted by the siren of empire. In Gaston's words, "The Anglo-Saxon race is united and has entered upon its world-mission" (440). North Carolina's whites, no longer fearful of federal interference—indeed, now confident of national consent—will proceed to eliminate the remnants of the "paper-made policies" that stripped them of self-determination (441). They will effectively "nullify the Fourteenth and Fifteenth Amendments to the Constitution of the Republic," relegating the syntax of equality to the dustbin of history (446). Every African American in the land, including educated ones, will "feel the clutch of the iron hand of the white man's unwritten laws on their throat" (263), but the figurative lynching will apply to northern holdouts as well as to blacks. As Dixon would put it in *The Clansman*, the South has "its hands tight-gripped on the throat of tyrant, thug, and thief."[7] Loudly and irresistibly declaiming the Truth of white sovereignty, a reborn Dixie is choking its ideological adversaries into stillness.

Dixon's romances are the metafictional analog to Gaston's "Speech That Made History." They contributed significantly to the changed climate of opinion. In the novelist, too, the former Confederacy attained world-changing utterance and overmastered the "army of cheap scribblers and demagogues" who traduced its way of life. Tourgée, Chesnutt, and, yes, the vindictive imaginer of Uncle Tom, more than met their match in *The Leopard's Spots* and *The Clansman*, books that became blockbusters above and below the Mason-Dixon Line and that spoke with one voice, the South's voice, for both sections. "There was no North, no South," says Dixon of the imperial nation that had, for the first time in its history, fulfilled the "beautiful dream called *E Pluribus Unum*" (406). Dixon's fictions would have a second life (or a third, because he turned his second novel into a stage play) as the screenplay for *The Birth of a Nation*, arguably the most influential movie ever made; and of course the Jim Crow doctrine that he advocated so tirelessly would harden into the republic's official position on race from the end of the nineteenth century until the middle of the twentieth. Only the most anodyne and regressive aspects of *Uncle Tom's Cabin*—black submission and suffering—would enjoy that kind of longevity.

From one perspective, this outcome could be understood as a regeneration of discursive agency, with the power that once belonged to New England reformers and idealists now wielded by the forces of reaction. Dixon, as I have been arguing, saw his novels as toppling the canon of activism and incorporating its effectiveness. But the displacement of Stowe's and Sumner's words by Gaston's and Dixon's could also be thought of as the culmination of a trend. The seizure of verbal authority by southern writers, or by the unified colossus that took its lead on race from the South, represented the fulfillment, the emergence into autonomy, of the unreconstructed voice that inhabits so many late nineteenth-century fictions as an insistent pressure from within: Tom Sawyer, Pudd'nhead Wilson, Basil Ransom, the town of Whilomville. And those who dissented from the ascendant monolith—Huck, Twain, Dr. Trescott, Douglass, Chesnutt, and Wells—would be stifled by the rough hands on the country's throat.

But perhaps the true acme of the cultural formation that replaced the statutory repression of the slave republic with the majoritarian prison house of segregation and disenfranchisement was "A Film That Made History": *The Birth of a Nation*. Griffith timed the release of his masterpiece to coincide with the fiftieth anniversary of the end of the Civil War, and its success established the movies as the twentieth-century successor and, in audience reach, the superior of the novel. Griffith's epic depicts Reconstruction as a monstrous revolution in the natural order of things that is repelled by the combined force of southern vigilantes and enlightened Northerners. Redemption asserted its ownership over the most demotic art form of the modern age, a species of entertainment, and an instrument of ideological indoctrination, unprecedented in its appeal. *Uncle Tom's*

Cabin sold three million copies before the Civil War; between 1915 and 1926, 100 million moviegoers watched *The Birth of a Nation*.[8] President Woodrow Wilson extolled the film, and its popularity jump-started the second incarnation of the Ku Klux Klan. It is all "so terribly true," the Virginia-born president is supposed to have said, and Dixon, who had attended graduate school at Johns Hopkins University with Wilson, vouched for the picture's "historical accuracy" on numerous occasions. Both were right in the sense that the film's interpretation of postwar events entered historical consciousness and, for generations of Americans, shaped understanding of the country's past. Almost everyone fell into line. As a contemporaneous critic of the movie remarked, "Even the most eminent historians suppress the truth about it [Reconstruction], in the interest . . . of national harmony."[9] The cinema, according to Dixon, constituted "a new universal language of man."[10] *The Birth of a Nation*, by strangling the African American voice, showed that it was a "universal" tongue not everyone would be permitted to speak.

A concluding irony arises from the hostile reception of *The Birth of a Nation* by a small band of racial progressives. Griffith, who had begun shooting on July 4, regarded himself as upholding American traditions, in his case white supremacy. An eruption of protest startled the director: the NAACP and a few prominent white liberals, such as Jane Addams, called for the movie to be banned. "Freedom of discussion"—the freedom, that is, to dehumanize the other—deserted to the side of reaction as Griffith rallied to his picture's defense. Having consolidated the cultural hegemony that marginalized and muzzled blacks, he reinvented himself as an implacable foe of censorship. Fervently championing "freedom of expression," he deplored the campaign against his film as the gravest threat to this basic right since the Sedition Act of 1798. (The trespasses of the Slave Power went unremarked.) Griffith denounced the Supreme Court's denial of First Amendment protections to the movies, and he insisted that the cinema deserved "the same constitutional freedom as the printed press." The title he chose for the pamphlet he published in 1916 to justify his film was *The Rise and Fall of Free Speech in America*.[11]

Antebellum

1791–1804	Haitian Revolution establishes world's first black republic	
1820–21	Missouri Compromise Timothy Fuller opposes extension of slavery	
1829		Walker, *Appeal to the Coloured Citizens of the World*
1831	Nat Turner's Rebellion	Garrison founds *The Liberator*
1833	American Anti-Slavery Society founded	
1833–34	Southern postmasters seize and burn abolitionist mailings	
1834	Slavery abolished in the British West Indies	
1835	William Lloyd Garrison mobbed in Boston	Emerson, "John Milton"
1836	Gag rule adopted by the House of Representatives	Emerson, *Nature*

1837	Elijah Lovejoy murdered in Alton, Illinois	Emerson, "The American Scholar"
1838		Lincoln, "The Perpetuation of Our Political Institutions"
1844	Repeal of the gag rule through the efforts of John Quincy Adams	Emerson, "Address on the Emancipation" Emerson, "The Poet" Fuller, *Summer on the Lakes*
1845	Annexation of Texas	Fuller, *Woman in the Nineteenth Century* Douglass, *Autobiography*
1846	War with Mexico Wilmot Proviso introduced	Melville, *Typee*
1848	Mexican-American War ends Free Soil Party founded Seneca Falls Convention	
1849		Thoreau, "Civil Disobedience" Thoreau, *A Week on the Concord and Merrimack Rivers* Melville, *Mardi*
1850	Compromise of 1850, including the Fugitive Slave Law	Hawthorne, *The Scarlet Letter* Melville, "Hawthorne and His Mosses"
1851	Rendition of Thomas Sims from Boston	Hawthorne, *The House of the Seven Gables* Melville, *Moby-Dick*
1852	Franklin Pierce elected president	Stowe, *Uncle Tom's Cabin* Hawthorne, *Life of Franklin Pierce* Hawthorne, *The Blithedale Romance*

1853		Melville, "Bartleby, the Scrivener"
1854	Return of Anthony Burns to slavery Kansas-Nebraska Act passed, repealing the Missouri Compromise	Thoreau, *Walden* Thoreau, "Slavery in Massachusetts" Emerson, "The Fugitive Slave Law"
1855	Fighting breaks out in Kansas Republican Party founded	Whitman, *Leaves of Grass* Douglass, *My Bondage and My Freedom* Melville, "Benito Cereno"
1856	Charles Sumner assaulted in U.S. Senate Sack of Lawrence, Kansas Territory Pottawatomie massacre led by John Brown James Buchanan elected president	Stowe, *Dred* Whitman, *The Eighteenth Presidency!*
1857	*Dred Scott* decision Buchanan supports discredited Lecompton Constitution	Melville, *The Confidence-Man*
1858	Lincoln-Douglas debates	
1859	John Brown's raid on Harpers Ferry Brown executed Stephen A. Douglas offers "Invasion of States" resolution in U.S. Senate	Thoreau, "A Plea for Captain John Brown" Emerson, Speech on John Brown Wilson, *Our Nig*
1860	Democratic Party fractures Abraham Lincoln elected president in a four-way race	Lincoln, Address at Cooper Institute

1861	Lincoln inaugurated Ft. Sumter fired upon Civil War begins	Jacobs, *Incidents in the Life of a Slave Girl*
1863		Lincoln, Emancipation Proclamation Lincoln, Gettysburg Address
1865	Robert E. Lee surrenders at Appomattox Lincoln assassinated Andrew Johnson becomes president Thirteenth Amendment ratified	Lincoln, Second Inaugural Address Emerson, "Abraham Lincoln" Whitman, *Drum Taps*

Postbellum

1866	Presidential Reconstruction Ku Klux Klan founded	Melville, *Battle-Pieces and Aspects of the War*
1867	Congressional Reconstruction	
1868	Fourteenth Amendment ratified	
1870	Fifteenth Amendment ratified	
1871	Congress passes enforcement acts dismantling KKK	Whitman, *Democratic Vistas*
1873	Massacre of blacks in Colfax, Louisiana *Slaughterhouse Cases* decision weakens protections of Fourteenth Amendment	
1875	Civil Rights Act	

1876		Melville, *Clarel*
1876–77	Rutherford B. Hayes elected president in disputed election against Samuel Tilden Federal troops withdrawn from the South	
1879		Whitman, "Death of Abraham Lincoln" Tourgée, *A Fool's Errand*
1880		Cable, *The Grandissimes* Tourgée, *Bricks without Straw*
1881		Douglass, *Life and Times* Harris, *Uncle Remus*
1883	Supreme Court decision overturning 1875 Civil Rights Act seen as giving a green light to segregation and disenfranchisement	Twain, *Life on the Mississippi*
1884	Grover Cleveland elected first Democratic president since Buchanan	Jackson, *Ramona*
1885		Twain, *Adventures of Huckleberry Finn*
1886		James, *The Bostonians*
1888	Benjamin Harrison elected president	
1889		Twain, *A Connecticut Yankee in King Arthur's Court*
1889–92	Dramatic increase in lynching	

1890	Lodge Force Bill Mississippi Plan	
1891	Senate defeats Force Bill	Melville, *Billy Budd* Whitman, "Deathbed edition" of *Leaves of Grass*
1892	Cleveland elected president for the second time	Wells, *Southern Horrors* Howells, *An Imperative Duty*
1893	Congress repeals all enforcement acts World's Columbian Exposition	Douglass, *Life and Times*, expanded edition
1894		Twain, *Pudd'nhead Wilson* Cable, *John March, Southerner*
1895		Crane, *The Red Badge of Courage*
1896	*Plessy v. Ferguson* decision	
1898	Spanish-American War "White riot" kills scores of blacks in Wilmington, North Carolina	Page, *Red Rock* Crane, *The Monster*
1901		Chesnutt, *The Marrow of Tradition* Twain, "The United States of Lyncherdom" (unpublished in his lifetime) Washington, *Up from Slavery*
1902		Dixon, *The Leopard's Spots*
1905		Dixon, *The Clansman* Chesnutt, *The Colonel's Dream*
1907		James, *The American Scene*

| 1912 | Woodrow Wilson elected president; proceeds to segregate the federal government | |
| 1915 | Fiftieth anniversary of the end of the Civil War American troops occupy Haiti | Griffith, *The Birth of a Nation* |

INTRODUCTION

1. The relevant works are W. J. Cash, *The Mind of the South* (1941; rpt., New York: Vintage Books, 1991); Clement Eaton, *Freedom of Thought in the Old South* (Durham, NC: Duke University Press, 1940); and Russel B. Nye, *Fettered Freedom: Civil Liberties and the Slavery Controversy, 1830–1860* (East Lansing: Michigan State College Press, 1949). The best subsequent study of southern despotism is William W. Freehling, *The Road to Disunion*, 2 vols., *Secessionists at Bay, 1776–1854* (New York: Oxford University Press, 1990), and *Secessionists Triumphant* (New York: Oxford University Press, 2007).

2. On Free Soil, see James M. McPherson, *Battle Cry of Freedom: The Civil War Era* (New York: Oxford University Press, 1988), 62. David Reynolds cites the Republican slogan in *John Brown, Abolitionist: The Man Who Killed Slavery, Sparked the Civil War, and Seeded Civil Rights* (New York: Alfred A. Knopf, 2005), 426. Important works on the campaign against free speech include David Grimsted, *American Mobbing, 1828–1861: Toward Civil War* (New York: Oxford University Press, 1998); William Lee Miller, *Arguing about Slavery: John Quincy Adams and the Great Battle in the United States Congress* (New York: Alfred A. Knopf, 1996); and John Nerone, *Violence against the Press: Policing the Public Sphere in U.S. History* (New York: Oxford University Press, 1994). On the Republicans, see Eric Foner, *Free Soil, Free Labor, Free Men: The Ideology of the Republican Party before the Civil War* (New York: Oxford University Press, 1970). Fifty years after Nye, we still await a comprehensive analysis of "fettered freedom" in the prewar North. The book that comes closest to a general overview is Michael Kent Curtis, *Free Speech, "The People's Darling Privilege": Struggles for Freedom of Expression in American History* (Durham, NC: Duke University Press, 2000).

3. Cash, *The Mind of the South*, 134. On reunion and the abandonment of the freedmen, see, among a host of studies, David W. Blight, *Race and Reunion: The Civil War in American Memory* (Cambridge, MA: Harvard University Press, 2001); and Edward J. Blum, *Reforging the White Republic: Race, Religion, and American Nationalism, 1865–1898* (Baton Rouge: Louisiana State University Press, 2005). On postwar white terrorism, see Stephen Budianski, *The Bloody Shirt: Terror after Appomattox* (New

York: Viking, 2008); and Nicholas Lemann, *Redemption: The Last Battle of the Civil War* (New York: Farrar, Straus and Giroux, 2006). On lynching, see Jacqueline Goldsby, *A Spectacular Secret: Lynching in American Life and Literature* (Chicago: University of Chicago Press, 2006).

4. C. Vann Woodward, *Origins of the New South, 1877–1913* (Baton Rouge: Louisiana State University Press, 1951), 321–49; also see Jack Beatty, *Age of Betrayal: The Triumph of Money in America, 1865–1900* (New York: Alfred A. Knopf, 2007), 377–89.

5. Foner, *The Story of American Freedom* (New York: W. W. Norton, 1998), 137; and Rabban, *Free Speech in Its Forgotten Years* (New York: Cambridge University Press, 1997). An excellent study of historical erasure and denial, with the focus on Haiti, is Michel-Rolph Trouillot, *Silencing the Past: Power and the Production of History* (Boston: Beacon Press, 1995).

6. Ezra Tawil also notes the silence of the Declaration and the circumlocutions of the Constitution about slavery in *The Making of Racial Sentiment: Slavery and the Birth of the Frontier Romance* (New York: Cambridge University Press, 2006), 26–29. He sees a sharp break between eighteenth- and nineteenth-century conceptions of race.

7. See Jacobs, *Incidents in the Life of a Slave Girl, Written by Herself*, ed. Jean Fagan Yellin (Cambridge, MA: Harvard University Press, 1987), 122; and James Turner, ed., *David Walker's Appeal* (Baltimore, MD: Black Classic Press, 1993), 74, 91, and Turner's introduction. William Lloyd Garrison regularly spoke of the oppression that "now holds millions of our colored countrymen by their throats." Garrison is quoted in Robert Fanuzzi, *Abolition's Public Sphere* (Minneapolis: University of Minnesota Press, 2004), 12.

8. See Takayuki Tatsumi, "Literacy, Literality, Literature: The Rise of Cultural Aristocracy in 'The Murders in the Rue Morgue,'" *Journal of American and Canadian Studies* 12 (1994): 1–23. Poe may have been thinking of the panic over free black sailors arriving in southern ports on ships from the North.

9. Whitman, *Leaves of Grass: The First (1855) Edition*, ed. Malcolm Cowley (New York: Penguin Classics, 1986), 16.

10. Wilson, *Our Nig; or, Sketches from the Life of a Free Black*, ed. Henry Louis Gates Jr. (New York: Vintage Books, 1983), 35.

11. Douglass, "Lessons of the Hour" (1894), in *The Frederick Douglass Papers*, series 1, *Speeches, Debates, and Interviews*, vol. 5, *1881–95*, ed. John Blassingame and John R. McKivigan (New Haven, CT: Yale University Press, 1992), 585; and Douglass, introduction to Ida B. Wells, Frederick Douglass, Irvine Garland Penn, and Ferdinand L. Barnett, *The Reason Why the Colored American Is Not in the World's Columbian Exposition: The Afro-American's Contribution to Columbian Literature*, ed. Robert W. Rydell (1893; rpt., Urbana: University of Illinois Press, 1999), 12. Lynching may have been peculiar to the United States, but the use of rape charges to vindicate "civilization" against "barbarism" was not. A similar pattern emerged simultaneously in post-Mutiny India, with the violated woman serving as a metonym for a colonial administration "that sees itself as the violated object of rebellion." See Jenny Sharpe, *Allegories of Empire: The Figure of the Woman in the Colonial Text* (Minneapolis: University of Minnesota Press, 1993), 7 passim.

12. See Morrison, *Playing in the Dark: Whiteness and the Literary Imagination* (1992; rpt., New York: Vintage Books, 1993).

13. Douglass, "The Anti-Slavery Movement" (1855), in *My Bondage and My Freedom* (1855), in *Autobiographies* (New York: Library of America, 1994), 449.

14. Du Bois, *Black Reconstruction in America* (1935; rpt., New York: Atheneum Books, 1992), 707.

15. James M. McPherson makes this point in *Abraham Lincoln and the Second American Revolution* (New York: Oxford University Press, 1991), 138.

16. For an extended treatment of this idea, see Louis Menand, *The Metaphysical Club: A Study of Ideas in America* (New York: Farrar, Straus, and Giroux, 2001).

17. The remark appears in Ellison, "Stephen Crane and the Mainstream of American Fiction" (1960), in *Shadow and Act* (New York: Vintage Books, 1965), 68.

18. A timeline appears before the index to this book.

19. The incident is described in Douglas A. Blackmon, *Slavery by Another Name: The Re-Enslavement of Black Americans from the Civil War to World War II* (New York: Doubleday, 2008), 237.

20. Tawil argues that because of the proscription on public debate about slavery, discussions of the Indian could be a displaced way of talking about the Negro. See *The Making of Racial Sentiment*, 26–68 passim.

21. Rafael Campo, "Patriotic Poem," in *Enemy* (Durham, NC: Duke University Press, 2007), 17.

22. The fiction and nonfiction of Reconstruction have attracted relatively little attention in scholarship. Amanda Claybaugh, "The Autobiography of a Substitute: Trauma, History, Howells," *Yale Journal of Criticism* 18:1 (2005): 45–65, notes that postwar novelists themselves shied away from the subject, partly because of unwillingness to address issues of social class.

23. See the notes on "The Two Temples," in *The Piazza Tales and Other Prose Pieces, 1839–1860*, ed. Harrison Hayford, Alma A. MacDougall, and G. Thomas Tanselle, vol. 9 of *The Writings of Herman Melville* (Evanston, IL: Northwestern University Press; and Chicago: Newberry Library, 1987), 700–703. Donna M. Campbell discusses Boyesen's term and its influence in *Resisting Regionalism: Gender and Naturalism in American Fiction, 1885–1915* (Athens: Ohio University Press, 1997), especially 51–53 and 109–45. On the genteel critics and editors, see John Tomsich, *A Genteel Endeavor: American Culture and Politics in the Gilded Age* (Stanford, CA: Stanford University Press, 1971).

24. Thoreau, "Resistance to Civil Government," in *Reform Papers*, ed. Wendell Glick (Princeton, NJ: Princeton University Press, 1973), 71. The rest of Thoreau's sentence reads: "but it is his duty, at least, to wash his hands of it, and, if he gives it no thought longer, not to give it practically his support."

PART I: SLAVERY, RACE, AND FREE SPEECH

1. "Address at Cooper Institute, New York City," in Abraham Lincoln, *Speeches and Writings*, vol. 2, *1859–1865* (New York: Library of America, 1989), 130. A detailed treatment of the Cooper Institute Address is Harold Holzer, *Lincoln at Cooper Union:*

The Speech That Made Abraham Lincoln President (New York: Simon & Schuster, 2004). Holzer does not discuss the free-speech issues examined here.

2. "Address at Cooper Institute," 128–29.

3. For skepticism about a slavocrat plot, see David Brion Davis, *The Slave Power Conspiracy and the Paranoid Style* (Baton Rouge: Louisiana State University Press, 2000). Support for Lincoln's argument can be found in myriad sources, among them Don E. Fehrenbacher, *The Slaveholding Republic: An Account of the United States Government's Relations to Slavery* (New York: Oxford University Press, 2001); David Grimsted, *American Mobbing, 1828–1861: Toward Civil War* (New York: Oxford University Press, 1998); and Leonard L. Richards, *The Free North and Southern Domination, 1780–1860* (Baton Rouge: Louisiana State University Press, 2000).

4. Wilson, *History of the Rise and Fall of the Slave Power in America* (1874; rpt., Boston: Houghton, Mifflin, 1884), 2:606–7. The "Invasion of States" resolution is also mentioned in Henry Mayer, *All on Fire: William Lloyd Garrison and the Abolition of Slavery* (New York: St. Martin's Griffin, 1998), 506–7; and James M. McPherson, *Battle Cry of Freedom: The Civil War Era* (New York: Oxford University Press, 1988), 211.

5. *The Congressional Globe*, 36th Congress, 1st Session, January 23, 1860, 553–54.

6. Ibid.

7. Ibid.

8. Ibid., 555 and 558.

9. Ibid., 558 and 560.

10. "Address at Cooper Institute," 127–28 and 130.

11. See David M. Rabban, *Free Speech in Its Forgotten Years* (New York: Cambridge University Press, 1997).

12. Webster is quoted in Albert J. Von Frank, *The Trials of Anthony Burns: Freedom and Slavery in Emerson's Boston* (Cambridge, MA: Harvard University Press, 1998), 21.

13. *The Border Ruffian Code in Kansas* (New York, 1855), 1–2.

14. For information on the Sumner assault, I have relied on David Donald, *Charles Sumner and the Coming of the Civil War* (New York: Alfred A. Knopf, 1961), 278–347; and Wilson, *History*, 2:478–95. William Cullen Bryant said of the beating: "Has it come to this, that we must speak with bated breath in the presence of our Southern masters?" Quoted in Mayer, *All on Fire*, 453.

15. Emerson, "Assault on Charles Sumner" (1856), in *Emerson's Antislavery Writings*, ed. Len Gougeon and Joel Myerson (New Haven, CT: Yale University Press, 1995), 107; and Whitman, *The Eighteenth Presidency!* (1856), in Walt Whitman, *Poetry and Prose* (New York: Library of America, 1996), 1333. Stephens is quoted in Grimsted, *American Mobbing*, 246.

16. The quotation is in Marat Halstead, *Three against Lincoln: Marat Halstead Reports the Caucuses of 1860*, ed. William B. Hesseltine (Baton Rouge: Louisiana State University Press, 1960), 54. For the 1860 election, see Ollinger Crenshaw, *The Slave States in the Presidential Election of 1860* (Baltimore, MD: Johns Hopkins University Press, 1945).

17. A relevant study of prophecy is George Shulman, *American Prophecy: Race and Redemption in American Political Culture* (Minneapolis: University of Minnesota Press, 2008).

18. Whitman, preface to *Leaves of Grass: The First (1855) Edition*, ed. Malcom Cowley (New York: Penguin Classics, 1986), 15.

19. For a different take on the continuity between the revolutionary and antebellum periods, see Jay Grossman, *Reconstituting the American Renaissance: Emerson, Whitman, and the Politics of Representation* (Durham, NC: Duke University Press, 2003).

20. Burke, *A Rhetoric of Motives* (New York: George Braziller, 1955), pp. 3–5 passim. See also Burke, *Language as Symbolic Action* (Berkeley and Los Angeles: University of California Press, 1966), especially the section entitled "Rhetoric and Poetics," pp. 295–307.

21. Whitman, *The Eighteenth Presidency!*, 1332.

22. "Address to the Young Men's Lyceum of Springfield, Illinois," in Abraham Lincoln, *Speeches and Writings*, vol. 1, *1832–1858* (New York: Library of America, 1989), 28.

23. George B. Forgie has written at length on Lincoln's filiopiety in *Patricide in the House Divided: A Psychological Interpretation of Lincoln and His Age* (New York: W. W. Norton, 1979).

24. This is the argument in William Lee Miller, *Lincoln's Virtues: An Ethical Biography* (New York: Alfred A. Knopf, 2002).

25. See James M. McPherson, *Abraham Lincoln and the Second American Revolution* (New York: Oxford University Press, 1991), viii.

26. The term "island communities" comes from Robert H. Wiebe, *The Search for Order, 1877–1920* (New York: Hill and Wang, 1967). See also Wiebe, *The Opening of American Society: From the Adoption of the Constitution to the Eve of Disunion* (New York: Random House, 1984), especially 353–84.

27. Lincoln, "'House Divided' Speech at Springfield, Illinois," in *Speeches and Writings: 1832–1858*, 426. For the information on the size of the military, see William Lee Miller, *President Lincoln: The Duty of a Statesman* (New York: Alfred A. Knopf, 2008), 49.

28. Tyler is quoted in Mayer, *All on Fire*, 197. Trish Loughran argues that the communications revolution of the antebellum era produced not nationalism, but rather the heightened sectionalism that led to disunion. See Loughran, *The Republic in Print: Print Culture in the Age of U.S. Nation Building, 1770–1870* (New York: Columbia University Press, 2007).

29. Material on antebellum publishers in this and the next paragraph can be found in John Tebbel, *Between Covers: The Rise and Transformation of American Book Publishing* (New York: Oxford University Press, 1987), 21–76. On the exclusion of Emerson, see Clement Eaton, *Freedom of Thought in the Old South* (Durham, NC: Duke University Press, 1940), 331–32.

30. Amanda Claybaugh discusses transatlantic fictions of social reform in *The Novel of Purpose: Literature and Social Reform in the Anglo-American World* (Ithaca, NY: Cornell University Press, 2007). Claybaugh's principal American examples are

James and Twain. As she observes, Twain wrote against slavery twenty years after the fact, and James's reformist novel *The Bostonians* was ambiguous about woman suffrage.

31. On the selective remembering and forgetting of the Civil War, the standard study is David Blight, *Race and Reunion: The Civil War in American Memory* (Cambridge, MA: Harvard University Press, 2001). The Whitman quotations are from "Death of Abraham Lincoln" (1879), in *Poetry and Prose*, 1061. The argument in this and the following paragraph has connections to the analysis of pragmatism in Louis Menand, *The Metaphysical Club: A Story of Ideas in America* (New York: Farrar, Straus & Giroux, 2001).

32. The quoted lines are from Whitman, "O Captain! My Captain!" (1865–66), in *Poetry and Prose*, 467. In the final edition of *Leaves of Grass* (1891–92), Whitman placed this poem in a section called "Memories of President Lincoln."

33. See, among the many studies on Reconstruction, Blight, *Race and Reunion*; Eric Foner, *Forever Free: The Story of Emancipation and Reconstruction* (New York: Alfred A. Knopf, 2005); Foner, *Reconstruction: America's Unfinished Revolution, 1863–1877* (New York: Harper & Row, 1988); and Joel Williamson, *The Crucible of Race: Black/White Relations in the American South since Emancipation* (New York: Oxford University Press, 1984).

34. For a thorough study of the freedmen and the ballot, see Xi Wang, *The Trial of Democracy: Black Suffrage and Northern Republicans, 1860–1910* (Athens: University of Georgia Press, 1997).

35. "Address at Cooper Institute," 129.

36. The 1880 platform is quoted in Rayford W. Logan, *The Betrayal of the Negro: From Rutherford B. Hayes to Woodrow Wilson* (1954; rpt., n.p.: Da Capo Press, 1997), 38 and 77 passim. Logan is excellent on the hypocrisy of rhetoric on black rights.

37. The Douglass quote is from *Life and Times of Frederick Douglass* (1893), in Douglass, *Autobiographies* (New York: Library of America, 1994), 967. The Harlan and Brown opinions are in Brook Thomas, ed., *Plessy v. Ferguson: A Brief History with Documents* (Boston: Bedford/St. Martin's, 1997); the citations are from 57 and 44; see also Thomas's informative introduction.

38. See, in general, Thomas Bender, *A Nation among Nations: America's Place in World History* (New York: Hill & Wang, 2006); the quote is from *Emerson's Antislavery Writings*, 7.

39. See Nancy Bentley, "Literary Forms and Mass Culture, 1870–1920," in *The Cambridge History of American Literature*, vol. 3, *Prose Writing, 1860–1920*, ed. Sacvan Bercovitch (New York: Cambridge University Press, 2005), especially 186–89; and Ida B. Wells, Frederick Douglass, Irvine Garland Penn, and Ferdinand L. Barnett, *The Reason Why the Colored American Is Not in the World's Columbian Exposition: The Afro-American's Contribution to Columbian Literature*, ed. Robert W. Rydell (1893; rpt., Urbana: University of Illinois Press, 1999). The phrase "imperial spectacle" comes from Bentley.

40. Letter of November 12, 1887, in William Dean Howells, *Selected Letters*, vol. 3, *1882–1891*, ed. Robert C. Leitz III with Richard H. Ballinger and Christoph K. Lohmann (Boston: Twayne, 1980), 201–6; quotation from 204.

41. See Ida B. Wells, *Southern Horrors and Other Writings: The Anti-Lynching Campaign of Ida B. Wells, 1892–1900*, ed. Jacqueline Jones Royster (Boston: Bedford/St. Martin's, 1997). Wells's autobiography is quoted by Royster in her introduction, 40; the second quote is from Wells's preface, 50.

42. See Logan, *The Betrayal of the Negro*, 262–63.

43. One clear exception is Chesnutt's *The Marrow of Tradition* (1901), which is based on a white race riot in North Carolina that had occurred three years earlier.

44. George Washington Cable, *The Grandissimes: A Story of Creole Life* (1880; rpt., New York: Penguin Classics, 1988), 96 and 339.

45. Cable, *John March, Southerner* (1894; rpt., Gretna, LA: Firebird Press, 2001), 508.

46. On Tourgée, see Mark Elliott, *Color-Blind Justice: Albion Tourgée and the Quest for Racial Equality from the Civil War to "Plessy v. Ferguson"* (New York: Oxford University Press, 2006).

47. Hawthorne, *The House of the Seven Gables* (New York: W. W. Norton, 1967), 8 and 122.

48. Crane, *The Monster*, in *The Red Badge of Courage and Other Stories*, ed. Anthony Mellors and Fiona Robertson (New York: Oxford University Press, 1998), 186 and 196–97.

49. McPherson, *Abraham Lincoln and the Second American Revolution* (New York: Oxford University Press, 1991), especially chapter 1, 3–22; the remark about the change from plural to singular subject appears in the preface, viii. For an interesting perspective on standardization in this period, see also Walter Benn Michaels, "Promises of American Life, 1880–1920," in Bercovitch, *Cambridge History of American Literature*, 3:285–409.

50. For the information in this paragraph, I have relied on Jennifer Carol Cook, *Machine and Metaphor: The Ethics of Language in American Realism* (New York: Routledge, 2007), 1–14; and Thomas J. Schlereth, *Victorian America: Transformations in Everyday Life, 1876–1915* (New York: HarperPerennial, 1992), 177–207. On the postal system in particular, see David M. Henkin, *The Postal Age: The Emergence of Modern Communications in Nineteenth-Century America* (Chicago: University of Chicago Press, 2006), and Richard R. John, *Spreading the News: The American Postal System from Franklin to Morse* (Cambridge, MA: Harvard University Press, 1995).

51. See John Tebbel, *Between Covers: The Rise and Transformation of American Book Publishing* (New York: Oxford University Press, 1987), 79–198. Also relevant, particularly on late nineteenth-century periodicals, is Nancy Glazener, *Reading for Realism: The History of a U.S. Literary Institution, 1850–1910* (Durham, NC: Duke University Press, 1997).

52. Commentary on the plantation school can be found in Walter Benn Michaels, *Our America: Nativism, Modernism, and Pluralism* (Durham, NC: Duke University Press, 1997), 10–40; and Kenneth W. Warren, *Black and White Strangers: Race and American Literary Realism* (Chicago: University of Chicago Press, 1993), 102–5.

53. Dixon, *The Leopard's Spots: A Romance of the White Man's Burden, 1865–1900* (1902; rpt., Gretna, LA: Firebird Press, 2001), 434–35.

54. Stoneman is based on the Radical Republican leader Thaddeus Stevens, who was in fact clubfooted; but Dixon describes the carpetbagger as satanic and wants us to make the symbolic connection.

EMERSON: PROSPECTS

1. See especially Len Gougeon, "Emerson's Abolition Conversion," in *The Emerson Dilemma: Essays on Emerson and Social Reform*, ed. T. Gregory Garvey (Athens: University of Georgia Press, 2001), 170–96; Gougeon, *Virtue's Hero: Emerson, Antislavery, and Reform* (Athens: University of Georgia Press, 1990); and Albert J. Von Frank, *The Trials of Anthony Burns: Freedom and Slavery in Emerson's Boston* (Cambridge, MA: Harvard University Press, 1998).

2. On Emerson's ambivalence toward Garrison, see T. Gregory Garvey, "Emerson, Garrison, and the Anti-Slavery Society," in *Emerson: Bicentennial Essays*, ed. Ronald A. Bosco and Joel Myerson (Boston: Massachusetts Historical Society, 2006), 153–82.

3. Herder is quoted in Ian Balfour, *The Rhetoric of Romantic Prophecy* (Stanford, CA: Stanford University Press, 2002), 111.

4. On Emerson's intellectual influences, see Lawrence Buell, *Emerson* (Cambridge, MA: Harvard University Press, 2003); and Philip F. Gura, *American Transcendentalism: A History* (New York: Hill & Wang, 2007). The phrase "long foreground" comes, of course, from Emerson's letter thanking Walt Whitman for the gift of *Leaves of Grass*.

5. On Garrison and the *Liberator*, see Henry Mayer, *All on Fire: William Lloyd Garrison and the Abolition of Slavery* (New York: St. Martin's Griffin, 1998). On reverence for the fathers in this period, see George B. Forgie, *Patricide in the House Divided: A Psychological Interpretation of Lincoln and His Age* (New York: W.W. Norton, 1979).

6. "Second Reply to Hayne, January 26–27, 1830," in *The Papers of Daniel Webster, Speeches and Writings*, vol. 1, *1800–1833*, ed. Charles M. Wiltse and Alan R. Berolzheimer (Hanover, NH: University Press of New England, 1986), 296; and William Lee Miller, *Arguing about Slavery: John Quincy Adams and the Great Battle in the United States Congress* (New York: Alfred A. Knopf, 1996), 124–25 passim.

7. The quotation is from Emerson, "Historic Notes of Life and Letters in New England" (1867, 1883), in *Complete Works*, centenary ed. (Boston: Houghton, Mifflin, 1903–4), 10:325. On the Constitutional process, see Michael Vorenberg, *Final Freedom: The Civil War, the Abolition of Slavery, and the Thirteenth Amendment* (New York: Cambridge University Press, 2001).

8. Emerson, quoted in James Elliot Cabot, *A Memoir of Ralph Waldo Emerson* (Boston: Houghton, Mifflin, 1887), 2:425–27.

9. Ralph Waldo Emerson, "John Milton" (1835), in *Early Lectures*, vol. 1, *1833–1836*, ed. Stephen E. Whicher and Robert E. Spiller (Cambridge, MA: Harvard University Press, 1959), 144–63; quotations from 148, 156, 158–59, and 161. A useful discussion of Emerson and Milton appears in Joel Porte, *Representative Man: Ralph Waldo Emerson in His Time* (New York: Oxford University Press, 1979), 64–75.

10. Quotations from *Nature* come from *The Selected Writings of Ralph Waldo Emerson*, ed. Brooks Atkinson (New York: Modern Library, 1950); page numbers are given in the text.

11. See Emerson, "John Milton," in ibid., 161. On the figure of Adam in Emerson, see James Perrin Warren, *Culture of Eloquence: Oratory and Reform in Antebellum Literature* (University Park: Pennsylvania State University Press, 1999), 29–51. Warren is especially good on Emerson and language, though he does not relate the language theme to contemporaneous attacks on free speech.

12. Quotations from "The American Scholar" are from *The Selected Writings of Ralph Waldo Emerson*, ed. Atkinson; page numbers are given in the text.

13. Quotations are from Abraham Lincoln, *Speeches and Writings*, vol. 1, *1832–1858* (New York: Library of America, 1989); page numbers in the text refer to this edition.

14. Quotations from the "Address" are from Len Gougeon and Joel Myerson, eds., *Emerson's Antislavery Writings* (New Haven, CT: Yale University Press, 1995); page numbers are given in the text. Subsequent references to Emerson's antislavery essays come from this edition, with the titles given parenthetically.

15. Quotations are from "The Poet," in *The Selected Writings of Ralph Waldo Emerson*, ed. Atkinson; page numbers are given in the text.

16. Emerson may be alluding to the shorthand title of Thoreau's essay "Resistance to Civil Government" (1849) when he denounces the "passive obedience" of Bostonians before the provisions of the 1850 Compromise (54).

17. Harold K. Bush examines Emerson's growing interest in the Declaration in "Emerson, John Brown, and 'Doing the Word': The Enactment of Political Religion at Harpers Ferry, 1859," in Garvey, *The Emerson Dilemma*, 197–217.

18. Studies of Lincoln's evolution are legion. Valuable examples include Henry V. Jaffa, *A New Birth of Freedom: Abraham Lincoln and the Coming of the Civil War* (Lanham, MD: Rowman & Littlefield, 2000); and James Oakes, *The Radical and the Republican: Frederick Douglass, Abraham Lincoln, and the Triumph of Antislavery Politics* (New York: W. W. Norton, 2007).

19. "Eulogy on Henry Clay," in Lincoln, *Speeches and Writings*, vol. 1, *1832–1858*, 269; "Sixth Lincoln-Douglas Debate," at Quincy, Illinois, in ibid., 734.

20. Page numbers refer to the copy of the eulogy "Abraham Lincoln," reprinted in *The Selected Writings of Ralph Waldo Emerson*, ed. Atkinson.

21. In a speech entitled "Books" from 1864, Emerson characterized the Declaration as "the greatest achievement of American literature," a statement that neatly captures the correlation of literature with politics in his later thought. See *Uncollected Lectures by Ralph Waldo Emerson*, ed. Clarence Gohdes (New York: William Edwin Rudge, 1932), 40.

22. Construction was not begun, however, until 1914, a salutary reminder that even in death Lincoln remained a lightning rod for controversy. On the postwar fixation with commemorating the past, see David Blight, *Race and Reunion: The Civil War in American Memory* (Cambridge, MA: Harvard University Press, 2001).

THOREAU: WORDS AS DEEDS

1. I have written on Thoreau and the market in *American Romanticism and the Marketplace* (Chicago: University of Chicago Press, 1985), 35–51.

2. See Lawrence Buell, *The Environmental Imagination: Thoreau, Nature Writing, and the Formation of American Culture* (Cambridge, MA: Harvard University Press, 1995).

3. Quotations from Thoreau's essays come from *Reform Papers*, ed. Wendell Glick (Princeton, NJ: Princeton University Press, 1973); page numbers refer to this edition. On antislavery activism in Concord, see Sandra Harbert Petrulionis, *To Set This World Right: The Antislavery Movement in Thoreau's Concord* (Ithaca, NY: Cornell University Press, 2006). Wai Chee Dimock examines the global ramifications of Thoreau's idea of civil resistance in *Through Other Continents: American Literature across Deep Time* (Princeton, NJ: Princeton University Press, 2006), 7–22.

4. Henry David Thoreau, *Walden*, ed. J. Lyndon Shanley (Princeton, NJ: Princeton University Press, 1973); page numbers given in the text refer to this edition.

5. Quotations are from Thoreau, *A Week on the Concord and Merrimack Rivers*, ed. Carl F. Hovde, William L. Howarth, and Elizabeth Hall Witherell (Princeton, NJ: Princeton University Press, 1980); page numbers are given in the text.

6. On the oppositional epic, see David Quint, *Epic and Empire: Politics and Heroic Form from Virgil to Milton* (Princeton, NJ: Princeton University Press, 1993). In this and the following paragraph, I rely on Quint's account. On Virgil in America, see John C. Shields, *The American Aeneas* (Knoxville: University of Tennessee Press, 2001).

7. For contemporary reflections on the idea of the poet who can act, see Allen Grossman, with Mark Halliday, *The Sighted Singer: Two Works on Poetry for Readers and Writers* (Baltimore: Johns Hopkins University Press, 1992).

8. On manliness in Thoreau, see Dana D. Nelson, "Thoreau, Manhood, and Race: Quiet Desperation versus Representative Isolation," in *A Historical Guide to Henry David Thoreau*, ed. William E. Cain (New York: Oxford University Press, 2000), 61–93.

9. In Lincoln, *Speeches and Writings*, vol. 2, *1859–1865* (New York: Library of America, 1989), 130.

10. On Thoreau's revisions, see Stephen Adams and Donald Ross Jr., *Revising Mythologies: The Composition of Thoreau's Major Works* (Charlottesville: University Press of Virginia, 1988), 51–63 and 165–91; and J. Lyndon Shanley, *The Making of "Walden": With the Text of the First Edition* (Chicago: University of Chicago Press, 1957).

11. The platforms are available online. "Final settlement" is from Henry Wilson, *History of the Rise and Fall of the Slave Power in America* (1874; rpt., Boston: Houghton, Mifflin, 1884), 2:360. Wilson, who lived through the period, was summarizing the contemporaneous view.

12. Much of the historical information in this paragraph comes from Wilson, *History of the Rise and Fall*, 2:360–77; quote from 2:372. Sumner is quoted from his speech "Freedom National; Slavery Sectional" (August 26, 1852), in Charles Sumner, *Recent Speeches and Addresses* (Boston: Ticknor & Fields, 1856), 69–171; quote from 80. Also see Albert J. Von Frank, *The Trials of Anthony Burns: Freedom and Slavery in Emerson's Boston* (Cambridge, MA: Harvard University Press, 1998).

13. The quotations are from *Speeches and Writings*, vol. 2, *1859–1865*, 108 (letter of December 20, 1859, to John W. Fell, "Enclosing Autobiography") and 167 ("Autobiography Written for Campaign," June 1860).

14. For a somewhat different view of *Walden*'s relation to the framing essays, see

George Shulman, *American Prophecy: Race and Redemption in American Political Culture* (Minneapolis: University of Minnesota Press, 2008), 39–88.

15. On water in the text, see Willard H. Bonner, *Harp on the Shore: Thoreau and the Sea*, ed. George R. Levine (Albany: State University Press of New York, 1985); and William E. Cain, "Henry David Thoreau, 1817–1862: A Brief Biography," in Cain, *A Historical Guide*, 11–57.

16. Still valuable on *Walden* as a heroic text is Stanley Cavell, *The Senses of Walden* (New York: Viking, 1972).

17. For good discussions of "Slavery in Massachusetts" and the reform essays generally, see Len Gougeon, "Thoreau and Reform," in *The Cambridge Companion to Henry David Thoreau*, ed. Joel Myerson (New York: Cambridge University Press, 1995), 194–214; and Deak Nabors, "Thoreau's Natural Constitution," *American Literary History* 19, no. 4 (Winter 2007): 824–48. Nabors is especially informative on the integration of nature with law in the essays.

18. For an analysis of Thoreau's investment in privacy see Milette Shamir, *Inexpressible Privacy: The Interior Life of Antebellum American Literature* (Philadelphia: University of Pennsylvania Press, 2006), 175–208.

19. Quoted in Joel Porte, *Consciousness and Culture: Emerson and Thoreau Reviewed* (New Haven, CT: Yale University Press, 2004), 145.

20. On Brown's impact on the Transcendentalists, see David S. Reynolds, *John Brown, Abolitionist: The Man Who Killed Slavery, Sparked the Civil War, and Seeded Civil Rights* (New York: Alfred A. Knopf, 2005), 334–69 passim.

FULLER: HISTORY, BIOGRAPHY, AND CRITICISM

1. Edgar Allan Poe, "Sarah Margaret Fuller," in "The Literati of New York City" (1846), in *Raven Edition of the Complete Works of Edgar Allan Poe* (N.p.: Lamb, 1902), 9:6–19; quotations from 9 and 17.

2. In fairness to Emerson, the presentist emphasis of *Nature* is uncharacteristic. "The American Scholar" (1837) lists books or the past as an essential influence on the scholar; and "History," from *Essays: First Series*, treats past events and thoughts as a congeries of portents.

3. Quotations are from Fuller, *Woman in the Nineteenth Century*, ed. Larry J. Reynolds (New York: W. W. Norton, 1998); page numbers in the text refer to this edition.

4. The definitive biography of Fuller is Charles Capper, *Margaret Fuller: An American Romantic Life*, vol. 1, *The Private Years* (New York: Oxford University Press, 1992), and *Margaret Fuller: An American Romantic Life*, vol. 2, *The Public Years* (New York: Oxford University Press, 2007).

5. On the Missouri Compromise and Jefferson, see Robert Pierce Forbes, *The Missouri Compromise and Its Aftermath* (Chapel Hill: University of North Carolina Press, 2007); and Peter S. Onuf, *Jefferson's Empire: The Language of American Nationhood* (Charlottesville: University Press of Virginia, 2000). The quote comes from Forbes, 104.

6. Wai Chee Dimock, *Through Other Continents: American Literature across Deep Time* (Princeton, NJ: Princeton University Press, 2006), discusses the Egyptian

Book of the Dead in relation to Fuller, noting that she lifts "the gag order that comes with mortality" (61). My claim is the more narrowly historical one that Fuller wrote in awareness of the contemporaneous gag on antislavery petitions. Adams is mentioned in "New Year's Day" (December 28, 1844), in *Margaret Fuller, Critic: Writings from the New-York Tribune, 1844–1846*, ed. Judith Mattson Bean and Joel Myerson (New York: Columbia University Press, 2000), 15.

7. For explications of woman's voicing in Fuller, see Jeffrey Steele, *Transfiguring America: Myth, Ideology, and Mourning in Margaret Fuller's Writing* (Columbia: University of Missouri Press, 2001), and Steele, "Margaret Fuller's Rhetoric of Transformation," in Fuller, *Woman in the Nineteenth Century*, 278–97; Christina Zwarg, *Feminist Conversations: Fuller, Emerson, and the Play of Reading* (Ithaca, NY: Cornell University Press, 1995); and especially Julie Ellison, *Delicate Subjects: Romanticism, Gender, and the Ethics of Understanding* (Ithaca, NY: Cornell University Press, 1990), 217–98.

8. Ellison refers to the "veritable binge of quotations from Xenophon" in *Delicate Subjects*, 285.

9. See *Summer on the Lakes* (1844), in *The Essential Margaret Fuller*, ed. Jeffrey Steele (New Brunswick, NJ: Rutgers University Press, 1992), 112.

10. Dall, *Margaret and Her Friends: Ten Conversations with Margaret Fuller upon the Mythology of the Greeks and Its Expression in Art* (Boston: Roberts Brothers, 1895), 142.

11. Fuller, "A Short Essay on Critics," in *The Writings of Margaret Fuller*, ed. Mason Wade (New York: Viking, 1941), 224.

12. On Fuller's translations, see Colleen Glenney Boggs, *Transnationalism and American Literature: Literary Translation* (New York: Routledge, 2007), 91–110.

13. The quoted phrase comes from Ian Balfour, *The Rhetoric of Romantic Prophecy* (Stanford, CA: Stanford University Press, 2002), 250. Balfour also cites these verses from Deuteronomy 18 (the speaker is God): "I will raise then up a Prophet from among their brethren, . . . and will put my words into his mouth, and he shall speak unto them all that I shall command him" (72–73). On Fuller and the prophetic, see Marie Mitchell Olesen Urbanski, *Margaret Fuller's "Woman in the Nineteenth Century": A Literary Study of Form and Content, of Sources and Influence* (Westport, CT: Greenwood, 1980).

14. Balfour quotes Schlegel in *The Rhetoric of Romantic Prophecy*, 15.

15. From *Narrative of the Life of Frederick Douglass, an American Slave*, in Douglass, *Autobiographies* (New York: Library of America, 1994), 42.

16. The first quotation is from "New Year's Day," reprinted along with "First of August, 1845," in *Margaret Fuller, Critic*, 16–18, 185, and 188.

17. Fuller, *"These Sad but Glorious Days": Dispatches from Europe, 1846–1850*, ed. Larry J. Reynolds and Susan Belasco Smith (New Haven, CT: Yale University Press, 1991), 165 and 230. On Fuller's Italian phase, the introduction to this book by Reynolds and Belasco (1–35) and the last chapter of Steele's *Transfiguring America*, "Phoenix Rising: The Transfiguration of Italy (and America)," 262–93, are helpful.

18. Fuller, *"These Sad but Glorious Days,"* 166.

19. Hawthorne, *The Scarlet Letter*, ed. Ross C. Murfin (Boston: Bedford/St. Martin's, 1991), 201. Sand, says Fuller, will not be the "parent" of the new order: "Those who would reform the world must show that they do not speak in the heat of wild impulse;

their lives must be unstained by passionate error; they must be severe lawgivers to themselves" (*Woman in the Nineteenth Century*, 45).

HAWTHORNE AND THE RESILIENCE OF DISSENT

1. On Hawthorne's politics, influential work has been done by Jonathan Arac, "The Politics of *The Scarlet Letter*," in *Ideology and Classic American Literature*, ed. Sacvan Bercovitch and Myra Jehlen (New York: Cambridge University Press, 1986), 247–66; Sacvan Bercovitch, *The Office of "The Scarlet Letter"* (Baltimore, MD: Johns Hopkins University Press, 1991); and Lauren Berlant, *The Anatomy of National Fantasy: Hawthorne, Utopia, and Everyday Life* (Chicago: University of Chicago Press, 1991). On Hawthorne and slavery, see Teresa A. Goddu, "Letters Turned to Gold: Hawthorne, Authorship, and Slavery," *Studies in American Fiction* 29 (Spring 2001): 49–76; and Jean Fagan Yellin, "Hawthorne and the Slavery Question," in *A Historical Guide to Nathaniel Hawthorne*, ed. Larry J. Reynolds (New York: Oxford University Press, 2001), 135–64. For an argument that Hawthorne was antislavery, closer in some respects to the (David) Wilmot wing of the Democratic Party than the Pierce wing, see Robert S. Levine, "Genealogical Fictions: Melville and Hannah Crafts in Hawthorne's *House*," in *Dislocating Race and Nation: Episodes in Nineteenth-Century American Literary Nationalism* (Chapel Hill: University of North Carolina Press, 2008), 119–78.

2. The best recent study of Hawthorne's career is Brenda Wineapple, *Hawthorne: A Life* (New York: Alfred A. Knopf, 2003).

3. All quotations from Hawthorne's work refer to *The Centenary Edition of the Works of Nathaniel Hawthorne*, ed. William Charvat et al., 23 vols. (Columbus: Ohio State University Press, 1962–97); volume and page numbers are given in the text.

4. On Zenobia's words as a variant of Dido's curse from *The Aeneid*, see my "Dido's Curse: Hawthorne's Unwilling Radicalism," in *Hawthorne Revisited: Honoring the Bicentennial of the Author's Birth*, ed. Gordon Hyatt (Lenox, MA: Lenox Library Association, 2004), 113–18.

STOWE: FROM THE SACRAMENTAL TO THE OLD TESTAMENTAL

1. Stowe, *Uncle Tom's Cabin; or Life among the Lowly* (New York: Barnes & Noble, 1995); page numbers given in the text refer to this edition. The classic study of Stowe's "sentimental power" is Jane Tompkins, *Sensational Designs: The Cultural Work of American Fiction, 1790–1860* (New York: Oxford University Press, 1985).

2. The quoted passage has been analyzed in some detail by Catharine E. O'Connell, "'The Magic of the Real Presence of Distress': Sentimentality and Competing Rhetorics of Authority," in *The Stowe Debate: Rhetorical Strategies in "Uncle Tom's Cabin,"* ed. Mason I. Lowance Jr., Ellen E. Westbrook, and R. C. De Prospo (Amherst: University of Massachusetts Press, 1994), 13–36. Another relevant discussion of "real presence" in Stowe's novel is Marianne Noble, *The Masochistic Pleasures of Sentimental Literature* (Princeton, NJ: Princeton University Press, 2000), 126–46. Noble also links the term to Calvinism, but her interest is in God's love as affliction and the erotic ecstasy of sentimental "wounding."

I am mindful that the relation between writing and presence occupies a central place in deconstructive criticism. The standard work on this subject is Jacques Derrida, *Of Grammatology*, trans. Gayatri Chakravorty Spivak (Baltimore, MD: Johns Hopkins University Press, 1976). My goal is practical rather than theoretical: I am trying to historicize the discussion of verbal presence by developing its filiations, in the American nineteenth century, with the Protestant sacrament of communion.

3. In Thoreau, *Reform Papers*, ed. Wendell Glick (Princeton, NJ: Princeton University Press, 1973), 87.

4. See Joan D. Hedrick, *Harriet Beecher Stowe: A Life* (New York: Oxford University Press, 1994), 213–14.

5. On Passover and its relation to Stowe's novel, see Jessica Lang, "Retelling the Retold: Understanding Repetition in *Uncle Tom's Cabin*," forthcoming, *Arizona Quarterly*.

6. Emerson, "The Lord's Supper" (1832), in *Selected Prose and Poetry*, ed. Reginald L. Cook (New York: Holt, Rinehart & Winston, 1950), 89. The scholarship on this subject is vast; a venerable and still useful example is Alexander Barclay, *The Protestant Doctrine of the Lord's Supper: A Study in the Eucharistic Teaching of Luther, Zwingli and Calvin* (Glasgow: Jackson, Wylie, 1927).

7. The experience is related in Hedrick, *Harriet Beecher Stowe*, 155–56.

8. I am not implying that Stowe endorsed her father's anti-Catholicism. Lyman Beecher was the author of an anti-immigrant tract, *A Plea for the West* (1835), but Harriet makes St. Clare's mother a devout Catholic and says that Cassy received religious training from nuns. My argument is the perhaps self-evident one that *Uncle Tom's Cabin* is the product of a Protestant sensibility.

9. James, *The Will to Believe and Other Essays on Popular Philosophy* (New York: Dover, 1956), 25.

10. The pioneering study of this phenomenon in *Uncle Tom's Cabin* is Karen Halttunen, "Gothic Imagination and Social Reform: The Haunted Houses of Lyman Beecher, Henry Ward Beecher, and Harriet Beecher Stowe," in *New Essays on "Uncle Tom's Cabin*," ed. Eric J. Sundquist (Cambridge: Cambridge University Press, 1986), 107–34. See also Teresa A. Goddu, *Gothic America: Narrative, History, and Nation* (New York: Columbia University Press, 1997), 140–44. On the eschatological dimension in Stowe's novel, see Helen Petter Westra, "Confronting Antichrist: The Influence of Jonathan Edwards's Millennial Vision," in Lowance, Westbrook, and De Prospo, *The Stowe Debate*, 141–58.

11. Good examples of such readings include Lawrence Buell, "Harriet Beecher Stowe and the Dream of the Great American Novel," in *The Cambridge Companion to Harriet Beecher Stowe*, ed. Cindy Weinstein (Cambridge: Cambridge University Press, 2004), 190–202; Robert S. Levine, *Martin Delany, Frederick Douglass, and the Politics of Representative Identity* (Chapel Hill: University of North Carolina Press, 1997), 144–76; and John Carlos Rowe, "Stowe's Rainbow Sign: Violence and Community in *Dred: A Tale of the Great Dismal Swamp*," *Arizona Quarterly* 58, no. 1 (Spring 2002): 37–55.

12. The quotation comes from Hedrick, *Harriet Beecher Stowe*, 258.

13. Stowe, *Dred: A Tale of the Great Dismal Swamp*, ed. Robert S. Levine (New York: Penguin Classics, 2000); page numbers are given in the text.

14. *Uncle Tom's Cabin*, 447.

15. The Kansas-Nebraska Bill was still being debated in Congress when Stowe began to voice her despondency over the direction of the country. In her "Appeal to the Women of America," she deplored the South's "unmitigated despotism" and had no doubt that the next step would be "the legalizing of slavery throughout the free States." The bill became law in 1854. See Charles Edward Stowe, *Life of Harriet Beecher Stowe: Compiled from Her Letters and Journals* (Boston: Houghton Mifflin, 1889), 257–59.

16. See Cindy Weinstein, "*Uncle Tom's Cabin* and the South," in Weinstein, *The Cambridge Companion to Harriet Beecher Stowe*, 39–57.

17. For English sales and reception, see Audrey Fisch, "Uncle Tom and Harriet Beecher Stowe in England," in Weinstein, *The Cambridge Companion to Harriet Beecher Stowe*, 96–112.

18. On the text's use of doubling or binaries, see Thomas R. Hovet, *The Master Narrative: Harriet Beecher Stowe's Subversive Story of Master and Slave in "Uncle Tom's Cabin" and "Dred"* (Lanham, MD: University Press of America, 1989).

19. For a reading of the novel that construes Milly's orphanage as civic action, see Elizabeth Duquette, "The Republican Mammy? Imagining Civic Engagement in *Dred*," *American Literature* 80, no. 1 (March 2008): 1–28.

20. William Lloyd Garrison wrote editorials with the title, "Watchman, What of the Night?" Cited in Robert Fanuzzi, *Abolition's Public Sphere* (Minneapolis: University of Minnesota Press, 2003), 67.

21. From "Speech at a Meeting to Aid John Brown's Family" (November 18, 1859), in *Emerson's Antislavery Writings*, ed. Len Gougeon and Joel Myerson (New Haven, CT: Yale University Press, 1995), 118.

SPEECH AND SILENCE IN DOUGLASS

1. All quotations from Douglass's accounts of his life come from Douglass, *Autobiographies* (New York: Library of America, 1994); page numbers given in the text refer to this edition.

2. For relevant discussions of the *Narrative*, see, among others, Gregg D. Crane, *Race, Citizenship, and Law in American Literature* (New York: Cambridge University Press, 2002), 112–16; Henry Louis Gates, Jr., *Figures in Black: Words, Signs, and the "Racial" Self* (New York: Oxford University Press, 1989), 80–124; and Lisa Yun Lee, "The Politics of Language in Frederick Douglass's *Narrative of an American Slave*," *Melus* 17, no. 2 (Summer 1991–92): 51–9. I have written previously about literacy in the *Narrative* in *Surface and Depth: The Quest for Legibility in American Culture* (New York: Oxford University Press, 2003), 159–64.

3. See Henry Mayer, *All on Fire: William Lloyd Garrison and the Abolition of Slavery* (New York: St. Martin's Griffin, 1998), 203–5.

4. Jefferson, *Notes on the State of Virginia* (rpt., New York: Harper Torchbooks, 1964), 155.

5. In *My Bondage and My Freedom*, this act of resistance becomes "I found my strong fingers attached to the throat of my cowardly tormentor." *Life and Times* repeats the second formulation more or less verbatim. The later autobiographies are unambiguous about the association of Covey with omnipotent speech. Douglass writes, "Whence

came the daring spirit necessary to grapple with a man, who, eight-and-forty hours before, could, with his slightest word have made me tremble like a leaf in a storm, I do not know" (283 and 588).

6. Lee describes this change in detail in "The Politics of Language."

7. On the second installment of Douglass's book, see John Stauffer's foreword to Douglass, *My Bondage and My Freedom* (New York: Modern Library, 2003), xix–xxviii; and Eric J. Sundquist, *To Wake the Nations: Race in the Making of American Literature* (Cambridge, MA: Harvard University Press, 1993), 83–134.

8. See Robert S. Levine, *Martin Delany, Frederick Douglass, and the Politics of Representative Identity* (Chapel Hill: University of North Carolina Press, 1997). Levine emphasizes the "overlapping and shared concerns" of Delany the emigrationist and Douglass the "representative" African American (5 passim).

9. On this point, see a lecture of 1853 by Douglass, "A Nation in the Midst of a Nation," in *The Frederick Douglass Papers*, series 1, *Speeches, Debates, and Interviews* (New Haven, CT: Yale University Press, 1982), 2:423–40. Although Douglass could express patriotic sentiments, he was also capable of saying, as he did in a letter to Garrison from England that he quotes in *My Bondage and My Freedom*, "As to nation, I belong to none" (372). Also relevant is Roosevelt Montas, "Meaning and Transcendence: Melville, Douglass, and the Anxiety of Interpretation," *Leviathan: A Journal of Melville Studies* 10, no. 2 (June 2008): 69–83.

10. For a detailed analysis of this speech, see James A. Colaiaco, *Frederick Douglass and the Fourth of July* (New York: Palgrave Macmillan, 2006).

11. Though I disagree with his conclusions, the reader should consult John Stauffer, "Frederick Douglass and the Aesthetics of Freedom," *Raritan* 25 (Summer 2005): 114–36, on Douglass's compromises. Stauffer also cites Douglass's marriage to a white wife, Helen Pitts, as reflecting a loss of identification with blacks. For more positive views of the later Douglass, see the essays by Ross Castronovo and Dana D. Nelson, Gregory Jay, Carolyn L. Karcher, and Maurice S. Lee in Robert S. Levine and Samuel Otter, eds., *Frederick Douglass and Herman Melville: Essays in Relation* (Chapel Hill: University of North Carolina Press, 2008).

12. Some retrospective embellishment is at work in this portrayal of Lincoln. In actuality, Douglass was so disheartened by Lincoln's conciliatory First Inaugural Address that he briefly considered immigrating to Haiti in 1861. The firing on Ft. Sumter changed his mind. See the discussion in John Stauffer, *Giants: The Parallel Lives of Frederick Douglass and Abraham Lincoln* (New York: Twelve, 2008), 215–22.

13. Compare Douglass's analysis to that of Emerson in his "Address . . . on . . . the Emancipation of the Negroes in the British West Indies" (1844). Emerson similarly sees discourse as vanquishing the West Indian planters.

14. Harris, *Uncle Remus: His Songs and His Sayings* (1881; rev. ed., New York: D. Appleton, 1906), vii–viii passim.

15. On the 1875 Act and the Supreme Court's voiding of it, see Eric Foner, *A Short History of Reconstruction, 1863–1877* (New York: Harper & Row, 1990), 226–27, 234–35, and 247; and David W. Blight, *Race and Reunion: The Civil War in American Memory* (Cambridge, MA: Harvard University Press, 2001), 309–11. Blight discusses Douglass's response to the Court's decision on 309.

16. A good treatment of this last phase of Douglass's life and of his movement toward a "hemispheric nationalism," is Robert S. Levine, *Dislocating Race and Nation: Episodes in Nineteenth-Century American Literary Nationalism* (Chapel Hill: University of North Carolina Press, 2008), 179–236.

17. The quotations are from Ferdinand L. Barnett, "The Reason Why," in Ida B. Wells, Frederick Douglass, Irvine Garland Penn, and Ferdinand L. Barnett, *The Reason Why the Colored American Is Not in the World's Columbian Exposition: The Afro-American's Contribution to Columbian Literature*, ed. Robert W. Rydell (1893; rpt., Urbana: University of Illinois Press, 1999), 80–81.

WHITMAN: FROM SAYER-DOER TO SAYER-COPYIST

1. Whitman's politics and the place of his antislavery beliefs in *Leaves of Grass* have received incisive attention since the late 1980s. Classic studies include Betsy Erkkila, *Whitman the Political Poet* (New York: Oxford University Press, 1989); and Martin Klammer, *Whitman, Slavery, and the Emergence of Leaves of Grass* (University Park: Pennsylvania State University Press, 1995). Also see David S. Reynolds, *Walt Whitman* (New York: Oxford University Press, 2005); Reynolds, *Walt Whitman's America: A Cultural Biography* (New York: Alfred A. Knopf, 1986); and James Perrin Warren, *Culture of Eloquence: Oratory and Reform in Antebellum Literature* (University Park: Pennsylvania State University Press, 1999), 169–95. Erkkila has drawn an illuminating comparison between the 1855 *Leaves* and Marx's *Communist Manifesto* as expressions of the global "1848" in "Whitman, Marx, and the American 1848," in *Leaves of Grass: The Sesquicentennial Essays*, ed. Susan Belasco, Ed Folsom, and Kenneth M. Price (Lincoln: University of Nebraska Press, 2007), 35–61.

2. For important work on Whitman and Lincoln, see Daniel Mark Epstein, *Lincoln and Whitman: Parallel Lives in Civil War Washington* (New York: Ballantine Books, 2004); and Allen Grossman, "The Poetics of Union in Whitman and Lincoln: An Inquiry toward the Relationship of Art and Policy," in *The American Renaissance Reconsidered*, ed. Walter Benn Michaels and Donald E. Pease (Baltimore, MD: Johns Hopkins University Press, 1985), 183–208.

3. From "The Fugitive Slave Law" (March 7, 1854), in *Emerson's Antislavery Writings*, ed. Len Gougeon and Joel Myerson (New Haven, CT: Yale University Press, 1995), 83.

4. Quotations are from *Leaves of Grass: The First (1855) Edition*, ed. Malcolm Cowley (New York: Penguin Classics, 1986); page numbers given in the text refer to this edition.

5. Philip Fisher calls Whitman's image of democratic interchangeability "an aesthetics of the subtraction of differences." See Fisher, *Still the New World: American Literature in a Culture of Creative Destruction* (Cambridge, MA: Harvard University Press, 1999), 69.

6. Quotations from other of Whitman's works than the 1855 *Leaves* come from Whitman, *Poetry and Prose* (New York: Library of America, 1996); page numbers given in the text refer to this edition.

7. Early readers of *Leaves of Grass*, including Emerson, were not sure which genre

Whitman's verses belonged to. See Ed Folsom, "Database as Genre: The Epic Transformation of Archives," *PMLA* 122 (October 2007): 1572.

8. "Dickens, Griffith, and the Film Today" (1944), in Sergei Eisenstein, *Film Form: Essays in Film Theory*, trans. and ed. Jay Leyda (San Diego: Harcourt Brace, 1949), 233. Eisenstein is mainly concerned with the influence of Dickens on Griffith, but he mentions Whitman briefly and notes that Griffith draws on "Out of the Cradle, Endlessly Rocking" in *Intolerance*. On Whitman and the image, see Ed Folsom, "Appearing in Print: Illustrations of the Self in *Leaves of Grass*," in *The Cambridge Companion to Whitman*, ed. Ezra Greenspan (New York: Cambridge University Press, 1995), 135–65. On Whitman and film, there are valuable studies stretching from Alice Ahlers, "Cinematographic Technique in *Leaves of Grass*," *Walt Whitman Review* 12 (December 1966): 93–97, to Kenneth M. Price, "Walt Whitman and the Movies: Cultural Memory and the Politics of Desire," in *Whitman East and West: New Contexts for Reading Walt Whitman*, ed. Ed Folsom (Iowa City: University of Iowa Press, 2002), especially 36–70.

9. Vachel Lindsay, *The Art of the Moving Picture* (1915; rpt., New York: Liveright, 1970), 93–94.

10. An argument can be made that Whitman was so disaffected from language by the horrors he saw in Washington that, except for "When Lilacs Last in the Door-Yard Bloom'd" (1865), he never again approached the level of his prewar poetry. See Robert Roper, "Collateral Damage," *American Scholar* 78, no. 1 (Winter 2008): 75–82.

11. Luke Mancuso argues that Whitman supported black political equality in *Drum-Taps* (1865) and *Democratic Vistas*, but I do not find his evidence persuasive. See *The Strange Sad War Revolving: Walt Whitman, Reconstruction, and the Emergence of Black Citizenship* (Columbia, SC: Camden House, 1997), especially 51–76.

12. See Epstein, *Lincoln and Whitman*, 64–66; Warren, *Culture of Eloquence*, 192–95, is insightful on the Lincoln speech.

13. About a decade earlier, Whitman had taken notes for a lecture on Hegel, Fichte, and Schelling. See Erkkila, *Whitman the Political Poet*, 248.

14. I acknowledge with gratitude the assistance of Ed Folsom, who helped me sort out the dates of Whitman's revisions. For further information, the reader should consult Walt Whitman, *Poems, 1860–1867*, vol. 2 of *Leaves of Grass: A Textual Variorum of the Printed Poems*, ed. Sculley Bradley, Harold W. Blodgett, Arthur Golden, and William White (New York: New York University Press, 1980).

15. Professor Folsom reminds me that Whitman's first commercial publisher, Thayer and Eldridge, brought out the 1860 edition of *Leaves*, and thus the poet had available to him a much greater array of type fonts than he did in 1855. The fact remains, though, that Whitman made a choice to italicize the speech of other persons; he could have left the punctuation unchanged.

SLIT THROATS IN MELVILLE

1. Good studies of Melville's life are Andrew Delbanco, *Melville: His World and Work* (New York: Alfred A. Knopf, 2005); and Hershel Parker, *Herman Melville: A Biography*, vol. 1, *1819–1851* (Baltimore, MD: Johns Hopkins University Press, 1996), and vol. 2, *1851–1891* (Baltimore, MD: Johns Hopkins University Press, 2005).

2. Melville, *The Confidence-Man*, ed. John Bryant (New York: Modern Library, 2003), 6; page numbers given in the text refer to this edition.

3. Page numbers refer to *Typee: A Peep at Polynesian Life* (New York: Signet Classics, 1964). On *Typee*, see T. Walter Herbert, *Marquesan Encounters: Melville and the Meaning of Civilization* (Cambridge, MA: Harvard University Press, 1980); Samuel Otter, *Melville's Anatomies* (Berkeley and Los Angeles: University of California Press, 1999), 9–49; and Geoffrey Sanborn, *The Sign of the Cannibal: Melville and the Making of a Postcolonial Reader* (Durham, NC: Duke University Press, 1998).

4. From Melville, *Mardi: And a Voyage Thither*, ed. Harrison Hayford, Hershel Parker, and G. Thomas Tanselle, vol. 3 of *The Writings of Herman Melville* (Evanston, IL: Northwestern University Press; Chicago: Newberry Library, 1970), chapter 162, 531–35; quotations are from 532–33 and 534.

5. Letter of March 3, 1849, to Evert A. Duyckinck, in Melville, *The Letters of Herman Melville*, ed. Merrill R. Davis and William H. Gilman (New Haven, CT: Yale University Press, 1960), 80.

6. Simms, review of *Mardi*, *Southern Quarterly* 16 (1849–50): 260–61. This review is also cited in Carolyn L. Karcher, *Shadow over the Promised Land: Slavery, Race, and Violence in Melville's America* (Baton Rouge: Louisiana State University Press, 1980), 18.

7. Melville, "Hawthorne and His Mosses," in *The Piazza Tales and Other Prose Pieces, 1839–1860*, ed. Harrison Hayford, Alma A. MacDougall, and G. Thomas Tanselle, vol. 9 of *The Writings of Herman Melville* (Evanston, IL: Northwestern University Press; Chicago: Newberry Library, 1987), 244.

8. *Moby-Dick; or, The Whale*, ed. Charles Feidelson Jr. (Indianapolis: Bobbs-Merrill, 1964); page numbers given in the text refer to this edition.

9. Garrison is quoted in Henry Mayer, *All on Fire: William Lloyd Garrison and the Abolition of Slavery* (New York: St. Martin's Griffin, 1998), 112. On Melville and slavery, the classic studies are Karcher, *Shadow over the Promised Land*, and Michael Paul Rogin, *Subversive Genealogy: The Politics and Art of Herman Melville* (New York: Alfred A. Knopf, 1983).

10. On New York, slavery, and antebellum politics, see Ira Berlin and Leslie M. Harris, eds., *Slavery in New York* (New York: New Press, 2005); and Philip S. Foner, *Business and Slavery: The New York Merchants and the Irrepressible Conflict* (Chapel Hill: University of North Carolina Press, 1941). The quotations are from *Business and Slavery*, 14 and 30.

11. The suggestion is from Rogin, *Subversive Genealogy*, 142–43.

12. The contrast I draw here should not be exaggerated. Boston was also a port with southern business and tended to be more conservative than the rest of the Commonwealth. In "Civil Disobedience," Thoreau complained that Massachusetts farmers and merchants were the main obstacles to antislavery reform. In New York, moreover, the western part of the state was more progressive than the city. Antislavery evangelicals clustered there, and the area was home to Frederick Douglass (in Rochester) and John Brown (in North Elba).

13. Writing in 1856 in *Frederick Douglass's Paper*, the black activist and physician James McCune Smith compared the *Pequod* to the Republican Party and, criticiz-

ing what he saw as a failure of resolve, called for a style of leadership like Ahab's, not Stubb's. See "Horoscope," in *The Works of James McCune Smith*, ed. John Stauffer (New York: Oxford University Press, 2006), 143–48.

14. Melville, *Mardi*, 535.

15. For suggestive discussions of silence in Melville, see John Bryant, *Melville and Repose: The Rhetoric of Humor in the American Renaissance* (New York: Oxford University Press, 1993).

16. On "Benito Cereno," see Philip Fisher, *Still the New World: American Literature in a Culture of Creative Destruction* (Cambridge, MA: Harvard University Press, 1999), 91–119; Maurice S. Lee, *Slavery, Philosophy, and American Literature, 1830–1860* (New York: Cambridge University Press, 2005), 133–64; and Eric Sundquist, *To Wake the Nations: Race in the Making of American Literature* (Cambridge, MA: Harvard University Press, 1993), 135–84. For a reading of Babo as modeled on Toussaint L'Ouverture, see Jonathan Beecher, "Echoes of Toussaint Louverture and the Haitian Revolution in Melville's 'Benito Cereno,'" *Leviathan: A Journal of Melville Studies* 9, no. 2 (June 2007): 43–58.

17. See Lincoln, "Speech on the Kansas-Nebraska Act," October 16, 1854, in *Speeches and Writings*, vol. 1, *1832–1858* (New York: Library of America, 1989), 315.

18. Quotations are from the reprint of "Benito Cereno" in Melville, *Billy Budd and Other Stories* (New York: Penguin Classics, 1986); page numbers given in the text refer to this edition.

19. Lee makes the suggestion that Melville is writing for a reader of the future better able to understand his controversial positions; *Slavery, Philosophy, and American Literature*, 156–64.

20. *David Walker's Appeal*, ed. James Turner (Baltimore, MD: Black Classic, 1993), 74.

21. See Elizabeth Renker, *Strike through the Mask: Herman Melville and the Scene of Writing* (Baltimore, MD: Johns Hopkins University Press, 1996), 61–100; and Renker, "'A——!': Unreadability in *The Confidence-Man*," in *The Cambridge Companion to Melville*, ed. Robert S. Levine (New York: Cambridge University Press, 1998), 114–34. Renker views the novel as part of Melville's lifelong ordeal with the compositional process, his difficulties at "the scene of writing."

22. On similar patterns of wording in *Pierre*, see Cindy Weinstein, *Family, Kinship, and Sympathy in Nineteenth-Century American Literature* (Cambridge: Cambridge University Press, 2004), 159–84.

23. I have touched on the "foundling" nature of speech in the novel in *American Romanticism and the Marketplace* (Chicago: University of Chicago Press, 1985), 150–53.

"SPEAK, MAN!": *BILLY BUDD* IN THE CRUCIBLE OF RECONSTRUCTION

1. The quotation is from Robert Milder, "Herman Melville, 1819–1891: A Brief Biography," in *A Historical Guide to Herman Melville*, ed. Giles Gunn (New York: Oxford University Press, 2005), 33.

2. See Robert S. Levine and Samuel Otter, eds., *Frederick Douglass and Herman Melville: Essays in Relation* (Chapel Hill: University of North Carolina Press, 2008).

The Jay essay is "Douglass, Melville, and the Lynching of Billy Budd," 369–95. I also allude to Russ Castronovo and Dana D. Nelson, "Cross Patriotism in Melville and Douglass," 329–48; Carolyn L. Karcher, "White Fratricide, Black Liberation: Melville, Douglass, and Civil War Memory," 349–68; and Maurice S. Lee, "Melville, Douglass, the Civil War, Pragmatism," 396–415. Also see Robert K. Wallace, *Douglass and Melville: Anchored Together in Neighborly Style* (New Bedford, MA: Spinner, 2005).

3. Melville quoted from the "Supplement" to *Battle-Pieces and Aspects of the War*, in *Poems of Herman Melville*, ed. Douglas Robillard (New Haven, CT: College and University Press, 1976), 162. James G. Randall is perhaps the best-known historian who took the "blundering generation"–intemperate rhetoric view of the war's causes; see Randall, *The Civil War and Reconstruction* (Boston: D. C. Heath, 1937).

4. Quoted words from the "Supplement" to *Battle-Pieces, Poems of Herman Melville*, 163. Besides the works cited in note 2, the following studies of Melville, the Civil War, and Reconstruction are particularly helpful: Daniel Aaron, *The Unwritten War: American Writers and the Civil War* (New York: Alfred A. Knopf, 1973), 75–90; Stanton Garner, *The Civil War World of Herman Melville* (Lawrence: University of Kansas Press, 1993); and Carolyn L. Karcher, "The Moderate and the Radical: Melville and Child on the Civil War and Reconstruction," *ESQ: A Journal of the American Renaissance* 45 (1999): 187–257.

5. Quotations are from *Poems of Herman Melville*, 145; and *Clarel: A Poem and Pilgrimage in the Holy Land*, ed. Harrison Hayford, Alma A. MacDougall, Hershel Parker, and G. Thomas Tanselle, vol. 12 of *The Writings of Herman Melville* (Evanston, IL: Northwestern University Press; Chicago: Newberry Library, 1991), 460.

6. See Woodward, *The Burden of Southern History*, 3rd ed. (Baton Rouge: Louisiana State University Press, 1993), 109–40.

7. My principal source on Lodge and the Force Bill has been Xi Wang, *The Trial of Democracy: Black Suffrage and Northern Republicans, 1860–1910* (Athens: University of Georgia Press, 1997), 216–52. For the general claim that Reconstruction persisted into the 1890s, see Heather Cox Richardson, *The Death of Reconstruction: Race, Labor, and Politics in the Post–Civil War North, 1865–1901* (Cambridge, MA: Harvard University Press, 2001). On the successor French revolutions and the American response to them, see Larry J. Reynolds, *European Revolutions and the American Literary Renaissance* (New Haven, CT: Yale University Press, 1988); and Philip M. Katz, *From Appomattox to Montmartre: Americans and the Paris Commune* (Cambridge, MA: Harvard University Press, 1998).

8. For information on postbellum New York and the South, I am indebted to David Quigley, *Second Founding: New York City, Reconstruction, and the Making of American Democracy* (New York: Hill & Wang, 2004); quotation from 41. The reader should also consult Edwin G. Burrows and Mike Wallace, *Gotham: A History of New York City to 1898* (New York: Oxford University Press, 1999).

9. Quigley, *Second Founding*, 76.

10. On Sumner, see Michael Vorenberg, *Final Freedom: The Civil War, the Abolition of Slavery, and the Thirteenth Amendment* (New York: Cambridge University Press, 2001), 51–58; on Tourgée, see *A Fool's Errand* (1879; rpt., Cambridge, MA: Harvard University Press, 1961), 177. Melville himself, in a note to his poem "The Conflict of

Convictions" (from *Battle-Pieces*), compared the lull after Lincoln's election to "the eclipse which came over the promise of the first French Revolution"; *Poems of Herman Melville*, 150.

11. See Claude G. Bowers, *The Tragic Era: The Revolution after Lincoln* (Cambridge, MA: Riverside, 1929); quotations are from vi, 67, 76, and 334.

12. The French Revolution hovers in the background of "Benito Cereno" too. San Domingo, for which Cereno's ship is named, was rechristened Haiti after experiencing the largest black slave uprising in history. The Haitian revolution was inspired by events in Paris. "Benito Cereno" takes place in 1799, two years after the action of *Billy Budd*.

13. Letter of March 7, 1877, to Catherine Gansevoort Lansing, in Melville, *The Letters of Herman Melville*, ed. Merrill R. Davis and William H. Gilman (New Haven, CT: Yale University Press, 1960), 255.

14. Page numbers refer to the Penguin Classics edition of *Billy Budd, Sailor (An Inside Narrative)*, in *Billy Budd and Other Stories* (New York: Penguin, 1986). This is a readily available reprint of the reading text prepared by Harrison Hayford and Merton M. Sealts in 1962 from Melville's surviving manuscript. The criticism on *Billy Budd* is voluminous. Among the many valuable studies, I would single out Eugene Goodheart, "*Billy Budd* and the World's Imperfection," *Sewanee Review* 114 (Winter 2006): 81–92, on Melville's tempered conservatism; Barbara Johnson, "Melville's Fist: The Execution of *Billy Budd*," in Johnson, *The Critical Difference: Essays in the Contemporary Rhetoric of Reading* (Baltimore, MD: Johns Hopkins University Press, 1980), 79–109, on language and self-reflexivity; Hershel Parker, *Reading "Billy Budd"* (Evanston, IL: Northwestern University Press, 1990), for its detailed examination of the text and its composition; Nancy Ruttenberg, *Democratic Personality: Popular Voice and the Trial of American Authorship* (Stanford, CA: Stanford University Press, 1998), 347–78, on articulateness and inarticulateness; and Brook Thomas, *Cross-Examinations of Law and Literature: Cooper, Hawthorne, Stowe, and Melville* (New York: Cambridge University Press, 1987), 201–50, on the role of law in the story.

15. Hawthorne, *The Scarlet Letter*, ed. Sculley Bradley, Richmond Croom Beatty, E. Hudson Long, and Seymour Gross (New York: W. W. Norton, 1978), 68.

16. *Clarel*, 460. For Henry James on America's loss of innocence, see James, *Hawthorne* (1879; rpt., Ithaca, NY: Cornell University Press, 1956), 12.

17. In fact, Vere was the last addition among the principal characters.

18. Goodheart is especially good on this aspect of Melville's thinking; see his "*Billy Budd* and the World's Imperfection."

19. There is a remarkable similarity between Melville's language about the French Revolution and that of one prominent historian of the anti-Reconstruction school, John W. Burgess of Columbia University. In a phrase quoted earlier, Melville said that Gallic innovations were "at war with the peace of the world and the true welfare of mankind." Burgess, in his *Reconstruction and the Constitution* (1902), argued that white supremacy had to be defended "for the civilization of the world and the welfare of mankind." Burgess is quoted in Nicholas Lemann, *Redemption: The Last Battle of the Civil War* (New York: Farrar, Strauss & Giroux, 2005), 192.

20. The preface is reprinted in *Melville's Billy Budd*, ed. F. Barron Freeman (Cambridge, MA: Harvard University Press, 1948), 131–32.

21. Melville, "The House-Top," in *Battle-Pieces*, from *Poems of Herman Melville*, 74.

22. Johnson speaks of "a place for reading beyond politics" in *The Critical Difference*, 107.

23. Sharon Cameron emphasizes the fact that the ballad is an impersonation in her treatment of *Billy Budd* in *Impersonality: Seven Essays* (Chicago: University of Chicago Press, 2006), 180–204.

24. It is worth mentioning that the English composer Benjamin Britten turned Melville's novella into an opera, and that he made a song out of Billy's stammer.

25. Compare Carolyn L. Karcher on the Black Handsome Sailor, *Shadow over the Promised Land: Slavery, Race, and Violence in Melville's America* (Baton Rouge: Louisiana State University Press, 1980), 304–7.

26. For an illustration, see Larry J. Reynolds, "*Billy Budd* and American Labor Unrest: The Case for Striking Back," in *New Essays on Billy Budd*, ed. Donald Yannella (Cambridge: Cambridge University Press, 2002), 21–48.

27. For statistics, see Joel Williamson, *The Crucible of Race: Black-White Relations in the American South since Emancipation* (New York: Oxford University Press, 1984), 117.

28. Melville, *Battle-Pieces*, 163.

INTERTEXT: "BARTLEBY, THE SCRIVENER"

1. Though it could be argued that "Bartleby" is about wage slavery and that its protagonist's walled-in condition rebuts the argument of Lincoln and the Republicans for the northern white workingman's (in this case, office worker's) opportunity for mobility. The story also has an interesting connection to "Benito Cereno," which does deal with slavery, in its emphasis on copying or taking dictation.

2. "Bartleby, the Scrivener," in Herman Melville, *Billy Budd and Other Stories* (New York: Penguin Classics, 1986); page numbers given in the text refer to this edition.

3. Enrique Vila-Matas, *Bartleby and Co.*, trans. Jonathan Dunne (2000; trans., New York: New Directions, 2004), 2 passim.

4. Quoted in Philip S. Foner, *Business and Slavery: The New York Merchants and the Irrepressible Conflict* (Chapel Hill: University of North Carolina Press, 1941), 41.

5. Lincoln, "Address at Cooper Institute," in *Speeches and Writings*, vol. 2, *1859–1865* (New York: Library of America, 1989), 126. Lincoln is first quoting Taney's words in *Dred Scott*.

TOURGÉE: MARGIN AND CENTER

1. Quoted from *Black Reconstruction in America, 1860–1880* (1935), in Mark Elliott, *Color-Blind Justice: Albion Tourgée and the Quest for Racial Equality from the Civil War to "Plessy v. Ferguson"* (New York: Oxford University Press, 2006), 310. I am

indebted to this excellent biography for information about Tourgée's life and career. On Tourgée, see also Daniel Aaron, *The Unwritten War: American Writers and the Civil War* (New York: Alfred A. Knopf, 1973), 193–205; and Edmund Wilson, *Patriotic Gore: Studies in the Literature of the American Civil War* (New York: Oxford University Press, 1962), 529–48.

2. The term is employed in Joel Williamson, *The Crucible of Race: Black-White Relations in the American South since Emancipation* (New York: Oxford University Press, 1984).

3. The neglect of Tourgée began with the end of the first Reconstruction and did not end until the rise of the second, almost a century later. John Hope Franklin's edition of the novel came out seven years after *Brown v. Board of Education*; see Tourgée, *A Fool's Errand*, ed. John Hope Franklin (1849; rpt., Cambridge, MA: Harvard University Press, 1961); page numbers given in the text refer to this edition.

4. Wilson, *Patriotic Gore*, 537.

5. On the fate of contract in the postwar South, see Brook Thomas, *American Literary Realism and the Failed Promise of Contract* (Berkeley and Los Angeles: University of California Press, 1997). *A Fool's Errand* begins with Servosse being outsmarted in a business deal. After his arrival in Dixie, he wants to buy a plantation known as the Warrington Place. Although he thinks he has made a good bargain, the seller, Colonel Vaughn, has taken advantage of his ignorance, and the carpetbagger pays more than the property is worth.

6. See Nina Silber, *The Romance of Reunion: Northerners and the South, 1865–1900* (Chapel Hill: University of North Carolina Press, 1993).

7. See Albion Winegar Tourgée, *The Invisible Empire*, introd. and notes by Otto O. Olsen (1880; rpt., Baton Rouge: Louisiana State University Press, 1989).

8. The 1880 songbook is quoted in Elliott, *Color-Blind Justice*, 187.

9. The piece appeared in the *Forum* in December 1888; it is reprinted in Ian Frederick Finseth, ed., *The American Civil War: An Anthology of Essential Writings* (New York: Routledge, 2006), 533–38. The quotations appear on 533–35 and 537.

10. Ibid., 536–37.

11. The formulation comes from Jeremiah 13:23: "Can the Ethiopian change his skin, or the leopard his spots?" Another inspiration for Dixon may have been *Ivanhoe* (1820), where Jews are the other to Saxons and Normans, and Friar Tuck observes, "The leopard will not change his spots, and a Jew he will continue to be." Cited in Peter Schmidt, "Walter Scott, Postcolonial Theory, and New South Literature," *Mississippi Quarterly* 56 (2003): 547. Tourgée's version suggests that the fierce and independent white man may be the leopard, a meaning that would have appealed to Dixon.

12. Elliott describes Tourgée's encounter with *The Leopard's Spots* in *Color-Blind Justice*, 17–22.

13. Ibid., 300.

14. On the separation of black and Indian reform in this period, see Susan Gillman, "*Ramona* in 'Our America,'" in *José Martí's "Our America": From National to Hemispheric Cultural Studies*, ed. Jeffrey Belnap and Raúl Fernández (Durham, NC: Duke University Press, 1998), 91–111. A demonstration of the split appears in the cinematography of D. W. Griffith, who left both the virulently antiblack classic *The Birth of a*

Nation and a pro-Indian film based on *Ramona* with the subtitle *A Story of the White Man's Injustice to the Indian* (1910). Gillman argues that Martí conjoins what in the United States was pried apart. My argument here, following Tourgée, is that a Stowe-Jackson, or black-Indian, interface emerged out of late nineteenth-century American realities. On *Ramona*, see also John M. Gonzalez, "The Warp of Whiteness: Domesticity and Empire in Helen Hunt Jackson's *Ramona*," *American Literary History* 16, no. 3 (Fall 2004): 437–65. On the superseding of the color line by the moving line of settlement, see Brook Thomas, "Turner's 'Frontier Thesis' as a Narrative of Reconstruction," in *Centuries' Ends, Narrative Means*, ed. Robert Newman (Stanford, CA: Stanford University Press, 1996), 117–37.

15. See the biographical note to Helen Hunt Jackson, *Ramona* (New York: Modern Library, 2005), viii; page numbers given in the text refer to this edition.

16. See Cynthia Jordan, *Second Stories: The Politics of Language, Form, and Gender in Early American Fictions* (Chapel Hill: University of North Carolina Press, 1989), 110–32.

17. Tourgée, "A Study in Civilization," *North American Review* 143 (September 1886): 252–53.

18. Ibid., 247 and 257.

19. Ibid., 258–60.

20. Ibid., 259 and 261.

JAMES AND THE MONOTONE OF REUNION

1. See especially Philip Fisher, "Appearing and Disappearing in Public: Social Space in Late-Nineteenth-Century Literature and Culture," in *Reconstructing American Literary History*, ed. Sacvan Bercovitch (Cambridge, MA: Harvard University Press, 1986), 155–88. Also relevant on the press and celebrity is Sara Blair, "Realism, Culture, and the Place of the Literary: Henry James and *The Bostonians*," in *The Cambridge Companion to Henry James*, ed. Jonathan Freedman (Cambridge: Cambridge University Press, 1991), 151–68. On fads and feminism in James's novel, see Jennifer L. Fleissner, *Woman, Compulsion, Modernity: The Moment of American Naturalism* (Chicago: University of Chicago Press, 2004), 123–60.

2. As Kenneth W. Warren puts it, James "finds his voice . . . carried away or stifled by an unreconstructed Southerner." See Warren, *Black and White Strangers* (Chicago: University of Chicago Press, 1995), 101. I believe that James is far more self-aware about the theme of silencing than Warren allows. The character of Verena may have been inspired by Anna Dickinson, the American "Joan of Arc" whose oratory electrified Republican audiences during and after the Civil War. Dickinson was the author of a pro-Reconstruction novel, *What Answer?* (1868). Her modern biographer, J. Matthew Gallman, believes that James was thinking of Dickinson's relationship with Susan B. Anthony when he imagined the "Boston marriage" of Verena and Olive Chancellor. See *America's Joan of Arc: The Life of Anna Elizabeth Dickinson* (New York: Oxford University Press, 2006), 103–4.

3. For the visit to Gilder, see Leon Edel, *Henry James, The Middle Years: 1882–1895* (Philadelphia: Lippincott, 1962), 75.

4. Quoted in Michael Anesko, *"Friction with the Market": Henry James and the Profession of Authorship* (New York: Oxford University Press, 1986), 87.

5. *The Bostonians: A Novel* (New York: Modern Library, 1965); page numbers given in the text refer to this edition.

6. *The Scarlet Letter*, ed. Ross C. Murfin (Boston: Bedford St. Martin's, 1991), 187.

7. James, *Hawthorne* (New York: Collier Books, 1966), 124.

8. See Louis Menand, *The Metaphysical Club: A Story of Ideas in America* (New York: Farrar, Straus & Giroux, 2001), 146.

9. Lynn Wardley notes the Booth allusion in "Woman's Voice, Democracy's Body, and *The Bostonians*," *ELH* 56 (Autumn 1989): 661–62.

10. On James and his relations with the market in the mid-1880s, see Anesko, *"Friction with the Market,"* 79–100; and Edel, *Henry James, The Middle Years*, 137–46. On Osgood and *The Bostonians*, see also Sheldon M. Novick, *Henry James: The Mature Master* (New York: Random House, 2007), 77–81.

11. James, *The American Scene* (Bloomington: Indiana University Press, 1968), 371, 374–76, and 387–90.

12. Ibid., 77 and 465; on the excision, see Edel's introduction, xxiii, and his *Henry James, the Master: 1901–1916* (Philadelphia: Lippincott, 1972), 318.

13. James, preface to *The American*, vol. 2 of the *New York Edition of the Novels and Tales of Henry James* (New York: Scribner's, 1907), xx.

14. He did publish some stories set in America and several volumes of autobiography dealing with the antebellum past, when no milestone was necessary to demarcate the North from the South.

WAS TWAIN BLACK?

1. Quotations are from Twain, *Pudd'nhead Wilson* (New York: Signet Classic, 1964); page numbers given in the text refer to this edition.

2. I am taking off on Shelley Fisher Fishkin's argument in *Was Huck Black? Mark Twain and African American Voices* (New York: Oxford University Press, 1993). See also Fishkin, *Lighting Out for the Territory: Reflections on Mark Twain and American Culture* (New York: Oxford University Press, 1997), and Fishkin, "Mark Twain and Race," in *A Historical Guide to Mark Twain*, ed. Shelley Fisher Fishkin (New York: Oxford University Press, 2002), 127–62. Fishkin argues that Twain refrained from expressing his frank opinions on race because "it was not the time to tell these stories—or at least, not the time for him to tell them" ("Mark Twain and Race," 152). I will argue in this chapter that the constraint on telling was a self-conscious theme in his work.

3. Twain, *Life on the Mississippi* (1883; rpt., New York: Signet Classic, 1961), 264–67.

4. Quotations from *Adventures of Huckleberry Finn* refer to the text edited by Sculley Bradley, Richmond Croom Beatty, E. Hudson Long, and Thomas Cooley (New York: W. W. Norton, 1977); page numbers given in the text refer to this edition.

5. A succinct and penetrating discussion of Twain and subscription publishing appears in Larzer Ziff, *Mark Twain* (New York: Oxford University Press, 2004), 26–30. For information on Twain's career, see also Ron Powers, *Mark Twain: A Life* (New York: Free Press, 2005); and Fred Kaplan, *The Singular Mark Twain: A Biography* (New York:

Random House, 2003). The best treatment of Twain's attitude toward the South remains Arthur G. Petitt, *Mark Twain and the South* (Lexington: University of Kentucky Press, 1974). Valuable studies of Twain's social thinking include, besides Fishkin's *Was Huck Black?*, Jonathan Arac, *"Huckleberry Finn" as Idol and Target: The Functions of Criticism in Our Time* (Madison: University of Wisconsin Press, 1997); and Louis J. Budd, *Mark Twain: Social Philosopher* (Bloomington: Indiana University Press, 1962).

6. My main source on these matters is again David W. Blight, *Race and Reunion: The Civil War in American Memory* (Cambridge, MA: Harvard University Press, 2001).

7. James S. Leonard, Thomas Asa Tenney, and Thadious M. Davis, eds., *Satire or Evasion? Black Perspectives on "Huckleberry Finn"* (Durham, NC: Duke University Press, 1992).

8. On Twain's complex reactions to the evasion see especially Charles H. Nilon, "The Ending of *Huckleberry Finn*: 'Freeing the Free Negro,'" in ibid., 62–76.

9. A dated but still illuminating analysis of the parallels can be found in Daniel G. Hoffman, *Form and Fable in American Fiction* (New York: Oxford University Press, 1961), 317–50.

10. Twain, *Life on the Mississippi*, 265.

11. Ibid., 266.

12. For this last point, see Amanda Claybaugh, *The Novel of Purpose: Literature and Social Reform in the Anglo-American Novel* (Ithaca, NY: Cornell University Press, 2007), 174–75.

13. After Cable wrote *John March, Southerner* (1894), Gilder complained that the novel tried "to fetch everything into literature save & except literature itself. . . . Shades of Tourgée!" Quoted in Kenneth W. Warren, *Black and White Strangers: Race and American Literary Realism* (Chicago: University of Chicago Press, 1993), 54.

14. See Xi Wang, *The Trial of Democracy: Black Suffrage and Northern Republicans, 1860–1910* (Athens: University of Georgia Press, 1997), 180–252; Lodge quote from 236.

15. See Joe B. Fulton, *Mark Twain in the Margins: The Quarry Farm Marginalia and "A Connecticut Yankee in King Arthur's Court"* (Tuscaloosa: University of Alabama Press, 2000), 82–100; quotes from 83 and 91.

16. Twain, *A Connecticut Yankee in King Arthur's Court* (New York: Signet Classics, 2004); page numbers given in the text refer to this edition.

17. Lincoln is quoted in Michael Lind, *What Lincoln Believed: The Values and Convictions of America's Greatest President* (New York: Doubleday, 2005), 101. The state legislator was James L. Petigru; see the entry under his name in *The Oxford Dictionary of American Quotation*, ed. Hugh Rawson and Margaret Miner (New York: Oxford University Press, 2008).

18. This is a subtheme in *A Fool's Errand* (1879; rpt., Cambridge, MA: Harvard University Press, 1961); see, for example, 377.

19. The best analyses of *Pudd'nhead Wilson* in context are Stephen Railton, "The Tragedy of Mark Twain, by Pudd'nhead Wilson," *Nineteenth-Century Literature* 56, no. 4 (March 2002): 518–44; and Eric J. Sundquist, "Mark Twain and Homer Plessy," in *Mark Twain's Pudd'nhead Wilson: Race, Conflict, and Culture*, ed. Susan Gillman and Forest G. Robinson (Durham, NC: Duke University Press, 1990), 46–72.

20. Two additional though minor similarities between author and character: both

sort of went to Yale, Tom dropping out and Twain receiving an honorary master of arts degree, and both are "the missing confederate" (147), Wilson's phrase for Tom's supposed accomplice, who is actually Tom himself in disguise. "Missing confederate" also suggests Twain's desertion from the Rebel forces.

21. Railton is excellent on this point; see "The Tragedy of Mark Twain, by Pudd'nhead Wilson." I differ from Railton in that I see Twain as not simply implicated in the "tragedy" of popularity but self-aware and self-critical of his implication.

22. Douglass made this point numerous times in his memoirs. An example can be found in *Life and Times* (1893), in Douglass, *Autobiographies* (New York: Library of America, 1994), 552–53.

23. Scott Moore remarks that the novel's ending implicates Twain's readers because our sympathies are with Wilson; we root for him to expose Tom. See "The Code Duello and the Reified Self in Mark Twain's *Pudd'nhead Wilson*," *American Transcendental Quarterly* 22, no. 3 (September 2008): 499–515, especially 512–13.

24. Tom muses that it was actually his "white blood" that corrupted him. But Twain excised this passage from the final version of the novel. See Fishkin, *Was Huck Black?*, 122–23.

25. See David Lionel Smith, "Black Critics and Mark Twain," in *The Cambridge Companion to Mark Twain*, ed. Forrest G. Robinson (New York: Cambridge University Press, 1995), 116–28. Smith notes that Washington wrote a warm tribute to Twain and finds "a surprising affinity between these two men" (119).

26. See Louis R. Harlan, *Booker T. Washington: The Wizard of Tuskegee, 1901–1915* (New York: Oxford University Press, 1983).

27. Washington, *Up from Slavery* (1901; rpt., New York: W. W. Norton, 1996), 97.

28. Twain, "The United States of Lyncherdom," in *Collected Tales, Sketches, Speeches, and Essays, 1891–1910* (New York: Library of America, 1992), 481–82.

29. See L. Terry Oggel, "Speaking Out about Race: 'The United States of Lyncherdom' Clemens Really Wrote," in *Prospects* 25, special issue, ed. Jack Salzman (2000): 115–58. The piece includes the original text of "The United States of Lyncherdom" and reflections on Twain and racism by Louis J. Budd. An unpublished article Twain wrote in 1905 underscores his concern with free speech. "The Privilege of the Grave" lists the hazards of espousing unpopular opinions while one is still alive: "it can ruin a man in his business; it can lose him his friends; it can subject him to public insult and abuse; it can ostracize his unoffending family, and make [of] his house a despised and unvisited solitude." (Reading these last words, one thinks of the fate of the Trescotts at the end of *The Monster*.) The essay also repeats Twain's inclination to substitute slavery for race. He mentions the widespread antipathy to abolitionists but says nothing about the discrediting of equality that made Dixon's coetaneous *The Clansman* so influential. See "The Privilege of the Grave," *New Yorker*, December 22 and 29, 2008, 50–51; quotation from 50.

CRANE AND THE TYRANNY OF TWELVE

1. For information on Crane's life, with salutary reminders about the limits of our knowledge, see Christopher Benfey, *The Double Life of Stephen Crane* (New York:

Alfred A. Knopf, 1992). John Berryman makes the "fallen women" argument in *Stephen Crane* (New York: Sloane, 1950); and William M. Morgan emphasizes Crane's humanitarianism in *Questionable Charity: Gender, Humanitarianism, and Complicity in U.S. Literary Realism* (Hanover, NH: University Press of New England, 2004), 68–99.

2. Ralph Ellison, "Stephen Crane and the Mainstream of American Fiction," in *Shadow and Act* (New York: Vintage Books, 1965), 60–76; quotes from 71, 76, and 68. I cited Ellison's judgment previously in the introduction, 10.

3. Quotations from *The Red Badge of Courage* and *The Monster* come from Crane, *The Red Badge of Courage and Other Stories*, ed. Anthony Mellors and Fiona Robertson (New York: Oxford World's Classics, 1998); page numbers in the text refer to this edition.

4. On Crane's writing of his novel, see Mellors and Robertson, "Composition and Publication History," in Crane, *The Red Badge of Courage and Other Stories*, xxxv–xlviii.

5. On the aversion of narrative to the injuries that warfare inflicts on humans, the classic study is Elaine Scarry, *The Body in Pain: The Making and Unmaking of the World* (New York: Oxford University Press, 1985).

6. Michael Fried discusses Crane's thematizing of writing in *Realism, Writing, Disfiguration: On Thomas Eakins and Stephen Crane* (Chicago: University of Chicago Press, 1987). For a general treatment of war and language, with a brief analysis of Crane, see James Dawes, *The Language of War: Literature and Culture in the United States from the Civil War through World War II* (Cambridge, MA: Harvard University Press, 2002). I am arguing that the landscape of war in Crane is saturated with language of all kinds and becomes an enclosing wall of sound. The novelist's parents both wrote; as Benfey suggests, language was everywhere in his life.

7. Stephen Crane, letter to William Howe Crane, October 29, 1897, in *The Correspondence of Stephen Crane*, ed. Stanley Wertheim and Paul Sorrentino (New York: Columbia University Press, 1988), 1:301.

8. Crane to William Howe Crane, letter of March 2, 1899, in *Correspondence*, 2:446.

9. On *The Monster* and race, the best studies are Jacqueline Goldsby, *A Spectacular Secret: Lynching in American Life and Literature* (Chicago: University of Chicago Press, 2006), 105–63; and Price McMurray, "Disabling Fictions: Race, History, and Ideology in Crane's 'The Monster,'" *Studies in American Fiction* 26 (Spring 1998): 51–72. Also informative is Jean Lutes, "Lynching Coverage and the American Reporter-Novelist," *American Literary History* 19, no. 2 (September 2007): 456–81. An incisive treatment of language in the novella is Jennifer Carol Cook, *Machine and Metaphor: The Ethics of Language in American Realism* (New York: Routledge, 2007), 45–61.

10. A connection noted by Bill Brown, *The Material Unconscious: American Amusement, Stephen Crane, and the Economies of Play* (Cambridge, MA: Harvard University Press, 1996), 217, who points out, however, that "Henry Johnson" was a fairly common name for blacks.

11. On the Frankenstein motif in the novel (and in American culture), see Elizabeth Young, *Black Frankenstein: The Making of an American Metaphor* (New York: New York University Press, 2008), 80–106 passim.

12. The finding, which was reported in the newspapers, is quoted in McMurray, "Disabling Fictions," 57.

13. On the representation of race in the *Century* (and other popular magazines), see Rayford W. Logan, *The Betrayal of the Negro: From Rutherford B. Hayes to Woodrow Wilson* (1954; rpt., n.p.: Da Capo Press, 1997), 159–395.

14. For the information in this paragraph, see Mellors and Robertson, "Composition and Publication History," in Crane, *The Red Badge of Courage and Other Stories,* xlvi–xlvii.

CHOKING IN CHESNUTT

1. The brief piece is reprinted in Charles W. Chesnutt, *Stories, Novels, and Essays,* ed. Werner Sollors (New York: Library of America, 2002), 872–73. Eric Sundquist discusses the role of the past in Chesnutt's fiction at length in *To Wake the Nations: Race in the Making of American Literature* (Cambridge, MA: Harvard University Press, 1993), 271–454.

2. The amount criticism on Chesnutt has grown dramatically. Besides Sundquist, I have learned from the work of William M. Andrews, *The Literary Career of Charles W. Chesnutt* (Baton Rouge: Louisiana State University Press, 1980); Sandra Gunning, *Race, Rape, and Lynching: The Red Record of American Literature, 1890–1912* (New York: Oxford University Press, 1996), 62–76; Dean McWilliams, *Charles W. Chesnutt and the Fictions of Race* (Athens: University of Georgia Press, 2002); and Matthew Wilson, *Whiteness in the Novels of Charles W. Chesnutt* (Jackson: University Press of Mississippi, 2004). For a review of recent Chesnutt scholarship, see Henry B. Wonham, "What Is a Black Author? A Review of Recent Chesnutt Studies," *American Literary History* 18, no. 4 (Winter 2006): 829–35.

3. See *Frederick Douglass* (1899; rpt., New York: Johnson Reprint, 1970), especially 107–18.

4. Quotations are from *The Marrow of Tradition* (New York: Penguin Classics, 1993); page numbers are given in the text.

5. See Wells, *Southern Horrors and Other Writings: The Anti-Lynching Campaign of Ida B. Wells, 1892–1900,* ed. Jacqueline Jones Royster (Boston: Bedford/St. Martin's, 1997).

6. *Marrow* teems with evidence not only of media technology, but also of an accelerated modernity "annihilating space and time" (the preferred nineteenth-century formulation): Dr. Miller is forced to sit in a segregated railroad car on his return from Philadelphia to Wellington, local communities schedule trains to bring spectators to Sandy's planned lynching, characters speak by telephone, and so forth. On these developments, see Thomas J. Schlereth, *Victorian America: Transformations in Everyday Life, 1876–1915* (New York: HarperPerennial, 1991), especially 177–207. Wilson, *Whiteness in the Novels of Charles W. Chesnutt,* 98–147, is perceptive on the South's domination of northern opinion.

7. In an essay published six months before *Marrow,* Chesnutt wrote that the South's "best people" are not free because they fear to give "public expression" to their disagreement with their region's racial policies. Ellis is a fictional illustration of this

fact. See Charles W. Chesnutt, "The White and the Black," in *Essays and Speeches*, ed. Joseph R. McElrath Jr., Robert C. Leitz III, and Jesse S. Crisler (Stanford, CA: Stanford University Press, 1999), 139–44; quote from 143.

8. On lynching and black corporeality, see Robyn Wiegman, "The Anatomy of a Lynching," *Journal of the History of Sexuality* 3 (January 1993): 445–67.

9. Howells's review is reprinted in Chesnutt, *The Marrow of Tradition*, ed. Nancy Bentley and Sandra Gunning (New York: Bedford/St. Martin's, 2002), 454–57; quote from 456.

10. The phrase, from Howells's review of "Mr. Charles W. Chesnutt's Stories" (1900), is quoted in Joseph R. McElrath Jr., "W. D. Howells and Race: Charles W. Chesnutt's Disappointment of the Dean," *Nineteenth-Century Literature* 51 (March 1997): 474. On Chesnutt and Howells, see also William L. Andrews, "William Dean Howells and Charles W. Chesnutt: Criticism and Race Fiction in the Age of Booker T. Washington," *American Literature* 48 (1976): 327–39. For an argument that Howells's model of socioethical fiction continued to influence Chesnutt after their break, see Paul R. Petrie, *Conscience and Purpose: Fiction and Social Consciousness in Howells, Jewett, Chesnutt, and Cather* (Tuscaloosa: University of Alabama Press, 2005), 109–48.

11. In Chesnutt, *The Marrow of Tradition*, ed. Bentley and Gunning, 457.

12. Letter of November 10, 1901, in W. D. Howells, *Selected Letters*, vol. 4, *1892–1901*, ed. Thomas Wortham with Christoph K. Lohmann and David S. Nordlow (Boston: Twayne, 1981), 274.

13. Chesnutt, *The Colonel's Dream* (New Milford, CT: Toby Press, 2004); page numbers given in the text refer to this edition. On *The Colonel's Dream*, see Brook Thomas, *American Literary Realism and the Failed Promise of Contract* (Berkeley and Los Angeles: University of California Press, 1997), 173–90; and Wilson, *Whiteness in the Novels of Charles W. Chesnutt*, 148–82.

14. Douglas A. Blackmon shows convincingly that the convict leasing system condemned thousands of African Americans to an involuntary servitude little different from that endured by their forebears. See *Slavery by Another Name: The Re-enslavement of Black Americans from the Civil War to World War II* (New York: Doubleday, 2008).

15. See Stephen Budiansky, *The Bloody Shirt: Terror after Appomattox* (New York: Viking, 2008), 284.

16. Review, *Nashville Banner*, October 29, 1905; quoted in Wilson, *Whiteness in the Novels of Charles W. Chesnutt*, 179.

DIXON AND THE REBIRTH OF DISCURSIVE POWER

1. Quotations are from Dixon, *A Leopard's Spots: A Romance of the White Man's Burden, 1865–1900* (Gretna, LA: Firebird Press, 2001); page numbers are given in the text. On Dixon, see Walter Benn Michaels, *Our America: Nativism, Modernism, and Pluralism* (Durham, NC: Duke University Press, 1995), 10–40; Leslie Fiedler, *The Inadvertent Epic: From "Uncle Tom's Cabin" to "Roots"* (Toronto: Canadian Broadcasting Corporation, 1979), 43–59; and Michele K. Gillespie and Randall L. Hall, eds., *Thomas*

Dixon, Jr. and the Birth of Modern America (Baton Rouge: Louisiana State University Press, 2006).

2. Dixon, *The Clansman: An Historical Romance of the Ku Klux Klan* (Lexington: University Press of Kentucky, 1970), 289. William Whipper was the name of a free black abolitionist from Philadelphia whom Douglass mentions several times in *Life and Times*.

3. For Scott's influence on Dixon, see Peter Schmidt, "Walter Scott, Postcolonial Theory, and New South Literature," *Mississippi Quarterly* 56 (2003): 545–54; on race pride in Scott, see Laura Doyle, *Bordering on the Body: The Racial Matrix of Modern Fiction and Culture* (New York: Oxford University Press, 1994), 35–53.

4. *The Clansman*, 342 and 2.

5. On the conflation of social and political, or private and public, in Dixon, see Walter Benn Michaels, "Local Colors," *MLN* 4 (September 1998): 734–56.

6. As Scott Romine puts it, Gaston has to learn "to speak Durham's untainted dialect of white supremacy." See Romine, "Things Falling Apart: The Postcolonial Condition of *Red Rock* and *The Leopard's Spots*," in *Look Away! The U.S. South in World Studies*, ed. Jon Smith and Deborah Cohn (Durham, NC: Duke University Press, 2004), 175–200; quote from 187. See also Romine, "Thomas Dixon and the Production of Whiteness," in Gillespie and Hall, *Thomas Dixon, Jr. and the Birth of Modern America*, 124–150.

7. Dixon, *The Clansman*, 341.

8. The figures come from Louis Menand, "Do Movies Have Rights," in Gillespie and Hall, *Thomas Dixon, Jr. and the Birth of Modern America*, 183–202, especially 201.

9. Wilson and the critic Albert E. Pillsbury, a white member of the NAACP, are quoted in Mark Elliott, *Color-Blind Justice: Albion Tourgée and the Quest for Racial Equality from the Civil War to "Plessy v. Ferguson"* (New York: Oxford University Press, 2006), 308 and 310.

10. Dixon is quoted in Jane M. Gaines, "Thomas Dixon and Race Melodrama," in Gillespie and Hall, *Thomas Dixon, Jr. and the Birth of Modern America*, 160.

11. The pamphlet is excerpted in Harry M. Geduld, ed., *Focus on D. W. Griffith* (Englewood Cliffs, NJ: Prentice-Hall, 1971), 43–45.